Foreign Trade Regimes and Economic Development: CHILE

Foreign Trade Regimes and Economic Development:

A Special Conference Series on Foreign Trade Regimes and Economic Development

VOLUME VIII

NATIONAL BUREAU OF ECONOMIC RESEARCH
New York 1976

CHILE

by **Jere R. Behrman**

UNIVERSITY OF PENNSYLVANIA

DISTRIBUTED BY Columbia University Press
New York and London

National Bureau of Economic Research

A Special Conference Series on Foreign Trade Regimes and Economic Development

Library of Congress Card Number: 74–82376
ISBN for the series: 0–87014–500–2
ISBN for this volume: 0–87014–508–8

Printed in the United States of America
DESIGNED BY JEFFREY M. BARRIE

Relation of the Directors of the National Bureau to Publication of the Country Studies in the Series on Foreign Trade Regimes and Economic Development

The individual country studies have not passed through the National Bureau's normal procedures for review and approval of research reports by the Board of Directors. In view of the way in which these studies were planned and reviewed at successive working parties of authors and Co-Directors, the National Bureau's Executive Committee has approved their publication in a manner analogous to conference proceedings, which are exempted from the rules governing submission of manuscripts to, and critical review by, the Board of Directors. *It should therefore be understood that the views expressed herein are those of the authors only and do not necessarily reflect those of the National Bureau or its Board of Directors.*

The synthesis volumes in the series, prepared by the Co-Directors of the project, are subject to the normal procedures for review and approval by the Directors of the National Bureau.

To
Lucy

Contents

Tables

Charts

Co-Directors' Foreword

This volume is one of a series resulting from the research project on Exchange Control, Liberalization, and Economic Development sponsored by the National Bureau of Economic Research, the name of the project having been subsequently broadened to Foreign Trade Regimes and Economic Development. Underlying the project was the belief by all participants that the phenomena of exchange control and liberalization in less developed countries require careful and detailed analysis within a sound theoretical framework, and that the effects of individual policies and restrictions cannot be analyzed without consideration of both the nature of their administration and the economic environment within which they are adopted as determined by the domestic economic policy and structure of the particular country.

The research has thus had three aspects: (1) development of an analytical framework for handling exchange control and liberalization; (2) within that framework, research on individual countries, undertaken independently by senior scholars; and (3) analysis of the results of these independent efforts with a view to identifying those empirical generalizations that appear to emerge from the experience of the countries studied.

The analytical framework developed in the first stage was extensively commented upon by those responsible for the research on individual countries, and was then revised to the satisfaction of all participants. That framework, serving as the common basis upon which the country studies were undertaken, is further reflected in the syntheses reporting on the third aspect of the research.

The analytical framework pinpointed these three principal areas of research which all participants undertook to analyze for their own countries.

Subject to a common focus on these three areas, each participant enjoyed maximum latitude to develop the analysis of his country's experience in the way he deemed appropriate. Comparison of the country volumes will indicate that this freedom was indeed utilized, and we believe that it has paid handsome dividends. The three areas singled out for in-depth analysis in the country studies are:

1. *The anatomy of exchange control:* The economic efficiency and distributional implications of alternative methods of exchange control in each country were to be examined and analyzed. Every method of exchange control differs analytically in its effects from every other. In each country study care has been taken to bring out the implications of the particular methods of control used. We consider it to be one of the major results of the project that these effects have been brought out systematically and clearly in analysis of the individual countries' experience.

2. *The liberalization episode:* Another major area for research was to be a detailed analysis of attempts to liberalize the payments regime. In the analytical framework, devaluation and liberalization were carefully distinguished, and concepts for quantifying the extent of devaluation and of liberalization were developed. It was hoped that careful analysis of individual devaluation and liberalization attempts, both successful and unsuccessful, would permit identification of the political and economic ingredients of an effective effort in that direction.

3. *Growth relationships:* Finally, the relationship of the exchange control regime to growth via static-efficiency and other factors was to be investigated. In this regard, the possible effects on savings, investment allocation, research and development, and entrepreneurship were to be highlighted.

In addition to identifying the three principal areas to be investigated, the analytical framework provided a common set of concepts to be used in the studies and distinguished various phases regarded as useful in tracing the experience of the individual countries and in assuring comparability of the analyses. The concepts are defined and the phases delineated in Appendix A.

The country studies undertaken within this project and their authors are as follows:

Brazil	Albert Fishlow, University of California, Berkeley
Chile	Jere R. Behrman, University of Pennsylvania
Colombia	Carlos F. Díaz-Alejandro, Yale University
Egypt	Bent Hansen, University of California, Berkeley, and Karim Nashashibi, International Monetary Fund
Ghana	J. Clark Leith, University of Western Ontario

India	Jagdish N. Bhagwati, Massachusetts Institute of Technology, and T. N. Srinivasan, Indian Statistical Institute
Israel	Michael Michaely, The Hebrew University of Jerusalem
Philippines	Robert E. Baldwin, University of Wisconsin
South Korea	Charles R. Frank, Jr., Princeton University and The Brookings Institution; Kwang Suk Kim, Korea Development Institute, Republic of Korea; and Larry E. Westphal, Northwestern University
Turkey	Anne O. Krueger, University of Minnesota

The principal results of the different country studies are brought together in our overall syntheses. Each of the country studies, however, has been made self-contained, so that readers interested in only certain of these studies will not be handicapped.

In undertaking this project and bringing it to successful completion, the authors of the individual country studies have contributed substantially to the progress of the whole endeavor, over and above their individual research. Each has commented upon the research findings of other participants, and has made numerous suggestions which have improved the overall design and execution of the project. The country authors who have collaborated with us constitute an exceptionally able group of development economists, and we wish to thank all of them for their cooperation and participation in the project.

We must also thank the National Bureau of Economic Research for its sponsorship of the project and its assistance with many of the arrangements necessary in an undertaking of this magnitude. Hal B. Lary, Vice President-Research (retired), most energetically and efficiently provided both intellectual and administrative input into the project over a three-year period. We would also like to express our gratitude to the Agency for International Development for having financed the National Bureau in undertaking this project. Michael Roemer and Constantine Michalopoulos particularly deserve our sincere thanks.

JAGDISH N. BHAGWATI
Massachusetts Institute of Technology

ANNE O. KRUEGER
University of Minnesota

Acknowledgments

I have been involved in this and related studies of the Chilean economy for over five years. Not surprisingly, the list of contributing individuals and organizations to which I am indebted is a long one. Among individuals special thanks are due to Ricardo Lira, who worked with me as a research assistant both in Santiago and in Philadelphia, and to Nancy Blossom, who contributed substantially to the computer programming and data processing. Considerable thanks also are due to a large group of economists with whom I worked or who provided suggestions while I was in Chile: Edmar Bacha, Juan de la Barra, Hollis Chenery, Peter Clark, Richard Eckaus, Alejandro Foxley, Eduardo García, Jorge García, Everett Hagen, Arnold Harberger, Ana Marie Jul, Cristian Ossa, Paul N. Rosenstein-Rodan, and Lance Taylor, all of whom were associated with the Oficina de Planificación Nacional (ODEPLAN)–Center for International Studies of the Massachusetts Institute of Technology–Ford Foundation project in 1967–70; Jorge Cauas, Ricardo Ffrench-Davis, and Carlos Massad of the Central Bank; Teresa Jeanneret, Joseph Ramos, and John Strasma of the University of Chile; and Sergio de la Cuadra of the Catholic University. A number of the same individuals provided assistance in the United States, as did F. Gerard Adams, Lawrence Klein, Joze Mencinger, James McCabe, Almarin Phillips, Robert Pollak, Robert Rasche, and Oskar Rufatt at the University of Pennsylvania; Markos Mamalakis of the Latin American Studies Center at the University of Wisconsin–Milwaukee; and Hans Bergendorf of the Development Research Center of the International Bank for Reconstruction and Development. All the members of the National Bureau of Economic Research project of which this study is a part provided insights directly or indirectly, but I owe special thanks to Jagdish Bhagwati, Carlos Díaz-Alejandro, Charles Frank, Anne Krueger, and Hal Lary. I also wish to thank Bela Balassa for his permission to reproduce the 1961 ITR and EPR estimates in Table 5.3. Ester Moskowitz of the NBER staff provided extraordinary editing services. H. Irving Forman skillfully drew the charts and figures. Finally, Sara Nunn, Andia Brown, Margo Richardson, Florence Barrow, and the Wharton Duplication Center under the guidance of Anna-May Busch provided essential bibliographical, secretarial, and organizational services.

Among organizations, I owe special thanks to the National Bureau of Economic Research Project on Foreign Trade Regimes and Economic Development, financed by the Agency for International Development, under whose auspices this study was conducted. I also wish to acknowledge with gratitude the financial support for this and related work that was provided by the Ford Foundation in Santiago, a Ford Faculty Fellowship in Economics in 1971–72, the Center for International Studies of the Massachusetts Institute of Technology, the University of Pennsylvania, the Development Research Center of the International Bank for Reconstruction and Development, and the National Science Foundation under Grant GS-36459. However, responsibility for the contents of this volume is entirely mine, and the aid rendered to me by the individuals and organizations mentioned above should not be construed as constituting endorsement of my findings, presentation, or point of view.

JERE R. BEHRMAN

Principal Dates and Historical Events in Chile

1536	Spanish discovery of Chile by Diego de Almagro.
1810–18	Wars of independence from Spain.
1865–66	War with Spain.
1879–83	War of the Pacific; Chile defeats Peru and Bolivia and becomes owner of rich nitrate and copper deposits.
1891	Civil War; President José Manuel Balmaceda killed.
1920–24	Presidency of Arturo Alessandri; initiation of substantial social legislation; creation of Central Bank; resignation of Alessandri.
1925	Revolution; reinstatement of Alessandri, approval of new constitution; abdication of Alessandri; election of Emiliano Figueroa Larraín as president.
1927	Resignation of Figueroa Larraín; election of Carlos Ibañez del Campo as president.
1931	Catastrophic impact of Great Depression; abandonment of convertibility; resignation of Ibañez; establishment of restrictive foreign economic regimes; succession of governments and great political instability.
1932–38	Re-establishment of political and economic order under President Arturo Alessandri (now more conservative than in 1920s).
1939	First year of Popular Front government under President Pedro Agiurre Cerda; major earthquake; creation of CORFO.
1941	President Agiurre dies.
1942	Juan Antonio Ríos elected president; copper price fixed at 12 cents per pound by agreement with United States government as part of war effort.

1946	President Ríos dies; Gabriel González Videla elected president with considerable support from leftist parties; copper price-fixing agreement terminated.
1947	Government moves toward right; Communist Party outlawed, diplomatic relations with Union of Soviet Socialist Republics broken.
1950	United States unilaterally fixes copper price because of Korean conflict.
1951	Washington Treaty signed after strong Chilean outrage.
1952	Chilean copper-sales monopoly started; Ibañez elected again to presidency.
1955	*Nuevo Trato* (new deal) legislated for large-scale copper mining, political and economic situation disintegrates considerably; Felipe Herrera made minister of finance; Klein-Saks consulting firm contracted for aid in stabilization program.
1956	Ibañez-Klein-Saks program of stabilization plus liberalization initiated.
1958	Jorge Alessandri Rodríguez elected president.
1959	Alessandri program of stabilization plus liberalization commences.
1960	Major earthquake in south.
1962	Stabilization-liberalization effort abandoned.
1964	Eduardo Frei Montalva elected president.
1965	Frei stabilization-liberalization effort begun; sliding-peg exchange rate policy adopted; foreign debt renegotiated.
1966	Chileanization of Kennecott's copper holdings.
1967	Collapse of stabilization attempt.
1969	Nationalization of Anaconda's copper holdings.
1970	Abandonment of sliding-peg exchange rate policy; Salvador Allende Gossens elected president as head of Popular Unity Coalition.
1971	Complete nationalization of large-scale copper mining; intensified quantitative restrictions.
1972	Foreign-debt renegotiation.
1973	Military coup in which President Allende killed.

Part I

Introduction

Chapter 1

The Foreign Sector and Chilean Economic Development: An Overview

1.1 INTRODUCTION

In discussions of economic development experience, considerable emphasis has been placed on the foreign sector. This emphasis partly reflects the view that the foreign sector can play a key role in the development process through the exploitation of dynamic comparative advantage, the transfer of technology and of command over resources, and inducements for efficiency,[1] and partly the fact that, in developing economies, the foreign sector is particularly subject to government influence.

Analyses of the foreign sector in actual economic development experience, however, usually have had definite limitations. In many cases the importance of quantitative restrictions in the foreign sector regime has been disregarded or understated. Historical perspective often has been lacking. Too frequently the supporting evidence is impressionistic, and available quantitative information has been ignored or not subjected to rigorous analysis. Repeatedly other macroeconomic policies and the problems to which they relate have not been kept in their proper perspective, with the result that foreign-sector considerations may be, or may appear to be, overstressed. At times partial-equilibrium conclusions have been misleading or wrong. In some cases very strong assumptions have been made about rigidities.[2] Considerable disagreement therefore remains about the impact of the foreign sector on developing economies.

In this study, I attempt to contribute to the analysis of the relations between international economic policies and various macroeconomic goals by a thorough examination of the experience of one specific developing country—Chile. Included among the macroeconomic goals are not only growth, but also other factors that are related to a broader definition of economic development: external position and the degree of national autonomy, stability in real and nominal terms, resource allocation and structural change, and the distribution of control over income and other resources. Some of these factors may be complementary and others may be competitive with the goal of growth.

Chile is a particularly interesting country for such a study for several reasons: (i) It has experienced a wide range of foreign-sector policies. (ii) Since the Great Depression, its attempts at industrial development under foreign-exchange control and trade restrictions have shown characteristics common to a number of other developing countries: a large and heavily protected industrial sector, recurrent balance-of-payment crises, a very large foreign debt, and high inflation which has helped to perpetuate overevaluation of the currency. (iii) Policy in the foreign sector has included responses to both substantial external and internal stimuli. (iv) Chile has had three major liberalization episodes in the past two decades, which provide a rich base for the evaluation of liberalization efforts in developing countries. (v) Recent Chilean governments have varied considerably in their political orientation. (vi) The Chilean experience has served as one of the major bases for the development of critiques of the conventional wisdom concerning development. To cite one important example, the "structuralist school" analysis of inflation and stagnation was based considerably on Chilean experience and was developed in substantial part by economists in Chile. According to the structuralists, the foreign sector is an important element in the vulnerability of certain Latin American economies to inflation and stagnation because slow and unstable export growth and a secular deterioration in the terms of trade for exports of primary products result in inadequate import capabilities and procyclical fluctuations in government revenues from foreign trade taxes.[3]

The interactions between the foreign sector and the rest of the Chilean economy have been quite complicated and have varied substantially over time. Moreover, in Chile more than in other countries, past events seem to have had unusually strong effects on recent policy decisions because of the catastrophic impact of some of those events, especially the Great Depression, and due to the unusually strong influence of Chilean economists who have attempted to understand the present in terms of the past.[4] In the next three sections of this chapter, I provide a chronological overview of the Chilean experience, in order to place the foreign sector in perspective both in a historical sense and as it relates to other areas of macroeconomic concern. In the last section, I furnish an outline of the study and a summary of my conclusions.

1.2 THE PERIOD BEFORE THE GREAT DEPRESSION[5]

Between the Spanish discovery of the land area that is now Chile, in 1535, and the War of Independence starting in 1810, Spain imposed a very mercantilistic regime on Chile. Trade could be conducted only with Spain and the Spanish colonies; goods were required to be carried in Spanish boats; manufacturing in Chile was discouraged, and the role of the mother country in government was substantial (although the geographic isolation of Chile resulted in considerable local autonomy). In the sixteenth century, exports consisted primarily of gold and silver; leather and animal fat were added in the seventeenth century; and copper and wheat were added in the eighteenth. From the beginning, then, mining products were an important component of Chilean exports and accounted for over half of the value of exports by the end of the eighteenth century. At that time imports consisted primarily of sugar (24 per cent of the total) and tobacco (24 per cent) from Peru, and textiles (16 per cent) and Paraguayan tea (24 per cent) from Argentina. Thus, Chile had relatively more of her trade with neighboring Latin American areas at that time than she was to have in the next 170 years. At the end of the colonial period, the population of about 1 million was approximately the same in size as when the Spanish first arrived, but its composition had changed from being almost entirely Indian to approximately 80 per cent Spanish and Creole. In comparison with most other Latin American countries, this population was relatively homogeneous and not dependent on agriculture. Furthermore, Chile had a relatively well-developed transportation system and urban structure.

From 1810 until 1830 the Wars of Independence and the subsequent political consolidation dominated events in Chile with substantial negative effects on the economy. By 1830 under the leadership of Diego Portales, banditry had been reduced considerably, public administration had been reorganized, public financing had been strengthened, and public works expenditure had increased. Chile then entered into a period of political stability which was unique in mid-nineteenth century Latin America. The period from 1830 to 1860 is widely thought to have been a "golden era" of great expansion and development.

Over the long term, international economic policy had moved from the extreme restrictiveness of colonial mercantilism, in 1810, through phases II and III and, by 1850–60, into Phase IV.[6] The most important change in the use of quantitative policy tools took place with the enactment of the Law of Free Commerce of 1811, which opened the ports of Talcahuano, Valparaíso, and Coquimbo to all trading nations. In 1849, the remaining ports were opened, and the prohibition on the participation of foreign boats in coastal trade was

TABLE 1.1

Exchange Rate and Selected Series on Exports, Imports, and Government Income and Expenditures of Chile, 1820–1930

Year	Exchange Rate (pesos, or 10^{-3} escudos, per U.S. dol.) (1)	Aver. Annual Exponential Growth Rate in Past 5 Yrs. (U.S. dol.) Imports (2)	Exports (3)	Total Govt. Income (4)	Ratios to Total Govt. Income: Foreign Trade Taxes Total (5)	Imports (6)	Exports (7)
1820					.44		
1825					.46		
1830	1.31				.50		
1835	1.29			.074	.57		
1840	1.29			.048	.62		
1845	1.29			.101	.52		
1850	1.06	.091	.138	.106	.57		
1855	1.09	.084	.081	.070	.56		
1860	1.14	.028	.046	.046	.56		
1865	0.70	.089	.100	.230	.23	.19	.04
1870	1.08	–.030	–.077	–.056	.33	.31	.02
1875	1.13	.053	.045	.008	.37	.36	.01
1880	1.61	–.118	.002	.078	.24	.20	.04
1885	1.95	.019	–.044	–.063	.60	.37	.23
1890	2.08	.086	.045	.067	.65	.26	.39
1895	2.93	–.064	–.053	.085	.52	.17	.35
1900	2.97	.122	.162	.021	.59	.21	.38
1905	3.19	.091	.108	.103	.41	.26	.15
1910	4.62	.093	.028	.030	.50	.19	.31
1915	6.07	–.134	–.000	–.078	.52	.13	.39
1920	5.73	.152	.110	.087	.40	.12	.28
1925	8.55	.036	.015	.086	.36	.15	.21
1930	8.26	.033	–.063	.081	.29	.19	.10

(*continued*)

TABLE 1.1 (*concluded*)

Year	Ratios to Total Govt. Income: Extraordinary Income[a] (8)	Ratios to Total Govt. Expenditures: Development Functions[b] (9)	Debt Service: Total (10)	Debt Service: Foreign (11)	Ratios of External Public Debt to: Ordinary Govt. Income (12)	Export Value (13)	Aver. Actual Import Tax Rates (14)
1820							
1825							
1830	.00				3.1		
1835	.14				2.5		
1840	.00		.06	.06	1.7		
1845	.04		.15	.12	2.7	1.16	.19[c]
1850	.05		.15	.13	1.8	0.42	.22[c]
1855	.06		.10	.08	1.1	0.35	.20[c]
1860	.14		.16	.13	1.9	0.56	.22[c]
1865	.56		.32	.10	1.5	0.44	.15
1870	.40		.24	.17	2.5	1.07	.21
1875	.24		.22	.16	2.7	1.22	.20
1880	.36		.16	.10	1.9	1.05	.17
1885	.09		.48	.35	1.5	1.08	.36
1890	.10	.36	.14	.07	1.8	1.38	.22
1895	.34	.28	.44	.10	2.3	2.66	.32
1900	.23	.26	.16	.15	2.2	1.48	.24
1905	.46	.28	.13	.13	2.0	0.88	.31
1910	.49	.33	.13	.13	1.9	1.03	.16
1915	.00	.31	.18	.17	2.5	1.35	.14
1920	.02	.47	.11	.09	1.0	0.49	.10
1925	.26	.31	.19	.16	1.4	0.69	.16
1930	.31	.21	.08	.07	1.9	1.86	.26

SOURCE: Calculated from data in Humud [1969:18, 100, 110, 130, 173, 205, 207, and 256].

a. Extraordinary income is from internal or external borrowing.

b. Includes expenditures by ministries of Industry, Public Works and Railroads, Agriculture and Industry, Land and Colonization, Commerce and Communications, and Development.

c. Overstates import tax rate since numerator includes import and export tax revenues.

suspended. Price-related policy tools were limited primarily to import and export taxes, with ad valorem–equivalent explicit rates of no more than 30 per cent. A unified and almost constant nominal exchange rate (NER)[7] (with some appreciation against the dollar) prevailed from 1830 to 1860 (column 1 in Table 1.1), during which time the value of the escudo-equivalent in 1960 United States dollars averaged 1,529 and never varied by more than 5 per cent from that average (a degree of stability not again attained).[8]

The dating of the switch from Phase IV to Phase V is somewhat arbitrary.[9] Domestic support of laissez faire policies was growing as the secular liberalization in foreign trade progressed. Prominent in both developments was a fervent French laissez faire advocate, Jean Gustave Courcelle-Seneuil, who was an adviser to the minister of finance and a professor at the University of Chile from 1855 through 1863. Courcelle-Seneuil directly participated in the drafting of important economic legislation during his years in Chile and is said to have had considerable indirect impact through the dogmatic application of his theories by Chilean disciples over the next fifty years. Among the pieces of legislation which he drafted, the 1860 banking law, which in the words of Hirschman [1963:164], "reflected distrust of the government" by establishing "the principle of free, almost wildcat, banking," has become at the least an important symbol of the acceptance of laissez faire by the Chilean body politic. Since the 1857–61 financial crisis, which reputedly originated in fluctuations in international markets and led, in some degree, to passage of the 1860 banking law, also resulted in a break with the past, 1861 has been selected as the year of transition to a new phase.

In the 1860s and on into the late 1870s, a very liberal international economic policy prevailed, except for the suspension of convertibility during the war with Spain (1865 to mid-1866). During this phase Chilean currency first appreciated against the dollar (partly because of the Civil War in the United States) and then started a long secular depreciation (Table 1.1, column 1). The average value of an escudo-equivalent in 1960 United States dollars, however, remained at about the average 1830–60 level (i.e., $1,512 for 1861–77 as compared to $1,529 for 1830–60).

A succession of events occurred between 1878 and 1882 which had a strong impact on the Chilean economy for the next half-century. First, convertibility was suspended in 1878 during a financial crisis largely brought on by a decrease of 27 per cent in the real value of exports between 1872 and 1878. This decrease, in turn, was primarily due to a succession of bad harvests and a sharp decline in copper prices. Hirschman [1963:169] probably is correct in hypothesizing that the 1878 financial crisis by itself probably would not have had substantially more impact on longer-run Chilean economic events and policies than did the temporary suspension of convertibility during the 1865–66 war with Spain had not a constellation of subsequent significant events followed so quickly. But other events did follow, and Chile never again returned to the gold standard for any period longer than six years.

Second, partially in response to the threat of having her rather substantial interests in the nitrate mines in the Atacama desert displaced, Chile fought the War of the Pacific with Peru and Bolivia from 1879 through 1882. Hope of an immediate return to convertibility was dashed by the war, and temporary restrictions on imports of nonwar materials were imposed which moved foreign trade policy back to Phase II or III. Such results were rather minor, however, in comparison with the longer-run impact of the war. Chile won and incorporated into her area Tarapacá and Antofagasta, which contained the world's only known sources of natural sodium nitrate. A new era began as nitrates dominated Chilean exports, becoming the major source of government revenue for the next half-century; and Chile became very integrated into the world economy.

Third, in 1882 the Chilean government denationalized the nitrate industry by returning ownership to the holders of certificates originally issued before the War of the Pacific by the Peruvian government.

Fourth, in 1882, after three centuries of wars, the Indian resistance in the south finally was crushed. The settling of this frontier together with the northern province won in the War of the Pacific led to the creation of new landholding and mining classes which were to join with the middle class to form a significant political power in the early twentieth century.

For the next half-century following the turbulent war years of 1878–82, a Phase IV or V international regime generally prevailed. Events and policies that resulted in some significant alterations in the foreign sector included (i) attempts to return to complete convertibility, (ii) the tariff revisions of 1897 and 1928, (iii) foreign debt accumulated in the War of the Pacific and the Civil War of 1891 and in the expanded public works programs of the 1920s, (iv) changes in world markets, (v) the resurgence of copper exports in the early twentieth century, (vi) and the establishment of the Central Bank in 1925. For this half-century preceding the Great Depression, nevertheless, foreign-sector policies were relatively homogeneous and predominantly liberal.

Five questions about that half-century of experience merit further consideration: (i) Why was complete and enduring convertibility not re-established after the War of the Pacific? (ii) Why did ownership of the major export commodities shift from Chilean to foreign hands? (iii) What was the evolution and impact of import-substitution policies? (iv) Did increased foreign dependence and vulnerability result from liberalization? (v) What was the relationship between liberalization and growth?

1.2.1 Failure to Re-establish Enduring Complete Convertibility.

On the face of it, the acquisition of control over the world's only nitrate source would seem to have made a return to convertibility rather easy after the War of the Pacific, given the critical role of nitrates in the manufacture of explosives and fertilizers. In the immediate postwar period, however, convertibility was not re-established because, for the reasons described below, there was a shortage of foreign exchange at the previous exchange rate level:

i. In the first half of the 1880s total export value actually declined (see column 3 in Table 1.1) because the increase in nitrate exports was more than offset by decreases in exports of copper and wheat.

ii. At the same time, government debt service on loans from abroad reached levels greater than one-third of total government expenditure, in part because of obligations incurred during the war (Table 1.1, column 11).

iii. Because of the 1882 decision to return nitrate ownership to certificate owners and because of earlier speculation in such certificates by foreigners, the Chilean share in nitrate ownership increased only from 20 per cent in 1875 to 36 per cent in 1882. Because the foreign speculation had been funded largely by the Chilean banking system, moreover, no substantial capital inflow accompanied the assumption of control of almost two-thirds of the nitrates by foreign interests.

iv. Because of internally financed government deficits and wildcat banking, the rate of inflation increased to a level of about 5 per cent per year at the same time that worldwide many prices were falling.[10]

Attempts to return to a metallic standard were made in 1887, 1895–98, and 1925–31. But all of these attempts were abortive because of a combination of factors, including the continuation of internal inflation, the setting of fixed NERs at overvalued levels, the large foreign debt incurred in the Civil War of 1891, and declines in external markets. Between 1878 and 1927 the value of Chilean currency depreciated steadily (Table 1.1, column 1). The escudo-equivalent in 1960 U.S. dollars decreased at a mean rate of 3.8 per cent per year with the result that in 1927 it was worth only approximately 15 per cent of its 1878 level.

1.2.2 Shift to Foreign Ownership of Major Exports.

Before the War of the Pacific the major exports were copper and wheat, both of which were almost entirely domestically owned. For three decades after the war, copper production fell steadily to a low in 1911 of less than 40 per cent of the 1876 peak level, and the Chilean share of world copper production fell from 44 per cent in 1878 to less than 5 per cent for 1900–15.[11] Agricultural exports (primarily wheat) also declined, from about 45 per cent of the total in 1844–80 (Pinto [1962]) to approximately 10 per cent in the 1920s.[12] Nitrates became the dominant export in the postwar decades,[13] but ownership was largely in foreign hands because of the 1882 denationalization decision. After 1910 there was a resurgence of copper production, but it occurred almost entirely in foreign-owned mines.[14] Production increased at a mean annual exponential rate of 11.8 per cent from 1910 through 1927; the Chilean share of world production increased from 4 to 16 per cent in the same period; and copper again became the leading Chilean export. Thus the weight in exports shifted from domestically owned copper and wheat to largely foreign-owned nitrates and then to almost completely foreign-owned copper.

This move to foreign control over exports reflected a number of factors:

i. Because of transportation costs, Chile could not compete effectively with new low-cost wheat producers in North America, Russia, and Argentina.

ii. The richest copper deposits had been exhausted by 1880, resulting in a substantial increase in Chilean copper-mining costs.

iii. Overvaluation of the currency after the War of the Pacific discouraged exportation of copper and wheat, the two previously dominant and domestically controlled export commodities.

iv. A shortage of government funds, arising from heavy service charges on war debts, was an important consideration in the 1882 denationalization decision.

v. In the early twentieth century, the lack of sufficient funds from domestic sources and the limited access to the international capital market precluded Chilean-controlled application of the new capital-intensive Jackling process to the remaining relatively low-grade copper ore.

vi. Before the discovery of a practical method for fixing nitrogen from the air, in 1914, Chile's nitrates were too important a war import material for the major powers to let control rest with Chile.

vii. An economic "open door" policy was thought to be useful in attracting desired immigrants.

viii. The philosophy of the ruling elite generally was laissez faire—partially because of the continuing influence of disciples of Courcelle-Seneuil. This viewpoint was instrumental in the 1882 decision to denationalize nitrates (so that the government would not be involved in direct production) and in subsequent decisions to leave the mining industry almost completely unregulated except for the collection of export taxes on nitrates.[15]

ix. The ruling and commercial elite apparently identified their interests strongly with those of foreign economic entities and with foreign trade. As a result, and despite the general laissez faire policies toward the export minerals, Humud [1969:38, 40, 217] notes, the government did attempt to aid the foreign-controlled nitrate companies in times of labor-market or international-market crises.[16]

Because of the shift of the export minerals to foreign ownership, large transfers of funds were made from Chile to the more developed countries. In the early twentieth century, there were also substantial capital inflows, which were used in developing foreign-owned, large-scale copper mines. The evaluation of these net flows [17] and of other costs and benefits is very difficult because the options cannot be determined with confidence on the basis of the scanty information available. However, from the nationalistic viewpoint of the 1960s and 1970s, which is *not* the same as that of the ruling elite of those times, it appears that Chile could have gained much more than she did from her mineral riches by exercising greater control, if not actual ownership.

1.2.3 Evolution and Impact of Import-Substitution Policies.

Conflicting claims about the pattern of import substitution before the Great Depression abound in the Chilean literature. The following data may aid in determining the actual evolution and impact of import-substitution policies:

i. From 1830 to 1960, the ad-valorem-equivalent import tax for final consumer goods ranged from 20 to 35 per cent; for intermediate goods, from 10 to 15 per cent; and for capital goods, zero (Humud [1969:122, 125]). Thus, the tariff structure resulted in higher effective than nominal protection rates for consumer and intermediate goods industries. Export taxes included an element of protection for thc processing of wheat in that the rate for flour was two-thirds that for grain. In the early part of the period from 1861 to 1896, some rationalization of the import tariff structure was made by reducing rate variances between categories. The highest ad-valorem-equivalent nominal rate also was decreased from 35 per cent to 25 per cent; so some decline in effective protection for final consumer goods resulted. Under Law 980 of 1897 the maximum import tariff rate was increased to 60 per cent for some final consumer goods and reduced to zero for some intermediate goods. Effective protection on final goods therefore increased substantially, although effective protection on some intermediate goods decreased.[18]

ii. Calculations based on data in Lagos [1966:26] indicate that the share of consumer goods in imports dropped from 89.6 per cent in 1870–72, to 76.2 per cent in 1878–82, and to 54.8 per cent in 1903–07. This secular decline in the relative importance of consumer goods imports is consistent with the claim of increasing substitution for such imports.

iii. The average actual import tax rates (Table 1.1, column 14) do not indicate a substantial decline immediately after 1860, but do show an increase from 1885 to 1905, a decline from 1910 to 1925, and an increase as of 1930; but these rates must be interpreted with some care because of changes in the composition of imports.

iv. Muñoz [1968:82] estimates that the total import substitution coefficient for the period from 1914–15 to 1927 was 0.431, as compared to a "normal" Chenery value of 0.194.[19]

v. For 1914–15 through 1929–30 Muñoz [1968:38] gives a mean annual rate of growth for real industrial GDP of 4.8 per cent. Other estimates range from 2.2 per cent to 6.0 per cent (see Table A.1, line 2.1; see also Ballesteros and Davis [1963] and CEPAL, in Muñoz [1968:38]).

vi. Both Lagos [1966:144] and Mamalakis [1971b:306] maintain that by the 1920s over a fifth of the total labor force was employed in manufacturing. For this sector to have been such a large employer, considerable industrialization must have taken place in the preceding seventy or eighty years.

Thus, the evidence suggests that at least moderate protection of final consumer goods had prevailed since the 1830s.[20] The degree of protection was reduced slightly in the 1860s, and a significant increase was instituted by the tariff law of 1897. The years from 1860 to the Great Depression were not characterized by substantially less protection than had prevailed before 1860, however, as Jobet [1955:42], Lagos [1966:19, 22–23, 38], Pinto [1962:16, 21, 49], and Sepúlveda [1959:36, 71–72] contend; nor did relatively low levels of protection prevail until just before the Great Depression, as Ellsworth [1945:49] and Jeanneret [1971:145] suggest. Moreover, industrial growth from 1860 to 1930 must have been substantial, although not extraordinary, in order for a manufacturing sector to have developed as large as that which existed in the 1920s. Much of this development took place, finally, through import substitution for consumer goods — a process which occurred at more than the Chenery "normal" rates, at least beginning with the outbreak of World War I and continuing thereafter.

1.2.4 Liberalization, Foreign Dependence, and Vulnerability.

The contention of the structuralist school (see section 1.1) is that because of liberalization Chile became extremely dependent on the foreign sector and, therefore, more vulnerable to instabilities abroad than would otherwise have been the case. The structuralist claim of great dependence is based on the following considerations:

i. *In the years immediately preceding the Great Depression, the economy was very dependent on exports and imports.* COMMENT: This hypothesis is based on observation of ratios of exports and of imports to GDP. Available estimates of these ratios range from 0.3 to 0.6, which are quite high compared with subsequent Chilean experience and with the experience of most other countries.[21]

ii. *As liberalization took place, the rates of growth of real exports and imports increased to relatively high levels.* COMMENT: A crude test of this hypothesis is provided by the following two regressions, in which the natural logarithms of the value of exports *(X)* and of imports *(M)*, both in 1960 dollars, are the dependent variables and dummy variables are utilized to test whether significant phase-related deviations in growth rates occurred in the period 1844–1927:[22]

$$\ln(X) = \underset{(7.2)}{0.037}\ TIME + \underset{(1.1)}{0.014}\ TIME{*}DUM(44\text{–}60) + \underset{(24.9)}{6.77} \quad (1.1)$$
$$\bar{R}^2 = 0.94,\ SE = 0.23,\ DW = 2.1,\ \rho = 0.79$$

$$\ln(M) = \underset{(5.7)}{0.048}\ TIME + \underset{(1.6)}{0.019}\ TIME{*}DUM(44\text{–}60) - \underset{(2.1)}{0.012}\ TIME{*}DUM(78\text{–}27) + \underset{(27.2)}{6.49} \quad (1.2)$$
$$\bar{R}^2 = 0.93,\ SE = 0.22,\ DW = 1.7,\ \rho = 0.73$$

where

TIME = time trend;
DUM(44–60) = dummy variable with value of 1.0 for 1844–60 and 0.0 for other years;
DUM(78–27) = dummy variable with value of 1.0 for 1878–1927 and 0.0 for other years.

These estimates suggest that real exports and imports in fact did *not* increase more rapidly in the more liberal, post-1860 phases. To the contrary, the growth rates were, if anything, significantly higher during the period before 1860. For exports, such a result might seem surprising because of the acquisition of a major new export—nitrates—in the War of the Pacific. But apparently the decline of wheat and copper (mentioned above) offset the expansion of nitrates. Finally, the implied growth rates for exports, 0.051 for 1844–60 and 0.037 for 1860–1927, and for imports, 0.067 for 1844–60, 0.048 for 1861–77, and 0.036 for 1878–1927, are less than those reported for some of the more restrictive, post-1940 phases (lines 1.2.4.1 and 1.2.4.2 in Table A.1), and undermine the assertion that exports and imports increased quite rapidly from 1860 to 1930.

iii. *In the period before the Great Depression, government income was very dependent on the foreign sector.* COMMENT: By any available index the reliance of government income on the foreign sector was considerable: between 1820 and 1930, foreign trade taxes ranged from 23 per cent to 65 per cent of total government income; for 1908–27, taxes related to foreign income (including income taxes on copper mining) averaged 83 per cent of total taxes; between 1820 and 1930, extraordinary income (including substantial foreign borrowing) was as high as 56 per cent of total government income; between 1840 and 1930, the resulting external public debt service was as high as 35 per cent of total government expenditures; in 1830–1930, the ratio of foreign public debt to ordinary annual government income was never below 1.0; and from 1845 to 1930, the ratio of external public debt to annual export value often exceeded 1.0 (Table 1.1, columns 5, 8, 11, 12, and 13, and Table A.1, lines 1.2.6.5 and 1.2.6.6). Regressions of ordinary (primarily taxes) and extraordinary (internal and external borrowing) government income on imports and exports for 1844–1927 provide further confirmation:[23]

$$OGY = 0.11M + 0.40X + 371.7 \qquad (1.3)$$
$$(1.7) \quad (11.7) \quad (1.0)$$
$$\bar{R}^2 = 0.96, SE = 703., DW = 1.8, \rho = 0.71$$

$$EGY = 0.33M - 0.10X + 293.9 \qquad (1.4)$$
$$(2.9) \quad (1.4) \quad (0.6)$$
$$\bar{R}^2 = 0.53, SE = 1{,}342., DW = 2.1, \rho = 0.58$$

where

OGY = ordinary government income (in thousands of 1960 dollars);
EGY = extraordinary government income (in thousands of 1960 dollars).

Variations in the foreign trade variables were consistent with a substantial proportion of the variance in ordinary government income and with over half of the variance in extraordinary government income.

Relation 1.4 merits further interpretation. The positive coefficient for the value of imports probably reflects both a secular trend in the use of extraordinary income[24] and the dependence of marginal imports on foreign exchange obtained from external extraordinary government income. The negative coefficient for the value of exports, although significantly nonzero only at the 10 per cent level, provides some support for the claim that the government substituted between extraordinary income sources and ordinary export tax revenues. When the latter declined the former were increased. To the extent that such extraordinary sources consisted of external debts (which were more important than internal ones), a decline in the value of exports resulted in an increase in foreign debt and in foreign dependence.

Although the foregoing evidence indicates that government income depended substantially on the foreign sector, it does not follow that this dependence was unavoidable. In fact, Humud [1969:151] reports that before the establishment of an income tax, in 1925, internal taxes generally declined as a percentage of total taxes as a result of deliberate decisions to eliminate most of these taxes.[25]

iv. *With increased liberalization, government revenues became more dependent on the foreign sector.* COMMENT: A test of this hypothesis is to include phase-coincident dummy variables in relations 1.3 and 1.4. In neither case, however, does such a procedure result in coefficients that are significantly nonzero even at the 15 per cent level.[26] Examination of the data in Table 1.1 also indicates the lack of association between dependence on the foreign sector for government revenues and phases of restrictionism. Foreign trade taxes accounted for over half of total government income both in the relatively restrictive years from 1830 to 1860 and in the more liberal and highly-nitrate-dependent period from 1885 to 1915 (columns 5, 6, and 7). The external public debt was relatively large primarily after wars and moderately so after borrowing abroad for infrastructural development (Table 1.1, columns 12 and 13).[27]

v. *With increased liberalization, foreign ownership increased.* COMMENT: As is discussed above, after the War of the Pacific,[28] foreign direct ownership of the key mineral exports increased considerably.

Thus the available evidence suggests that dependence on the foreign sector was quite substantial before the Great Depression, although not necessarily correlated with the degree of liberalization. The assertion that the economy became more vulnerable to externally generated fluctuations is more difficult to explore, but the following observations have some bearing on this issue.

i. Deviations from the secular time trend provide a measure of fluctuations, some of which, of course, originate in internal events and wars or reflect government decisions. The mean absolute proportional deviations of actual export value levels relative to the levels predicted by equation 1.1 are 0.10 (standard deviation of 0.06) for 1844–60, 0.11 (0.12) for 1861–77, and 0.19 (0.24) for 1878–1927. The mean for the last period is significantly larger at the 5 per cent level than those for the two earlier periods.[29] The implication of these fluctuations is that the actual value of exports fell 20 per cent below the value predicted by the model of secular time trend (equation 1.1) in eleven of the fifty years covered.[30] As the structuralists claim, it would be difficult correctly to anticipate the availability of foreign exchange if exports differed greatly from their anticipated levels. However, such fluctuations in exports did not increase significantly in the Phase V years 1860–77, contradicting the structuralists' contention.[31]

ii. The results for imports are similar. The mean absolute proportional deviations of the level of actual import values from the levels predicted by equation 1.2 are 0.09 ($\sigma = 0.08$) for 1844–60, 0.10 (0.10) for 1861–78, and 0.20 (0.20) for 1878–1927. Once again, fluctuations did not increase significantly between 1844–60 and 1861–77 (test statistic $= 0.3$), but they did increase significantly between 1844–77 and 1878–1927 (test statistic $= 2.7$).

iii. An analogous calculation for the mean absolute proportional deviation from a secular trend for ordinary government income, however, gives 0.15 for 1878–1927 ($\sigma = 0.15$), and this figure is not significantly different from the figure of 0.10 ($\sigma = 0.09$) for the earlier period (test statistic $= 1.6$). The structuralists' contention is, therefore, not supported: the significantly greater fluctuations in exports and imports after the War of the Pacific did not cause significantly increased fluctuations in government revenue, which would have had inflationary effects because the government would have had to finance its debts locally, since it could not readily reduce its expenditures.

iv. After the War of the Pacific, inflation apparently was higher than before, although the evidence is quite fragmentary, but lower, nevertheless, than the rates observed after the Great Depression (Table A.1, line 2.1). Since substantial portions of these relatively moderate rates were due to such factors as wildcat banking, supply disruptions, and internal deficit financing originating in the Civil War of 1891, the structuralist claim that substantial price instability originated in the foreign sector seems to be overstated.

v. Of course, price changes are but one aspect of cyclical fluctuations. Perhaps of more importance are fluctuations in the utilization of productive capacity. The mean rate of capacity utilization for the 1908–27 period was 93 per cent, an average level not exceeded again until the 1960s for the periods included in Table A.1 (line 2.2). Thus, on the average, at least during the twenty years before the Great Depression, no evidence exists of unusually large forgone output due to fluctuations in foreign markets (or to any other possible source). However, international market conditions were associated with the two lowest troughs in capacity utilization in the period: in 1914–15, because of wartime shortages of imported intermediate supplies, and in 1919–22, because of the 1921 depression.[32]

1.2.5 Liberalization and Economic Growth.

Chilean analysts have presented two quite different characterizations of growth before the Great Depression. Conflicting policy recommendations have been made because of the different interpretations of that experience. On the one hand, Hurtado [1966:57], Lagos [1966:38–39], Pinto [1962:16], and a number of structuralists contend that the relatively important role of the government in general and of government controls on international economic transactions in particular before 1860 resulted in much greater industrialization and economic development than occurred in the more liberalized period after 1860. In contrast, de Castro and de la Cuadra [1971:1] describe the decades immediately prior to 1929 as having one of the highest growth rates on record "in an environment of free trade which made it possible to take advantage of the opportunities created by the international markets while demanding, at the same time, efficiency in the domestic allocation of productive resources."

The conclusion that relatively high growth rates were experienced before 1860 as a result of the restrictive international trade regime seems doubtful from a number of points of view.

i. The characterization of rapid over-all economic growth is based primarily on the growth of exports, imports, and government revenues. But the presumption that these growth rates were unusually high before 1860 is not well founded. For exports the pre-1860 growth rate was found to be significantly higher than the post-1860 growth rate only at the 15 per cent level in relation 1.1. Again, for government revenues, the difference in growth rates between the two periods was not significant even at the 25 per cent level. Moreover, the rates of growth of exports and imports for 1844–60 that are implied by relations 1.1 and 1.2 were exceeded in a number of periods after the Great Depression (Table A.1, lines 1.2.4.1 and 1.2.4.2).

ii. Subsequent experience (including that during 1908–27, when imports and exports were much more important relative to over-all product than in the more agrarian and self-sufficient economy before 1860) indicates that the relations between the over-all rate of growth and the rates of growth of exports and of imports are not simple ones characterized by high correlations.[33]

iii. Much of the growth which did occur apparently originated not in industry, but in agriculture and mining, partly because of export opportunities in these sectors.

iv. The industrial expansion may have been an adjustment from a below-"normal" industrial sectoral share (in the Chenery [1960] sense) resulting from the effects of the Spanish colonial mercantilist policy to a "normal" share which would have occurred under a wide range of international economic regimes once Spanish control was eliminated. If so, subsequent slowing down of industrial expansion (if indeed it did occur[34]) may only have indicated that the relatively easy "catching up" period was over.

v. The existing data refer primarily to the years 1844–60, when substantial liberalization of international trade was occurring. Perhaps, therefore, the rapid rates of growth of imports and exports only reflected increasing propensities to trade because of the trade liberalization or high income elasticities for foreign trade.

On the other hand, even if such propensities were not increasing and income elasticities were not high, with the result that equivalent rates of growth of national income did occur, to attribute that growth to the liberalizing of foreign trade policy seems at least as consistent with the available data as to attribute it to the earlier, somewhat protectionist policies.

For the two or three decades preceding the Great Depression, more evidence is available about the probable relation of the international economic regime to growth. For savings, the impact was mixed, in that the effect of the regime was a continued shift of resources to the government, which apparently had a fairly high propensity to save;[35] however, in addition, under that regime a level of negative net foreign savings was tolerated which on average was not exceeded in any period before 1965 (see Table A.1, line 1.2.6.1).[36] The effect of the regime on investment seems to have been positive, generally resulting in a shifting of resources from sectors of average labor productivity[37] to higher ones (with the one exception noted below).[38] Relative domestic efficiency was raised by subjecting local industry to foreign competition (at least according to de Castro and de la Cuadra [1971:1]). In addition, in the early twentieth century, new technology and substantial amounts of foreign capital were allowed to enter, so that copper mining could be developed on a large scale.

On the other hand, the regime seemed to have negative consequences because it induced the movement of some resources into the manufacturing sector, in which productivity was relatively low.[39] Moreover, the development of the largely foreign-owned export mining sector was allowed to proceed with little regulation to protect the interests of Chile in cases where these interests might differ from those of the owners. Finally, excessive upper-class consumption and resource transfers abroad were allowed. As a result, the returns from the mineral export booms, which might otherwise have been utilized for substantial capital accumulation, were dissipated.[40] The net result of these internal and external factors was a mean annual growth rate in real per capita product of 1.5 per cent for 1908–27 [41] and, probably, a rate of about the same magnitude for the preceding decades.[42] Such a growth rate is not low for the Chilean experience, but it is exceeded by the rates recorded in several subsequent periods (Table A.1, line 5.1). Even if one is willing to assume a very strong relationship between trade policies and growth, therefore, this order of magnitude seems to justify neither the Hurtado-Lagos-Pinto characterization of that relationship as low and due to the failure of free trade, nor the de Castro-de la Cuadra claim of it as high and due to the very positive effects of free trade in the years before the Great Depression.[43]

1.3 THE IMPACT OF THE GREAT DEPRESSION

The Great Depression began to affect Chile in 1930. The resulting substantial change in the over-all economic situation is clear from the following observations. In 1930 the capacity to import fell 28 per cent,[44] the real value of imports fell 13 per cent, capacity utilization fell 11 per cent, and real mining product fell 27 per cent (with declines of 32 per cent in copper production, 47 per cent in nitrate production, and 25 per cent in nitrate employment);

per capita real GDP fell 14 per cent. Sectoral increases in real product per capita occurred only in agriculture and in government. Because of "misguided stubbornness in defending the gold standard" (Hirschman [1963:179]), monetary policy was contractionary because of a 29 per cent decline in gold reserves. Credit was restricted, wholesale prices declined 13.4 per cent, the real Central Bank interest rate increased 3.4 per cent, and the NER remained constant. The only significant anticyclical policy was an increase of 10 per cent in real government production, and this was financed by foreign borrowing.[45]

The extensive negative impact of the Great Depression on the Chilean economy in 1930 was intensified even further in 1931 and 1932. By the latter year, in comparison with 1929, the export capacity to import was 18 per cent, the real value of imports was 13 per cent, nitrate production was 23 per cent, nitrate employment was 15 per cent, copper production was 32 per cent, capacity utilization was 55 per cent, and per capita GDP was 49 per cent.[46] Even granted that 1929 was a boom year for the Chilean economy, and even though authorities differ in their estimates for this period (see, for example, Mamalakis [1971b:40; 1965:384] and Ballesteros and Davis [1963]), the conclusion that the declines were catastrophic is incontestable on any basis. Indeed, a League of Nations report characterized Chile as the hardest hit of any country by the Great Depression.

For the purposes of this study the most important reaction to the Great Depression was the abrupt change in the prevailing economic philosophy and policy from liberalism to restrictionism and, somewhat more slowly, to interventionism. Tremendous frustration resulted from too much *dependencia* on the external sector.[47] In hopes of reducing that dependence and the associated vulnerability, acceleration of internal industrial development was desired. Restrictive policies, especially for the foreign sector, were seen as the most effective means of encouraging domestic industry, reducing dependence on the foreign sector, and conserving scarce foreign exchange. Therefore quite restrictive policies were imposed in 1931.

Before the Great Depression, as is noted in the previous section, some tendencies toward greater control of international economic relations and reduced dependence on the foreign sector had existed. For example, industrial import substitution apparently was a major aim of the 1897 and 1928 tariff laws and the 1925 tax legislation served to lessen the dependence of government revenues on the foreign sector. Despite these elements of continuity, however, the periods before and after the Great Depression differed substantially in the range and nature of the policy tools used. For the eighty years before the Great Depression, the major policy tools were a unified NER and indirect taxes on foreign trade; the characteristics of phases IV and V dominated. For the forty years after the Depression, the economy was characterized by the more restrictive phases—I, II, and III—except for a brief experience of Phase IV in 1959–61. The major policy tools (see Part II, below) included multiple exchange rates, a myriad of indirect taxes and surcharges on imports, direct taxes on the major export producers, licensing, quotas, permitted and prohibited lists, prior deposits on imports, special regimes for exports and imports, explicit and implicit subsidies, tax rebates, bilateral and compensation agreements, and regulations concerning direct investment and related flows and capital movements. Not only was there great expansion in the variety of policy tools utilized in the attempt to run the more highly controlled system of the post-depression era, but also there were great increases in both the frequency of policy changes and specificity of policy. The Great Depression, thus, delineated the most important break in the history of the Chilean experience of quantitative restrictions.

1.4 PHASES OF EXCHANGE CONTROL AFTER THE GREAT DEPRESSION[48]

1.4.1 1931–55: Phases I and II—A Quarter Century of Quantitative Restrictions.

Phase I restrictions were imposed in 1931 and followed by twenty-five years of Phase II ad hoc adjustment in the foreign trade regime in attempts to offset the perceived negative results of the restrictions. The degree of quantitative restrictions was relatively constant throughout the quarter century, but policy in other areas of economic activity was less consistent.[49] Four subphases[50] of the basically Phase-II-type foreign-sector regime may be distinguished: 1931–39, 1940–46, 1947–51, and 1952–55.

1931 TO 1939.

The first years were characterized by the sharp economic decline discussed in the previous section. The subsequent recovery was only partial: by 1939, real per capita GDP was 76 per cent of the 1930 level and 66 per cent of the peak-1929 level, and the value of exports in constant United States dollars was 53 per cent of the 1930 level and 29 per cent of the peak 1920 level.[51] The resulting subphase means for the growth rate in real per capita GDP (Chart 1.1) and for the level of capacity utilization were the lowest among all post-1907 phases and subphases. The subphase mean for the index of export capacity to import was tied for second lowest (Chart 1.1). Moreover, even though prices declined initially (as mentioned above), the rate of inflation rose to a mean level of 8.5 per cent (Chart 1.1).[52] Despite definite improvements since the early 1930s, therefore, at the end of this subphase the over-all economic situation remained substantially worse than that which had prevailed before the Great Depression.

1940 TO 1946.

This subphase was dominated by two features: First, the Popular Front government pursued a generally expansionary policy, especially in regard to the activities of CORFO (Corporación de Fomento), a quasi-public development corporation established in 1939. Second, World War II had the effect of substantially increasing the demand for Chilean copper and reducing the availability of imports.[53]

Economic activity increased considerably because of heightened aggregate demand. Mean capacity utilization returned to its pre-Depression level, which was not exceeded again until the 1960s (Chart 1.1). The mean rate of growth of real GDP per capita was the highest recorded in 1908–64 (Chart 1.1). The mean annual rate of growth of real industrial product, 7.5 per cent, was the highest attained in 1908–70 (line 5.2 in Table A.1).

The factors leading to these gains in real terms, however, also led to substantial inflationary pressures. Aggregate demand pressures, moreover, were reinforced by worldwide price increases: over the seven years 1940–46, unit import values in foreign currency and the imported component of the wholesale price index increased at mean annual rates of 15.2 and 38.8 per cent, respectively. The mean annual rate of change in the GDP deflator increased to 15.1 per cent (Chart 1.1).

Despite the much higher physical quantities of copper exported, the index of export capacity to import fell slightly to the lowest mean value among the periods for which data is available, 1928–66 (Chart 1.1).[54] This decline reflected the combination of fixed copper prices in 1942–46 (due to an agreement with the United States as part of the war effort) and rapidly rising import prices (line 1.1.5.1 in Table A.1). The PLD-NER, moreover, dropped almost 40 per cent because devaluations did not match the internal inflation (Chart 1.1). The exchange control system nevertheless loosened up somewhat. One possible indication is that the ratio of the free- or black-market exchange rate to the average exchange rate actually declined by 11 per cent (Chart 1.1).[55] The lack of more pressure on foreign exchange despite the declines in the capacity to import and in the PLD-NER was due to two factors mentioned above—the increase in the international price of imports and the limited availability of imports—and to considerable CORFO-related net capital inflows.

1947 TO 1951.

This immediate-postwar subphase was characterized by reduced capacity utilization and growth, but accelerated inflation at an average annual level of

CHART 1.1
Selected Macroeconomic Variables During Phases and Subphases of the Chilean Exchange Control Regime, 1908–71

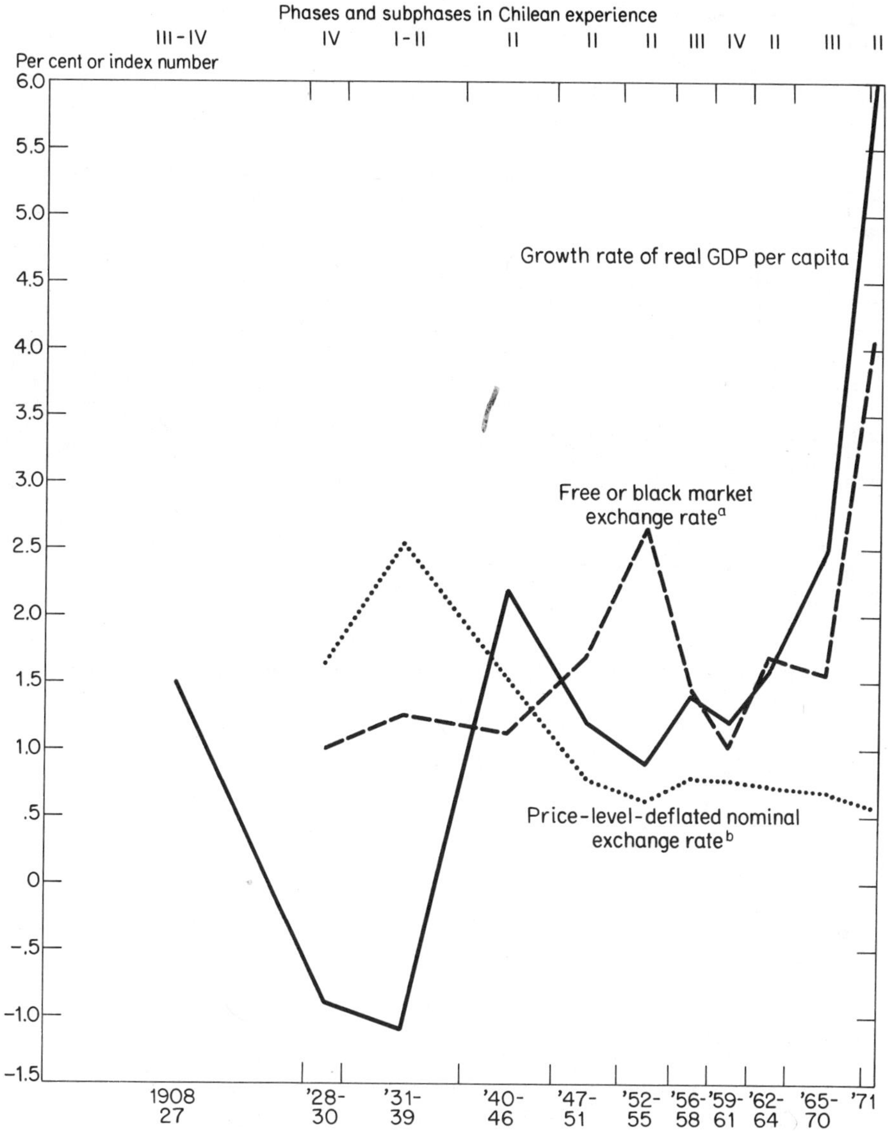

(continued)

CHART 1.1 (*concluded*)

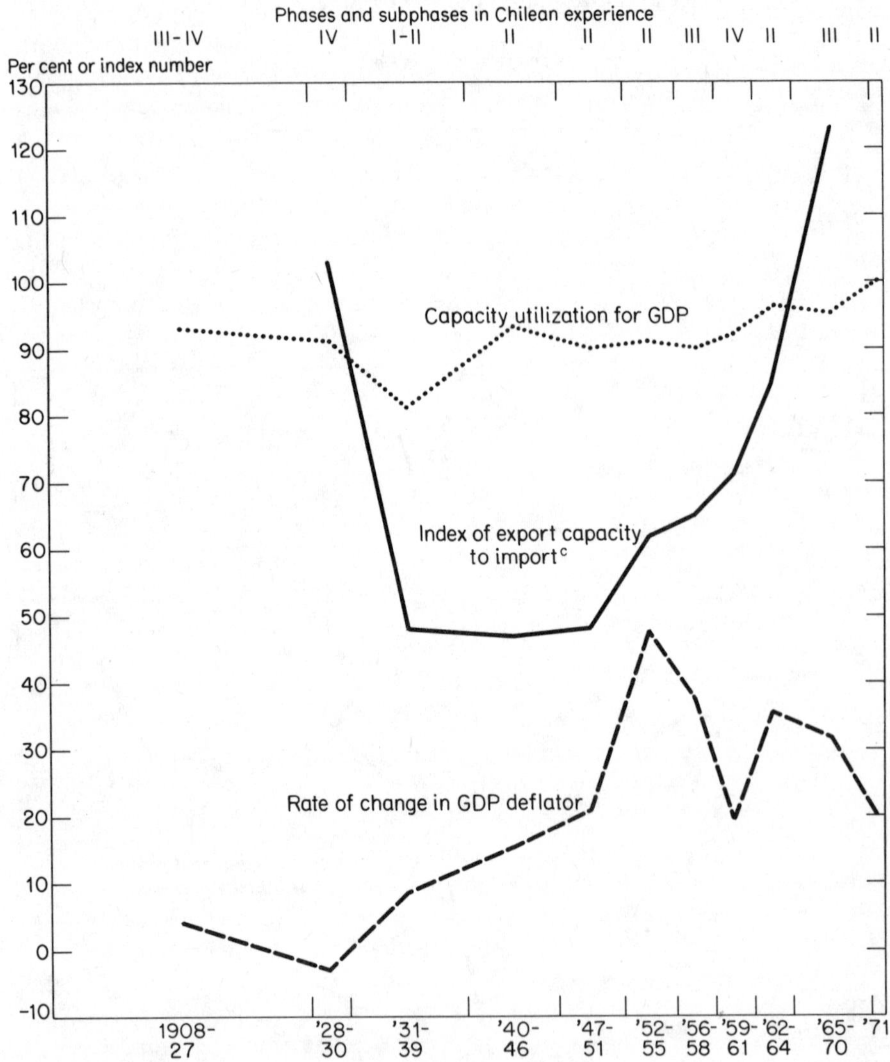

SOURCE: Table A.1, lines 1.1.1, 1.1.3, 5.1, 1.2.6.3, 2.1, and 2.2.

a. Expressed as a multiple of the national accounts rate.

b. January 1, 1959 = 1.00 (see note to line 1.1.1 in Table A.1).

c. 1965 = 100. In 1965–70 phase, average is for 1965–66 only.

20.8 per cent (Chart 1.1). The stagnation partially reflected the depression in the world copper market in 1948–49. Some of the inflationary pressure likewise originated in the foreign sector (i.e., the unit value of imports increased 23.6 per cent in 1947 and 16.8 per cent in 1951; the unit value of exports increased 31.4 per cent in 1947 and 26.5 per cent in 1951). A midperiod attempt under Finance Minister Jorge Alessandri to revitalize the economy and reduce inflation was abortive.

The constant-dollar value of both exports and imports increased at very high mean rates (Table A.1, lines 1.2.4.1 and 1.2.4.2).[56] The former rose initially because of the termination of the fixed copper price, dropped in the intermediate years because of recessionary conditions abroad, and increased in 1951 because of the Korean War boom. The latter grew because of a 48 per cent fall in the PLD-NER (Chart 1.1)[57] and pent-up demand from the war. In fact, imports would have increased even more had not exchange control increased somewhat due to the scarcity of foreign exchange (Table A.1, lines 1.1.3 and 1.2.6.2.).

1952 TO 1955.

The predominant features of these years included rising economic and political instability and rampant inflation. The mean growth rate in per capita GDP sank to a postwar trough, mean capacity utilization remained relatively low, and the mean annual inflation rate skyrocketed to 47.8 per cent (Chart 1.1).

Near the end of this subphase, the internal situation deteriorated greatly. In 1954 and 1955, real per capita GDP decreased by a total of 4 per cent, capacity utilization fell to an average level of 89 per cent (the lowest level since the mid-1930s), real wages fell by a total of 17 per cent below the historic high of 1953, annual strikes and labor conflicts increased an average of 25 per cent above the previous all-time high of 1953, and the mean annual increase in the GDP deflator was 71.7 per cent. In May 1954, a major blue-collar strike took place, and a state of siege was declared in September. In 1955, three different ministers of finance held office in the first half of the year. In July, a general strike occurred, the long-silent Central Bank issued a report on the inflation which recommended forceful anti-inflationary measures, and rumors of a military-backed suspension of the Constitution abounded.[58]

In the external sector, in contrast, the immediate situation was relatively favorable in many respects. The mean export capacity to import increased 29 per cent (Chart 1.1). The mean deficit on the goods and services account was the smallest in absolute value in the postwar period (Chart 1.2). In 1954 and 1955, furthermore, the constant-dollar value of net foreign loans to the Chilean government increased rapidly. In 1955 exports and imports in con-

CHART 1.2

Major Components of Chile's Balance of Payments During Phases and Subphases of Her Exchange Control Regime, 1947–71

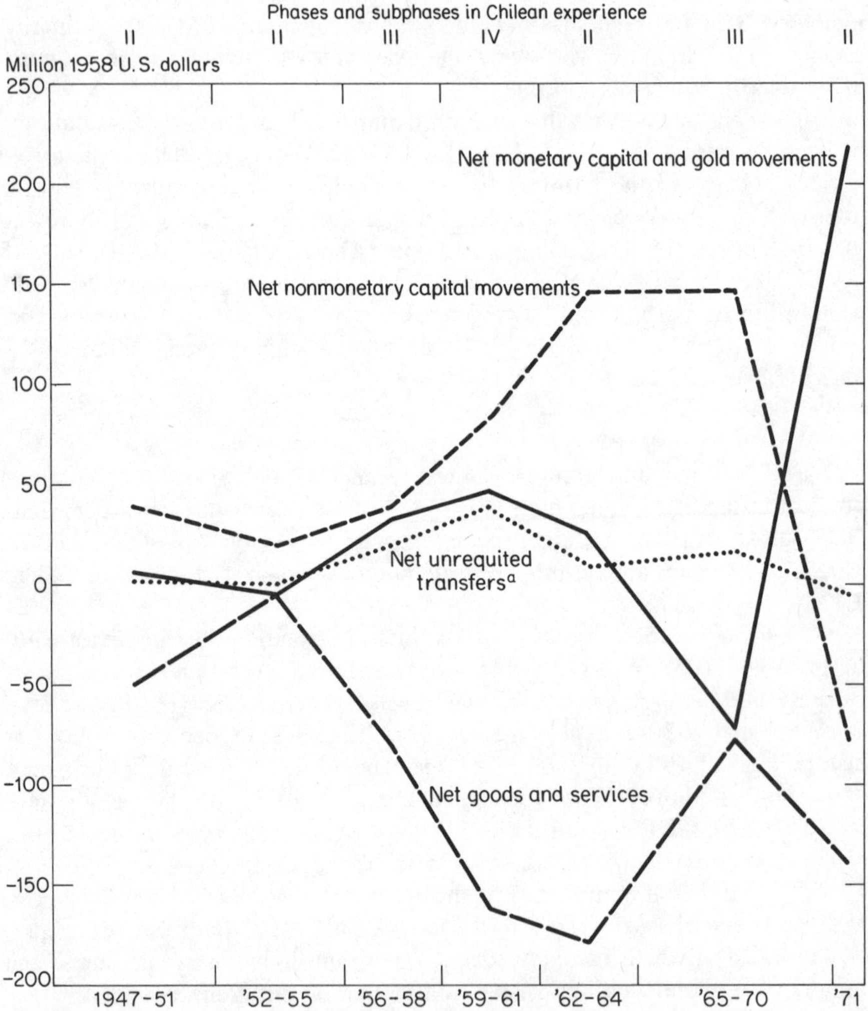

SOURCE: Table 8.1. Values for 1965–69 and 1970 from that table have been combined in order to obtain the 1965–70 averages shown here.

a. Value for 1971 calculated from data in Table 8.1 under assumption that errors and omissions were nil.

stant dollars rose 18.4 and 11.0 per cent, respectively, and the terms of trade were the most favorable since 1937.

But the PLD-NER declined to the lowest level of the whole period from 1908 to 1970 because devaluation lagged behind inflation (Chart 1.1). The resulting high demand for foreign exchange was augmented by the effects of capital flight prompted by internal instability. Exchange control therefore was intensified, reaching a postwar high (line 1.2.5.2 in Table A.1). The average ratio of the black-market to the legal exchange rate reached a record high of 2.66, a level not attained again until 1971 (Chart 1.1).

1.4.2 1956–58: Phase III—The Ibañez-Klein-Saks Stabilization and Liberalization Program.

Because of the rapidly deteriorating internal situation, in mid-1955 the government hired the Washington-based Klein-Saks consulting firm to advise in the formulation of a stabilization program. The effort of stabilization plus liberalization that commenced in early 1956 was strongly identified with the Klein-Saks mission.

A number of indices suggest that this stabilization attempt met with at least initial success. The mean rate of rise of prices was reduced from 47.8 per cent in 1952–55 to 37.6 per cent in 1956–58 (Chart 1.1), with annual rises declining from 58.3 per cent in 1956 to 28.3 per cent in 1957 and to 26.3 per cent in 1958. Although the mean rate of capacity utilization declined slightly below the 1952–55 average, it was higher than the 1954 and 1955 levels (Chart 1.1). The mean rate of growth of per capita real GDP was the highest recorded among the phases and subphases since the end of the Second World War (Chart 1.1), as a decline in industry was more than offset by increases in agriculture and other sectors (lines 5.1, 5.2, and 5.3 in Table A.1). However, in most respects, the economy worsened in 1958.

In the foreign sector, liberalization resulted in a shift to a Phase III regime. Accompanying this liberalization was a fall of 46 per cent in the mean ratio of the black-market NER to the over-all average NER, a rise of 30 per cent in the PLD-NER, and an increase of 5 per cent in the mean export capacity to import (Chart 1.1). Imports grew so much more rapidly than exports, however, that the mean deficit on the goods and services account in millions of 1958 dollars increased from −5.6 to −81.7 (Chart 1.2). This enlarged deficit was partially offset by mean increases in net unrequited transfers from −0.1 to 19.6 million 1958 dollars (largely due to foreign official support for the stabilization effort) and in net nonmonetary capital inflows from 18.6 to 37.4 million 1958 dollars (Chart 1.2). But mean net monetary capital and gold movements also increased—from −5.6 to 32.7 million 1958 dollars (Chart 1.2)—which placed growing pressure on the dwindling foreign exchange reserves. Among the causes of this pressure were a reduction in export value due to a decline in the terms of trade, which reflected recessionary conditions in foreign markets (line 1.1.5.1 in Table A.1) and increased demand for foreign exchange for imports due to the decline in the PLD-NER after the fixing of NERs at constant levels in mid-1957. As a result of the increasing pressure on foreign exchange reserves, exchange controls were intensified in the last half of this phase, although probably not to the same degree as in 1955.

1.4.3 1959–61: Phase IV—The Alessandri Stabilization and Liberalization Policies.

In the presidential election of late 1958, Jorge Alessandri, a conservative, narrowly defeated Senator Salvador Allende Gossens, the Socialist candidate. The new government had no formal stabilization program, but generally hoped to achieve price stabilization and to revitalize the economy through increased supplies of all goods, to be induced by liberalized internal and external policies. In comparison with the Klein-Saks program of the previous phase, the Alessandri government seemed to place revitalization above price stabilization [59] and to place greater importance on the role of a liberalized foreign sector.

The Alessandri policies had mixed results during this period. The mean capacity utilization rate was the highest since the Second World War, although lower than rates attained in the 1960s and early 1970s (Chart 1.1). The mean rate of inflation was the lowest in the entire postwar period, 1946–71 (Chart 1.1). In all the twenty-six postwar years through 1971, rates as low as the ones in 1960 and 1961—9.5 and 7.9 per cent—were recorded only two other times. The rate of growth of real GDP, however, fell to the lowest mean level of any phase after 1955, although it did exceed the means for the subphases between 1928 and 1940 and 1947–55.

Liberalization of the foreign sector proceeded steadily. The result was a Phase IV regime, the most liberal since the Great Depression. One index of the relative lack of restrictions is the drop in the mean ratio of the black-market NER to the average legal NER; it fell 30 per cent to a post-Depression low of approximately 1.0 (Chart 1.1 and line 1.2.6.2 in Table A.1).

The mean export capacity to import rose by 9 per cent (Chart 1.1) despite a small decline in the mean terms of trade (line 1.1.5.1 in Table A.1). The fall in the mean PLD-NER, which resulted from the maintenance of a fixed NER after the January 1959 devaluation (Chart 1.1), and the reduction of restrictions on imports, however, resulted in an increase of over 18 per cent in the mean value of imports in constant dollars (line 1.2 in Table 8.1). The mean deficit on the goods and services account, therefore, rose from −81.7 to −163.0 millions of 1958 dollars (Chart 1.2). Despite partially offsetting increases in mean net unrequited transfers, which resulted from international support of the stabilization program, and in mean net nonmonetary capital inflows, which resulted from new foreign investment and capital repatriation, compensatory mean net monetary movements reached the highest level of the 1947–70 period (Chart 1.2). Mean net foreign reserves held by the banking system fell from $29.9 million in the previous phase to –$60.0 million in this one (line 1.2.6.4 in Table A.1). At the end of 1961 these reserves amounted to –$164.8 million.

1.4.4 1962–64: Phase II—Reversal to Restrictionism, Interventionism, and Inflation.

In December 1961 the Central Bank's liquid foreign reserves were equal to the value of about ten days of imports, a considerable number of import applications were pending, and the Central Bank could no longer borrow abroad because of the substantial outstanding foreign debt. Near the end of that month, therefore, the Central Bank revoked all grants of authority to deal in foreign exchange and established temporary 10,000 per cent prior-deposit requirements on all imports. The Alessandri stabilization attempt and the Phase IV type of foreign-sector regime thus came to an end. The next three years were characterized even less than the 1959–61 period by a systematic over-all economic program. Instead, piecemeal policies led to a generally more complicated and restrictive system.

The general performance of the economy in 1962–64 was in some respects quite satisfactory. The mean rate of growth of real GDP was the highest since the Second World War (Chart 1.1). The mean rate of capacity utilization was the highest it had been in any phase or subphase from 1908 to 1964 (Chart 1.1). However, there were problems. The mean annual rate of change of prices increased to 35.4 per cent (Chart 1.1), with levels recorded in 1963 and 1964 that were exceeded in the Chilean experience only in the near-hyperinflations of 1954–56 and 1972–76. The relatively high mean rate of growth, moreover, was due almost entirely to events in 1962. On a per capita basis, the economy in real terms almost stagnated in 1963 and 1964.

Inflation outpaced even the rather substantial devaluations; so the PLD-NER fell another 5 per cent (Chart 1.1). The increased inducement to import was restrained only by the return of quantitative restrictions to a Phase II level. The mean ratio of the black-market NER to the average of the legal NERs rose to 1.70 (Chart 1.1), providing one measure of the increase in exchange control. Bacha and Taylor [1963:144] estimate that the degree of overvaluation averaged 47 per cent in this phase.

The export capacity to import increased about 20 per cent (Chart 1.1) because of an improvement of almost 10 per cent in the terms of trade (line 1.1.5.1 in Table A.1) and an expansion in the physical quantity of copper exports. Even though exports grew more rapidly than imports, however, the mean net deficit on the goods and services account rose to its largest value in the postwar period primarily because of the large augmentation in net factor payments abroad (Chart 1.2, and line 5 in Table 8.1). Mean net unrequited transfers fell, but mean net nonmonetary capital inflows increased substantially because mean net inflow of loans to the central government was the highest recorded in any period since World War II (Chart 1.2 and line 13.1 in Table 8.1). As one result, mean net monetary capital and gold movements fell to almost half the level of the previous period (Chart 1.3). As another result, foreign debt by the end of 1964 had risen to $1,896 million—278 per cent of the export value or 36.1 per cent of GDP for that year.

1.4.5 1965–70: Phase III—The Frei Stablization and Liberalization Program.

In the presidential election of late 1964 the Christian Democratic candidate, Eduardo Frei Montalva, won by a substantial margin (the runner-up, once again, was Senator Salvador Allende, the leftist-front candidate). The new government had as its goals substantial changes in the economic, political, and social fabric of the country. Among the major objectives were (i) increases in the rates of economic growth through higher capacity utilization and capacity expansion;[60] (ii) gradual programmed price stabilization; (iii) redistribution of income and of political power toward the lower economic classes; (iv) increased national control over the national destiny and the elimination of balance of payments problems by changing the nature of control over Chilean mineral resources, by increasing the capacity to export both traditional and nontraditional products, and by increasing domestic production in "dynamic" sectors; and (v) structural changes including reforms in agriculture, social security, education, the Constitution, housing, taxation, government, and (later) industrial organization; and popular promotion (*promoción popular*) of wider participation in decision making.

These broad objectives had firm roots in the structuralist analysis of the Chilean economy. Price stabilization was included as one of the major objectives for the third time in a decade, but was not given priority over all other aims. Foreign-sector liberalization was initiated in some ways almost immediately. A sliding-peg NER policy was introduced in April 1965, with weekly or biweekly devaluations (section 3.2). Exchange control was reduced much more, however, in the last half of the period, after the Vietnam War–related copper boom had provided increased foreign exchange and the momentum for internal reform had died. The result was a Phase III regime over the period as a whole, with perhaps some Phase IV characteristics appearing in the last years.

The indication of a number of indices is that the average general economic performance was relatively satisfactory during the Frei regime (Chart 1.1). The mean growth rate of per capita real product was the highest attained in any phase or subphase since 1908. The mean capacity utilization level had been exceeded only once before. The mean rate of change in the GDP deflator declined significantly from the level of the 1962–64 phase.

Once again, however, the mean values disguise a deteriorating intraphase situation. Almost all of the per capita real growth, the highest capacity utilization rates, and the lowest rates of inflation occurred in 1965 and 1966. Thereafter, the economy was relatively stagnant with increasing inflation.

The mean value of exports in constant dollars rose almost 60 per cent because of the copper-market boom of the late 1960s (line 1.1 in Table 8.1). For the first time, the export capacity to import exceeded the pre-Depression level (Chart 1.1). Because of the continuing fall in the mean PLD-NER (Chart 1.1) and the reduction in exchange control, mean PLD-EERs dropped considerably. Mean imports in constant dollars increased 21 per cent (line 1.2 in Table A.1). The net impact of the changes in exports and imports was a reduction of almost 60 per cent in the mean deficit on the goods and services account (Chart 1.2), despite an increase of 75 per cent in the mean net outflow of investment income (Table 8.1, line 5). The reduction in this deficit, together with slight increases in mean net unrequited transfers and nonmonetary capital inflows, resulted in a drop in mean compensatory capital and gold movements to post-World War II lows (Chart 1.2). By the end of this phase, net international reserves of the banking system had reached the highest level in at least two decades. But the foreign debt nevertheless grew at an average rate of 7.3 per cent per year to a level of approximately $3 billion by late 1970—248 per cent of annual export value or 27.2 per cent of GDP.[61] The debt position thus was ominous despite the benefits from the copper-market boom.

1.4.6 1971–73: Phase II—Allende and Popular Unity Policies.

In the presidential election of late 1970 Salvador Allende, the candidate of Popular Unity (a coalition of the Communist, Socialist, Radical, and several minor parties), narrowly defeated former president Alessandri (thus reversing the results of the 1958 election). According to Américo Zorrilla [1970:1477], the first minister of finance, the central long-run aim of the new government was "to transform the present economic structure, terminating the power of foreign and domestic monopolistic capital and of the latifundia, in order to initiate the construction of socialism."[62] Related medium- and long-run goals included: (i) the redirection of benefits of the economy more to lower- and middle-income classes; (ii) the development of an extensive multilevel planning system with wide participation; (iii) the reduction of external dependence in all of its possible forms; and (iv) the establishment of a new ownership structure for the means of production—state (basic natural resources, large monopolies, banks, foreign commerce, and other strategic activities for development), mixed (parts of the industrial, fishing, mining, and trade sectors), and private. The government proposed to move toward these goals gradually and constitutionally in "the Chilean way," not by extralegal means.

To broaden support for the long-run attempt to transform society, the government recognized that some short-run successes were essential. The components of short-run policy, as outlined in the 1971 plan, were the following:

i. Revitalization of the economy by reducing uncertainty through the use of guaranteed production contracts with the state and by increasing aggregate demand through increased exports, a substantial redistribution of income, and a large increase in government expenditures on public works, housing, and human capital;

ii. Constraint of inflation by strict price controls, by freezing the NER, and by increasing supplies from domestic production (by means of increased capacity utilization) and from imports (which would be financed through expanded exports and the available international reserves accumulated during the 1960s copper boom);

iii. Redistribution of income to the lower and middle classes by a minimum readjustment of wages and salaries of 100 per cent of past price increases (and larger adjustments for lower wages and salaries) in combination with reduced inflation; by increased lower-income housing; by increased human-capital investment (especially in education and in health); by increased employment; by reductions in returns to national and foreign higher-income groups through the nationalization of key subsectors in the economy; by accelerated agrarian reform; and by the democratization of the distribution of credit;

iv. Redistribution of control over resources from the private to the public sector in hopes of providing the basis for planned "harmonized and balanced growth" which would favor the lower and middle classes by expanding the planning apparatus and by extending state control into the productive sector;

v. Initiation of structural reform, which would lay the basis for high long-run growth and for the transformation to socialism by means of accelerated investment of public-sector enterprises,[63] by the enlargement of the role of the state in the economy, and by acceleration of agrarian reform;

vi. Expansion of state activities in all aspects of international economic interchange by the reintroduction of a Phase II regime in order to reduce foreign dependence of all types and to utilize the foreign sector in the pursuit of the other aims mentioned above.

In 1971 the performance of the economy was quite positive in a number of important general respects. Capacity utilization rose to a very high level

(Chart 1.1). Unemployment dropped substantially (Table A.1, line 2.3).[64] The rate of change of prices fell to 20 per cent (Chart 1.1). Imports in constant dollars increased over 6 per cent (Table 8.1, line 1.2). The rate of growth of per capita real product soared above the means of any phases or subphases since 1907 (Chart 1.1) and exceeded annual means of every year but one after the Second World War.

In the same year the new government also succeeded in several ways in its aims of transforming ownership relations and of extending state control. With unanimous legislative support, Chile completely nationalized large-scale copper mining, which previously had been subject to considerable foreign control.[65] The state extended its direct control over a number of other formerly foreign- and domestically-owned enterprises, including most private banks. The government accelerated agrarian reform. Exchange control increased, and the public-sector share in approved import registration rose from 34 per cent in 1970 to 44 per cent in 1971 (and to 65 per cent in the first eight months of 1972).

Some of these short-term gains, however, were purchased at significant long-term costs:

i. The high growth in 1971 reflected higher capacity utilization resulting from expansion of current consumption more than it did an increase in productive capacity. In fact, in that year the rate of augmentation of capacity declined. Real physical investment dropped by 7.7 per cent (Table A.1, line 5.4),[66] and the constant-dollar value of imported machinery and equipment fell 16.8 per cent.[67] The fall in the rate of growth of industrial production from values ranging from 10.8 to 14.7 per cent in 1971 to 2.5–2.8 per cent in 1972 may reflect in part the approach of the economy to capacity limits.[68]

ii. The decline in the rate of change of prices in 1971 occurred despite a 121 per cent increase in the money supply because of greater supplies of goods from domestic production and imports, more extensive price controls, the maintenance of a fixed NER, and an upward shift in the demand for real monetary balances resulting from income redistribution and changed expectations. Given the augmentation of the money supply and of labor payments, these measures could not suppress inflation for long. In late 1971, the pace of price increases began to accelerate. In 1972 the consumer price index rose 178 per cent, an all-time high. Inflation increased even more in 1973. Black markets flourished for many commodities.

iii. The constant-dollar value of exports dropped 12 per cent in 1971 (Table 8.1, line 1.1) and declined again in 1972[69] because of the slump in the world copper market[70] and the failure of Chilean production to reach planned levels (e.g., in 1971, production was less than 80 per cent of that planned for the year). In part because of United States reaction to the terms of the copper nationalization, net unrequited transfers in constant dollars also fell, and net nonmonetary movements in constant dollars plummeted (Chart 1.2). At the same time imports in constant dollars increased over 6 per cent in 1971 (Table 8.1, line 1.2) and approved import registrations apparently rose even faster in 1972.[71] As a result, international reserves held by the banking system fell by over $300 million in 1971, net monetary capital and gold outflows in constant dollars reached a post-World War II high (Chart 1.3), and a severe foreign exchange shortage existed by the end of 1971. Therefore, the escudo was devalued by 30 per cent in December 1971 and by 58 per cent in August 1972, exchange control became much more restrictive, and the large foreign debt obligations were renegotiated in 1972.[72] Nevertheless, the country continued to be on the verge of foreign-exchange crises.

iv. The attempt to transform the power and ownership relations of society caused considerable politicization and polarization in Chilean society. In 1972 martial law had to be invoked several times, and the economy ground to a halt in October because of a 25-day work stoppage by the Truck Owners' Association (supported by many business and professional groups) which was terminated after the government added three military members to the cabinet. Internal instabilities increased in 1973. Copper miners went on strike in May. An attempted military coup was squelched on June 29, 1973. Truckers, businessmen, and professionals again struck. On September 11, Allende died in a military coup.

1.5 MAJOR CONCLUSIONS

Not all of the detailed results of this book can be presented here in a sufficiently brief form. The following points, however, integrate and summarize many of the major thrusts of this analysis of the Chilean experience.

i. *Early origins of exchange control and import substitution.* The introduction of exchange control as an element of Chilean international economic policy was *not* a post-World War II phenomenon, as apparently was the case in a number of other developing economies. Instead, exchange control was introduced in the early 1930s in response to the devastating impact of the Great Depression on a previously quite open economy.[73] Moreover, fairly continuous conscious attempts to industrialize by import substitution dated back at least to the 1897 tariff law (and, perhaps with less continuity, to before 1860). Most of the aggregate industrial import substitution which had been accomplished by the mid-1960s had in fact been achieved before the end of World War II. Thus, although the exhaustion of foreign reserves accumulated during World War II and the end of the Korean War boom intensified exchange control and efforts to induce import substitution, both of these phenomena originated much earlier.

ii. *Cyclical pattern of restrictions and overvaluation in a system in disequilibrium.* After the Second World War disequilibrium combined with an overvalued NER prevailed because of the perceived negative impact of devaluation on income distribution, inflation, and the cost of imported capital goods. The intensity of exchange control, however, varied considerably. The system, in combination with external stimuli, generated cycles in the degree of complexity and restrictiveness. Subsequent to devaluation and rationalization, ad hoc changes of greater specificity were made with increasing frequency because of the perception of unintended side effects of quantitative restrictions, the attempt by the government to use such restrictions for a multitude of reasons additional to managing the balance of payments, and the growing overvaluation due to internal inflation. In each cycle the government resisted formal devaluation for some time because of the perceived negative impact of the action. However, inflation was so fast that, despite accelerated ad hoc changes in Chile's international economic policy, devaluation of the NER(s) to new fixed rates (generally accompanied by considerable rationalization and some liberalization) could not be avoided. At that point the cycle would begin anew. Moreover, even when the government operated a sliding-peg NER policy with frequent devaluations, the NER(s) remained overvalued so that the cycle was only moderated, but not eliminated.

iii. *Motivations for shifts in exchange control.* External developments have been influential in the decisions to alter foreign-sector policies. Extensive exchange control was reintroduced in reaction to the Great Depression. No other course was judged to be possible at the time. The experience of the 1930s also led to some general attitudes which have shaped the evaluation of policy possibilities in the ensuing decades: export pessimism and a desire to establish greater domestic control over the national economic destiny, even at the cost of forgoing possibly considerable static comparative advantage. Specific policies, however, often have been ad hoc responses to immediate foreign market conditions. Precarious foreign-exchange situations have developed repeatedly because of the disequilibrium system with its limited inducements for export expansion and extensive needs for intermediate and capital goods imports for the import-substitution industries. Instead of establishing greater independence from the international market, therefore, the trade regime in some respects caused the economy to become more vulnerable to foreign-market fluctuations. Thus, restrictiveness tightened during slumps in the world copper market and loosened during booms in that market (such as those related to the Second World War, the Korean War, and the Vietnam War).

The importance of external conditions, however, should not be overstated. Most of the recent shifts from one phase to another have been but a part of much larger policy programs for which the dominant causal factors have been internal political changes and policy considerations (especially those concerning cyclical fluctuations and income distribution).

iv. *Nominal versus effective devaluations.* Except when the sliding-peg exchange-rate policy was in effect, in 1965–70, effective devaluations were smaller in magnitude than the nominal devaluations from which they resulted because devaluations usually have been accompanied by partial removal of import restrictions, surcharges, and export subsidies. Another factor of considerable importance, however, is that devaluations have led to substantial and fairly immediate responses in the domestic price level. Thus, care must be taken in the assessment of liberalization attempts not to confuse formal alterations in exchange rates with effective devaluations.

v. *Problems in evaluating the impact of foreign-sector policies.* The difficulties in assessing the effects of foreign trade and payments policies are many, as is well-known. Several, which are made quite clear in the present study, however, merit mention because they are often ignored in other analyses. (a) Partial-equilibrium conclusions about the impact of changes in the magnitude and, in some cases, even the direction of the foreign-sector regime may be very misleading. The general-equilibrium analysis below, for example, suggests that the impact of devaluation on the balance of payments and on employment is much less positive than has been suggested by partial-equilibrium analyses because of indirect offsetting effects transmitted in large part through the monetary and price system. (b) The time patterns of responses to policy changes vary considerably from one area of concern to another. In some cases, moreover, the direction of the response reverses over time. An evaluation of the success or failure of such policies, therefore, may depend crucially upon what time period is relevant. (c) If the empirical measures derived from the Chilean experience are appropriate indicators, substantial effort may have been misplaced in the considerable recent literature on alternative protection and resource-cost estimates. Intrameasure differences in the treatment of the cost of capital, for example, apparently are about as important a source of disparities among sectors as are the much more debated distinctions between EPRs and DRCs. Some of the other intrameasure concerns which have received relatively great emphasis (e.g., the treatment of nontraded inputs), moreover, do not make much difference. Within a general-equilibrium context, finally, the pattern of changes in the prices ratios of final to intermediate products frequently differs from patterns of changes in either capacity utilization or capacity creation. Measures related to the price ratios, therefore, may be quite misleading indicators of short- and long-run resource shifts.[74]

vi. *Wide variations in economic costs.* Variations in DRCs are quite large both between and within sectors. Some industries appear to be quite efficient, while others require a large multiple of all resources in order to save an identical amount of foreign exchange. This large variation apparently reflects the failure of the exchange control system to indicate differences in social profitability to individual decision makers. Industries are encouraged indiscriminately. The result is a much higher social cost than might obtain if the low-cost industries could be given preference.

vii. *Short- and medium-term constraints on exchange liberalization.* In light of the short- and medium-term impact (i.e., within one to three years) on major areas of the economy, the repeated reluctance of Chilean governments to devalue and to reduce exchange control is understandable, especially if a high enough discount rate is used. In the short run, the results of tightened quantitative restrictions have been to enlarge the net command over international resources from trade; extend national autonomy by some measure; increase capacity utilization; and favor industry over other goods sectors and goods over services. In the short run, devaluation makes a smaller positive contribution to the balance of payments than is often suggested, causes an immediate reduction in capacity utilization, has a substantial inflationary impact, is discriminatory against industry, and has substantial unwanted effects by shifting control over income and over resources away from labor and the government and toward foreigners.[75] In many respects specific liberalizations adopted toward previously foreign-owned large-scale mining, e.g., the *Nuevo Trato* of 1955, which is discussed in subsection 4.2.1, did not on balance work to Chile's advantage.

Exchange control to maintain an overvalued NER is, of course, hardly without undesirable features even in the short run: Exports have been discouraged.[76] Variations in imports have been increased, with disruptive effects on supplies in wide areas of the economy. The composition of imports has been altered in unwanted ways. Government deficits have been enlarged because revenues from exports and imports were reduced;[77] as a result, inflation has been increased and income distribution changed for the worse. Finally, substantial resources have been needed to operate the system.

Thus the point is not that overvaluation plus exchange control is without costs, but that there are substantial costs as well as possible benefits to moving away from the type of payments regime which has been dominant in Chile for the past four decades. Without a specific welfare function, it is not clear that the benefits outweigh the costs. The repeated reluctance of Chilean governments to liberalize the foreign sector may be quite rational, or at least understandable. Even if the government is convinced that the long-run net benefits of eliminating exchange control and overvaluation are positive and substantial, it might reasonably hesitate to proceed with such changes because of the high short- and medium-term costs as seen either from the broad viewpoint of the nation or from the narrower political interests of the governing group.[78] Given the history of past failures of programs of liberalization plus stabilization, future significant liberalization probably will be attempted only if the government is convinced of the following: that the long-run net benefits will be substantial, that it had unusually broad internal political support derived from a widespread perception that it could resolve a severe economic or political crisis, and that it had expectations of a very large command over foreign resources from capital inflows or from a copper-market boom.

viii. *Development and exchange liberalization.* Many interrelationships exist between the trade and payments regimes and economic development. Although foreign-sector policies affect many aspects of the economy, the evidence to be presented in this study does not indicate overwhelming support for either of two polar positions, (a) that exchange control accelerates development, since resources can be allocated directly to the uses where developmental payoffs are the highest or (b) that liberalization quickens development because of international transfer of knowledge, comparative advantage, and market pressures for efficiency. Instead, the evidence is mixed and indicates that both of these positions may overstate the contribution that changes in the foreign trade regime could make to development.

It is possible that the underlying evidence is too closely tied to short-run situations, despite my attempts to incorporate adjustments to longer-run phenomena. A liberalization which was viewed as permanent might have substantially greater positive impacts on growth through large nonmarginal changes such as Fishlow [1974] reports in the Brazilian case. Perhaps Bruton [1967] is correct in his speculation that exchange control has resulted in substantially less productivity growth in Chile and other Latin American countries because much of the economy has been isolated from international market pressures for increasing efficiency.

I am fairly sympathetic to the notion that the Chilean exchange control system may have dampened development achievements. The system has not seemed sufficiently flexible to adapt to changing conditions. Protection, once granted, has been very difficult to reverse. In the early 1960s, some of the most protected industrial subsectors included the traditional ones which had received deliberate protection—in some cases since the 1897 tariff law—and in which import substitution had been achieved largely before the Second World War. The exchange control system seems to have an inner logic of its own which perpetuates its existence because of the costs of dismantling it despite the limitations it may impose on development achievements.

On the basis of the present study alone, however, it would be primarily speculative to assert that really substantial development benefits can be attained through the selection of a particular foreign-exchange regime. Although there is plenty of evidence of interaction between such regimes and variables which are widely thought to be related to the development process, the results do not warrant a firm conclusion about the preferred type of regime. Part of the problem, of course, is that our knowledge of what really underlies the process of development is limited.

ix. *Gradual versus abrupt liberalizations.* If liberalization is to have a substantial long-run development payoff, expectations that the policy will be permanent must be strengthened. Otherwise, efforts will be devoted not to increasing productivity, but to obtaining the private benefits of greater protection. Given the failure of three liberalizations and four stabilization attempts in less than two decades, it will not be easy to make new programs credible.

Gradual attempts have the advantage of allowing some short-run gains. But they probably would not cause sufficient short-run benefits to enable the maintenance of the necessary political momentum until longer-run returns became clear. The best hope for a successful liberalization, therefore, probably is an abrupt imposition which incurs certain short-run costs, but also alters expectations so that longer-run advantages may become obvious before political momentum falters.

NOTES

1. Some analysts have developed the contrary view—that the role of the foreign sector in economic development is not necessarily positive. In some cases, these views, which are mentioned below, have been based on the Chilean experience.

2. Different studies have different weaknesses. Those with broader historical and macroeconomic perspectives often tend to be less rigorous analytically (for example, Pinto [1962]). Those with a more careful and detailed data analysis often tend to have a limited historical perspective (for example, Jeanneret [1971]). (The bibliography provided at the end of this book contains publication details for all works cited.)

3. For fuller presentations and critiques of the structuralist analysis, see Baer [1967], Behrman [1974], Corbo [1971], Edel [1969], Campos [1964], Pazos [1972], Prebisch [1961], Seers [1963], Sierra [1969], Sunkel [1958] and Wachter [1974].

4. Analyses of Chilean economic history which have had substantial impact in recent years include Ahumada [1956], Pinto [1962, 1964], Sunkel [1958], and Instituto de Economía [1956, 1963]. Part of this impact is due to the important political and advisory positions which economists have held in Chile for more than a century. A few examples include Jean Gustave Courcelle-Seneuil (see section 1.2, below); Felipe Herrera, who served as minister of finance in 1953 in the Ibañez government; Carlos Massad and Jorge Cauas, who served as president and vice-president of the Central Bank in the Frei administration of 1964–70; and Pedro Vúskovic, who was minister of economics for the first twenty-two months of the Allende government.

5. Basic sources for this section include Ballesteros and Davis [1963], Cohen [1960], Ellsworth [1945], García [1964], Hirschman [1963], Humud [1969], Hurtado [1966], Lagos [1966], Mamalakis [1971b], Mamalakis [1965], Marshall [1957], Muñoz [1968], Pinto [1962], Reynolds [1965], and Rufatt [1972].

6. The phases are defined in Appendix D. These phases are descriptive only; *no* causal inference is intended.

7. For a definition of this and all other terms and abbreviations relating to the foreign trade regimes, see Appendix D.

8. The value of the escudo-equivalent in 1960 U.S. dollars at time t is the purchasing power in terms of 1960 dollars of one escudo (or, equivalently, 1,000 pesos) at time t.

(In 1960, the basic currency unit was changed from the peso to the escudo at a conversion rate of 1,000 pesos per escudo.) For more recent periods, see Table A.1, line 1.1.2.

9. Pinto [1962:15], in fact, suggests that the next phase (i.e., Phase V) may have started as early as 1848.

10. For the decades from 1880 to 1930, Hirschman [1963:160] reports average annual rates of change of prices ranging from 3 to 8 per cent (see also Table A.1, line 2.1, below). For extensive discussions of the causes of this inflation see Fetter [1931], García [1964:12–15], Hirschman [1963:160–183], Humud [1969:64–72], Mamalakis [1971b:97–98, 117–120], Marshall [1957:4–9], and Pinto [1962:59–64].

11. Unless otherwise noted, data in this study on long-run trends in the copper subsector are based on Senado, Oficina de Informaciones [1971:20–21].

12. The estimate by Hurtado [1966:38–59] is lower than Pinto's. On either count, however, a substantial postwar decline in the share of agriculture is implied.

13. In fact the foreign-owned share of nitrates increased from 64 per cent in 1882 to 85 per cent in 1901. See Mamalakis [1971b:105–115, 415–498] and Pinto [1962:53–57] for these and other details about nitrates in this era.

14. Mamalakis [1971b:498] estimates that Chilean ownership was 4.5 per cent of the total in 1918. Reynolds [1965:219] estimates that the Chilean share was 11 per cent in 1920.

15. For example, before the establishment of an income tax, in 1925, the tax incidence on the gross value of copper production was 0.8 per cent, and neither copper nor nitrates were subject to the impact of significant nontax government policies. Even after the imposition of the income tax on copper, less than 40 per cent of the total value of production of large-scale copper mining remained in Chile (of which over three-fourths was for local operating expenses), and less than 1 per cent of the labor force was employed in large-scale copper mining. The comparatively low value of series 1.1.5.2 in Table A.1 despite high copper prices also reflects limited linkage. For further details see Reynolds [1965:223, 226, 376, and 378].

16. For further discussion of these factors, see Gunder-Frank [1969:17–84, 89–98], Mamalakis [1971b:105–115, 465–498] and Pinto [1962:53–57].

17. Mamalakis [1971b:106–115] suggests that in the early twentieth century factor payments abroad for mining (copper as well as nitrates) were largely offset by capital inflows and probably were less in magnitude than the amounts involved in the flights of domestic capital resulting from internal instability. This analysis seems to be at least partially misleading in that the capital inflows to which he refers were primarily for large-scale copper mining from which substantial net outflows were to occur for at least four decades subsequent to the end of this period.

18. Muñoz [1968:19] claims that a substantial increase in average tariff rates was implemented earlier in 1878. Humud's [1969:100, 122, 130] data, however, indicates that the general legal tariff rate was 25 per cent both before and after 1878 and that the average actual nominal rate did not increase substantially at that time.

19. These import substitution coefficients are defined as $(u_0 - u_1)\ (D_1 + M_1)/(D_1 - D_0)$, where D equals domestic production, M equals imported supply, $u = M/D$, and the subscripts refer to the endpoints of the time period over which the comparison is made. For a critique of this measure based on the exclusion of impacts on intermediate products, see Morley and Smith [1970].

20. Mamalakis [1971b:84] suggests that the increased taxes on industrial imports in the 1830–60 period reflected not a deliberate intent of the government to protect domestic industry per se, but a desire on the part of the powerful agricultural elite to shift the tax burden to the economy as a whole. However, considerable evidence exists,

both for this and for later periods, that protection was an important motivation for upward adjusments in the tariff structure. For examples, see Ellsworth [1945:49], Jeanneret [1971:145], and Mamalakis [1971b:14].

21. For the import-to-GDP ratio, Ellsworth [1945:3] presents a range of 0.30 to 0.40 for before the Great Depression, and CEPAL (as reported in Muñoz [1968:83]) estimates 0.31 in 1929. A comparison of the Humud [1969] trade data and the Ballesteros and Davis [1963] product data suggest that by 1929, the ratio had fallen substantially from previous levels. In Table A.1, for the period from 1908 to 1927, the import ratio (line 1.2.6.7) is 0.52, and the export ratio (line 1.2.6.8) is 0.58: both seem somewhat high. The discrepancy in the same table between the export ratio and the ratio of mining GDP (line 3.1.1.2) to over-all GDP also raises similar doubts. However, some discrepancies would be expected because of the considerable size of positive net factor payments abroad and because the GDP estimates are based on real quantity data while the real value of exports reflects secularly increasing relative prices for nitrates over the period.

22. Throughout this study all regression estimates presented are based on ordinary least squares techniques, except when the Cochrane-Orcutt procedure has been utilized to estimate a first-order autocorrelation coefficient (ρ). The absolute values of t statistics are presented in parentheses beneath the point estimates. $\overline{R}^2$ is the coefficient of determination (corrected for degrees of freedom), *SE* is the standard error of estimate, and *DW* is the Durbin-Watson statistic. The data source for this and all other regression estimates presented in this subsection is Humud [1969].

23. Additive and multiplicative dummy variables for different phases were excluded because the coefficients of the dummies were not significantly different from zero even at the 15 per cent level.

24. A simple autocorrelated time trend model, however, is consistent with only 14 per cent of the variation in extraordinary government income over the sample.

25. Moreover, deliberate decisions were made to change the tax structure in ways which increased the susceptibility of government income to fluctuations in world markets. For example, Law 23 of 1897 liberated all exports from taxes except for nitrates and iodine. If it is assumed that there was less than perfect correlation among fluctuations in revenues from the different exports, the risk of fluctuations in government revenues was thereby increased.

26. The estimation of regressions analogous to relations 1.1 and 1.2, but with ordinary and extraordinary government income as the respective dependent variables, also did not yield evidence of a significant phase-coincident shift in growth rates.

27. Higher debt ratios were recorded in 1830–35 after the War of Independence, in 1870–75 after the war with Spain of 1865–66, and starting in 1895 after the Civil War of 1891. A particularly high debt ratio was not maintained in 1885 after the War of the Pacific because the acquisition of control over revenues from nitrates made rapid amortization possible (see column 11). The relatively high ratios in 1830–45, 1870–75, 1900–15, and 1930 also partially reflected foreign borrowing for infrastructure construction.

28. After the War of the Pacific, foreign trade policy was relatively liberal, although convertibility generally was not maintained and the 1897 tariff law substantially increased industrial protection.

29. The critical value for a normally distributed series is 2.0; the test statistic is 2.5.

30. The years are 1885, 1886, 1891–94, 1899, 1914, 1919, 1921, and 1922.

31. The test statistic of 0.3 is far below the critical value of 2.0.

32. The low capacity utilization rates in 1914–15, however, may be due to in-

adequacies in the industrial-sector data used in the underlying series (see Muñoz [1968:66, 82]).

33. For a satisfactory examination of such interrelationships a general-equilibrium model is required. See section 2.1 below.

34. Muñoz [1968:13–23] suggests that the post-1860 experience in industrial growth may have been substantially better than Pinto and others have claimed.

35. The average proportion of government expenditure devoted to development ranged from 0.26 to 0.47 after 1890 (Table 1.1, col. 9). For a listing of the external government borrowings and their uses (which included substantial construction of infrastructure) see Humud [1969:73–80]. Information on investment in human capital is scarce, but Mamalakis [1971b:128] does report that literacy increased from 13.5 per cent in 1854 to 56.1 per cent in 1930 and that compulsory primary education was introduced (at least de jure) in 1920.

36. Savings also may have been affected positively by the transfer of resources out of agriculture or by forced savings induced by the inflation (both of which may have been partly brought on by the international economic regime), but no concrete evidence is available.

37. Of course marginal, not average, products are of real interest, but to the extent that the production process can be approximated by a Cobb-Douglas production function, the marginal and average products are proportional.

38. The following estimates of the sector share of the labor force in Census years are from Ballesteros and Davis [1963:176], and may be compared with the estimates for the sector share of GDP in Table A.1, lines 3.1.1.1 to 3.1.1.3; but see also note 20, above:

	1907	*1920*	*1930*
Agriculture	37.7%	36.2%	34.7%
Mining	2.8	4.1	5.1
Industry and construction	17.6	15.2	18.3
Transportation	3.4	4.8	3.8
Government	5.3	4.2	7.6
Commerce and services	33.2	35.5	30.5

39. Not only was industry a sector of lower than average labor productivity, but Muñoz [1968:61] estimates that average industrial labor productivity declined 14.4 per cent between 1914–16 and 1922–24.

40. I do not imply that the Chilean elite did not act in their own best interests in this period, but that they did not act in the best national interests of Chile as viewed decades later by such commentators as Hurtado [1966:70], Lagos [1966:40], Mamalakis [1971b:133, 488] and Pinto [1962:73–74].

41. The data presented in Ballesteros and Davis [1963] imply this growth rate (Table A.1, line 5.1). This estimate may be on the low side. Mamalakis [1971b:40] argues that if the more rapidly growing services sectors are included (Ballesteros and Davis include only the goods sectors) the rate may be closer to 2.0 per cent. Moreover, Muñoz [1968:35–40] maintains that for industry the Ballesteros and Davis estimates are biased downward because of the inclusion of artisan industry in the 1907 base-year census, but not in subsequent censuses, and because of the assumption of almost no industrial growth during World War I (owing to a lack of data) instead of the 8–9 per cent annual estimate which Muñoz makes. On the other hand, Muñoz also claims that the Ballesteros and Davis estimates may be high in the early 1920s because of insufficient adjustment for depressed international market conditions. Moreover, the extremely high ratios for imports and exports relative to GDP (lines 1.2.5.7 and 1.2.5.8

in Table A.1) suggest that the estimates of the level of GDP for the early part of this period may be low relative to those for foreign trade. Since the foreign trade estimates are probably more securely based, this last observation implies a higher level of GDP in the earlier years and a lower rate of growth.

42. Evidence for earlier decades is very limited, but the growth of government income and expenditures and exports and imports (all in constant dollars) in conjunction with measures of the importance of related variables relative to total product in 1908–27 (lines 1.2.6.7, 1.2.6.8, and 3.1.2.3 in Table A.1) are suggestive. For 1844–1927 mean exponential growth rates for ordinary government income and expenditures were 0.043 and 0.044 respectively (with no significant phase-coincident deviations). Government income and expenditure may have grown somewhat faster than total product during this period, but probably not very much so, or the estimate for government current expenditures relative to GDP for 1908–27 (line 3.1.2.3 in Table A.1) would have been higher. Adjustment for probable population growth implies a growth rate in per capita product of about the same or slightly higher magnitude as that in the text. Analogous considerations for exports and imports (including the growth rates in relations 1.1 and 1.2 and the high ratios in lines 1.2.6.7, and 1.2.6.8 in Table A.1) imply a growth rate in per capita product of about the same or slightly lower magnitude.

43. De Castro and de la Cuadra [1971:1] also refer to the Ballesteros and Davis estimates, but ignore the warning that the 1928 and 1929 figures probably are misleading because of high nitrate prices and the large transitory inflow of foreign capital. Therefore, they emphasize the 2.7 per cent growth rate for 1908–29 instead of the 1.5 per cent growth rate for 1908–27.

44. The 1929 capacity-to-import level, in fact, was not attained again until 1966.

45. See Cohen [1960:8–9], Ellsworth [1945:34–35], Hirschman [1963:179], Marshall [1957:8–11], and Pinto [1962:109–119] for more detailed discussions of this period. For data in the text that are not included in Table A.1, see Cohen [1960:8–9] for gold reserves, Hurtado [1966:Tables 13 and 23] for the mining data, Mamalakis [1965: Appendix Table 1] for the real interest rate, and Ballesteros and Davis [1963:160] for real government production.

46. For the sources for these and other measures of the decline in the Chilean economy due to the Great Depression, see Table A.1, lines 1.1.5.1, 1.2.4.1, 1.2.4.2, 1.2.6.3, 1.2.6.7, 1.2.6.8, 2.2, and 5.1 to 5.3; Hurtado [1966:Table 23]; and Senado, Oficina de Informaciones [1971:21].

47. Moran [1970] presents an interesting discussion of *dependencia* in Chilean decisions concerning large-scale copper mining in recent decades.

48. Basic general studies which summarize Chilean economic policies and performance since the Great Depression include Behrman [1974], Cauas [1972], Corbo [1971], Ellsworth [1945], Ffrench-Davis [1971], García [1964], Gunder-Frank [1972], Hirschman [1963], Instituto de Economía [1956, 1963], Lagos [1966], Luders [1968, 1970], Mamalakis [1971b], Marshall [1957], Muñoz [1968], Pinto [1962], Pisciotta [1971], and Sierra [1969].

49. During this quarter century Chile also was headed by a fairly wide range of governments. One immediate result of the catastrophe of the Great Depression was a short period of political instability. The violent economic contraction in mid-1931 gave opponents of what Hirschman [1963:179] refers to as General Carlos Ibañez del Campo's "thinly veiled military dictatorship" an opportunity to force Ibañez to resign on July 26, 1931. Fifteen months of instability followed, including the "100 days of Socialism" in 1932 under Carlos Davila. In October 1932, Arturo Alessandri was elected with support from the right to head a new government which succeeded in restoring

political and economic stability. Near the end of 1938 a Popular Front government was elected under Pedro Aguirre Cerda, who was succeeded (after his death in 1941) by Juan Antonio Ríos. In 1946 Gabriel Gonzalez Videla was elected with considerable support from the left, but during the six years of his administration, the government moved substantially to the right. In 1952, Ibañez again was elected as an independent candidate who, it was widely hoped, would be a strong man capable of eliminating internal instability. Ibañez served through the end of this quarter century and through the liberalization attempt of 1956–58.

50. The availability of national accounts starting in 1940 also entered into the choice of 1940 as the start of the second subphase.

51. Unless otherwise noted, the sources for the data in this section may be found in Tables 8.1 and A.1.

52. This was probably the highest decadal mean in at least a century, although information is very scanty for before 1880 (see note 1, above, and Table A.1, line 2.1).

53. The relatively high mean rate of growth of the constant-dollar value of imports for 1940–46 (Table A.1, line 1.2.4.1) reflects the high rates of growth in 1940 and 1946 (the latter apparently related to pent-up demand) which offset the substantial declines (40.5 per cent in 1942) resulting largely from shortages of imported supplies during the war.

54. Import capacity is somewhat understated because the variable does not adequately reflect the increase in the proportion of each dollar of Chilean copper sales which was returned to Chile (compare lines 1.1.5.1 and 1.1.5.2 in Table A.1).

55. This ratio equals 1 if there is no exchange control and tends to be correlated with the degree of exchange control, although the correlation is less than perfect because of the relative narrowness of the black market in foreign exchange and because of the impact of illegal activity on supply and demand in this market.

56. The index of export capacity to import, however, rose much less (Chart 1.1) than the constant-dollar value of exports because the Chilean unit value of imports used in the former index increased more rapidly than the United States deflator used in the latter index.

57. After 1946, and continuing to the present, devaluations have been a regular part of the Chilean experience. They generally did not, however, keep up with the inflation. See section 3.2 and Table A.7.

58. For further descriptions of economic conditions in these years see Cohen [1960: 23–24], Ffrench-Davis [1971:160], and Hirschman [1963:199–202].

59. Of course, in this period, price increases were substantially below the range of 70–80 per cent that prevailed when the 1956 stabilization effort was started, which may explain the difference in the degree of preoccupation with price stability between the two administrations.

60. In a comparative sense, Chilean economic growth had not been particularly high for some time. According to unpublished 1970 UNCTAD calculations, for the 1950–65 period Chile ranked twenty-ninth among 45 developing countries in the degree of increase of its per capita GDP. For 1960–65, Chile ranked thirty-eighth among 56 countries.

61. These relative measures indicate a slight decline in the importance of the debt during 1965–70.

62. In addition to Zorrilla [1970], sources on which this summary of the objectives of the Allende government is based include Allende [1971], Cauas [1972:46–56], CORFO [1970–71], Gunder-Frank [1972:16–18], Hobsbaum [1971:23–32], ODEPLAN [1971a, 1971b], Pisciotta [1971:236–237], and Vúskovic [1971:385–399].

63. The imported component of such investment, however, would be lower than in the past in order to reduce external dependence.

64. June 1972 unemployment had dropped further, to a level of 3.7 per cent.

65. Before the Chileanization and nationalization policies of the previous phase, large-scale copper mining had been entirely foreign-owned. Under Frei, however, a substantial share of ownership had been returned to Chile. For details, see subsection 4.2.1, below.

66. De Castro [1972:45] suggests that actual investment may in fact have declined more than 7.7 per cent because much of the construction investment was done by the government and measured at factor cost. It was, therefore, overvalued in real terms because of the very high rate of increase of wages.

67. On the other hand, investment in human capital may have increased. Minister of Economics Vúskovic also suggested that the changing of the structure of ownership, which was accelerated in this period, was a prerequisite to sustained long-run Chilean development.

68. The ranges refer to the alternative estimates given in Banco Central [1973b].

69. In the first three quarters of 1972, shipments were down 21 per cent in current dollars and export returns increased only 1.5 per cent in current dollars.

70. To provide some perspective, however, the 1971 and 1972 copper prices still were higher than those received for any year before 1965 and, according to Cauas [1972:52], were higher than the price which had been used in 1970 in the Central Bank in its projections for 1971.

71. In the first eight months of 1972 current-dollar registrations were 17.9 per cent above the level of the comparable period for 1971.

72. The Allende government inherited $3 billion of foreign debts with amortization and interest payments of $433 million due in 1971, $409 million due in 1972, $410 million due in 1973, and $388 million due in 1974. In April 1972 the Paris Club (the United States and ten other major creditors) recommended the adoption of a new payments program over an eight-year period, including a two-year grace period on 70 per cent of the Chilean debts which were due between November 1, 1971, and December 31, 1972. The creditors promised to study "with good will" the refinancing of those debt payments due in 1973, but no agreement on further rescheduling had been reached by the end of the Allende government.

73. Perhaps one should say that exchange control was reintroduced, since substantial control had existed a century earlier.

74. That changes in measures based on price ratios of final to intermediate products do not induce resource allocation changes except under very special assumptions has been well-established for some time on a theoretical level. The present results illustrate how such measures also may be quite inadequate in empirical applications.

75. The recent reduction of foreign ownership which is described in subsections 4.2.1 and 4.3.2 may have reduced the impact of this effect.

76. Nontraditional exports, the expansion of which has long been desired in order to reduce risks by diversifying, have been particularly discouraged (section 7.2).

77. Revenues from imports have fallen more than total imports because of the tendency to favor "essential" imports with relatively low tariff rates when restrictions have been intensified.

78. In the past, of course, pressures resulting from internal inflation have forced the government to devalue despite the costs, but then generally an attempt was made again to maintain an overvalued NER.

Chapter 2

An Annual Macroeconometric Model for Chile, 1945–65

Changes in the international economic regime have substantial effects throughout the Chilean economy. Foreign-sector policies interact in complex ways with fiscal, monetary, and income policies. Prices are the most important transmittal mechanism, but the magnitudes of available physical quantities also have direct impact on other real variables in the system; the underlying structure is not linear; responses are not homogeneous across sectors; [1] since feedbacks often are quite important, partial-equilibrium analysis may be misleading.

Given these conditions, a general-equilibrium macroeconometric model is the most appropriate tool for analyzing their aggregate effects.[2] I have prepared an annual econometric model containing 172 endogenous variables estimated for the 1945–65 period. Because it is referred to frequently in the subsequent text—in particular, it is used extensively in parts III and IV to explore the implications of foreign-sector changes for factors that are of major concern to macroeconomic policymakers—a brief description of the model is provided in section 2.1, below. Some of the components of the model are presented and discussed below in Part III; a complete presentation and examination of the model is contained in Behrman [1974].

For the purposes of the present study, the model includes a number of desirable features: (i) nonlinear technological and behavioral responses of real quantitative variables to prices and policies;[3] (ii) lags in adjustments and in the formation of expectations; (iii) a wide range of government policy instruments and the interactions among them; (iv) emphasis on the direct and indirect consequences of changes in the foreign sector;[4] (v) adding-up constraints on fiscal and monetary behavior; (vi) disaggregation to the nine-sector level[5] to reflect sectoral heterogeneities; and (vii) inclusion of intermediate demands and intermediate prices, based on input-output tables, to link the sectors; and (viii) simultaneous and lagged feedbacks.

2.1 STRUCTURE OF THE MODEL

The model has its roots in the Keynes-Tinbergen-Klein tradition. However, it is distinguished from that tradition by the following modifications in order better to reflect the structure and goals of the Chilean economy:

i. Sectoral production capacities are determined within the model by physical investment and labor allocation decisions and by secular technological trends.[6] The implications of a set of policies for long-run growth thus can be investigated by examining changes in these capacities.

ii. Short-run output is *not* determined by final demand. Instead, sectoral capacity utilization decisions determine real production in response to prices of products relative to inputs (adjusted for the impact of fiscal policies), import and credit availabilities, and total demands. The difference between total production and (noninventory) final demand determines the change in inventories, which feeds back on short-run capacity utilization and balance-of-payments functions and on long-run decisions on capacity creation.

iii. The agricultural and services sectors absorb residual labor.

iv. The foreign sector is pervasive in its effects—not only through current prices and quantities, but also through expectations.

v. The impact of inflation and of inflationary expectations also is very widespread because of the experience of very rapid price changes (e.g., an average annual increase of over 30 per cent in the GDP deflator for the sample period).

vi. Substitution between domestic and foreign savings is incorporated.[7] Increases in the command over foreign resources, therefore, go in part to increased current consumption.

vii. The specification of policies reflects the specific institutional constraints under which the government operates. Money supply basically responds passively to government deficits and changes in international reserves because of legal requirements to accept government debt and the lack of a developed open market. The effective internal monetary instruments are limited to average and marginal reserve rates, rediscount rates, bank interest rates, restrictions in the use of dollar bonds and deposits, credit ceilings, and institutional changes such as the creation of the State Bank (Banco de Estado) in 1953. Tax revenues from a given activity depend not only on the level of that activity and legal tax rates, but also on the degree of inflation and expectations thereof. Government consumption is primarily endogenous because the short-run latitude of the government is limited given the annual legal determination of its wage structure. Government expenditure policy, therefore, operates primarily through changes in public direct and indirect investment. Foreign-sector policies include a multitude of both price-related and quantity-based tools.

These seven features and the previous comments give much of the flavor of the model. However, some further detail is useful.

2.1.1 Policy Variables.

The model includes the primary macroeconomic policy tools which the Chilean government used with a substantial degree of discretion in the sample period. In the long run, of course, not all of these instruments are independent.[8]

FISCAL POLICIES.

Revenue instruments include legal tax rates or their proxies for eleven tax categories,[9] import prior-deposit rates, and the legal cost of production for large-scale mining. The last of these determines how many dollars the large-scale mining companies have to convert into escudos for local expenditures at a generally disadvantageous NER. The profits from the resale of those dollars at a higher rate go to the government.

Expenditure instruments include domestic or export subsidies, current government consumption (but see the discussion of the seventh point above), and direct and indirect public financial investment.

INTERNAL MONETARY POLICIES.

The monetary base changes mainly because of internally financed government deficits and changes in international reserves. The Central Bank shapes the impact of changes in the monetary base on the monetary supply by its determination of the marginal and average reserve requirements for time and demand deposits, the rediscount rate, the bank interest rate, quantitative restrictions on total credit, and the requirements for dollar deposits. The nominal money supply is determined by these factors, together with behavioral relationships for the net free reserves held by the commercial banks and for the composition of assets held by the private sector. These behavioral relations depend upon expectations concerning inflation and devaluation, interest rates, and the relevant activity variables, i.e., the level of deposits for bank reserves and the level of product for privately held assets.

INCOME POLICIES.

The minimum wage (*sueldo vital*) is the major direct tool in this area, but obviously, many other policies, such as those on taxes, also affect income distribution.

FOREIGN-SECTOR POLICIES.

The price-related tools included in the model are the average ad-valorem-equivalent nominal tariff rate, which incorporates all the taxes and exemptions discussed in section 4.1, the import prior-deposit cost rate, a subsidy rate for nontraditional exports, three legal NERs (one for large-scale mining, another for services, and a third for other transactions),[10] and copper price and surtax policies. Among the last are included the establishment of the Chilean sales monopoly in 1952–54; the introduction of the Chilean producers' price in 1964; and the imposition of surtaxes in 1951 (see section 4.2.1).

Quantitative policies in the foreign sector are represented by the Ffrench-Davis quantitative restrictions index (line 1.2.6.2 in Table A.1), ratios of aggregate internal prices to EERs,[11] variables which relate to the short-run availability of foreign exchange (such as the export capacity to import and the net foreign-exchange reserves of the banking system), the legal cost of production in large-scale mining, and dummy variables for a number of particular policy changes which are discussed in Part II below.

In Chapter 1, I suggested that major changes in foreign-sector policy instruments generally have been implemented only as part of an over-all economic program with an internal focus. Between initiations of such programs, large numbers of smaller often ad hoc adjustments have been made in order to offset some of the negative effects explored in Part III below. Although there is some latitude for independent choice about international economic policies in the short run, therefore, the ranges of alternatives are narrow. On the whole, such policies have had more of a passive than an active nature.

2.1.2 Model Relationships.

For the most part, the model consists of a set of relationships for each of the nine sectors indicated above. In some cases, however, the lack of necessary data precludes estimation on the same level of disaggregation in all cases.[12]

The *sectoral capacity for real GDP production*[13] is determined by a CES production function of the secular sectoral labor force and of the sectoral capital stock. The function incorporates constant returns to scale and Hicks's neutral technological change. The use of the secular sectoral labor force and of total capital stock makes possible the representation of production capacity instead of production. The estimated sectoral elasticities of substitution between capital and labor are significantly nonzero and substantial in some important sectors, namely, agriculture, 0.31; mining, 0.51; industry, 0.76; utilities, 0.32; and government, 0.89 (see Behrman [1972a] for a detailed discussion).

The *sectoral secular labor allocation*[14] is based on long-run adjustment, assuming competitive conditions, in the expected ratio of the price of labor, including employers' social security taxes, to the product price. Agriculture and services absorb any excess labor, given the exogenous total supply.[15]

Sectoral real physical capital investment consists of responses to replacement needs, changes in the desired stock of capital, availability of government financial investment, and availability of imported machinery and equipment. The desired stock of capital, in turn, depends on a neoclassical term, expected utilization rates, and price uncertainty (for detailed discussion of these determinants, see subsection 12.2.3.1).

Sectoral capacity utilization rates determine real sectoral GDP for a given sectoral capacity. Domestic determinants of utilization rates include ratios of product prices to input prices after adjustments for taxes, indices of the change in current economic activity, the relative availability of credit, natural conditions (e.g., the level of rainfall and the impact of earthquakes), the state of infrastructure development, the average indirect tax and subsidy rates, the rate of inflation, the real value of monetary balances, and a number of sector-specific factors. Foreign determinants include the ratios of intermediate goods imports to total domestic product and of competing imports to product; quantitative restrictions indices; and sector-specific factors. Section 9.2 contains further discussion of these relations. Because sector-specific data on unemployment fluctuations for the sample period are lacking, sectoral capacity utilization rates are used instead.

The *sectoral product price* reflects general and sector-specific factors both of domestic and of international origin. General domestic factors include the monetary supply, real GDP, indices of economic activity, indices of sectoral and factoral distribution, and dummy variables for the initiation of stabilization programs. Sector-specific domestic factors include several measures of sectoral capacity utilization, sectoral intermediate input prices, sectoral unit labor costs (including the employers' social security tax contribution), and average real sectoral labor productivity. General foreign-sector determinants include the NER, the deflator for imports, indices of quantitative restrictions, and prior-deposit requirements on imports (which, when increased, absorb banking system credit and reduce inflationary pressures). Sector-specific international factors include the ratio of the premium-inclusive EERs for sectoral intermediate inputs to the general NER, EERs for sectoral imports or exports, and the level of sectoral imports relative to domestic absorption. For estimates and comment, see subsection 9.1.3.

The *sectoral intermediate input price* is the price the sector must pay for domestic and imported intermediate inputs. This price is a weighted average of all sectoral product prices and of imported intermediate goods prices. The weights are based on aggregation from the 1962 input-output table in ODEPLAN [1970].[16]

The *sectoral wage* primarily reflects domestic considerations: sectoral nominal and real average labor productivities, sectoral capacity per laborer, sectoral unionization, indices of sector-specific or general economic activity, employers' social security contribution rate, the institution and timing of minimum wages, and expectations for leading prices (and the Harberger [1963] "accelerator" variant). The international economic regime directly enters only through the expectational impact of legal and black-market NERs.

The *price for sectoral investment* is a weighted average of sectoral product prices and of imported machinery and equipment prices. The weights are the average of the 1960–66 estimates of the sectoral origin of sectoral investments by Meza [1967].

The *deflators for final demand components* are weighted averages of sectoral product prices and of relevant EERs, with an adjustment in the latter for the effects of quantitative restrictions.

Sectoral real exports are determined for the following breakdown (the relative percentage share in exports over the sample period is given in parentheses): agriculture (8), large-scale mining (62), small- and medium-scale mining (11), industry (7), and services (11). Export determinants can be divided into three groups: (i) Levels and standard deviations of relative prices (i.e., EERs relative to factor input costs or PLD-EERs); (ii) quantitative supply factors, including the effects of quantitative restrictions; and (iii) quantitative demand considerations reflecting the level of activity in the destination countries. See section 7.2 for the estimates and their interpretation.

Real imports are included for the following categories (the relative percentage share in imports over the sample period is given in parentheses): services (12), staple consumption goods (19), durable consumption goods (6), secondary consumption goods (3), machinery and equipment investment goods (18), transportation equipment investment goods (10), and intermediate goods (32). In the model, real imports depend on relative price characteristics, other demand characteristics, and the degree of policy restrictiveness. The relative prices are the levels and standard deviations (as a proxy for uncertainty) of PLD-EER(PI)s, PLD-EERs, and PLD-NERs. The other demand characteristics include a relevant activity index (e.g., real consumption in the consumption goods import relations), total real credit, and direct and proxy measures of domestic inventories and income distribution. The degree of policy restrictiveness is represented by the Ffrench-Davis quantitative restrictions index, the export capacity to import, the net foreign exchange reserves held by the banking system relative to the unit value of imports, and dummy variables to represent such events as the operation of the Public Law 480 food program. Section 6.2 contains a discussion of the underlying estimates.

Real domestic savings relationships are included for the government, business, and households and nonprofit institutions. Real savings depend on the relevant real net revenue variable (e.g., real disposable income for households) and real foreign savings. In addition, private real savings respond to the level of real monetary balances, the means and standard deviations for expected inflation and exchange rate movements, and the sectoral and factoral distributions of income. (See subsection 12.2.3.2 for further discussion.)

Factoral income distribution depends on the relationships, mentioned above, for production (or capacity utilization), labor allocation, product price, and wages. Given the values calculated from these relationships and given government policies, especially on taxation, nonwage income can be calculated as a residual.

2.2 SIMULATION PROCEDURE

In parts III and IV extensive use is made of the Chilean macroeconometric model to simulate the general-equilibrium impact of changes in the foreign sector. Eight characteristics of the simulation procedure are especially important:

i. The structure of the model outlined in the previous subsection is assumed to be the true structure of the Chilean economy in the periods to which these simulations are applied. If biases exist in the estimated coefficients, such biases have an impact on the simulation results. Sensitivity analysis, of course, can be utilized to explore the effect of any such expected biases in specific parameter values or in particular relations in the model. Nevertheless, some possibly very important phenomena—such as changes in psychological and political attitudes or the effects of Krueger [1974] competitive rent-seeking—are not well incorporated into the model.[17]

ii. The simulations presented in this study are all nonstochastic.[18]

iii. All the simulations are dynamic in that in the *n*th simulation period, simulated lagged endogenous values from the first $n-1$ simulation periods are used instead of actual lagged endogenous values. This procedure permits the tracing out of the time path of the responses to a given change.

iv. For each simulation only an explicitly indicated alteration in foreign-sector policies or foreign-sector conditions is explored. All other variables and parameters, including internal policy instruments, are fixed at their base simulation values in order not to confuse the impact of the foreign-sector changes with that of other changes.[19]

v. Because the model is nonlinear, it cannot be solved by simple matrix inversion. Instead, a two-step Gauss-Seidel iterative procedure is utilized (with the two steps referring to iterations back and forth between the real and the monetary sectors, both of which also are solved iteratively).

vi. In each simulation, unless otherwise noted, the indicated foreign-sector changes are maintained not for a number of years, but for the initial year only. The results therefore give the time pattern of response to such once-and-for-all shocks.

vii. In most cases the important consequences of a particular foreign-sector change occur within three or four years. Therefore, Table A.11 includes the results for the first and the third year after the designated change. These two years are presented in order to include the short- and medium-term effects of the indicated change without the voluminous presentations which would be required if the year-by-year effects for a longer period were included. In the few cases in which two-year cycles or effects after the third year are important, such features are noted explicitly in Part III, below.

viii. In Part III, a chapter each is devoted to examining the effects of foreign-sector changes on each of five major macro policy areas. However, the reader should realize that for each foreign-sector change real trade-offs exist. The consequences are positive in at least one area and also are negative in at least one other area. No particular change is uniformly beneficial.[20]

The results of a number of simulations of the impact of foreign-sector changes are presented in Table A.11. To summarize the simulations, ex-post general-equilibrium elasticities are given for responses to the change indicated in the column headings for the first and third years.[21] Elasticities are presented in order to have a measure of the responses independent of the particular units in which the underlying data are reported. For variables which are defined to be differences between flows (e.g., savings, net reserves, and deficits), however, the implied elasticities may be very high because of the small absolute value of the base difference relative to the magnitudes of the two underlying flows.[22]

Elasticities are included for variables associated with each of the five major policy areas to be discussed in Part III: (i) balance-of-payments factors, i.e., exports and their major components, imports and their major components, and other related variables; (ii) real and nominal cyclical fluctuations in capacity utilization, price levels, monetary supply, monetary base, government deficit, and net foreign reserves; (iii) resource allocation among the major goods-producing sectors and measures of goods sectors versus service sectors, i.e., product prices relative to intermediate prices, the secular labor force, and capital distributions, and distributions of capacity and of real product; (iv) distribution of income and of control over resources (factoral, international, intertemporal, and public versus private); and (v) economic growth in product, capacity, savings, and investment.

The elasticities are calculated from deviations from a base simulation which is identical to the other simulations except as is indicated in the column headings. The first two columns of Table A.11 contain proportional deviations from the actual values for 1962 and 1964, the first and third year of this base simulation. The proportional deviations are fairly large for some of the variables that are defined as differences between two flows and for some of the disaggregated variables.[23] In general, however, these deviations are small enough so that one can proceed to use the model with considerable confidence. For a dynamic simulation covering 1962–68, root mean square errors computed for some of the major aggregate variables indicate that the model seems to duplicate the Chilean experience of the 1960s rather well. For a thorough exploration of the properties of the model, see Behrman [1974].

NOTES

1. For econometric evidence of the sectoral heterogeneity in responses, see Behrman [1972c].

2. Several other quite competent general-equilibrium analyses of impacts of changes in Chilean international economic policies are available. Linear programming models are used by Cabezón [1969], Clark [1970], and Foxley [1971]. Black [1971] and Taylor and Black [1973] use a log-linear, Johansen-type model. For the purposes of the present investigation, however, these models have definite inadequacies. The linear programming studies assume zero elasticities of factor substitution and proceed with the maximization of a global objective function which leads to the exploration of the question "what *could* happen if socially optimal readjustment of the economy occurred in response to policy changes," rather than "what *would* happen if independent economic units which make up the economy followed their traditional behavioral patterns in response to such changes." The Taylor-Black approach includes only one primary factor (labor), does not require consistency in the final demand and factor payments sides of the national accounts (i.e., relations linking factor payments, savings, and consumption are not included), and assumes short-run perfectly competitive behavior on the production side. More important, the usefulness of both types of approach in exploring the short- and medium-term impact of policy changes is very limited because immediate adjustments are assumed, the government policy tools incorporated in the analysis are few, and the entire fiscal-monetary-incomes-international policy-inflation nexus is ignored. Given the dominance of adjustment and cyclical problems in the Chilean economy, the intimate relations between major changes in domestic and foreign-sector policies, and the repeated failure of reforms of the international economic regime because of internal cyclical problems (see Chapter 13, below), such deficiencies are very important.

3. Table 5.3 and the tables in Appendix A provide the basis for analyzing the effects of the foreign-sector regime on prices, costs, and value added. What is of fundamental interest, however, is the response of real quantities (e.g., capacity, capacity utilization, imports, exports, and other final-demand components) to those price-related variables.

4. The indirect effects, especially those transmitted through the monetary and price system, are very large in some cases. See Part III, below for examples.

5. The sectors and their respective mean percentage shares in GDP and in the labor force in the sample period are agriculture, 13, 31; mining, 7, 5; construction, 2, 6; industry, 20, 19; transportation, 7, 5; utilities, 1, 1; housing, 7, 0; government, 8, 8; and other services, 35, 35.

6. Attempts to incorporate the effects of changing human capital on the basis of estimates by Harberger and Selowsky [1966] were not fruitful.

7. Rahman [1967], Griffin and Enos [1970], and Weisskopf [1972], among others, have emphasized the importance of such substitution. For a counterview, see Papanek [1972, 1973].

8. For example, long-run exchange rate and exchange control policies must be coordinated with internal fiscal and monetary policies because of effective limits on foreign debt accumulation. In the short run, however, there is a greater degree of independence among such policies.

9. The tax categories are employer social security contributions, with a mean percentage share in total taxes of 19 for the sample period; employee social security contributions, 17; direct personal income taxes, 6; direct taxes on large-scale mining, 9; direct taxes on other businesses, 6; sales taxes, 7; import taxes, 12; production taxes, 8; legal taxes, 3; service taxes, 6; and other taxes, 6.

10. The black-market NER also is included in the model, in part to represent the impact of quantitative restrictions (see the equation in note c to Table A.7).

11. This ratio differs from 1.0 whenever the import premium rate is nonzero, but this may occur because of adjustment lags rather than effective quantitative restrictions (see note to line 1.1.6 in Table A.1).

12. The estimation technique primarily used for these relationships is ordinary least squares, although in some cases nonlinear maximum likelihood procedures are utilized for autocorrelated structures or nonlinear functions. The expected returns on the use of more sophisticated methods are less than the expected costs of doing so given the nature of the data, some questions about the robustness of alternative estimators, and the opportunity costs of sophistication in estimation procedure in terms of exploring various model structures. Annual data are utilized for the following reasons: much of the data, especially the national accounts data, are available only on an annual basis; the relevant responses are those of more than very transitory impact such as might dominate with shorter observation periods; and strong seasonal patterns exist owing to the timing of agricultural production and of annual wage (and related price) readjustments. The 1945–65 period is used because a consistent set of national accounts is lacking before 1940 and after 1965. In addition, the existence both of lagged responses and of a possibly altered structure for the Second World War years suggests the necessity or wisdom, or both, of dropping the 1940–44 observations. Finally, the switch to the Brussels nomenclature associated with the adoption of the new tariff law at the start of 1967 also was associated with a widespread reclassification of all international trade data; as a result series consistent with earlier definitions are in many cases not available after 1966. Of course, some of the estimated functions can be utilized to comment on the implications of the policies adopted in the postsample period (such as the sliding-peg NER and the export subsidies under the Frei administration discussed in Chapters 3, 4, and 7). All the estimates and more detailed comment are given in Behrman [1974].

13. Capacity is defined by the trend-through-the-peaks method. For discussions of the strengths and weaknesses of this approach, see Behrman [1973b] and the references given there.

14. Data on the allocation of the secular labor force are based on interpolations between observations in census years. Such series are useful for determining long-run capacity trends, but do not reflect short-run employment fluctuations.

15. Lewis [1954] is the seminal article about the implications of such a role for traditional sectors in many developing economies. In this connection, the Instituto de Economía [1963:6] places particular emphasis on the role of the services sector in the Chilean experience.

16. The lower the elasticities of substitution among intermediate inputs and between

intermediate and primary inputs, the more satisfactory are these weights. Theil and Tilanus [1966] and Balassa, Guisinger, and Schydlowsky [1970] claim that the available empirical evidence reveals very low substitutibility on an aggregate level between intermediate and primary factors.

17. For example the psychological and political impact of the nationalization of copper or of participating in a possibly unique experiment in the democratic transformation to socialism are very difficult to incorporate. However, the model can be used to give some insights about such effects. To the extent that psychological and political attitudes are related to collective consumption which should enter into the social maximand, the model can be used to explore the trade-offs (if any) between such collective consumption variables and other variables in the objective function. To the extent that these attitudes affect parameters such as those related to labor productivities, moreover, those parameters can be changed appropriately, although the direction of change is not obvious since the increased real income resulting from the collective consumption good may be associated with reduced labor productivity but the increased pride of the workers may result in an increase in productivity.

18. Young [1972] presents an interesting exploration of the impact on policy choices of including or excluding the stochastic aspects of a macroeconomic model.

19. Behrman [1974] uses the same basic model to explore the consequences of changes in internal policies.

20. Taylor [1973b] presents an interesting analysis, based in large part on the Chilean experience, of the difficulties in certain developing economies of pursuing stabilization, balance-of-payments, growth, and distributional objectives even when all of the available major policy instruments are manipulated simultaneously.

21. The elasticities are based on deviations of 0.01 in the relevant exogenous variable(s). Because of the nonlinearities in the model, the magnitudes of the elasticities might change with considerably different proportional deviations. The simulations in columns 2.1.1–2.1.3 of Table A.11 provide an example.

For some simulations, proportional deviations are given because elasticities cannot be defined. Such cases are indicated explicitly in the table.

22. The sign of the elasticity indicates whether the particular variable changes in the same (positive) or opposite (negative) *algebraic* direction as the exogenous variable(s) the value(s) of which is (are) altered for that simulation. If the level of the variable is negative (as is the case for some of the variables which are defined to be the difference between two flows), a positive elasticity implies that this variable increases algebraically (and decreases absolutely) in response to an increase in the exogenous variable(s) with which it is being compared.

23. For example, the deviation for the government deficit financed abroad (line 1.3.3) is large in the first year because the actual value of this variable for the base year was almost zero. As a result, small deviations for the underlying flows result in very large deviations relative to this small base.

Some of the deviations, moreover, reflect the particular time period selected for this base simulation. For example, the proportional deviation in industrial exports (line 1.1.3) is much larger in the 1962–64 period used for this base run than for earlier or subsequent periods because the underlying single-equation estimate for these exports has large residuals in these years. The simulations in Table A.11 can still indicate the responses in industrial exports within the context of the general-equilibrium model under the assumption that those residuals are not causally related to the changes under exploration.

Part II

Evolution of the Structure of Exchange Control Regimes in Recent Decades

Chapter 3

Exchange Control Institutions and Patterns in the Nominal Exchange Rates

In this part, I consider the evolution of foreign-sector regimes in the period since the Great Depression. Since more information is available for recent years (at least through 1970), and recent policies more directly constrain future choices, I emphasize the later years of the period. The discussion has two major foci: (i) presentation of the policies utilized during the phases of this period; and (ii) analysis of the effects of such policies on price- and cost-related variables—PLD-NERs, PLD-EERs, PLD-EER(PI)s, ITRs, EPRs, and DRCs.

SUMMARY AND CONCLUSIONS

In section 3.1 of this chapter, I delineate the institutional responsibility for exchange regulation since 1931, thus providing a framework for the subsequent consideration of foreign-sector policies. It should be noted that the loci of decision-making power have varied substantially over time, with the Central Bank often having little power. Exchange-rate policy, therefore, generally has not been the sole component of the Central Bank's discretionary monetary policy.[1] To the contrary, the Central Bank has at times had a very limited influence over exchange-rate policy.

In section 3.2 I examine the patterns of the major NERs and PLD-NERs for the 1931–72 period, the former because they are a major component of EERs—although clearly not the only one, as will be discussed in Chapter 4—

the latter because of the considerable inflation which Chile has experienced for years (see line 2.1 in Table A.1):

i. Repeatedly, NERs have been devalued and then held constant at the new level. Even if the initial devaluation in a cycle was to an equilibrium level, however, the internal inflation caused the associated PLD-NERs to decline quickly. Therefore, a disequilibrium situation soon developed, usually leading to a loss in reserves, an increase in restrictiveness, and an eventual de facto devaluation (thus beginning another cycle).

ii. De facto devaluations often have been implemented by switching items from one NER to another instead of actually changing the NERs.

iii. The sliding-peg NER policy of 1965–70 resulted in a relatively stable PLD-NER, but its level was probably below the long-run equilibrium level.

iv. The secular trend in the over-all mean PLD-NER has been downward at an exponential average of over 5 per cent per year for over three decades. Even during the sliding-peg period, the weighted average of all legal PLD-NERs fell a total of 8 per cent (in contrast to the intended increase of 2 per cent per year). The steady and substanial decline has vastly outpaced the long-run expansion of Chile's receipts of foreign exchange through exports and capital inflows. Therefore, the NER has been more and more overvalued in a long-run sense, although export booms and capital inflows sometimes masked this disequilibrium in the short run.

v. Some phase-coincident patterns have been evident. Each liberalization started with an increase in the over-all PLD-NER (23 per cent in 1956, but only about 4 per cent in 1959 and 1965). Each switch to a more restrictive phase started with a decrease in the over-all PLD-NER. The black-market PLD-NER increased and the over-all average of legal PLD-NERs decreased near the end of each phase, with one exception: the black-market PLD-NER decreased until the very end of the Phase IV period in 1959–61 because convertibility at a fixed NER was maintained to the end of that phase.

vi. The dispersion among legal NERs sometimes was quite considerable. For example, the ratio of the gold NER to the official NER was 9.8 in 1953. Such variances generally were reduced on average during liberalization attempts but not eliminated, except in 1959–61.

vii. The legal NER used for invisibles (i.e., the broker rate) generally was increased substantially relative to the NERs for merchandise at times of exchange shortages and extensive exchange control.

viii. The ratio of the black-market NER to the weighted average of all legal NERs ranged from about 1.0 in 1959–61 to 10.0 in 1972. Generally, the black-market PLD-NER moved inversely to the over-all average of legal PLD-NERs. This negative correlation reflects the greater severity of exchange control and, therefore, stronger demand in the black market when the legal PLD-NERs were high compared to times when they were low.

3.1 INSTITUTIONAL RESPONSIBILITY FOR EXCHANGE CONTROL

Decree Law 4973 of July 30, 1931 supplemented by Law 5107 of April 19, 1932 instituted exchange control and established the Exchange Control Commission (Comisión de Cambios Internacionales).[2] The effect of the five main provisions of the enacting legislation was to shift considerable control over foreign-exchange operations from the Central Bank to the new commission and to limit substantially the scope of private operations: (i) the Central Bank alone could buy and sell foreign exchange; (ii) the Central Bank fixed the official rate used by large-scale mining enterprises; (iii) the commission determined other rates; (iv) the commission allocated foreign exchange, with preference to be given to raw materials, prime necessities, and drugs; (v) the commission had control over exports. Nitrate, iron, iodine, and copper exporters were required to purchase domestic currency to cover "legal costs of production." All other exporters were required to obtain export permits and to return all foreign-exchange earnings to Chile.

Over the next decade the control system became quite complicated, with a multitude of rates, specified uses, and independent agencies involved. An example is given by the summary in Table 3.1 of the sources and uses of foreign exchange in February 1942. This complex system was perceived to have caused many inefficiencies. Moreover, it reputedly was administered in an arbitrary manner, with frequent unanticipated and unpublicized changes. The Emergency Power Act (Law 7200 of July 21, 1942) was intended to simplify the system somewhat. The Consejo Nacional de Comercio Exterior (CONDECOR; National Council of Foreign Commerce) was created to replace the Exchange Control Commission, the Export Control Service (Servicio de Control de Exportaciones), the Import License Commission (Comisíon de Licencia de Importaciones), and the National Supply Agency (Junta Nacional de Abastecimientos). In addition, the power to fix all exchange rates was returned to the Central Bank.

Law 8403 of December 29, 1945 (by which Chile ratified the Bretton Woods Agreement) introduced further procedural reforms. One of these was that an annual foreign-exchange budget (*presupuesto de devisas*) was to be drawn up each September for the following calendar year to aid in the distribution of foreign exchange.

Law 9839 of November 1950 further altered the exchange control system by (i) redefining the membership of CONDECOR in an attempt to make it more technical and less subject to specific private interests; (ii) replacing the annual foreign-exchange budget by a more flexible system in which expected future exchange-rate movements were incorporated (*calculo estimado del*

TABLE 3.1
Sources and Uses of Foreign Exchange in Chile in February 1942

Source	Sold to	Use
1. Exchange of dollars for escudos to pay domestic cost of production in large-scale mining at 0.01937 escudos per dollar	Caja de Amortización (government debt-funding agency)	To provide exchange at 0.031 escudos per dollar
2. Small- and medium-scale copper mining (Caja de Crédito Minero)	Central Bank	To provide exchange at 0.031 escudos per dollar
3. Nitrates and iodine (CONVENSA)		
a. Amounts agreed upon with government at 0.01937 escudos per dollar	Caja de Amortización	To provide exchange at 0.031 and 0.025 escudos per dollar
b. Cost of production from compensation "A" account exchange	Compensation Office	To provide exchange for compensation countries
c. Remainder at 0.025 escudos per dollar	Caja de Amortización	To provide exchange at 0.025 escudos per dollar
4. Gold sales at 0.031 escudos per dollar	Central Bank	To provide exchange at 0.031 escudos per dollar
5. Other commodity exports		
a. Quotas from 1.0–20.0 per cent of value at 0.01937 escudos per dollar	Central Bank	Government foreign expenses
b. Specified important agricultural exports at 0.031 escudos per dollar	Commercial banks	To provide exchange at 0.031 escudos per dollar
c. Other exports at 0.025 escudos per dollar	Commercial banks	To provide exchange at 0.025 escudos per dollar

(*Continued*)

TABLE 3.1 (*concluded*)

Source	Sold to	Use
6. Private funds		
a. Legally sold funds at free-fund rate	Caja de Amortización	To provide funds at free-fund rate
b. Illegal or black-market funds	Black-market dealers	To provide funds at black-market rate
7. Tax revenues, payable in foreign exchange		
a. 18 per cent tax on profits of large-scale copper mining	Government	Service of foreign debt or sold at 0.031 escudos per dollar
b. 15 per cent tax on profits of large-scale copper mining (earmarked for CORFO) and 1.25 cents per pound of increased price paid by Metal Reserve Corporation	Government	Use of CORFO or sold at 0.025 or 0.031 escudos per dollar
c. 25 per cent of profits of Nitrate and Iodine Marketing Corporation, part of duties on imports of petroleum, and on copper and nitrate production	Government	Foreign debt service
8. Export-Import Bank $12 million credit to CORFO	Government	Use of CORFO or sold at 0.025 or 0.031 escudos per dollar

SOURCE: *Ellsworth* [1945:60–62].

movimiento de devisas); and (iii) giving commercial banks and other entities the right to undertake foreign-exchange operations with the prior authorization of CONDECOR.

The switch to a Phase III regime as part of the Klein-Saks-Ibañez stabilization program was accompanied by further changes in the institutional responsibility for overseeing exchange operations. Law 12084 of August 19,

1956, replaced CONDECOR by the Foreign Exchange Commission (Comisíon de Cambios Internacionales; COCAIN) and gave the Central Bank much more control over the exchange market. The obligation to approve an annual budget of expected exchange needs was eliminated. Commercial banks were authorized to operate in the bank spot market, but could sell foreign exchange only in amounts indicated on prior-deposit certificates (see subsection 4.1.4, below). Various exchange dealers, tourist agencies, and hotels were authorized to operate in the free brokers' market.

The liberalization to a Phase IV regime as part of the Alessandri stabilization program resulted in additional changes in institutional responsibilities. After January 27, 1959, commercial banks were allowed to deal in all classes of foreign exchange and monetary instruments in the brokers' market. Decree Law 250 of April 6, 1960, moreover, incorporated the Foreign Exchange Commission into the Central Bank. The Central Bank thus had more control over exchange operations than it had had since 1931.

The reversal to a Phase II regime in 1962 diminished somewhat the role of the Central Bank vis-à-vis the rest of the government but not relative to the private sector. Exchange control remained under the supervision of the foreign trade department of the bank, but the Treasury began to receive foreign loans without Central Bank intermediation. Only commercial banks were allowed to operate in the bank spot market (until December 17, 1963, when commercial banks were restricted to the bank future market). Commercial banks and authorized dealers (until the latter were excluded on May 3, 1963) were allowed to operate in the brokers' market.

For the return to Phase III associated with the Frei stabilization attempt, which began in 1965, the institutional arrangements remained basically the same. The foreign trade department and the department of international transactions of the Central Bank continued to be in charge of the exchange control system. Some functions of the former department were delegated to local commissions in important cities. Control over all imports of the copper industry was entrusted to the Copper Corporation (CODELCO). Imports for the public sector were supervised by the Interministerial Import Committee for the Public Sector (which included Central Bank representatives). Beginning July 31, 1965, hotels were permitted to accept foreign exchange in payment of travelers' normal hotel charges, and certain hotels in remote areas were permitted to accept foreign exchange for other purposes as well. Beginning December 7, 1967, all transactions in foreign securities were made subject to Central Bank authorization. Such modifications in institutional responsibilities, however, were relatively minor.

The initial institutional arrangements for exchange control under the Allende government were the same as in the previous phase, with operations centralized in the Central Bank, but with supervision of certain foreign-exchange transactions the responsibility of other government agencies. Subsequent modifications were made, however, when the regime reverted to a Phase II type as part of the over-all attempt to increase government control. Central Bank Circular 1510 of April 28, 1971, excluded all but state-owned banks from operations in the brokers' market. Under Superintendent of Banks Circular 31 of September 6, 1971, all banks were required to inform the Central Bank regularly about the magnitude of credit lines abroad. Under Central Bank Executive Committee Circular 1015 of December 22, 1971, banks authorized to deal in foreign exchange lost the right to maintain positions in foreign exchange or in gold (although on August 4, 1972, this right was reinstated subject to quotas).

3.2 MAJOR TRENDS IN NOMINAL EXCHANGE RATES (NERs) AND PRICE-LEVEL-DEFLATED NERs (PLD-NERs)

Exchange-rate policy is a principal component of any foreign-sector regime. For most of the years since 1931, Chile has had an explicit multiple-exchange-rate system. The main average annual NERs for 1931–72 are shown in Table A.7. Because of the substantial inflation (cf. line 2.1 in Table A.1), however, PLD-NERs are of much more interest than the NERs.[3] Table 3.2 contains the major average annual PLD-NERs for the same period. In the following column-by-column discussion, primary emphasis is given to the bank spot rate and the brokers' rate because these have been the most important ones during the past two decades.

3.2.1 Official PLD-NER.

The official NER (called the special rate after 1942) was set by the Central Bank for the following uses: (i) government imports; (ii) the legal cost of production and local costs of investment (until 1947) for large-scale mining; and (iii) the conversion of proceeds of almost all other exports at a varying quota (1–20 per cent) after September 1932.[4] The official NER was reduced substantially in the 1932–34 period, then increased to the level at which it remained fixed for the next two decades (column 1 in Table A.7). The *Nuevo Trato* of 1955 ended the use of this rate for large-scale copper mining (see subsection 4.2.1). Law 12018 of April 23, 1956, eliminated the last use of this rate, which was for part of the proceeds from nitrate exports.

A constant NER for two decades—given the substantial domestic price increases—implies a tremendous decline in the official PLD-NER (column 1 in Table 3.2). The PLD-NER for 1956 was only 2 per cent of that for 1939.

TABLE 3.2
Major Average Annual Price-Level-Deflated Nominal Exchange Rates of Chile, 1931–72
(1965 escudos per U.S. dollar)

Phase and Year	Official (special after 1942) (1)	Export Draft (2)	Gold (3)	Wine (4)	Free Funds (parity after Dec. 1946)[a] (5)	Black or Free Market[b] (6)
I-II						
1931	6.301					10.679[d]
1932	7.050	16.959				12.544[d]
1933	4.450	11.067				11.341
1934	3.232	8.404				8.381
1935	6.480	8.133				8.381
1936	5.901	7.932	10.658[d]			8.526
1937	7.318	9.664	12.845[d]		10.578	9.822
1938	7.677	9.889	13.480[d]		11.205	10.702
1939	7.900	10.188			12.614	13.051
1940	7.174	9.251			11.451	12.156
1941	5.869	7.575			9.393	9.558
1942	4.966	6.410			7.948	8.110
1943	4.210	5.434			6.739	6.991
1944	3.654	4.716			5.849	5.949
1945	3.521	4.545			5.636	5.827
1946	2.980	3.846			4.769	5.297
1947	2.333	3.012			3.734	5.681
1948	1.956	2.525			3.131	6.136
1949	1.641	2.118	10.470		2.627	6.361
1950	1.403		9.901		2.246	6.637
1951	1.159		8.048	6.582	1.856	5.377
1952	0.944		8.027	6.491	1.512	5.951
1953	0.750		7.341	6.582	4.263	7.286
1954	0.446			5.641	2.534	7.718
1955	0.256			4.625	1.456	7.483
III						
1956	0.162				0.920	4.401
1957					0.717	5.218
1958					0.568	5.684
IV						
1959					0.404	3.891
1960						3.548
1961						3.295

Bank Market		Special		Central		National
Spot (7)	Future (8)	Commercial (9)	Provisional (10)	Bank (11)	Brokers' (12)	Accounts[c] (13)
						6.301
						7.025
						10.674
						10.727
						8.046
						7.308
						9.445
						9.909
						10.196
						9.259
						9.090
						7.692
						6.521
						5.660
						5.454
						4.615
						3.855
4.343						3.636
3.644						3.220
3.115					6.513	3.695
5.389[d]		3.623	4.347		5.118	3.413
5.522		2.994	3.592		6.042	3.219
4.272		2.439	2.926		6.744	2.945
2.830		1.937	2.325		6.682	2.396
2.716					7.152	2.397
3.790				4.175	4.468	2.937
4.050				4.044	4.527	4.070
4.098				4.072	5.167	3.695
3.847				3.840	3.877	3.855
3.528				3.521	3.528	3.521
3.271				3.264	3.271	3.264

TABLE 3.2 (*concluded*)

Phase and Year	Official (special after 1942) (1)	Export Draft (2)	Gold (3)	Wine (4)	Free Funds (parity after Dec. 1946)[a] (5)	Black or Free Market[b] (6)
II						
1962						4.812
1963						5.776
1964						6.091
III						
1965						5.350
1966						4.637
1967						3.934
1968						4.398
1969						4.896
1970						5.780
II						
1971						10.989
1972						17.049
Mean	3.836	7.315	10.096	5.984	4.921	7.279

SOURCE: The sources for the NERs and EERs are given in Table A.7. The deflator for 1931–39 is the wholesale price index; for 1940–71 it is the GDP deflator from the CORFO and ODEPLAN national accounts; and for 1972, a weighted average of the consumer and wholesale price indices (with weights of 0.667 for the former and 0.333 for the latter).

a. After June 1959 calculations of the IMF for Chilean reserves and balance of payments have been based on the bank rate.

Bank Market						
Spot (7)	Future (8)	Special Commercial (9)	Provisional (10)	Central Bank (11)	Brokers' (12)	National Accounts[c] (13)
3.140				3.140	4.815	3.171
3.539	4.629			3.537	5.684	3.532
3.041	3.515			3.043	4.108	3.100
3.128	3.310			3.131	3.739	3.237
3.082	3.117			3.082	3.623	3.117
3.045	3.045			3.045	3.448	3.075
3.142	3.142			3.142	3.619	3.175
3.083	3.083			3.083	3.486	3.106
2.954	2.954			2.954	3.453	2.989
2.482[e]	2.482			2.482	4.095[f]	2.706
1.527[e]					2.748[f]	1.698[g]
3.764	3.236	2.749	3.298	3.347	4.605	5.024

b. End of June for 1948–72.
c. Weighted average of legal exchange rates.
d. End of year.
e. See note f in Table A.7.
f. See note g in Table A.7.
g. Weighted average of the bank market and brokers' market rates described in notes f and g of Table A.7.

Over the years, the decline in this rate manifested itself, ceteris paribus, in increasing incentives for government imports, decreasing incentives to use local factors in large-scale mining, and decreasing incentives to export generally.

3.2.2 Export Draft PLD-NER.

The export draft NER was first quoted in August 1931. It was initially a free rate at which exporters other than those in large-scale mining could sell directly to importers or use their proceeds to do their own importing. Banks were sometimes intermediaries in these transactions. In 1935, however, because of the scarcity of exchange, the Exchange Control Commission required that beginning in September 1936 all transactions be handled by the banks at a fixed rate.

The export draft NER followed approximately the same pattern as the official NER, but generally at about a 30 per cent higher level (column 2 in Table A.7). A decline in 1933–35 was followed by an increase in 1936 because the NER was fixed at a high level in that year owing to an exchange shortage in late 1935 and early 1936. Then the export draft NER was reduced in 1937 to the level at which it remained about constant for the next twelve years.

Although the export draft PLD-NER (column 2 in Table 3.2) rose in the late 1930s, it was 10 to 24 per cent lower than the new free funds PLD-NER (column 5 of the table). Pressures therefore increased for use of the former for imports and the latter for exports. The Exchange Control Commission responded in 1939 first by allowing only imports of goods designated as "essential" at the export draft NER and then by continually reducing the number of goods so designated. After 1939 the commission also yielded to pressure from exporters to reclassify their nonquota returns (i.e., those which were not required to be converted at the official rate) from the export draft NER to the free funds NER. The export draft NER subsequently was used less and less and not at all after 1949, by which time the export draft PLD-NER had declined to about a fifth of the 1939 level.

3.2.3 Gold PLD-NER.

The gold NER was established after the exchange shortage of late 1935 and early 1936 to cover luxury imports and travel abroad. The source of exchange was sales from the government-run gold office. Since this office purchased gold at the equivalent of 0.02711 escudos per dollar, and the gold NER was at first 0.0300 escudos per dollar and subsequently (after October 30, 1936) 0.0350 escudos per dollar, the government acquired revenue directly from these transactions. The gold rate was legally abolished in December 1936, but sales continued de facto at 0.030 and 0.035 escudos per dollar. In August 1937 these rates were lowered, respectively, to 0.029 and 0.034. At the beginning of 1938 the special NER for gold exports was discontinued and the export draft NER was applied to gold exports.

Almost eleven years later, in response to pressure from gold-mine owners, Law 9270 of December 1948 was passed, authorizing CONDECOR to allow the importation of any articles paid for by foreign exchange received from the sale of domestically produced gold (subject to a semiannual quota set by presidential decree). Thus, the gold rate was reinstated. In 1954 it became inoperative as a result of the government's decision not to announce the semiannual quota.

Throughout its existence the gold NER exceeded all other NERs including the black-market rate. In the 1949–53 period, for example, the gold NER averaged 2.6 times the weighted average of all legal rates (i.e., the national accounts rate) and 1.3 times the black-market rate (cf. columns 3, 6, and 13 in Tables 3.2 and A.7). The differential between the gold and black-market rates reflected the high cost of smuggling the type of goods, e.g., consumer durables, for which the former was used.

3.2.4 Wine PLD-NER.

The wine NER was established in 1951 by CONDECOR for a list of nonessential items which, if import licenses were granted, could be imported with foreign exchange received from wine exports. Initially this rate was kept at 0.020 escudos per dollar above the flexible bank spot NER. For the last quarter of 1952 and part of 1953, use of the wine NER was suspended, and wine export proceeds were converted at the lower free funds NER because CONDECOR and the Central Bank decided that foreign exchange could not be spared for nonessential goods. In February 1953 the wine NER was set at 0.060 escudos per dollar above the fixed free funds NER. In May 1954 it was adjusted to 0.150 escudos per dollar above the free funds dollar rate and at 0.120 escudos per dollar above the conversion rate for all other currencies. In October 1955 it was replaced by the special-area NER under which listed nonessentials could be imported, using the export proceeds of wine and a few other products, at almost double the old wine rate (again, subject to the granting of import permits).

The wine NER averaged about 16 per cent below the gold rate for overlapping years, but about 109 per cent above the weighted average of all legal rates. The added return for wine exports, as in the case of gold exports, was quite substantial because these activities were accorded preferential exchange-rate treatment.

3.2.5 Free Funds PLD-NER.

The free funds NER (*disponibilidades propias*) was established in 1937 to serve the same basic functions as the gold rate. However, over the years, this NER covered more and more imports as the Exchange Control Commission declared increasing numbers of goods to be luxuries due to the shortages of exchange at the export draft NER. The excess demand for exchange at the latter rate was intensified in 1940, when all minerals produced by domestically owned companies were reclassified from the export draft to the free funds NER, and in 1941, when certain agricultural exports (e.g., fruits and wines), manufactured goods, and specified returns on services were similarly reclassified. By the end of 1941 most imports, except for those traditionally deemed essential (e.g., drugs, sugar, newsprint), were transacted at the free funds NER.

In 1946, in response to an IMF inquiry, the parity free funds NER was given as 0.031 escudos per dollar. In that same year this rate was established for use of the 1–20 per cent quotas on the conversion of proceeds from small- and medium-scale mining mentioned above in the discussion of the official NER.

Because of serious balance-of-payments problems in 1948, approximately the same exports which had been reclassified to the free funds rate in 1940 and 1941 plus machinery and equipment, some invisibles, and "necessary" imports (i.e., neither luxuries nor goods of primary importance) were reclassified to the new higher bank spot NER. At the same time essential imports and less favored exports (e.g., wool and fish products) were raised to the free funds rate from the export draft rate.

The free funds NER was maintained at 0.031 escudos per dollar and subsequently was used less and less, although at the end of 1951 it was still utilized for the liquidation of some insurance, minimum quotas on the proceeds of certain agricultureal exports (35 per cent for bran, hides, skins, wax, and wool and 20 per cent for lentils, frozen meat, and chick peas); and for imports of certain government items, necessities (drugs, antibiotics, sugar, newsprint, tallow, wheat, and flour), and some invisible items. On October 5, 1953, the IMF sanctioned an increase from 0.031 to 0.110 escudos per dollar for the parity rate, which thereafter remained fixed at this level. But after several years the PLD-NER had declined so much (see below), that the parity was no longer utilized. After 1959 quotations were no longer given for the free funds NER.

The free funds PLD-NER declined monotonically from 1939 through 1952, with a value in 1952 of less than 12 per cent of the 1939 value (column 5 in Table 3.2). The parity change in 1953 increased this PLD-NER by a factor of 2.8 in comparison to the previous year—but only to about a third of the 1939 level. By 1959 the PLD-NER had declined to 9 per cent of the 1953 value and to 3 per cent of the 1939 value.

3.2.6 Black- or Free-Market PLD-NER.

The black- or free-market NER varied substantially over the years. Operations in this market were not legally recognized before November 1950, when CONDECOR was authorized to use it for capital transferred to Chile in the form of foreign exchange for uses other than in large-scale mining, or after 1961. Nevertheless, this NER has played important roles as an index of the tightness of exchange control in the other foreign-exchange markets and as an index of economic and political expectations.[5]

The black market developed immediately after the initiation of exchange control, in mid-1931. It originally was the only source of foreign exchange for many invisible imports as well as for imports of unauthorized goods, and was utilized quite extensively in the early and mid-1930s. The subsequent establishment of the gold and free funds NERs provided alternative legal markets for many foreign-exchange operations; so demand shifted downward in the black market.

When exchange control was tightened after World War II, black-market activity expanded again—especially during the near-hyperinflation in 1954 and 1955. In the first decade after the war, the black-market PLD-NER tended to increase regularly except during the boom years in the copper market, touched off by the Korean War (column 6 in Table 3.2). In the period of political and economic chaos of 1954–55, substantial capital flight occurred through this market. As a result, the ratio of the black-market NER to the national accounts NER reached 3.17—the highest level recorded before 1971 (also see Chart 1.1).

During the post-1955 phases, four characteristics of the evolution of the black-market PLD-NER stand out: (i) During the 1959–61 Phase IV period exchange control decreased so much that the black-market rate did not differ significantly from the legal rates. (ii) At the start of each of the three stabilization programs this PLD-NER fell considerably below its level of the preceding year: 31 per cent in 1956, 32 per cent in 1959, and 12 per cent in 1965 (but to 35 per cent below the 1964 level by 1967). These drops partially reflected declines in exchange control in the legal markets. (iii) In each of the three presidential election years—1958, 1964, and 1970—the black-market PLD-NER increased somewhat because of related political uncertainties. (iv) After the 1970 election of Allende, the black-market PLD-NER soared to historical highs because of fears and uncertainty about the attempt to transform the economy to socialism.[6] The 1972 black-market PLD-NER was 2.2 times the previous post-World War II peak of 1954. The ratio of the black-market NER to the national accounts NER in 1972 averaged over 10.0 compared to a mean of 1.45 for the entire 1931–72 period.

3.2.7 Bank Spot PLD-NER.

In February 1948, in response to a balance-of-payments crisis, the bank spot NER was set by Decree 255 of the Ministry of Economics at 0.043 escudos per dollar. Those categories of exports and imports mentioned above in the discussion of the free funds NER were immediately transferred to this rate, and large-scale mining companies were allowed to use this rate for converting new investment funds. In January 1950 a provisional NER of 0.060 escudos per dollar largely replaced the bank spot rate. Subsequently, in 1951, the bank spot NER was increased to 0.0900 and, in turn, replaced the special-commercial and provisional rates.

In 1953, in probably the single most important attempt to rationalize the exchange-rate system in the 1931–55 phase, decrees 741 and 742 made the bank spot NER applicable to almost all merchandise imports and to a substantial portion of merchandise exports. This NER covered approximately 36 per cent of the inflows and 40 per cent of the outflows in the foreign-exchange budget in the first half of 1953 and approximately 90 per cent of the outflows in the second half of the year. Substantial excess demand soon developed for exchange at this rate, however, partly because the price of dollars it implied relative to the price of the currencies covered in bilateral agreements was quite low. Moreover, the bank spot PLD-NER declined rapidly (column 7 in Table 3.2). Therefore, the relatively unified exchange-rate system quickly evaporated as new restrictions were introduced and items were moved to other NERs.

After 1955 the bank spot NER again was the dominant rate for goods transactions. In the 1956–58 Phase III period, it was used for almost all imports and related invisibles, government invisibles, education-related invisibles (up to certain limits), and capital transfers (subject to the decree of November 10, 1953, discussed below). Exceptions included large-scale mining trade and imports of certain necessities (e.g., sugar, tea, Paraguayan tea, kerosene) worth up to $30 million, which were given a rate of 0.300 escudos per dollar prior to July 1957. Because of frequent devaluations during this phase, including a series of incremental changes in the first half of 1957, the bank spot PLD-NER increased to its highest level since 1953. The 1957 and 1958 levels, moreover, have not been attained again since that time.

On January 27, 1959, the Alessandri government introduced a Phase IV regime, instituting a unified NER of 1.051 escudos per dollar and in effect devaluating the currency. The Instituto de Economía [1963:203] and Leftwich

[1966:407] suggest that, given the trade regime in operation at the time, this rate was close to equilibrium. From that date until the end of this phase, the Central Bank maintained fixed NERs (Table A.7) as a symbol of stability. However, because of continual internal inflation (albeit at a greatly reduced rate), the PLD-NERs declined steadily (by over 20 per cent between 1958 and 1961 for the bank spot PLD-NER).

After a foreign-exchange crisis at the end of 1961, a Phase II regime with multiple exchange rates was reintroduced. The bank spot NER initially was kept constant as a symbol of price stability despite obvious, ever-increasing disequilibrium. Finally, it was supposedly (but not actually) freed after a 33 per cent devaluation, on October 15, 1962, an act which was encouraged by the IMF. Because of the continuing foreign-exchange shortage and the Central Bank's continued prevention of adjustments in the bank spot market, shortages existed at that rate. Therefore the Central Bank increasingly switched transactions to the bank future NER (see below). The bank spot NER also was raised, but not enough to arrest the decline in the bank spot PLD-NER more than temporarily.

In 1965 the new Frei government initiated a Phase III regime. As one component of that regime, in April 1965 the Central Bank adopted a sliding-peg or programmed exchange-rate policy in which small devaluations—about 1 per cent at a time—were announced every 15 or 30 days with the intent of increasing the PLD-NER by about 2.0 per cent per year. That the bank spot NER was adjusted with great frequency in itself was not such a novelty. Monthly adjustments were made in that rate between April 1952 and January 1953, between April 1956 and January 1959, and between October 1962 and the initiation of this new policy. The novelties of such a policy in the Chilean experience lay in the explicit intent slowly to increase the PLD-NER and in the official claim that such a policy was advantageous.

A number of a priori advantages have been claimed for the Chilean sliding-peg exchange-rate policy of this period: [7] (i) Exporters would not be subjected to wide variations in their returns because of unanticipated exchange-rate policies or because of substantial fluctuations in the PLD-NER. Instead they could plan ahead confidently with the guarantee of a slightly increasing PLD-NER. (ii) Import-substitution activities would not be subjected to fluctuating protection with relatively high EPRs after a large devalution, then decreasing EPRs as competitive imports became ever cheaper due to declining PLD-NERs.[8] Such a pattern had occurred repeatedly in the Chilean experience because of the combination of fixed NERs and internal inflation. Operators of import-substitution enterprises therefore could plan ahead with much greater certainty. (iii) Speculators acting with knowledge of frequent small devaluations would have a less destabilizing effect on the market than if there were infrequent, but large (and profitable, if correctly anticipated) devaluations.

(iv) Desired inventory holdings would be lowered owing to the relative unlikelihood that severe restrictions would be placed on future imports, given the improved balance of payments resulting from the sliding-peg policy. (Actual inventories, however, might increase despite a decline in desired inventories if actual inventories had previously been below desired inventories because of exchange restrictions.) (v) Average capacity utilization would be increased because of the constant availability of required imported inputs. (vi) Direct inflationary pressures would not be increased, except possibly in the short run, by the series of frequent small devaluations in place of infrequent large devaluations; and the psychological impact of devaluation on inflationary expectations might be less under the former than under the latter policy.

In Part III, I evaluate some of these claims. At this point it is pertinent to note, however, that in the six-year experience with the sliding-peg exchange rate the bank spot PLD-NER generally declined (except in 1968)—despite officially announced intentions of achieving the contrary (column 7 in Table 3.2).

In July 1970 the sliding-peg policy was discontinued because of the traditional claims raised by the opposition in the presidential election campaign—that it was inflationary and that it favored rich foreign and national exporters. After the election Minister of Finance Américo Zorrilla [1970:1488] of the new Allende government announced, on November 27, 1970, that the escudo would no longer be periodically depreciated and, also, that exchange control would be intensified.[9] The government adopted a fixed bank spot NER as a symbol of stability[10] and proposed to serve as a buffer between external and internal markets in order to protect the domestic economy from any external disequilibriums or fluctuations.[11] For the first year of the new administration the bank market NER was in fact kept constant (see Table A.7), although during this period changes were made in access to that market.[12] As a result the bank spot PLD-NER dropped 16 per cent in 1971 to the lowest level recorded since the establishment of the rate in 1948.

The fixed NER symbol was abandoned in December 1971 with a nominal devaluation of approximately 30 per cent. Exchange control was intensified and the bank spot rate was replaced by four rates for four detailed lists: (A) primarily agricultural and petroleum imports, at 12.21 escudos per dollar; (B) the basic rate for exports, for principal merchandise imports of necessities, pharmaceuticals, fertilizers, and agricultural inputs, and for invisible imports and exports related to credits from international organizations and services from international news agencies and postal and parcel post agencies, at 15.80 escudos per dollar; (C) imports of machinery and parts, imports of nonessential primary materials, and imports of manufactured products, indemnification and premiums for insurance on ships and planes, and inflows and outflows of financial capital under articles 15 and 16 of Decree 1272 and

Decree Law 259, at 19.00 escudos per dollar; and (D) luxuries and other nonnecessities, at 25.00 escudos per dollar. This new structure was intended to favor imports of mass-consumption goods and intermediate inputs.

Because of the accelerating inflation, a further devaluation was implemented, on August 7, 1972, equivalent to a 58 per cent nominal change in the basic rate. At the same time, several additional lists were established, making a total of seven altogether, with rates for the seven ranging from 20 to 80 escudos per dollar. Moreover, the executive committee of the Central Bank announced that it would establish higher rates for foreign currencies deriving from nontraditional exports, the promotion of which would be in the national interest. Despite these two major devaluations in less than eight months, however, the basic bank market PLD-NER in 1972 fell 38 per cent below the 1971 level to an all-time low. On August 3, 1973, still further changes were made: the new rates ranged from 25 to 890 escudos per dollar. Nevertheless, owing to the raging internal inflation, the PLD-NER continued to fall on the average in 1973.[13]

3.2.8 Bank Future PLD-NER.

The bank future NER was introduced in 1963. Because shortages existed at the bank spot NER the Central Bank authorized commercial banks to sell exchange at a bank future NER for necessities (i.e., items with a prior-deposit requirement not greater than 10 per cent) and to buy exchange at this rate from the proceeds of exports other than from large-scale mining with delivery to be effected in less than 90 days. Starting on November 8, 1963, the Central Bank began quoting the bank future NER at a 20.3 per cent differential from the spot NER. Effective December 18, 1963, commercial banks were no longer permitted to buy exchange at the bank spot NER. The effect of this change, together with a series of changes in 1964 that increased the upper limit of prior-deposit categories for import items that qualified for the bank future rate, was to shift almost all merchandise exports other than those from large-scale mining and all nongovernment merchandise import operations to the bank future NER. Importers preferred this rate even though it was higher than the bank spot NER because of the increasing uncertainty and delays they experienced in trying to do business at the latter rate. Thus an effective devaluation occurred, with large-scale mining once again faced with a discriminatory exchange rate since it was legally bound to effect all exchange operations with the Central Bank at the bank spot NER.

In the early part of the Phase III regime of the Frei government even greater access to the bank future NER was granted by a series of ten announcements in 1965 and January 1966. On January 10, 1967, the bank spot and future NERs were unified as part of the attempt to simplify the exchange-control system. Separate but identical quotations were given for each rate until the December 1971 exchange-rate realignment.

During 1963–66, the four years in which the bank future NER was distinct from the bank spot NER, the percentage difference declined steadily; it was 31 per cent in 1963, 16 per cent in 1964, 6 per cent in 1965, and 1 per cent in 1966. Over the same period of time the bank future PLD-NER dropped by a third (column 8 in Table 3.2).

3.2.9 Special-Commerical PLD-NER.

The special-commercial NER of 0.050 escudos per dollar was introduced in August 1950 to favor the importation of certain petroleum products, agricultural machinery, raw cotton, and india rubber. By the end of 1951 it covered approximately 98 per cent of the export proceeds from nitrates and iodine, as well as imports of crude oil, gasoline, tea, Paraguayun tea, paraffin, antibiotics, kerosene, rubber, jute, cellulose, ships, etc., and certain invisible items. In 1953, it was replaced by the bank spot rate, and has not been in use since. The special-commercial PLD-NER fell 47 per cent in the four years during which it was quoted (column 9 in Table 3.2).

3.2.10 Provisional PLD-NER.

The provisional NER of 0.060 escudos per dollar, which is discussed above in the section on the bank spot rate, was instituted in January 1950 and not utilized after 1953 except for the conversion of new investment funds for large-scale mining. The provisional PLD-NER also fell 47 per cent in the four years during which it was utilized (column 10 in Table 3.2).

3.2.11 Central Bank PLD-NER.

The Central Bank NER was first quoted in 1956 at a level 10 per cent above the bank spot NER. In subsequent years, however, the differential was much smaller. After 1961 the two rates were identical except in 1965.

3.2.12 Brokers' PLD-NER.

The brokers' NER was established in November 1950 for a number of invisible transactions and for the transfer of capital in the form of foreign exchange, except for that related to large-scale mining.[14] This was the only legal NER that was allowed to fluctuate more or less without quantitative restrictions for any significant period of time. It was relatively free in 1950–55; at the start of the Phase III period, in 1956; and during the first part of the Phase II period, in 1962 and 1963. When it was free and during the 1959–61

Phase IV years it was virtually identical to the black-market NER (cf. columns 6 and 12 in Table A.7). When the brokers' NER was fixed, the black-market NER rose to levels as much as 6.2 times as high (in 1972).

Except during the period 1959–61, when exchange rates were unified, the brokers' NER always has been above the weighted average of all legal NERs. By the middle of each of the two Phase III periods (1956–58 and 1965–70) such discrepancies had declined to 11 or 12 per cent. In both cases, however, they increased thereafter. During the three Phase II periods (1950–56, 1962–64, and 1971 on), such discrepancies were much higher—almost 200 per cent in 1955 and about 60 per cent in 1963 and in 1972. These patterns reflect the practice of using NERs more to limit invisible imports than to limit merchandise imports at times of exchange shortages.

The secular trend of the brokers' PLD-NER was downward during 1950–72. However, this pattern is distinct in two respects from that of the over-all legal PLD-NER (see the discussion of the national accounts rate, below): (i) The relative decline has been somewhat greater because the brokers' NER was a free rate at the beginning and was fixed at an overvalued level at the end of this period, while the other legal rates were fixed at overvalued levels at both the beginning and the end. (ii) The brokers' PLD-NER has increased much more frequently because at times this NER was free and at other times the brokers' NER was devalued both more and earlier than NERs applicable to merchandise transactions.[15]

As was the case for the bank spot NER, in late 1971 the brokers' NER was split into several rates: the basic rate remained at 28.00 escudos per dollar, but operations in some invisibles were allowed at the B-list rate of 15.80 escudos per dollar or at the C-list rate of 19.00 escudos per dollar.[16] Furthermore, on August 2, 1972, the brokers' NER was devalued and subdivided into the following three rates:

Area I. 36.00 escudos per dollar: for re-export of capital investments under Article 14 of Decree 1272, expenditures for study abroad, and noncommercial medicines;

Area II. 46.00 escudos per dollar: for broker market operations not designated as Area I or Area III;

Area III. 85.00 escudos per dollar: for travel and transportation, pensions and family help to nonstudent nonresidents, obligatory payments in foreign currency abroad by residents in Chile, and extraordinary remittances.

3.2.13 National Accounts PLD-NER.

The national accounts NER is a statistical entity only. It is calculated by the national accounts office as a weighted average of all of the legal NERs. As such, it is a useful composite index of over-all exchange-rate movements. Examination of the national accounts PLD-NER (column 13 of Table 3.2) suggests two important features: (i) The weighted average of all PLD-NERs did not change as sharply as did many of the individual PLD-NERs. This characteristic reflects the frequent shifting of items to higher exchange-rate categories in lieu of formal devaluation—all in an environment of considerable inflation. (ii) From 1940 on, the secular movement in the national accounts PLD-NER was downward at a mean exponential rate of 5.4 per cent per year (also see Chart 1.1). During the 32 years from 1940 to 1972, the annual PLD-NER increased only seven times. In only three of those years—1950, 1957, and 1963—was the increase as large as 5 per cent. The value for 1972 was less than one-sixth of the value for 1940. The strong downward secular trend in the weighted average of legal PLD-NERs implies that even if the exchange-rate system had been near equilibrium in the early 1940s, it was unlikely to have remained there long.[17] The resulting disequilibrium system could not be supported for any significant period of time except through the use of quantitative restrictions.[18]

3.2.14 Other Rates.

A large number of additional NERs also were in use at various times. Bilateral and compensation agreements (see subsection 4.1.6) implied the existence of distinct NERs. From March 30, 1954, until the start of a Phase III regime in 1956 imports of certain specified products (e.g., liquor, tobacco, truck chassis, tires) were permitted, subject to authorization, using the export proceeds of small- and medium-scale mining with different fixed exchange-rate differentials for *each* individual import and export item. At the time of the August 1972 alignment, as is noted above, the Central Bank announced it would establish special NERs on an individual basis for certain nontraditional exports.

In general these special NERs did not substantially affect the over-all average NER. But they did add considerably to the complexity of the system, increase distortions, and have substantial income distribution implications for those directly affected.

NOTES

1. Johnson [1971], McKinnon [1971, 1972], and Mundell [1971], among others, have recently argued that exchange-rate policy is best considered as simply one facet of monetary management.

2. With the July decree, Chile abandoned the gold standard, thus acting two months before the pound was devalued, in September 1931, rather than, as Hirschman [1963:179] has claimed, in March 1932, six months after the devaluation.

3. Of even more interest are the PLD-EERs which incorporate the effects not only of exchange rates per se, but also of all the other policy tools to be discussed in chapters 4 and 5. In section 5.1, I explore the evolution of PLD-EERs and PLD-EER(PI)s in the years since the Great Depression.

4. The existence of varying quotas on exports other than from large-scale mining and of varying legal costs of production rates on large-scale mining in effect implied a different de facto NER for each export good.

5. The latter role is emphasized in Instituto de Economía [1956:28]. The determinants of the black-market PLD-NER are investigated in Table A.7, note b.

6. The election was on September 4, 1970. Between the end of August and the end of September 1970 the black-market NER increased from 22.8 to 35.0 escudos per dollar, although it subsequently declined somewhat to a year-end level of 28.0 escudos per dollar. Picks' [1971:124] also reports considerable postelection black-market activity in Chilean escudos in Buenos Aires (almost $13 million's worth in one week with the cross rate up to 50.0 escudos per dollar at one time) and in Bogotá and Quito.

7. Ffrench-Davis and Carrasco [1969:901–904] include many of the following points in their *Central Bank Bulletin* explanation of the government rationale for the policy.

8. EPRs will not necessarily decline as the PLD-NERs decrease even under ceteris paribus assumptions because the price of inputs might decrease more than the price of products. However Ffrench-Davis and Carrasco [1969:901–904] claim that in the Chilean experience the EPRs for the import-substitution industries in fact did decrease in such circumstances. If quantitative restrictions are effective, moreover, PLD-EER(PI)s may not decline even if PLD-NERs drop substantially.

9. According to de Onis [1971b:9]: "When President Salvador Allende Gossens ran for office last year, one of his promises was that Chile would 'terminate agreements with the International Monetary Fund and put an end to the scandalous devaluations of the escudo.' "

10. The adoption of a fixed NER as a symbol of stability had a certain ironical aspect to it in that Allesandri, the runner-up in the close presidential election of September 1970, had himself adopted such a symbol twelve years earlier after he had narrowly defeated Allende in the presidential election of late 1958.

11. For example, the government proposed to protect exporters from any disequilibrium due to domestic price increases and a fixed NER by an expanded drawback program (see subsection 4.2.2, below).

12. Substantial changes were also made in the use of import prior deposits (see subsection 4.1.4., below).

13. After the coup that ousted the Allende government, yet another devaluation was made, on October 1, 1973.

14. Starting in November 1953, however, the NER for each new foreign investment project was negotiated individually.

15. In 1962, for example, the brokers' NER was devalued by 35.1 per cent in January and a total of 110.2 per cent for the year. The bank spot NER, in contrast, was held constant until the 33 per cent devaluation of October 15. In July 1971, the brokers' NER was devalued by 95 per cent, but the bank spot NER was unchanged until the 30 per cent devaluation in December.

16. Circulars 1672 and 1677 of April 13 and 20, 1972, also established an exchange rate of 42 escudos per dollar for UNCTAD personnel for the duration of UNCTAD III.

17. Two assumptions underly this statement: (i) imports and exports were somewhat price responsive; (ii) exports or other sources of foreign exchange did not expand

sufficiently rapidly to allow such a great decline in the equilibrium NER. See Chapters 6–8 for consideration of both of these assumptions.

18. For indicators of the degree of disequilibrium in recent decades see line 1.1.1 in Table A.1 and the estimate in Bacha and Taylor [1973] that the NER was overvalued by 25 to 80 per cent in the 1960s.

Chapter 4

Supporting Policies for Exchange Control Regimes

In the years since 1931, Chile has utilized a large number of policy tools to support the exchange-rate systems presented in the previous chapter. In this chapter, the evolution of those policies is described. An awareness of such developments is important because the levels of EERs, EER(PI)s, and EPRs depend upon how the NERs are adjusted for the impact of such policies.

4.1 IMPORT POLICIES

Some general characteristics of these policies must first be noted.

i. A wide range of import policies has been used in Chile because the administration was attempting to restrain imports in a disequilibrium system at the same time that it was pursuing a number of objectives not connected with the balance of payments.

ii. Owing to the attempt to maintain a disequilibrium system with an overvalued exchange rate, cyclical fluctuations have occurred in the extent of restrictiveness of the import control system and the degree of its complexity. When favorable external conditions have prevailed and the exchange rate has not been too far below the long-run equilibrium level, the import control system has been relatively simple. Once external conditions have deteriorated and the PLD-NER has declined under pressure of inflation combined with a fixed NER, the system has been made much more complex and restrictive in response to ex ante balance-of-payments deficits.

iii. Because of this pattern, a number of policy tools that initially were introduced to liberalize and rationalize the system subsequently were altered in their basic character and used to make the system more restrictive and specific. The prior-deposit system on imports, for example, was initiated in 1956 with liberalizing and rationalizing intents. As the liberalization attempt faltered in 1957 and 1958, however, prior-deposit requirements were raised in order to limit imports and were made more varied in order to discriminate more among different imports. Therefore, in the next liberalization attempt, the additional tax was imposed to replace the prior-deposit system. When that liberalization attempt failed, prior deposits were reinstituted and the additional tax was maintained. Next, the added additional tax was introduced with the same intent, but eventually prior deposits, the additional tax, and the added additional tax were all three in effect.

iv. Some major policy changes have been associated with the switches from phase to phase which are delineated in section 1.4 above.

v. Most policy changes have been small, ad hoc adjustments made in response to specific problems that have arisen in the disequilibrium system or to concerns other than those related to the balance of payments. Those changes often have been very specific in their impact, which probably has increased distortions. Overriding general motives for the increased restrictiveness have included export pessimism and the desire for greater national control over the Chilean destiny, both of which have strong roots in the catastrophic experience of the Great Depression (see section 1.3). The motivation for many of the detailed policy alterations, however, has been the desire to limit short-run inflationary effects and to alter income distribution or to favor a particular interest group.

vi. Taxes have always been an important part of the foreign-sector regime. Because of accumulative effects they have often been quite high. They have not been very flexible, however, in response to changing conditions. They also have not been used to absorbing the entire import premium (see subsection 5.1.1). In fact, some taxes have been fixed in domestic currency, with the result that they have absorbed less of the premium as inflation has occurred. For example, Leftwich [1966:405] estimates that the ad valorem equivalent of the average specific tariff rate was 70 per cent in 1935, but declined to approximately 30 per cent by the late 1930s because of inflation. Also the tax of 0.015 escudos on foreign-exchange transactions was equivalent to more than 9 per cent when it was first applied, in 1954, but declined to the equivalent of less than 2 per cent by the time it was abandoned, in 1957.

vii. Quotas have been utilized with varying degrees of intensity since 1931. Nonprohibitive quotas, however, have not generally been an integral part of the regimes since 1955, except in 1965. The system utilized in that year was abandoned relatively quickly because of the perceived negative effects (e.g., penalizing rapidly growing industries and encouraging collusion). When nonprohibitive quotas have been in effect, the recipients of premiums generally have been the traditional traders, since allocations have been made on the basis of past import patterns. Complete prohibition has been used to provide protection to a changing group of industries.

viii. Delays and time constraints have been widely utilized to regulate short-run foreign-exchange disbursements, especially at times of foreign-exchange crises.

ix. Prior deposits on imports have been the major policy tool since they were introduced in 1956. At times of foreign-exchange shortages, such deposits have been raised to prohibitive levels on many items and the whole structure has been altered to favor specific mass-consumption necessities. During the more liberalized phases (i.e., 1959–61 and 1965–70), the prior-deposit system was gradually eliminated, only to be reintroduced abruptly with the abandonment of the liberalization attempt.

x. A large number of exceptions to the general regime have always been in force: special regimes, bilateral trading and compensation arrangements, exemptions for government agencies, and regional accords. These exceptions have tended to become more important during less-liberalized phases (although many of the special regimes were established during the Phase III and Phase IV years of 1956–61). Such exceptions have been quite important at times in terms of the proportions of total imports covered. They have caused considerable distortions and have substantially weakened the capability of the Central Bank (and related agencies) to operate a consistent exchange-control system.

4.1.1 Tariffs and Related Indirect Taxes.

Law 4321 of 1928 established the legal basis for specific import tariffs for the next four decades. Before the institution of exchange control, in mid-1931, the President had used the power delegated to him by this law to raise the rates significantly (i.e., by the end of 1930, increases averaging 71 per cent on the 73 per cent of imports affected—and further increases were made in March 1931). Subsequent modifications in the early 1930s included, in 1932, a rise of 10 per cent in the rates for luxuries (primarily as a revenue measure); in 1933, a 50 per cent increase in all duties to counterbalance devaluation; in 1934, a 100 per cent gold surcharge to replace the 50 per cent increase of 1933; and in 1935, an increase in the gold surcharge to 300 per cent because of further devaluation.

Ad valorem duties on the landed price, i.e., c.i.f. price plus all other duties and costs of clearing goods into the country, were added in 1936, 1941, and

1942. In 1943, Law 5786 created a structure which was maintained until 1967: 3 per cent on prime necessities, 30 per cent on ordinary consumption goods, and 62 per cent on luxuries.

By the early 1940s the system had become somewhat complex, and the sum of customs and landing charges had become quite large. Ellsworth [1945:50] provides an example for an automobile tire with c.i.f. value of 0.605 escudos (1 escudo = 1,000 pesos) in early 1942:

Basic duty	0.300
Warehouse charge (4 months)	0.018
Embarkation and disembarkation charges (Law 3852)	0.002
Statistical duty	0.0212
Additional duty (Law 4851)	0.030
Port fiscal duties	0.005
Total	0.3744
300 per cent gold surcharge	1.1232
	1.4976
Ad valorem tax (Law 5786)	0.1959
Total	1.6935

It is evident that the nominal protection in this case is very high because of the multitude of charges and the accumulative effects of the surcharge and that the ad valorem tariff adds significantly to the final price.

No other major revisions of import tariffs were made before 1959. The piecemeal modifications which were introduced, however, generally tended to increase the explicit tariff-equivalent, for example: (i) As mentioned earlier, from 1954 through 1957 a tax of 0.015 escudos per dollar (equivalent to 9.4 per cent initially) was collected on all exchange transactions classified as not for necessities. (ii) At the end of 1955 the exchange-rate base used to calculate customs costs in domestic currency was switched from that of the previous half-year to that of the previous quarter. (iii) In 1956, a tax of 1 per cent was introduced on all sales of foreign exchange. After being increased to 5 per cent, reduced to 1 per cent, and increased to 2 per cent, this charge was abolished in 1959. (iv) In 1957, special import taxes on vehicles were established.

In 1959, Law 13305 altered the tariff structure in a major way by imposing an additional tax (*impuesto adicional*) of from 5.0 to 200.0 per cent of the c.i.f. value for six import categories, payable in United States dollars. This tax was intended gradually to replace the prior-deposit system (see subsection 4.1.4, below) so as to rationalize the regime. At least until May 2, 1960, an amount equal to the additional tax had to be placed on deposit with the

Central Bank (and transferred to the Treasury) at the time when the import was registered with the Foreign Exchange Commission. When the import arrived, the deposit was applied against payment of the additional tax.

During the Phase IV period of 1959–61 the list of imports for which additional taxes were due in lieu of prior deposits was steadily expanded. The maximum additional-tax rate remained at 200.0 per cent, although the minimum was lowered to 0.1 per cent, and new categories were established. In May 1960, a small number of goods was shifted to lower additional-tax categories.

After the reversal to a Phase II regime, in 1962, the additional-tax rates were increased substantially in each category: in the formerly tax-free category, rates were imposed of from 5 to 30 per cent; rates of 10 to 30 per cent were raised to 100 per cent; rates of 50 per cent, to 100 per cent; and rates of 75–100 per cent, to 200 per cent. The maximum limit also was raised from 200 to 400 per cent in November 1962. In February 1963, many of these increases were reversed by the Ministry of Finance, apparently in an attempt to offset partially the inflationary impact of the devaluation of late 1962.

In November 1964, one of the first acts of the new Frei government was to institute an added additional tax (*impuesto adicional agregado*) ranging up to 300 per cent of the c.i.f. value. The government then eliminated the previous legal link between increases in additional and added additional taxes and reductions in prior deposits. Consequently, the former taxes could be changed independently of prior-deposit requirements. Subsequently, the Ministry of Finance modified these tax rates for many commodities. The most important modification, in June 1966, was a reduction of the additional and added additional taxes on machinery imports: declines from about 90 per cent to 1–10, 20–30, or 50 per cent for industrial machinery; from 90–100 per cent to 20 per cent for agricultural machinery; and from 6 per cent to 1 per cent for mining machinery.

In January 1967 Law 16464 replaced Law 4321 of 1928 as the basic Chilean tariff legislation and instituted a major rationalization. In the new law, the simpler Brussels nomenclature was adopted, a 5 per cent charge was established on items previously exempted from tariffs, and the multitude of previously existing taxes [1] was consolidated into specific taxes defined in terms of 0.183057 grams of gold-equivalent per unit and ad valorem taxes on the c.i.f. value.

Some changes were made after January 1967 which were directed toward further rationalization. The most important one, made in August 1969, was that tariff charges generally were increased by 5, 10, 20, or 35 per cent to replace prior deposits of 15, 40, 90, or 180 per cent. However, most subsequent changes were of a much more ad hoc nature, as the following four cases illustrate: (i) The registration tax on the c.i.f. value of all imports (which had been established at 1.0 per cent in 1969) was increased to 2.0 per cent in 1967 and to 3.0 per cent in 1969. (ii) In July 1967, the percentage of ad valorem customs charges on capital goods paid out of the proceeds of foreign loans was reduced by twenty points for goods imported before the end of the year. (iii) In January 1968, ad valorem duties on all private imports (including those previously exempt, except for specified foodstuffs and specified commodities covered by international agreements) were raised by five percentage points. (iv) In September 1968, ad valorem duties on capital goods were reduced in proportion to the length of the repayment period for foreign credit obtained by the importer.

4.1.2 Quotas, Licenses, Foreign-Exchange Budgets, and Permitted Lists.

Integral to the attempt to partition the foreign-exchange market were explicit quantitative restrictions limiting access to import subdivisions of that market. Decree Law 138 of July 1932 (superseded by Law 5202 in July 1933) inaugurated the system of import quotas and licenses. The initial purpose of this system was to conserve foreign exchange by rationing and other means. Soon it was also used for other ends: to bring pressure on other countries with exchange control systems in hopes of promoting Chilean exports (e.g., to force Peru to buy Chilean exports; import quotas on Peruvian sugar were limited); to redistribute income by subsidizing "necessities" and prohibiting "luxuries"; and to provide additional protection (e.g., in the 1930s for flat glass, light bulbs, calcium carbide, jute bags). The Import License Commission (established in October 1933) determined the allocations of quotas and licenses primarily on the basis of past patterns, with some modifications in response to political influence. The Exchange Control Commission administered the system. The recipients were largely traders.

At times quotas exceeded available foreign exchange; as a result, by 1939 large quantities of goods were being held in customs because no foreign exchange was available. Therefore, the requirement was added that imports receive an additional permit before the goods were shipped to Chile. The institutional arrangements subsequently were rationalized somewhat through the establishment, in 1942, of CONDECOR; the establishment, in 1945, of an annual foreign-exchange budget; and the 1950 reform of CONDECOR and of the foreign-exchange budgeting system, which temporarily allowed the importation of certain machinery, raw materials, and replacement parts at the free-market rate without prior authorization.

During the Phase II period of 1931–55, nevertheless, the underlying pattern of operation remained the same. First, an attempt was made to make the system more rational and unified by setting up a fixed or controlled exchange rate for a significant proportion of international trade. Then, because of internal inflation and lags in exchange-rate adjustments, balance-of-payments crises occurred and the foreign-exchange budget was exhausted. In response, ad hoc measures were implemented: the suspension of licensing for some import or exchange-rate categories (especially luxuries and the gold and wine rates); the piecemeal reclassification of goods to higher rates; and the ad hoc reduction of permitted lists of imports. As a result of these modifications the system remained as complex as it had been initially.[2]

With the introduction of a Phase III regime in 1956, arrangements were altered significantly. In August 1956, Law 12084 abolished the previous system with its specific quotas in the foreign-exchange budget and its import licensing. Under this law, there was established a fairly broad list of goods which could be imported freely by any economic entity upon payment of duties, taxes, and the prior deposit without licenses, except for a few items which required a certificate of necessity from the Ministry of Economics. The newly established Foreign Exchange Commission proposed the original list of permitted imports and subsequent modifications to the Ministry of Finance, which enacted the same by decree. The permitted list generally was expanded throughout the period, although occasionally items that had formerly been on the list were excluded from it.

Early in the Phase IV period of 1959–61, further liberalizations were introduced. In April 1959, Decree 5474 of the Ministry of Finance expanded the permitted list to include almost all commodities (although those not previously included were subject to a 5,000 per cent, 90-day prior-deposit requirement). At the end of 1959 the permitted list effectively was expanded to all imports by making the 3,500 per cent prior-deposit category applicable to all items not mentioned explicitly on the permitted list.[3] A few exceptions to the generally less restrictive system existed: government agencies were still required to obtain permission from the Ministry of Finance for nondefense imports; a quota of 200 vehicles for use as taxicabs was fixed in August 1959; and from July 15 to August 9, 1961, a prohibition was imposed on non-domestically transformed re-exports, which remained in effect for the rest of the year for scrap iron. But generally the regime was the least restrictive one imposed since the Great Depression.

The reversal in 1962 to Phase II policies was accompanied by new import bans. In January 1962, Decree 41 of the Ministry of Finance prohibited the importation of about 700 items considered to be nonessential or in sufficient production in Chile. Application had to be made to the Central Bank for permission to import goods remaining on the permitted list. Approval was usually granted automatically, but sometimes there were considerable delays.

Early in the Frei regime, restrictions were tightened because of foreign-exchange shortages and impending foreign-debt payments. In January 1965, Law 16101 empowered a Central Bank committee to reject import applications for any commodity group for which total import applications during any month exceeded by more than 5 per cent the average monthly import registrations of the past twelve months for that group. When applications for any commodity were rejected, those for all other commodities in the same customs tariff category had to be rejected. Between January and November 1965, such power was used to reject $92 million of import applications.

This new procedure had a number of negative effects: (i) Relatively rapidly growing industries and activities were penalized. (ii) Holders of relatively large inventories within a particular category were favored, since they could submit very large requests and count on pressure from their competitors to ensure eventual acceptance without themselves incurring substantial relative costs because of delays. (iii) Inventory accumulation in excess of actual needs was encouraged because of concern that future dollar applications would not be approved. (iv) A certain random element was introduced into the process in that an "unreasonably" high request for dollars would have to be approved if it did not exceed the allowable limit for that month. But the same request (or a "reasonable" one) *might* be rejected if it was made in a month in which the criterion was not met. (v) Collusion was encouraged among firms in an industry in their attempt to ensure that total requests from that industry would not exceed the allowable limits. (vi) Control by other government agencies over allocation of approved applications within a tariff category had been surrendered in order to avoid charges of favoritism. (vii) Discrimination occurred against items with large seasonal fluctuations. (viii) Very costly delays were introduced, especially in regard to spare parts. (ix) The review committee was subjected to considerable political pressure for approval of certain applications.[4]

Such defects soon became apparent to the authorities. Almost immediately modifications were made so that spare parts worth up to $500 were exempted from the need for prior approval. Once the immediate foreign-exchange crisis had passed, rejections of import applications were less and less frequent. After February 1966 the whole procedure was no longer used.

Throughout the Frei years the permitted list of merchandise imports continued to be used. Initially this list was reduced because of the immediate foreign-exchange crisis. In early 1965, for example, 49 items were removed. Later in that year, however, the list was expanded, especially for machinery and medicine. This expansion continued over the next several years and then accelerated during the last two years of the Frei administration.[5] In January 1970, a Presidential Decree provided for the gradual (so as not to cause undue transition problems) elimination of virtually all import restrictions with the intents of limiting special advantages to imports from LAFTA; encouraging greater domestic efficiency by eliminating undue protection, but retaining the possibility of higher protection for one or two years for infant industries;

and using indirect taxes on luxuries instead of the import regime to limit consumption of items deemed socially undesirable. Throughout the rest of the year, a large number of items were added to the permitted list. By late in the year, virtually the only items not included were automobiles, television and radio receivers, cigarettes, guns, jewelry, alcoholic beverage, carpets, and toys.

The Allende government made no general changes in the use of the permitted lists and related tools. During the first two years of this government, however, a large number of specific modifications were made which discriminated against luxuries,[6] favored mass-consumption imports, and on balance increased the number of permitted items. Many of the added items, however, carried a prohibitive prior-deposit requirement of 10,000 per cent. The Central Bank included them on the permitted list because exceptions could be made more readily from the prior-deposit requirement than from the permitted list for imports generally deemed undesirable, but in specific cases judged advantageous.

4.1.3 Time Constraints on Foreign-Exchange Cover for Imports.

In some times of foreign-exchange shortages, informal delays in the delivery of foreign-exchange cover for imports increased, for example, in the first half of 1964 (Ffrench-Davis [1971:88]). The 1965 procedure for obtaining approval of import applications, which is described in the previous subsection, also had the effect of pushing foreign-exchange needs forward by increasing processing lags, even though the procedures announced in January 1965 limited the period between receipt and acceptance or rejection of any application to 90 days.

For the same purpose at other times such delays were formally introduced. In 1958 lags of 20 and then 30 days were instituted as the Phase III regime faltered because of exchange shortages. In the subsequent Phrase IV period such lags were reduced, in 1959, to 15 days after shipment for imports from Western Hemisphere countries and in 1961, to the date of arrival of the shipping documents. At the start of the Phase II period of 1962 the Central Bank reintroduced a compulsory deferred payment period of 90 days, which was increased to 120 days in September of that year. This deferment period remained in force through 1965. Given the lags in other steps of the procedure, such as in the consideration by the authorized Central Bank committee of whether to accept or reject applications, in that year 265 to 315 days elapsed between the initial presentation of an application by an importer and the actual transfer of foreign exchange. The compulsory deferment period subsequently was reduced in small steps until it was eliminated in 1969.

The lag in delivery on sales by the Central Bank to commercial banks provided another time constraint on the availability of foreign exchange. Under the Frei government of 1965–70, for example, this lag ranged from 56 to 82 days, with its peak occurring during the foreign-exchange shortage of late 1967.

Yet another time restriction was introduced in December 1965. Under Central Bank Circular 590 exchange for specified imports had to be purchased at the bank future rate corresponding to the full registration value to provide for immediate cash payment in local currency within 60 days after shipment (which was reduced to 30 days in October 1967). From January 1966 through January 1967, more commodities were added to the list covered by this circular until approximately 80 per cent of private-sector imports were included. For much smaller lists of commodities similar restrictions with maximum time periods of 120, 240, and 360 days also were established in 1967 and 1968.

From the point of view of importers, all these time constraints could result in higher costs. For example, if no part of the cost of the delay was borne by exporters, a 120-day delay implied an increase of 2 to 3 per cent in the real c.i.f. cost of Chilean imports. From the point of view of the Central Bank the primary purpose of these constraints, as noted above, was to push forward foreign-exchange requirements in times of shortages. Several of these time constraints were also introduced, however, to absorb domestic liquidity as part of anti-inflation programs.[7]

4.1.4 Prior Deposits on Imports.

In 1956 CONDECOR introduced a new tool into the set of Chilean foreign-sector policies in the form of import prior deposits. Such deposits have been among the most important and most altered measures in the regimes from that time to the present.

The original system included 30-day prior deposits in domestic currency on goods imported on a consignment basis (5 per cent deposit), goods imported on a deferred basis (amount of downpayment), and goods imported on a cash basis. Goods in the last group were divided into six categories. Some examples of the goods included in each category are given below, with deposits specified as percentages of the c.i.f. values:

Category A (5 per cent): cellulose, raw rubber, crude oil, wheat, Paraguayan tea, sugar, lubricants, gasoline, kerosene

Category B (50 per cent): sewing machines, wool tops, cotton, coffee, asbestos, chassis for trucks and buses, buses, tires, spare parts for motor vehicles

Category C (100 per cent): most antibiotics, chemicals, paraffin wax, plastic raw materials, tubes, newsprint, business machines

Category D (150 per cent): tin plate, films
Category E (200 per cent): pickup trucks
Category F (400 per cent): glassless station wagons

Capital-goods imports and imports by large-scale mining enterprises and by the public sector were exempt from the prior-deposit requirements. Banks were allowed to sell foreign exchange only in the amounts specified on the prior-deposit certificates.[8]

At first the use of this new tool implied a substantial liberalization of imports with the same general order of priorities as before, but without the extreme discrepancies among goods. There also was an initial, one-shot anti-inflationary impact as the new system absorbed substantial credit.

Subsequently, however, as the escudo became more overvalued and foreign-exchange reserves declined, the prior-deposit system was modified substantially. In 1957, three new categories were established:

Category G (600 per cent): automatic scales, photographic equipment, etc.
Category H (1,000 per cent): pineapples, poplin, elastic fabrics, aircraft, buses, etc.
Category I (1,500 per cent): spices, locks, trucks, automobiles, etc.

In 1958 the minimum deposit period was increased to 90 days,[9] the percentage required for imports on consignment was increased to 100, almost all items were shifted upward among categories, and a new category was established:

Category J (5,000 per cent): automobiles, station wagons, buses, pickup trucks, jeeps, typewriters, calculators, etc.

As a result of these major modifications in 1957 and 1958, as well as a host of minor ones, the basic character of the prior-deposit system was substantially altered. Changes were made more and more on an ad hoc basis. Discrimination among goods increased because of the spread in the rate structure and the differences in the deposit periods. Alterations ocurred quite frequently. Favoritism of specific products became more rampant. Some prior deposits became almost prohibitively high.[10] The whole system became much more restrictive.

In the Phase IV years of 1959–61, the dominant tendency was to reduce dependence on prior import deposits by substituting additional taxes in their place. A parallel tendency was to lower deposits on those items for which they were still required. In 1959, for example, deposits were first reduced and then eliminated on deferred payment imports, and all imports carrying prior-deposit requirements of 150 per cent or more were moved to lower categories, i.e., from 150 to 100 per cent, from 600 to 400 per cent, from 1,500 to 1,000 per cent, from 5,000 to 1,000 per cent, and from "not permitted" to 3,500 per cent. In 1960 and 1961 further downward shifts were made in classifications among categories and in the percentage rates for various categories. In November 1961 prior deposits on most imports were abolished.

One major anomaly, however, was introduced into the prior-deposit system in this period. In August 1960 imports of all used merchandise were made subject to a prior deposit of 5,000 per cent on the c.i.f. value of equivalent merchandise in unused condition. Although lower rates were established in January 1961 for certain construction items and boats, the strong general discrimination against the importation of second-hand machinery and vehicles precluded their profitable use as an alternative to new goods.

Another important change in the prior-deposit system in this period was the shift from payment in domestic currency to payment in dollars or in government bonds denominated in dollars. Near the end of 1958 the Foreign Exchange Commission sanctioned prior-deposit payments in short-term Treasury dollar bonds or in dollars in addition to domestic currency. In March 1959 the commission eliminated the eligibility of domestic currency for such purposes. Subsequently it permitted use of medium-term Treasury dollar bonds and obligations of the government debt finance agency (Caja de Amortización de la Dueda Pública). The motivations for these changes were twofold: to lessen the domestic currency liquidity of banks as part of the change toward a more restrictive monetary policy and to shift command over resources to the central government, since the dollar prior deposits were held by the Treasury, not by the banking system (which held prior deposits in domestic currency).

The reversal to a Phase II regime during the foreign-exchange crisis of December 1961 was initiated by the imposition of a 10,000 per cent prior-deposit requirement on all items. For most items deposits were reduced from these prohibitive levels early in 1962, but a system then was established of 90-day prior deposits in fiscal bonds at rates ranging from 10 per cent to 10,000 per cent of the c.i.f. value of imported merchandise.[11] Ffrench-Davis [1971:86] and Jeanneret [1971:150] report that the limited number of eligible bonds effectively constrained import applications. The scarcity rent on the bonds was as much as 30 per cent (which accrued, of course, to the bond owner and not to the government). Later in this phase the restrictiveness of the deposit requirements was slightly reduced.

At the start of the Phase III period of 1965–70, prior deposits in fiscal dollar bonds were replaced by escudo deposits equal to the value of the additional tax plus the added additional tax. At the same time commercial banks were prohibited from directly or indirectly financing prior deposits. The purposes of these changes were to transfer to the fiscal sector the rents previously received by dollar-bond owners without affecting the cost of imports for importers; to rationalize the system by preparing the way for the elimination of the additional and added additional taxes; and to redirect credit from commerce to "directly productive" activities.

During the first four years of this phase, a number of alterations were made which increased the restrictiveness or specificity of the system. Such modifications provided added protection for domestic production of a number of particular items.

The clearly dominant trend throughout this phase, however, was toward simplification of the system and reduction of its impact. After the exchange crisis of 1965, items were frequently reclassified to lower categories or exempted from the prior-deposit requirements; as a result, the importance of prior deposits declined steadily.[12] In 1967 the number of categories was reduced to six (10, 20, 50, 100, 200 and 10,000 per cent). After September 1968, prior deposits could be released and used to pay import duties and other import charges instead of being blocked for at least 90 days as was previously the case (therefore reducing the need for double financing). In 1969, the percentages of the deposits were reduced in four steps from 10 and 20 to 0, from 50 to 15, from 100 to 30, and from 200 to 50. On July 30, 1970, all prior-deposit requirements were eliminated except for the prohibitive 10,000 per cent category.

The demise of prior-deposit obligations once again was of short duration. Less than a month after taking office, late in 1970, the new Allende government established prior deposits of 10,000 per cent for refined sugar, cigars, pipe tobacco, tinplate, commercial aviation aircraft, certain rayon yarns and fibers, merchant ships, fishing vessels, and navigational equipment. This broadening of the use of prohibitive prior deposits was relatively minor in scope, but it represented a definite reversal from the prevalent trend of the previous phase of reducing the use of this policy instrument. In April 1971 (Central Bank Circular 1508), moreover, the 10,000 per cent prior-deposit requirement was extended to over 60 per cent of the import categories included on the permitted list. Subsequently the coverage of this requirement was steadily expanded. The only significant exception to this new trend was the exclusion of parts from the requirement of a 10,000 per cent deposit and prior Central Bank approval. Thus, prior deposits were the major means on the import side by which the government attempted to create a buffer between the international and domestic economies and to increase government control. The increase in the use of prohibitive import prior deposits was the most important single policy change in the move to a much more restrictive foreign-sector regime.

4.1.5 Special Regimes.[13]

Import policies have been further complicated by a number of exceptions to the general rules. The most significant probably have been those explicitly recognized as "special regimes." These usually have accorded favorable import treatment to particular regions or industries.[14] The importance of these regimes in the early 1960s is indicated by the fact that they affected 41 per cent of total imports in 1961. Further evidence of their importance at that time is the estimate by Beca, Galvez, and Imperatore [1969:136] that in 1962 customs duties actually collected were only 43.4 per cent of what they would have been had the legal rates applied to all imports, with special regimes accounting for about 80 per cent of the shortfall. The special regimes declined in relative importance during the 1960s, but still affected 18 per cent of imports in 1969 and 1970.

4.1.5.1 Special Regimes For Particular Regions.

These accounted for 30 per cent of the value of imports under special regimes in 1961 and 74 per cent of such imports in 1970. The motive for establishing these regimes was to achieve better integration of remote areas of northern and southern Chile into the national life. The four major areas covered, in order of the value of imports affected, are the following:[15]

Arica. In 1953 Decree Law 303 established a special regime for the department of Arica.[16] This regime is described in some detail because it has been the most important of all of the special regimes and it has served as a prototype in a number of respects for the other regional regimes.

As of 1961, special provisions for this department included: exemption from indirect taxes for industries; exemption from customs duties on imports of raw materials and capital and a single customs duty of 10 per cent on other products with an additional duty of 15 per cent for some luxury goods; a system of drawbacks on the exportation of products assembled or produced in Arica; a special credit system (not subject to the general margins established by the Central Bank) for all industrial enterprises that used only raw materials produced in the area; a 90 per cent reduction in profit and real-estate tax rates for all new industries established in 1959–69; and a geographical monopoly for the Chilean automobile industry.

Movement of goods from Arica to the rest of the country was governed by the general trade regime with the following exceptions: (i) Once in every six months, tourists in Arica could take out goods worth about $40 in duty without paying the duty and goods worth up to about $110 in duty on payment of only the specific and ad valorem charges. (ii) Goods produced in Arica and not produced in the rest of the country were subject to only one-half of the specific and ad valorem duties on the import content and were exempt from additional taxes and prior deposits. (iii) Goods produced in Arica and also produced in the rest of the country (but in inadequate quantities in the judgment of the Ministry of Economics) were subject to 75 per cent of the specific and ad valorem duties on the imported component and were exempt from additional taxes and prior deposits.

In the 1962–64 period import privileges for Arica were restricted, and almost all imports on the general prohibited list were subjected to a 200 per cent additional tax if imported into Arica. At the same time the government effectively created a category of otherwise prohibited luxury imports which could be imported only into areas such as Arica and which could be shipped to the rest of the country only if processed or assembled in the special regions.[17]

During 1965–70 some attempts were made to integrate the special regimes into the over-all trade regime as part of the general trade liberalization. In 1966 a tax was applied on all imports otherwise exempt (but much of this tax was eliminated in March 1968). Also in 1966 the Central Bank was given the authority to adjust the approval of import registrations for the television receiver, automobile, and sewing machine industries in Arica to the need to stimulate the development of similar industries elsewhere. In late 1969, regulations were changed so that any new items on the permitted list imported into Arica were subject to 80 per cent of the normal tax and prior-deposit requirements instead of the previous 25 per cent. After August 1970 import duties and taxes were applied to all but specified classes of goods when imported into Arica for local use.

Under the Allende government, attempts were made to remedy part of the perceived regressive income impact of the Arica regime. The government therefore immediately instituted a requirement that goods be certified by the appropriate government ministry before they could be imported into Arica. Shortly thereafter it required that importers seeking to benefit from the special regime for Arica establish that they had resided there without interruption for at least three years.

Despite modifications under the Frei and Allende governments, Arica has remained the most important of the special-regime areas. In 1971 it accounted for over a third of the value of total approved special-regime import applications. It has continued to provide a means for evading at least part of the general trade regime apparatus. It also has continued to be the home of some of Chile's most inefficient industries.

Provinces of Chiloé, Aysen, and Magallenes. In 1956 Law 12008 established a special regime for these three very isolated southernmost provinces of Chile. The area was exempted from import duties on all nonluxury products. The reshipment of imports to the central part of Chile was made subject to the same rules that applied to the department of Arica. In 1958, motor cars, whiskey, wine, beer, and cider were reclassified as nonluxury goods for this purpose and thereby freed from the restrictive quota on luxury imports into this area. Thereafter changes in this regime generally paralleled those for Arica.[18]

Provinces of Tarapacá and Antofagasta and Department of Chanaral. In 1958, Law 12858 established a special regime for these northern areas. It authorized duty-free importation of a number of food products, which were not in sufficient production to supply the local demand, in order to compensate in part for the impossibility of substantial agricultural production in these areas because they are located in the Atacama Desert.

Northern Area. Also in 1958 Law 12937 established a special trade regime for the northern departments of Iquique, Pisaqua, Tattal, and Chanaral (except for the El Salvador copper deposits) and for all small- and medium-scale copper mining in the province of Antofagasta. Under this regime, all productive enterprises in the area were exempted from import duties and prior deposits on capital goods, fuels, and raw materials (with normal customs duties for reshipments to other areas); a special credit plan was established for industrial enterprises that exclusively used raw materials produced in the area; and a system of drawbacks was instituted for products assembled or produced in the area.

4.1.5.2 Special Regimes for Particular Industries.

Individually, the value of imports covered by these regimes generally has not been as large as that for regions. However, the value of imports coming under (i), below, was second only to that of the department of Arica at times in the 1950s and early 1960s. The value of imports under the special regime for the nitrate industry (see subsection 4.2.2) also was substantial over a long period of time. The following were among the most important special regimes for industry.

i. In 1944, under Law 7896, exemption from all taxes, including customs duties and profit taxes, was granted to the then new (and only) enterprise producing iron and steel ingots (Compañía Acero de Pacífico; CAP).

ii. In 1950, under Law 9618, total tax exemption (including customs duties) was granted to the then newly established National Petroleum Enterprise (Empresa Nacional de Petróleo; ENAP).

iii. Also in 1950, under Law 9839, exemption from customs duties was granted for imports of machinery destined for agriculture, small- and medium-scale mining and fishing, and new industries at least 80 per cent of whose raw materials were of domestic origin. In 1953, Decree Law 208 expanded the special regime for the fishing industry, with broad tax exemptions, special import privileges, and the right directly to use its own foreign-exchange proceeds. Further provisions, favoring fishing and ancillary industries, were added in 1960 and 1961.

iv. In 1956, under Law 12084 the sugar industry was granted total exemption from import duties on beet-refining machinery in order to promote domestic self-sufficiency in sugar production.[19]

v. In 1960 Decree Law 255 established a special regime to promote the modernization of the coal industry. Accelerated depreciation was permitted, and exemptions were granted from all customs duties on imports of machinery and equipment under CORFO-approved investment programs, all customs duties on industrial or domestic coal-using equipment, profit taxes on profits reinvested in CORFO-approved plans, and production taxes in the coal-mining industries.

4.1.6 Bilateral, Compensation, and Barter Agreements.

These three forms of agreement constitute a second important class of exceptions to the general international economic regimes of Chile. After foreign credits were frozen, in 1931 (see subsection 4.3.3), a number of importers of Chilean nitrates threatened retaliation. As a result, compensation agreements along the following model were signed with a number of countries.

Two compensatory accounts with fixed, but different, exchange rates, "A" for new business and "B" for frozen credits, were established in each country.[20] In Chile, foreign nationals paid debts in Chilean currency into the B account at the Central Bank. A fixed percentage of the value of nitrate exports (and sometimes other exports) was paid for out of these deposits. Upon arrival of the nitrates in the importing countries, this same percentage of the sale was paid into local B accounts and transferred to creditors whose Chilean credits had been frozen. Commodity imports from the partner country provided deposits for the Chilean A account which were used to compensate nitrate exporters for the part of their shipments not paid for from the B account. In the partner country, credits to the A account came from proceeds of imports from Chile and disbursements were made to exporters to Chile.[21]

Thus, distinct bilateral exchange rates were in effect with each partner country.[22] Since these rates were not adjusted regularly to offset relative price changes, large sums often accumulated in the Chilean or partner country's compensation account. For example, in 1933 Chile had a large positive balance in francs in the A account for the agreement with France. In order to avoid the penalty for not utilizing this balance within the allotted period of time, Chile tried to induce more imports from France by lowering the escudo price for francs from this account, by allowing such francs to be used for previously excluded luxuries (e.g., champagne, wine, silk, cognac, and perfumes), and by promising that French francs would be made immediately available for all imports from France.

The first bilateral agreement was signed with France in 1932. Before a decade had passed, official compensation agreements had been made with Belgium, Germany, Holland, Spain, Sweden, and Switzerland. Private compensation agreements (in which generally only the proceeds for nitrates were blocked) had been made with Austria, Czechoslovakia, Denmark, and Italy. Barter arrangements also had been established with Argentina, China, Costa Rica, Ecuador, Finland, Guatemala, Japan, Peru, Sweden, and the USSR. The trade value of these agreements in the 1930s was evidently significant: Baerresen [1966:6] estimates that they covered 30 to 40 per cent of total Chilean trade in the mid-1930s; Wilson [1937] estimates that in 1936 such agreements covered 60 per cent of Chilean imports and 25 per cent of Chilean exports.

A large number of such agreements continued into the 1950s, and new ones were signed until near the end of that decade. With Chilean liberalization attempts, initiated in 1956 and in 1959, and concurrent worldwide liberalization efforts, the importance of these arrangements declined. In 1963, the last agreement then in operation expired. The Allende government, however, had shown interest in establishing new bilateral and barter arrangements, especially with socialist countries.

4.1.7 Government Agencies.

A third group of exclusions from the general foreign-sector regime are those enjoyed by various government agencies, in part to permit independent action by specific government entities, especially government trading and development agencies. At times exemptions also have been granted to the government in general.

4.1.7.1 Specific Government-Agency Exemptions.

A number of government trading and development agencies were established in the 1930s to provide better regulation of international trade and to guide economic development.

Petroleum distribution is an example of an area in which government trading agencies became involved. In 1932 Law 5124 introduced a state monopoly on petroleum imports. Later that year Decree Law 519 established price fixing and rationing for petroleum. Neither law, however, had much immediate impact (although the latter was used for rationing in 1942). Therefore in late 1934 the Compañía de Petróleo de Chile (COPEC) was formed to share petroleum trade with subsidiaries of the Shell and Standard Oil companies, and has continued in that role ever since.

The Agricultural Export Agency (Junta de Exportación Agrícola), established in late 1930, is an example of a combined trading and development agency. This organization subsidized agricultural production and exportation and set minimum agricultural prices. More specifically, in 1933 it established export bounties for oats and barley. In 1934–35 it was empowered to export and import wheat, to fix prices for wheat and related products, and to invest in export-related agricultural production. In 1935 it introduced export bounties for wine.

A number of pure development agencies also were created in the early

1930s (and some in the 1920s), although with very limited funding: Caja de Crédito Agrario, Instituto de Crédito Industrial, Caja de Crédito Minero, Instituto de Fomento Minero e Industrial de Tarapacá y de Antofagasta, and the Caja de Colonización Agrícola. These organizations became much more important in the 1940s when they were able to obtain more money through mandatory Central Bank loans at *nominal* rates of interest of from 1.0 to 4.0 per cent.

Law 6334 of 1939, however, established by far the most important of the development agencies: CORFO (Corporación de Fomento). The new Popular Front government evidently was able to have the necessary legislation passed only because it was linked to relief for the great earthquake of January 1939. In any case CORFO was given broad powers and ample financial resources. In subsequent decades, it became the most important single agency in the policy of substantially increased government economic intervention.

Functionally CORFO basically was (and still is) an investment bank. It financed investment primarily through loans and stock purchases and legally was instructed to use improvements in the standard of living and in the balance of payments as its investment criteria.

CORFO's power originated in its substantial financial resources which enabled it to control over 30.0 per cent of the imports of machinery and equipment in each of ten years in the period between 1939 and 1954 and more than 25 per cent of public investment and more than 10 per cent of total investment in all but three years (1945–47) of the same period. The sources of CORFO's finances included the government, through initial access to funds previously allocated by law to the Caja de Amortización, increased income taxes earmarked for CORFO including a 15 per cent additional tax on the profits of large-scale copper mining, and general-purpose contributions and loans from general revenues; the banking system, through loans, sometimes obtained on CORFO's behalf by the central government; the general public, through stock sales; returns from earlier investments; and foreign official credits, including $17 million from the Export-Import Bank in 1939–40 and a total of $969 million from foreign sources up to 1969.[23]

In recent years CORFO has continued in its primary role as an investment bank. It has also expanded its activities in planning and in plan implementation. An example of the latter function is provided by the 1967 requirement that subjected authorization of import licenses for specified capital imports to the approval of CORFO. Under the Allende government the scope of CORFO was further increased, especially in overseeing the large expansion of the state sector in commerce, finance, and production.

The power which CORFO has had since its inception has resulted in a certain degree of autonomy in its foreign-sector operation. Such independence at times has lessened the capability of the Central Bank, and of related exchange-control organizations, to create and pursue a consistent over-all foreign-sector strategy.

4.1.7.2 General Exemptions.

Exemptions granted to the government and quasi-governmental organizations have centered on the prior-deposit requirement for imports and on related taxes, i.e., the additional and added additional taxes mentioned in subsection 4.1.1. Such privileges have been inversely related to the degree of over-all liberalization. They were reduced in the 1959–61 and 1965–70 phases and increased in 1962–64 and after 1970. In restrictive phases these exclusions have substantially favored the recipient institutions over the rest of the economy.

4.1.8 Regional Agreements.

In the 1960s, Chile became party to two regional agreements, which have resulted in increased trade under special arrangements.

In early 1960 Chile signed the Treaty of Montevideo which instituted the Latin American Free Trade Association or LAFTA (Asociación Latinoamericana de Libre Comercio; ALALC). The signatories agreed to eliminate gradually all barriers to intraregional trade over a twelve-year period. Decree 22220, issued by the Ministry of Finance in 1961, established the Chilean national list of imports from LAFTA countries with special specific tariff rates and exemptions from ad valorem taxes, prior deposits, charges for embarkation and disembarkation, and consular charges. Subsequent acts extended LAFTA in some limited respects. In late 1965 complementary agreements were signed for the exchange of automobile components with Argentina and Mexico. A LAFTA multilateral clearing arrangement became effective in mid-1966. Under the Allende government a number of bilateral trade and credit agreements with other LAFTA nations were initiated (e.g., credit agreements with Uruguay and Peru in March 1971, with Paraguay in April 1971, with Mexico in January 1972, and with Brazil in February 1972). Chile's national list was revised biennially.

Progress was much slower than had been originally hoped for, however. Agreements were difficult to make. The share of LAFTA in Chilean trade remained constant in the last half of the 1960s. Moreover, in 1969, as part of the over-all trade liberalization program, some of the previous discrimination in favor of LAFTA countries was reduced. Prior-deposit requirements for third countries were eliminated in cases in which imports from LAFTA exceeded $30 million, and the lists of permitted imports were expanded to include all the items covered by LAFTA agreements.

However, in part because of the apparent stagnation of LAFTA, the Frei government took an active role in the promotion of the Andean subregional group throughout the period of its formation which was initiated by the Bogotá agreement of August 1966, right through to the signing of the final accord, in 1969, by Bolivia, Chile, Colombia, Ecuador, and Peru. This agreement had as its aim the creation by 1981 of a free-trade zone, common external tariffs, and uniform policies.

The Allende government continued to encourage the development of Andean economic relations. In mid-1971 a common investment code was established to regulate foreign capital movements, royalties, licenses, patents, and brand names. In 1972, the Andean group reached a decision on how to allocate 73 industrial divisions among the five member countries, thus passing what many observers had considered the most difficult test for this relatively new trade-aid-investment grouping.[24] Moreover, when the list of goods subject to the requirement of a 10,000 per cent prior-import deposit was greatly expanded, in April 1971, imports from LAFTA and from the Andean group were exempted. As a result, effective preferences for imports from regional suppliers became fairly considerable.

4.2 EXPORT POLICIES

Major features of Chile's export policies include the following:

i. The over-all export regimes have not been as complicated as the import regimes because total export value is mainly concentrated on just a few products.

ii. For the same reason, major changes in the over-all export regimes have often not coincided with major revisions of the import regimes.

iii. Over the long run, control over the most important export source, large-scale copper mining, has shifted steadily (albeit with short-run reversals) from the foreign-owned copper companies and the U.S. government to the Chilean government. This process culminated in the nationalizations of 1971.

iv. For the first quarter-century after the Great Depression, large-scale mining was subject to a curious combination of very unfavorable NERs for local costs and very favorable NERs for imported components. Moreover, at that time and up until nationalization, returns on foreign-owned factors of production and amortization were practically unregulated.

v. Quantitative restrictions generally have been imposed on specific export products only at times of domestic supply shortages. Most commonly, the restricted products have been agricultural in origin.

vi. Since the beginning of the 1930s, special favorable treatment has been given to nitrates, the former queen of Chilean exports but long a faltering industry. This example suggests that not only vested interests created by import-substitution policies but also those created by export-promotion policies may be difficult to ignore once they are entrenched.

vii. Export-promotion attempts have accelerated in recent phases, but still have had limited coverage and probably have not compensated for the disequilibrium NER policy (see section 5.2). Most of the limited resources involved in such programs, moreover, has been used to subsidize industries for reasons other than their export potential.

4.2.1 Large-Scale Copper Mining.

In the 1930s, copper reclaimed from nitrates the position it had held before the War of the Pacific as the dominant Chilean export. Since 1931, the output of large-scale copper mining has accounted for over half of Chilean exports. In 1934, the Chilean share of world copper production also exceeded 20 per cent for the first time in more than half a century. The resurgence of copper occurred almost entirely among the foreign-owned, large-scale companies.

Prior to the Great Depression—and especially before the income tax law of 1925—government policy toward large-scale copper mining had been almost nonexistent. In the Phase II quarter-century from 1931 to 1955, however, government policy favorable to the industry was expanded considerably, and numerous policies were specifically tailored for this industry. Major tools included the multiple exchange-rate system, taxes, international price agreements, and a Chilean copper sales monopoly.

Exchange-rate policy had four basic components:

i. Dollars for local production costs were converted into domestic currency at the official NER, which remained constant at 0.01937 escudos per dollar from 1937 on (column 1 in Table A.7). The amount converted was called the legal cost of production. It supposedly reflected actual production costs. But the annual determination of legal costs of production included an element of bilateral bargaining between the government and the companies because of the ever-greater incentive for the companies to reduce domestic currency outlays. The increase in this incentive is clear from the decline in the official PLD-NER—from 7.900 escudos per dollar in 1939 to 0.256 in 1955 (column 1 in Table 3.2).

ii. Dollars for local costs of new investment were converted at the official NER until 1948, at the bank spot NER of 0.043 escudos per dollar from 1948 through 1950, and at the provisional 0.060 NER thereafter. After 1947 a higher NER was allowed for these expenditures than for local labor and variable inputs in hopes of encouraging capacity expansion. As a result, the decline in the PLD-NER for such investment costs was not as great as for local operating expenses, but it still was quite substantial (columns 1, 7, and 10 in Table 3.2).

iii. Direct taxes and imported inputs and investment goods were paid for in dollars without any government intermediation. The incentive to use imported inputs (including labor paid in dollars) in place of domestic inputs increased tremendously because of the above-mentioned declines in PLD-NERs for domestic currency expenditures.

iv. Except for local purchases and taxes and while under the sales monopoly discussed below, the foreign-owned large-scale mining companies generally were *not* required to return their proceeds to Chile. Payments for foreign-owned factors, thus, were unregulated. In this respect these companies enjoyed a unique position among Chilean exporters.

Taxes on large-scale copper mining were increased steadily in this quarter-century. Direct taxes were the most important in magnitude, but other taxes also were significant. A sampling of relevant tax-rate changes illustrates the steadily increasing tax burden. In 1939, Law 6334 added a 15 per cent tax for the use of CORFO. In 1940, Law 6457 raised the fourth-category income tax to 9 per cent on mining plus 6 per cent on companies incorporated outside of Chile. In 1941, Law 7145 instituted a 3 per cent surcharge to both relevant components of the fourth-category income tax. In 1942, Law 7160 established an additional tax of 50 per cent on any added income due to increases in the price of copper beyond the base levels established by the same law. In 1944, Law 7750 introduced a temporary fourth-category income tax of 2 per cent for two years. In 1952, Law 7160 increased the additional-tax rate from 50 to 60 per cent. In 1954, Law 11575 imposed a 30 per cent surcharge. The employee contributions to the social security system, moreover, were increased in several steps from 16.43 and 3.1 per cent in 1940 for white- and blue-collar workers, respectively, to 34.36 and 34.20 per cent in 1955.

Copper *price agreements* were in effect in 1942–46 and in 1950–52, although not at the instigation of the Chilean government in the latter case. In 1942 the Chilean and United States governments signed a wartime agreement which lasted until the end of 1946. This agreement fixed the price of copper at 12 cents per pound and waived the United States tax of 4 cents per pound on Chilean copper going to the United States government stockpile.

In 1950, because of the Korean conflict, the U.S. Office of Economic Mobilization unilaterally set the price of copper at 24.5 cents per pound. The failure even to consult with Chile (in contrast to the 1942 price fixing) caused major indignation there. Because of this reaction a conference was arranged, resulting, in 1951, in the Washington Treaty, which established a three-cent-per-pound surcharge for the Chilean government; excluded 20 per cent of large-scale mining copper production from the price ceiling; set up a wage bonus for production increases; and conferred United States credits for imports of machinery and equipment for domestically owned small- and medium-scale copper mining companies. Despite this temporary resolution, the arbitrariness with which the United States had acted left a bitter taste.

In 1952, in response to the 1950–51 copper-price-fixing experience, Law 10255 was enacted. It superseded the Washington Treaty and established the Chilean *monopoly on copper sales.* The Central Bank was authorized to set quotas on copper exports from large-scale mining companies and to buy copper from them at the New York price of 24.5 cents per pound for resale at 35.5 cents per pound, with all profits credited to the Treasury. In 1953 the international copper market weakened considerably owing to the termination of the Korean War, but the Central Bank continued trying to apply the same policy. The result was that large stocks accumulated, most of which were sold at world market prices at the end of the year. In 1954, international copper market conditions further deteriorated. The government announced its intention of selling to the Union of Soviet Socialist Republics. However, a (coincidental?) purchase of 100,000 tons for the United States government stockpile in March reduced the backlog. Soon thereafter the Chilean government abandoned its sales agency.

By the 1950s dissatisfaction with the large-scale copper mining companies was considerable and widespread. From the point of view of the companies, the trade regime had limited the control of their operations, reduced the returns from their investments, and made maintenance of market shares difficult (especially for Anaconda). From the point of view of the Chilean government, negative features included the fall in Chile's share of world copper production from 20.2 per cent in 1934 to 19.2 per cent in 1944–46 and to 11.8 per cent in 1953–54, the drop in net returned value over the 1952–54 period of 16.7 per cent because of reduced sales, and the attenuation in the linkages of large-scale mining to the rest of the economy.

In 1955, therefore, the large-scale copper mining companies and the Chilean government agreed on a *Nuevo Trato* ("new deal") for large-scale copper mining. The *Nuevo Trato* was a considerable rationalization and liberalization of the treatment of large-scale copper. This agreement changed the regime in a number of significant respects: (i) All previous charges were replaced by a single direct tax on profits. (ii) The basic tax rate was to be 50 per cent, with a surtax no greater than 25 per cent. The surtax was an inverse function of quantities and became zero when production reached approximately 190 per cent of the 1949–53 levels (or 140 per cent of previous peak levels). (iii) The limit on depreciation allowances was increased from 5 to 20 per cent of the value of plant and equipment. (iv) Exchange-rate discrimination against large-scale copper mining companies was ended.[25] (v) A government copper corporation (Corporación del Cobre; CODELCO) was established to create national expertise in copper, control exports and quantities, encourage the use of local factors of production, and prepare statistics.

The *Nuevo Trato* was the basic law governing large-scale copper mining for more than a decade. Changes were made during that time, but they did not modify the basic character of the regime. After a few years, however, dissatisfaction once again was widespread. Many Chileans thought that too many benefits had been given to the companies.[26] On the other hand, the companies wanted further guarantees before they expanded their capacities. They shelved new investment plans in 1960 and 1961 because the government would not agree to a twenty-year guarantee against changes in the tax rates and against expropriation. In late 1961, after an impasse had been reached, the legislature responded by authorizing two special surtaxes totaling 13.0 per cent on the profits of large-scale mining. The Socialist party also introduced a bill (which was not passed) to nationalize large-scale copper mining with compensation of $209 million in the form of 3.0 per cent, thirty-year bonds.

In the 1962–64 phase, discriminatory exchange-rate policy was reintroduced as transactions other than with large-scale mining were shifted from the bank spot NER to the bank future NER (see section 3.2). In 1964 CODELCO established a Chilean copper producers' price for use in Chilean sales instead of the United States producer price.

In 1965–70 under the Frei government the frustrations with the results of the *Nuevo Trato* culminated in several major changes:

Price policy was altered substantially. The Chilean producer price had been established in 1964, but on the average the price for that year was 0.6 cents per pound less than the United States producer price and 13.3 cents per pound less than the LME (London Metal Exchange) price. On the average in 1965 the Chilean producer price was 0.7 cents per pound more than the United States producer price, but was 23.2 cents per pound less than the LME price. In 1966, however, CODELCO broke sharply with the United States producer price by establishing a Chilean price equal to the average of the LME spot and future prices in August and to the LME future price in October. Subsequently, in 1968, in agreement with the other major copper-exporting developing nations (Zambia, Peru, and the Congo) the Chilean producer price was set equal to the LME spot price. As a result of these price changes, the Chilean producer price per pound exceeded the monotonically increasing United States producer price on the average by 18.0 cents in 1966, 11.7 cents in 1967, 11.4 cents in 1968, 19.1 cents in 1969, and 5.9 cents in 1970.[27]

The government raised *tax rates* on large-scale copper mining. In 1966 it established a 100 per cent surtax on the first 55,000 tons sold at over 42 cents per pound.[28] In 1967 Law 16624 increased the direct-tax base rate from 50.0

to 52.5 per cent. In 1968 the government levied a surtax according to a graduated scale for all sales at prices greater than 40 cents per pound, with the marginal rate ranging from 54 per cent at 40 cents per pound to 70 per cent at 50 cents per pound and higher.

Much more fundamental changes occurred in regard to the *control of Chilean copper*. In his 1964 election campaign, Frei had promised to seek a large increase in copper production capacity and some kind of Chilean participation in the ownership of large-scale copper mining. Even before the inauguration, his representative, Raul Saez, began to negotiate with Kennecott. In 1966, after long negotiations with each of the foreign companies involved and equally long debates in Congress, large-scale copper mining was "Chileanized" under Law 16425 and Decree Law 16624.

These laws included four major provisions. (i) Large-scale copper mining capacity was to be expanded from 580,000 short tons in 1964 to 957,500 short tons in 1970–72 with investments of $147 million in Anaconda properties, $230 million in Kennecott properties, and $157 million in Cerro Corporation properties.[29] (ii) The Chilean government became a 51 per cent owner of El Teniente (with 49 per cent remaining with Braden, a Kennecott subsidiary), a 25 per cent owner of the new Anaconda venture at Exótica (but not of Chuquicamata, the major Anaconda mine, nor of El Salvador), and a 25 per cent owner of the Río Blanco mine being developed with the Cerro Corporation. (iii) Base tax rates were lowered to 44 per cent for El Teniente, 52 per cent on the Anaconda properties (but with accelerated depreciation and the tax rebate for refining in Chile removed so that most benefits would not be received until the late 1970s), and 15 per cent (plus 30 per cent on Cerro's dividends) for the Río Blanco venture. (iv) The share originating in Chile of total world production of each company was not to be reduced when the company's total world production fell.

Two years later, in June 1969, Chile nationalized the Anaconda properties of Chuquicamata and El Salvador. This nationalization gave the Chilean government 51 per cent ownership as of January 1, 1970 (but with participation in profits as of September 1, 1969). The cost of the purchase of 51 per cent ownership was $197 million to be paid in 24 semiannual installments at 6 per cent interest starting on June 30, 1970. The other 49 per cent was to be purchased starting sometime after 1972 but before 1982 and continuing for twelve years more on terms which were to depend on net profits after January 1, 1970. Immediate government participation in profits was instituted for prices above 40 cents per pound. Owing to this nationalization, in 1970 the respective legal participation rates of the Chilean government in profits from the two former Anaconda properties were 75.647 and 76.676 per cent plus the surtax for prices above 40 cents per pound.

Allende, as well as most members of his Popular Unity coalition, had been quite critical of the terms of Chileanization and nationalization of copper under the previous government. In his first month of office the Central Bank revoked access to the bank future rate for any company entitled to only partial surrender of its export proceeds. In his second month of office, Allende sent to Congress a proposed constitutional reform which, together with a general affirmation of the absolute dominion of the state over all subsoil deposits, established specific mechanisms for the complete nationalization of large-scale copper mining. On July 11, 1971, this constitutional reform was unanimously approved by Congress. Five days later the state assumed complete control of the mines.

The constitutional amendment authorized the government to pay the previous owners the book value[30] of the companies minus debts to the state, unpaid taxes, alleged damage to the mines, and "excess profits" since the 1955 *Nuevo Trato*. This payment was to be made over a period of not more than thirty years at an interest rate of not less than 3 per cent. An appeal procedure was established with a special five-man copper tribunal[31] (whose decision would be final) for the foreign companies if they did not agree with the payments so determined. Subsequently the Chilean government publicly pledged to pay off foreign-debt obligations, totaling more than $700 million, which had been assumed by the companies in the large investment program for expanding capacity initiated during the previous phase.[32]

On September 28, Allende stated that the two principal foreign copper companies involved, Kennecott and Anaconda, owed Chile $774 million in excess profits. On October 11, the Comptroller General announced that Kennecott and Anaconda were due no compensation and that Cerro was due a compensation of $14 million.[33] Anaconda and Kennecott appealed these decisions to the special tribunal. In August 1972 the tribunal disallowed the appeals of the copper companies.

Meanwhile, another controversy arose. On December 31, 1971, Chile failed to meet the first installment of $5.8 million in promissory notes due to Kennecott because of still-pending decisions concerning the usefulness of the investment undertaken with the proceeds of these notes. At the same time Chile failed to meet a $14 million obligation due to Anaconda (at least in the judgment of Anaconda) because the government interpreted the decision of the Comptroller General to mean that such obligations were void. In response, Anaconda and Kennecott sought and obtained United States court orders embargoing the New York bank accounts of nine Chilean government agencies. Chile reacted by embargoing all remaining properties of the two companies in Chile, but also announced it would honor $84.6 million of the $92.7 million in promissory notes held by Kennecott.[34] In 1972 and 1973, in further reaction to the nationalization and debt repayment issues, the United States companies succeeded in obtaining court orders that delayed the unloading of Chilean copper in Europe.[35]

4.2.2 Other Exports.

In 1932 Law 5107 established license requirements for all exports except those from large-scale mining to ensure the return to the government of a predetermined sum of foreign exchange at a stipulated price or the return by exporters of imports of "primary necessities" previously agreed upon. The NERs for such exports were more favorable than those for large-scale copper mining, but usually not as favorable as for many other imports (see section 3.2).

Throughout the next four decades the general characteristics of the regimes for these exports remained basically the same, although the option of using export proceeds directly for imports was not generally continued. Export licenses were granted automatically if the exporter agreed to ship the exports within a specified period, repatriate all the proceeds within a second specified period after shipment, and liquidate them within a third specified period.[36] As is described in section 3.2, exports steadily were moved to higher NERs, although the applicable PLD-NERs tended to decline.[37] As is also indicated in section 3.2, variations in the PLD-NERs among exports were at times quite considerable. Baerresen [1966:3] claims that the favored exports were determined largely by political influence.

Three exceptions to the general export regimes have been important: quotas on specific products, special regimes for traditional mining exports, and special regimes to promote nontraditional exports:

Quotas on specific products (sometimes completely prohibitory) have been a part of export policy since the early 1930s. Their purpose has been to ensure sufficient domestic supplies. The list of quota goods has been changed on the average at least once a year. The quotas have primarily been on agricultural and food products, although the export of other industrial products also has been constrained at times.[38] The government has tended to use such restrictions more when the over-all regime has been relatively restrictive. Even during the most liberal phases, however, quotas have been enforced on specific products in short supply—especially after poor harvests of agricultural commodities. Such quotas have been very important for the affected commodities[39] but generally have not been very broad in their impact.

The most important *special regime for traditional mining exports* (except for large-scale copper mining, on which see subsection 4.2.1, above) has been that for nitrates. In fact, the very first important special regime, established in 1931, was for the nitrate industry, which had once been dynamic, but by then was ailing.[40] In 1931 a monopoly (Compañía de Salitre de Chile) controlling approximately 95 per cent of Chilean nitrate production was formed to attempt (unsuccessfully) to affect world nitrate prices. There was a strong negative public reaction to this attempt because of the associated takeover of $25 million in Guggenheim financial obligations. In any case, President Alessandri dissolved the company in 1933.

In 1934 Law 5340 ratified an agreement between nitrate enterprises and the government which established the basic framework for the special regime in nitrates that was to prevail for the next several decades. This law created the Nitrate and Iodine Marketing Corporation (Corporación de Venta de Salitre y Yodo; CONVENSA) with representatives of both the nitrate enterprises and the government (the latter had veto power) on its board of directors. CONVENSA was given monopoly power over Chilean nitrate sales and entered into the international nitrate cartel. The government was to receive 25 per cent of the profits. Among other things, the major nitrate enterprises received exemptions from indirect taxes on their imports of equipment, machinery, fuel, electrical detonators, chemical imports, and containers. Indirect taxes on nitrate exports—once a major source of government revenue—were eliminated. Thus, a long-enduring policy of subsidizing production and exports of nitrates by special tax exemptions was begun, although such advantages may have been more than offset by the overvalued exchange rate and the government share of profits, at least in more recent years (see the estimates of the nitrate EPRs in section 5.2, below).

Subsequently, further benefits were added,[41] and the name was changed in 1968 to the Chemical and Mining Company of Chile (Sociedad Química y Minera de Chile S.A.; SOQUIM). The basic characteristic of the special regime for nitrates, nevertheless, has remained the same since the 1930s. In the 1960s and early 1970s, it accounted for 6 to 7 per cent of all imports under special regimes. In the late 1960s it was also one of the primary beneficiaries of the drawback program discussed below.

A second important special regime for traditional mining exports has been that for small- and medium-scale copper mining. This sector has been under Chilean ownership and control since before the War of the Pacific, at which time it accounted for as much as 40 per cent of total world production. Provisions of this special regime have included tax exemptions and special investment credits.[42] In 1970 it accounted for 8 per cent of total imports under special regimes.

Special regimes to promote nontraditional exports have existed since the 1930s. In that decade, some exporters, as is noted above, were free to utilize their foreign-exchange proceeds directly. Gold exports, for another example, were made at a favorable NER.

A number of special regimes established in the early and mid-1950s also incorporated an element of export promotion. In 1953 the fishing industry was allowed directly to utilize the foreign exchange it generated. Drawbacks were given for products made exclusively from raw materials originating in Arica, Iquique, Pisaqua, Tattal, and Chanaral, which were under regional special regimes (see subsection 4.1.5.1). Special favorable NERs for gold and wine also were available (see section 3.2).

Starting in the late 1950s, however, more general attempts at export promotion were initiated. In 1958 Law 12861 established a special regime for specific exports including (i) exemptions from indirect taxes and customs duties on material inputs applied to operations directly concerned with exports; (ii) rebates of taxes if an exporter could demonstrate that they affected the cost of his exports; and (iii) automatic refunds of taxes, after exportation, at fixed percentages of f.o.b. values, ranging from 0.015 per cent for copper or brass plates or sheets to 26.8 per cent for bulk wine shipments (but from 3 to 6 per cent for most other products). In 1960 these tax exemptions were modified. In 1961 special pre- and post-shipment credits were added.[43] In 1963 a new regime designed to increase exports was established for foreign capital investments.[44] Also in 1963 new lines of preshipment credit were established for agricultural and nontraditional exports.[45]

Despite these greatly expanded provisions, export promotion was not notably successful in the early 1960s. Agricultural exports for 1960–64 remained at about the 1955-59 level. Industrial exports other than of copper declined from 1959 through 1963, although they rose in 1964.

The Frei government, therefore, created a new export-promotion regime. Its basis was established in 1966 by Law 16528 and Central Bank Circular 734. The provisions of Law 16528 included the following: (i) For a specific list of exports[46] refunds of up to 30 per cent of the c.i.f. or f.o.b. value were made on the basis of tax incidence. (ii) The list or the percentage rates could be increased at any time, but could be decreased only after three years.[47] (iii) Foreign exchange from such exports was converted into escudos at the most favorable legal rate from the point of view of the exporter as of the date of export or the date of the return of the export proceeds (at the choice of the exporter).

Central Bank Circular 734 established two types of export-promotion credits: (i) preshipment credits in domestic currency for 126 specific products for up to 80 per cent of the f.o.b. value for 180 days at 9 per cent interest, refinanced entirely by the Central Bank;[48] and (ii) postshipment credits in foreign exchange for a smaller group of products for up to 80 per cent of the f.o.b. value for from 180 days (lowered to 90 days in July 1967) to two and a half years at 9 per cent interest, refinanced entirely by the Central Bank. For those 52 mostly industrial products eligible for both pre- and postshipment credits, the latter cancelled the former.

In late 1966 Decree 1224 of the Ministry of Economics implemented the new regime. It created a list of about two hundred new drawback rates ranging from 0.282 per cent to 29.29 per cent.[49] Products with rates over 10.0 per cent included bulk wine, 29.29 and 27.787 per cent; calcium carbonate, ferromagnesium, and ferrosilic magnesium, 26.0 per cent; newsprint, 20 per cent; champagne and cider, 18.838 per cent; ferrosilicone, 18.0 per cent; bottled wine, 14.038 per cent; and lead minerals and lead concentrates, 11.127 per cent.

Subsequently, more items were added to the list until in mid-1969 it totaled 331 products. Jul [1969:114–117] distinguishes three categories of listed products: (i) Group A—those items on the list as of October 1964 which legally had to be retained at least at the same rates; (ii) Group B—products included explicitly by Law 16528 or by petition of some government agency "for reasons independent of the promotion of exports;"[50] and (iii) Group C—products included for export promotion after the completion of technical studies concerning their potential. In 1966, 1967, and 1968, the respective shares of total drawbacks accounted for by each of these three categories were as follows: A—10, 10, and 3 per cent; B—80, 65, and 66 per cent (with fish meal and fish flour alone accounting for 60, 34, and 27 per cent); and C—10, 25, and 30 per cent (with agricultural and sea products alone accounting for 5, 18, and 23 per cent). An increasing but small proportion of the drawbacks, thus, was devoted to products in which Chile was deemed to have potential comparative advantage.

In 1969 Decree 124 of the Ministry of Economics lowered the rates for 40 products and eliminated the rates entirely for 160, primarily in Group A. These reductions were allowed because the rate of increase in the exchange rate had exceeded the rate of increase in the relevant domestic price index. Selowsky [1971:9] reports that the major drawbacks in effect after this modification were for paper and fish flour (30 per cent); steel and iron (26 per cent); wood (24 per cent); wool (22 per cent); matted rye, fresh fruits, and oils (20 per cent); cardboard, semi-elaborated copper, and beans (16 per cent); onions and garlic (14 per cent); frozen fish products, cellulose, and ferromolybdenum (12 per cent); and molybdenum oxide (9 per cent). According to unpublished Central Bank data, the distribution of drawbacks across sectors for 1969–70 was 23.0 per cent for agriculture, 16.5 per cent for mining, 50.4 per cent for industry, and 9.6 per cent for others. Paper and related products, food products (including fish meal and oils), and nitrates accounted respectively for 24.2, 19.3, and 11.7 per cent of the total.

In mid-1969 preshipment credits accounted for about 0.6 per cent of total credits. They were distributed primarily to cement (33 per cent), agricultural products (22 per cent), sea products (18 per cent), vehicle parts (17 per cent),[51] and paper products (11 per cent). At that time, $104,273 in postshipment credits were outstanding (equal to 0.6 per cent of the value of promoted exports in 1969). They were distributed primarily to machinery parts (55 per cent), chemical products (29 per cent), wood products (9 per cent), and bronze products (8 per cent).

The Allende government from the start stated that it would use expanded drawbacks and credits to promote exports and to help provide a protective buffer between world markets and exporters. In 1971 a number of decrees of the Ministry of Economics and Circulars of the Central Bank generally increased the scope of the drawback system and of the pre- and postshipment credit programs. In that year drawbacks increased approximately 50 per cent in constant escudo terms.[52]

4.3 POLICIES FOR OTHER INTERNATIONAL ECONOMIC TRANSACTIONS

Basic characteristics of these policies include the following:

i. Tourism and other personal expenditures have been treated as nonessential luxuries and have been among the first to be restrained at times of foreign-exchange shortages. As a result, the pattern of restraints on these expenditures has coincided quite closely with the over-all restrictiveness of foreign-sector policies.

ii. A number of regimes for foreign investment have prevailed in recent decades. The regulations in these regimes often have been quite specific, and many agreements have been negotiated on a case-by-case basis. A basic objective of most of them is to limit short-term capital movements. This concern, perhaps somewhat paradoxically, has resulted in much greater constraints being placed on capital repatriation and related payments for new investments than for large-scale copper mining.

iii. There was a resurgence of capital inflows on government account after 1955 as part of stabilization and public works programs. As a result, foreign debt increased to one of the highest per capita levels in the world in the 1960s and early 1970s. Therefore, debt payments and debt renegotiations have greatly constrained the options of recent governments.

Three features of NER policies for nongoods transactions should be noted (for details, see section 5.1.1): (i) The applicable NERs generally have been higher than those for most goods trade. (ii) The applicable NERs generally have been increased earlier than those for most goods trade at times of foreign-exchange crises. (iii) The gap between the NERs for goods and for nongoods transactions has narrowed in the early part of all of the more liberal phases.

To obtain EERs for nongoods transactions, of course, other policies must be considered, for example, indirect tax policy. As the following brief review of tax policy suggests, tax rates became significantly high only in recent years.

In August 1954 a tax of 0.015 escudos per dollar was levied on nonmerchandise international transactions. At that time it was equivalent to a 9.4 per cent tax rate, but by the time it was abolished, in 1957, it was equivalent to a 1.9 per cent tax. In August 1956, a 1 per cent tax was established. It was increased to 5 per cent in January 1957, reduced to 1 per cent in July 1957, increased to 2 per cent in February 1958, and abolished in April 1959. In 1964 a 4.0 per cent tax was applied on all purchases of exchange in the brokers' market (except those for which the Central Bank had approved a transfer application). The tax was increased to 6.0 per cent in July 1966, to 10 per cent in January 1967, to 15.15 per cent in January 1970, and to 33.15 per cent in March 1971. In late 1969 the tax was extended to cover capital imported in the form of foreign exchange and re-exported within a year of entry (as well as any related interest and profits on such capital). The minimum waiting period for avoiding this tax was increased to 18 months in May 1970 and eliminated entirely in December of that year.

Most nontax policies affecting nongoods transactions have varied substantially among the different categories of such transactions.[53] In the rest of this section, policies for some of these major categories are reviewed.

4.3.1 Tourism and Other Invisibles and Imports for Personal Use.

In recent years quantitative limits on this category of foreign-exchange use have been modified quite frequently. In May 1964, for example, maximum foreign-exchange allocations for travel were established at $300 for Latin American trips and $1,000 for all others. During the foreign-exchange shortage of 1965 these maximums were reduced. In September 1966 they were increased.[54] In the last half of 1968 they were reduced below the 1965 levels. In May 1969 they were increased to the 1966 levels. Between June and September 1970 the Central Bank openly ignored the limits. In October 1970 the maximums were again lowered; at the same time, children under seven were allowed only 50 per cent of the maximum, and a minimum period of 30 days between purchases was established.

Under the Allende government the maximum travel allocations generally were reduced, and the restrictions were made more specific. In November 1970, for example, Central Bank Circular 1454 established maximums of $100 (but no more than $25 per day) for travel within 500 kilometers of the Chilean border, $300 (with a maximum of $30 a day) for travel to other parts of Latin America and the Caribbean, $480 (with a maximum of $30 a day) for travel to the United States and Canada, and $720 (with a maximum of $30 a day) for travel beyond the Western Hemisphere.[55] During the next year a series of Central Bank circulars lowered these limits by 25 to 40 per cent, established an annual total maximum of $540, and introduced more complicated administrative procedures for travelers. Also, the export of Chilean bank notes was limited to 20 per cent of the travel allocation for residents and was prohibited for nonresidents. In addition, all foreign tourists were required to declare all foreign currency that they brought into Chile and to exchange a minimum of $10 per day for adults and $5 per day for children ($8 and $4 per day, respectively, for stays of over a week).[56]

Quantitative restrictions on foreign exchange for other personal uses followed the same general pattern over time as did those on travel. The limits in effect early in the Allende regime are suggestive of the types of transactions so restricted: $100 a month (with an annual maximum of $600) for each beneficiary of family maintenance; $50 a month for books, $200 a year for periodicals; $50 a year for student registration fees; $50 a month for medicine not available in Chile; $1,200 a year for previously contracted insurance premiums; approval of the Superintendency of Insurance for newly contracted insurance premiums; and to obtain foreign exchange for medical treatment abroad, certification of the need for such treatment plus a 200 per cent deposit guarantee.

4.3.2 Foreign Investment Other Than in Large-Scale Copper Mining.

Ellsworth [1945:79] claims that a conscious campaign to reduce the rights of foreign investors was pursued vigorously in the 1930s. As supporting evidence, he points to the above-mentioned attempts to establish a state trading monopoly in petroleum and to obtain national ownership and control in the nitrate industry. The default on foreign-debt payments in 1931 (see below) and the existence of exchange control also may have discouraged foreign investment. The prospects for attracting substantial new net foreign investment before the late 1940s were dim in any case, however, because of the Great Depression and the Second World War.

In the early postwar period, as is described in section 3.2, more favorable NERs were allowed for capital inflows in the form of foreign exchange. In late 1950, moreover, transfer guarantees for foreign investment registered upon entry were introduced in a further attempt to encourage foreign direct investment. CORFO also was attempting to facilitate such investment by providing information and other services.

In late 1953 a government decree substantially modified the terms under which new foreign capital could be brought into Chile. Such capital was granted favorable treatment when invested in export industries that could compete on the international market without government assistance; in production for the domestic market of goods that had previously been imported; or in industries in which at least 80 per cent of the raw materials were Chilean in origin and were used in the production of goods for the domestic market at reduced cost to the consumer. The Foreign Investment Commission supervised each application on a case-by-case basis and decided whether or not a particular applicant met the necessary conditions and, if so, exactly what the nature of the terms would be. For approved enterprises the following general guarantees and exemptions were allowed: (i) repatriation of capital after five years in annual quotas not exceeding 20 per cent per year of the value of the investment; (ii) transfer abroad of earnings on the investment for a period of at least ten years and possibly up to twenty years; (iii) exemption from all customs duties and charges on imported machinery and equipment; (iv) a guarantee that no applicable taxes would be changed for at least ten years; (v) freedom for at least ten years from price-fixing regulations and from controls affecting industries in which the investments were made; (vi) the right to re-evaluation of capital for tax purposes in accordance with exchange-rate fluctuations; and (vii) the rights and exemptions in ii and vi above for the reinvestment of earnings on such capital.

Decree Law 258 of 1960 (supplemented by Decree Law 1272 of 1962) established more favorable terms for bringing some capital into Chile. This decree covered new capital brought into Chile in the form of foreign currency, credits, or plant and equipment for the purpose of introducing, developing, improving, or resuming activities related to agriculture, mining, fishing, or any other industry officially defined to be in the national interest. Such capital was exempted from all customs duties and fees on related imported machinery and equipment. It also could receive many specific presidential decree privileges and guarantees for ten years (and in special cases, twenty years), covering such matters as future taxation, depreciation allowances, withdrawal of capital, and remittances of profits.

In 1962 Decree Law 1272 established an alternative set of regulations under which capital brought into the country in the form of foreign exchange could be sold freely in the brokers' market after registration with the Central Bank. These regulations included a nontransferable guarantee of free withdrawal of principal through the brokers' market, but prior authorization by the Central Bank was required for remittance of profits or interest. The foreign investor also could enter into a capital participation agreement with a Chilean entity and have the option of the bank or the brokers' market for entry and subsequent exit of capital and related flows (but exit had to take place in the same market as that chosen for entry), subject to a minimum investment period of three years.

In 1966 the Central Bank modified Decree Law 1272: foreign exchange for repatriation of all earnings on imported capital would be guaranteed under this decree provided that (i) the investment was deemed to be of importance to the Chilean economy; (ii) it had a value of at least $100,000; (iii) the capital stayed in the country for at least three years and subsequent repatriation occurred at a maximum rate of 20 per cent per year; (iv) the exchange was sold in the bank market; and (v) the interest rate on credit to Chilean firms did not exceed the rate prevailing in the domestic market of the investor. The apparent motivation for these changes was the same as for a number of other policies of this phase: export promotion, minimization of transitory capital movements, and governmental control over the form of capacity expansion in order to attempt to assure the most socially productive uses.

Under the Allende government, official policy was to encourage foreign investment, especially in mixed enterprises in which the government had majority control. Such investment, however, was subject to two important provisos: that it did not replace domestic investment and that it helped in the fulfillment of the economic plan. Foreign concerns which already operated in the state area of activity or which were otherwise not consistent with the economic goals of the government were to be nationalized.[57]

4.3.3 Official Capital Flows and Foreign Debts.

Before the Great Depression Chile had considerable official foreign-debt obligations (columns 12 and 13 in Table 1.1). With the Great Depression, however, foreign sources quickly dried up. Payments on past debts soon were depleting foreign-exchange reserves. Therefore, in mid-1931 Chile suspended payments of the service charges on foreign debts. In 1936 such payments were resumed at lower interest rates.

Over the next quarter-century or so, official capital inflows were welcomed. Sources included bilateral flows from the United States and Western European countries and flows from international agencies such as the International Monetary Fund.[58] A large proportion of this capital was destined for CORFO-sponsored projects or for stabilization funds related to the 1956 and 1959 attempts at stabilization plus liberalization. Official foreign debt increased substantially during the 1956–61 period because of the conscious decision to finance continuing government deficits abroad in order to lessen short-run inflationary pressures. In the early 1960s the Alliance for Progress provided further official inflows—which also increased the foreign debt (line 1.2.6.5 in Table A.1).

At the start of the Frei administration, foreign-debt payments were of considerable concern. Estimated debt-related obligations in 1965 of $367 million—together with the estimated outflow of $114 million for profits and amortization—would have absorbed almost 70 per cent of the value of exports for that year. As a result the foreign economic regime in some respects was made more restrictive at the start of 1965, as is discussed above. Chile successfully renegotiated the payment of her foreign debt in that year. Immediately thereafter the government became at least verbally concerned about contracting any future foreign debt. In December 1966, for example, the government renounced the acceptance of any more program loans from abroad—although such loans apparently were being accepted again by mid-1967. Also in 1967 a new external source of funds was established with the signing of an agreement with the USSR for the equivalent of $57 million in credits at terms apparently favorable to Chile.

In part because of the debt rescheduling in 1965, the Allende government inherited a fairly large foreign debt—approximately $3 billion at the end of 1970. According to Minister of Finance Zorrilla [1970:1478,1489] (also see Cauas and Corbo [1972:22] and Gunder-Frank [1972:16–18]), the aims of policies regarding official capital flows and foreign debts were to honor past obligations;[59] reschedule payments on foreign loans; reduce future dependence on foreign sources by resorting to them as little as possible and only under centralized state procedures; diversify the sources utilized in the future; and cease to be constrained by IMF policies and procedures.

Through most of 1971, Chile met her scheduled debt obligations. However, in November President Allende announced that Chile would request a renegotiation of debt payments with a consolidation of payments, a three-year grace period, and a long schedule of repayment.[60] Debt payments due later in that year were not made on schedule.[61]

In January and February 1972 Chile conducted negotiations in New York with forty-four private United States banks to which Chile owed more than $600 million. The result was a deferred schedule for payments due between 1972 and 1974.

From February through April 1972 Chile conducted negotiations in Paris with the so-called Paris Club (the United States and ten other major creditor nations).[62] A secret accord in April provided that Chile pay as scheduled 30 per cent of all the debt and interest payments due between November 1971 and December 1972, with six years' grace subsequently to pay those deferred payments in full; the creditors promise to study "with good will" the refinancing of those debt payments due in 1973; and the IMF periodically review Chile's monetary, credit, and trade performance.

In addition to debt renegotiation questions, another policy of the Allende government in this area was to welcome official inflows both from traditional sources, e.g., the IMF, the United States, and from new sources, e.g., the Socialist nations (on the latter, see Chapter 8).

4.3.4 Miscellaneous Transactions.

Most of the policies discussed in this subsection did not have a strong general impact nor a long-lasting one. At least for certain subsectors, however, they were very important for a while. Their effects are discussed in Part III, below.

In 1959 Law 13305 established a tax immunity for capital repatriated from abroad to buy tax-exempt dollar bonds. It also granted banks the authority to make loans expressed in terms of foreign currency and to pay interest on foreign-currency time deposits. With the end of the Phase IV period, in December 1961, these provisions were terminated.

In 1962 Law 14949 authorized the government to pay its internally held dollar debts in escudos at the bank spot NER, which was about two-thirds of the brokers' rate which would otherwise have been used.

In 1963 Law 15192 reserved all gold operations to the Central Bank. Later that year the Central Bank announced that it would continue to buy gold coins and bars from individuals and firms, but that it would sell gold only to industrial and professional users associated with the bank and not to other individuals and firms. In 1970 the exclusive power of the Central Bank to deal in gold was extended to all nonjewelry imports.

In 1963, the Central Bank also began to limit the rate of interest allowable on import credits for which it would provide foreign exchange. This maximum was altered a number of times in the 1960s until it was limited to the lower of the prevalent interest rate in the country of export or 1.5 per cent above the New York prime rate in 1969.

At the end of 1970 Central Bank Circular 1464 prohibited paying remuneration in foreign currency to Chileans or to non-Chileans of more than two years' residence. It also prohibited paying more than half of such remuneration in foreign currency to non-Chileans of less than two years' residence and then only with Central Bank approval.

NOTES

1. These included specific taxes based on the 1928 law; ad valorem taxes of 3, 30, or 62 per cent of the landed value; consular charges of 3 per cent; disembarkation and embarkation charges or port charges of 1 per cent; special taxes on agricultural machinery and parts, cotton, tea, sugar, gasoline, and related imports; additional taxes; and added additional taxes.

2. For example, in February 1951, after the December 1950 reforms, CONDECOR loosened the system further by publishing a reduced list of prohibited imports. Other changes in 1951, however, increased the restrictions in a piecemeal fashion: the list of luxuries which could be imported against gold sales was revised four times, with automobiles put on the prohibited list in the last revision; a new list of imports against the proceeds of wine exports was published; and importation of certain commodities previously permitted from all countries was restricted to countries with which Chile had payments or compensation agreements. In 1952, further restrictions were introduced: on April 24, imports previously quantitatively uncontrolled at the bank spot rate or at fixed rates were suspended or transferred to quantitatively controlled fixed rates (which effectively was a reversal to the system in effect before the reforms of December 15, 1950); on June 4, the importation of luxury items was suspended; and on June 26, an expanded list of prohibited imports was published with exceptions to be made by CONDECOR if domestic supplies were insufficient or if domestic costs were more than 50 per cent above foreign costs. For details, see IMF [1950–56b] and Banco Central [1950–56b].

3. Licenses continued not to be required for permitted imports, but registration with the Foreign Exchange Commission at the time of shipment from abroad was necessary in order to receive foreign-exchange cover.

4. Some of these results would occur with almost any rationing system. Others might have been ameliorated with modifications in the system as it existed, e.g., the allowable percentage increase could be a function of past or planned growth in order not to penalize the faster-growing activities so much.

5. Exceptions to this growing liberalization were primarily of a political nature. All nonhumanitarian direct and indirect trade with Cuba was suspended between April 27, 1966, and November 19, 1970. All direct and indirect nonhumanitarian trade with Rhodesia was prohibited as of February 9, 1967. Direct and indirect nonhumanitarian trade with the Union of South Africa was banned as of June 2, 1968, with a modification as of March 5, 1968, to ban invisible transactions as well, but copper exports were allowed!

6. For example, at the end of 1970 the importation for private use of automobiles valued at over $2,500 (later reduced to $2,200) c.i.f. was prohibited.

7. Some other changes in the 1965–70 regime were motivated in large part by the need to absorb liquidity: in June 1966, the establishment of a minimum downpayment of 20 per cent of the c.i.f. value for imports on a deferred payment basis (terminated in September 1967); and establishment, in June 1967, of special terms with a rebate at a 5.0 per cent annual rate for exchange contracts for import payment cover negotiated at the time of import registration (terminated in November 1970). The former requirement also probably resulted in real costs to the importers.

8. After several months banks were limited to financing a maximum of 100 per cent of deposits for category A, 60 per cent for category B, and 30 per cent for category C. Financing of the other categories was not permitted. These percentages were reduced in 1957.

9. Exceptions were made for some items on consignment, deposits made in dollars or in 120-day no-interest Treasury dollar bonds, and some items in categories A, B, and C.

10. A 5,000 per cent prior deposit for 90 days at a real interest rate of 10 per cent cost the importer 125 per cent of the value of the import.

11. Exempt were the government, municipalities, exporters subject to the "free port" and earthquake special regimes, large-scale mining, and imports from LAFTA countries.

12. The declining importance of prior deposits is indicated, for example, by the steady fall in the ratios of the value of deposits to registered imports from 14.3 per cent in 1964 to 2.9 per cent in 1968 (Joó [1969:17]). Ffrench-Davis [1971:101] reports that the value of imports requiring prior deposits decreased approximately 40 per cent in 1967 and another 40 per cent in 1968 to a level of only about 21 per cent of all imports at the start of 1969.

13. This subsection is heavily based on the work of Jeanneret [1971:349–362]. Special regimes related primarily to exports are discussed in section 4.2.

14. A few special regimes do not fall into these categories. For example in 1960 Law 14117 established a special regime for reconstruction after the May 1960 earthquake by permitting enterprises in the affected area to import machinery and equipment with a single customs duty of 15.0 per cent of the c.i.f. value until 1965.

15. In the first ten months of 1970, for example, 34 per cent of the value of imports under special regimes went to the department of Arica, 17 per cent to the provinces of Chiloé, Aysen, and Magallenes, 16 per cent to the provinces of Tarapacá and Antofagasta, and (under a different special regime) 7 per cent to the departments of Iquique, Pisagua,

Taltal, and Chanaral and the province of Antofagasta. A similar ordering occurred in other years, although the position of the last two groups was at times reversed.

16. Arica borders on Peru, was won in the War of the Pacific, has about 0.6 per cent of Chile's population, and is 1,500 kilometers (900 miles) across the Atacama desert from Santiago.

17. Some prohibited import items, such as most vehicles, could be imported for use in the special areas alone, but could not be shipped to the rest of the country.

18. Recently there have been some exceptions to this statement. For example, in 1970 Law 17382 established a tax of 8.0 per cent on the customs value of goods imported through Chiloé. After the 1971 devaluation, moreover, the southern area received favorable exchange-rate treatment for imports already registered and for certain newly registered imports. Also in 1971 a special point system was established for automobile imports into this area, with positive weights given to the age of any currently owned vehicles, the number of years' residence in the zone, family income, and the number of quarters in which applications had been filed (all subject to the limit of $2,200 c.i.f. in value and the existence of appropriate repair and service facilities for the vehicle being imported).

19. Fontaine [1964] concludes that the net economic benefits from the sugar industry set up under this shelter were negative.

20. For example, the original ratio of the rate for A account transactions to that for B account transactions in the agreement with France was 0.463.

21. Import premiums commanded by any licensing under such agreements generally were, of course, less than those which "free-foreign-exchange" licenses would command.

22. To illustrate, at the end of 1953 accounting dollars established under the terms of payments agreements with the Federal Republic of Germany and Brazil, implied respective rates of 38 and 28 per cent above the dominant bank spot rate, and the free-sterling rate implied a cross exchange rate 35.3 per cent above the spot rate, which had increased to 158 per cent by October 1954.

23. Ellsworth [1945:95–96] reports that because of this funding, CORFO's outstanding loans at the end of 1942 already were approximately double the combined total of all the other development agencies, even though the other organizations had been in existence much longer and had substantial resources at their disposal derived from mandatory Central Bank loans.

24. Difficult decisions remain to be made for petrochemical production, automobiles and trucks, and chemicals and pharmaceuticals, but progress has been much more rapid than had been anticipated in many quarters. See, for example, Novitski [1972].

25. However, large-scale copper mining continued to enjoy the third and fourth components of the exchange-rate treatment outlined above. Moreover, this subsector was exempted from prior deposits on imports, additional taxes, and added taxes.

26. In subsection 7.1.2.3, I evaluate both the short- and the long-run effects of the *Nuevo Trato*.

27. However, the Chilean producer price was below the United States producer price for some time after July 1970.

28. However, the additional taxes of 5 and 8 per cent which had been established in 1961 were eliminated in 1966.

29. Of the investments in Anaconda properties, $58.8 million were from the United States Export-Import Bank, $5.75 million were from the Chilean government, and the rest from Anaconda. For the Kennecott properties $110 million were from the United States Export-Import Bank and guaranteed by the Chilean government, $27.5 million were from the Chilean government, and $92.7 million were on loan from Kennecott and

insured by AID (but of that $80 million in fact were from the Chilean government as the price of 51 per cent control). For the Cerro Corporation properties, $56.4 million were from the Export-Import Bank with a Chilean government guarantee on $35.4 million and $20.1 million were from a Japanese consortium with a Chilean government guarantee on $10.1 million.

30. Hector Humeres, the politically independent Comptroller General, subsequently estimated the book value to be $629 million.

31. The tribunal was composed of a representative of the Chilean Supreme Court, a representative of the court of appeals, and three officials named to their posts by Allende.

32. Welles [1971] reports that these debts amounted to $550 million of principal (including $180 million to the Export-Import Bank, $92 million to Kennecott, $100 million to five major New York financial institutions—Chase Manhattan, Manufacturers Hanover Trust, Chemical Trust, First National City, and Morgan Guaranty Trust—$50 million to the Banca Commerciale Italiana, $18 million to the Cerro Corporation, $15 million to the Japanese Mitsui group, $17 million to the Japanese Sumimoto group, plus some smaller obligations), plus $220 million in interest.

33. Adding to the confusion was a statement by Chilean Foreign Minister Clodomire Almeyda in Washington on October 7 (after Allende's announcement of the excess-profit estimate, but before the announcement of the decision of the Comptroller General) that suggested that Kennecott and Anaconda would be assessed 49 per cent of their excess profits since that was their share in the ownership of the mines prior to the 1971 nationalization (see Welles [1971]). De Onis [1971a, 1971e] claims that in May Allende committed himself to signing a negotiated settlement for $56 million for the purchase of the Cerro properties. However, he reversed his decision and never signed the agreement partly because militants in the government coalition were dissatisfied with terms of the agreement and partly because the U.S. Export-Import Bank refused to grant Chile a credit of $21 million to purchase Boeing airplanes.

34. After surveys by French and Soviet mining experts, $8.1 million were deducted from the original sum of $92.7 million because that much was judged not to have been usefully invested.

35. The post-Allende government has indicated that it might reconsider the question of compensation for the former owners, but not the possibility of returning control to them.

36. The period for shipment usually was 60 days. The period for repatriation varied from 30 to 90 days, depending somewhat upon the restrictiveness of the over-all regime. The period for liquidation generally was 10 days. Longer periods were allowed for certain promoted exports, e.g., in 1970 the shipment limit was 120 days for wood, 180 days for industrial goods and minerals, and 360 days for iron ores, and the repatriation limit ranged from 120 to 480 days for exports on consignment and for specified processed exports. Penalties were imposed for delayed returns. Such penalties were increased during the more restrictive phases. Not all of these time limits were enforced all the time, however.

37. In some cases, such as for gold and wine exports, even the NERs fell.

38. For example, in February 1971 Decree 33 of the Ministry of Economics prohibited the export of industrial products through June of that year. In January 1972, Decree 27 of the same ministry prohibited the export of certain iron products through June of that year.

39. Because of the existence of such quotas, export prices of the constrained commodities have at times exceeded domestic prices, but Chileans have not been able to

arbitrage. In such cases the ratio of foreign to domestic prices overstates the EER because it includes the premium received by the quota recipients.

40. The secular decline in the Chilean share of world nitrate production has been huge: from 66 per cent in 1901–02 to 1.5 per cent in 1960.

41. For example, in 1956 Law 12018 allowed CONVENSA to include amortization, interest, and transportation in its production costs, guaranteed a better NER, and established an investment program for the industry.

42. For example, this subsector received the special credits from the United States that were negotiated in the Washington Treaty of 1951 (see subsection 4.2.1).

43. Credits were made available to favored exporters either 90 days before shipment for up to 100.0 per cent of the returns at 4.0 per cent or with the presentation of shipping documents for 180 days for up to 100.0 per cent of the returns at 3.0 per cent. In November 1961, such credits were extended only to exporters who did not have time deposits in the banking system.

44. This regime included guarantees on access to various exchange rates and on the speed of capital withdrawal. Incoming capital was sold in the brokers' market and servicing and withdrawal was in the bank market. Remittance of profits or interest of up to 7.0 per cent per year of the invested capital was permitted. Withdrawal was allowed to start two years after entry in annual amounts up to 12.5 per cent of the invested capital, subject to the restriction that the total of servicing and withdrawal did not exceed 50 per cent of the increase in repatriated export proceeds.

45. For eligible exports, credit was available in domestic currency equal to 80 per cent of the value for a maximum of 90 days (increased, a year later, to 180 days for industrial products). This credit was refinanced in its entirety by the Central Bank.

46. This list did not include exports from large-scale mining, those which entered the country under special exemptions, semimanufactured copper products, nitrates (until 1968), or services (except for shipping which was added later).

47. However, after January 1967, downward adjustments in the rates were allowed as long as they were not greater than the amount by which the rate of increase in the exchange rate exceeded the rate of increase in the wholesale price index. At the end of 1968 the maximum downward adjustments were limited to the amount by which the rate of increase in the exchange rate exceeded the rate of increase in the consumer price index, except that fish meal and fish oil were guaranteed no decrease for three years.

48. The interest rate later was increased to 12 per cent, but still was below the rate of change of prices; so this credit carried a negative real interest rate. The period for this credit was increased to 360 days in December 1967. The periods in use in 1969 were 90 days for agricultural products, 180 days for most industrial products, and 360 days for cement sent to Argentina and Brazil.

49. A large portion of these new rates established an inverse relation between the drawback rate and the international copper price for small- and medium-scale copper mining. This decree also maintained the previously existing drawbacks at least at the same levels.

50. Among these products were fish meal and oil, paper for periodicals, cellulose, and cardboard, included as a result of solicitations by CORFO prompted by low international prices; steel, as a result of solicitation by the Minister of Economics because of low domestic prices for CAP; shipping, because of losses suffered by the merchant marine; and nitrates, because in 1968, a transfer was arranged to SOQUIM of $5 million in drawbacks, to take place over a period of three years.

51. In early 1970, however, all products of the automobile industry were excluded from these credits.

52. The impact of the export-promotion attempts is examined further in chapters 5, 7, and 11, below.

53. Some other general policies also have applied, but have been relatively unimportant for the purposes of this study. For example, since 1963 private persons buying exchange in the brokers' market have been required to show proof of prior income tax payments.

54. At about the same time the tax of 30 escudos a trip on travel by Chilean residents to other Latin American countries was abolished and the tax on travel to all other locations was increased from 60 to 310 escudos a trip.

55. The relative shift in these maximums favored travel to Latin America and discriminated against travel to the United States and Canada. This shift was consistent with the over-all aims of the Allende government regarding changes in the geographical pattern of international economic and political interactions.

56. These last measures were in part directed at limiting black-market activity in escudos.

57. The value of United States investment alone (including large-scale mining) at the time of the election of Allende was over a billion dollars. The largest nonmining operations included Anglo-Lautaro Nitrate, Boise Cascade, International Telephone and Telegraph, Coca-Cola, Standard Oil of New Jersey, General Motors, Crown Zellerbach International, General Cable, and RCA International, all of which had 1968 Chilean sales of about $10 million at the least, although some were owned partially by Chilean entities. See Szulc [1970] for a complete listing of such enterprises and their sales value.

58. Imports financed by those flows were at times exempted from some import regulations such as the additional taxes and prior deposits.

59. In the case of large-scale copper mining the nature of such official obligations was redefined, however, as is indicated above in subsection 4.2.1.

60. In his announcement Allende noted that in the previous six months the foreign debt actually had been reduced; the foreign debt inherited from the previous government plus the $728 million in obligations taken over from the foreign copper companies made Chile second only to Israel in terms of per capita national debt; and debt payment obligations for 1971–1973 were approximately 40 per cent of total Chilean exports. Furthermore, he claimed that the fulfillment of Chile's scheduled debt payment commitment to date had been made much more difficult by its failure to receive more than $100 million in dividends and taxes from the foreign copper companies prior to nationalization; the closing of approximately $190 million in credit lines by United States banks in part because of the Edward Bank's failure to fulfill its contractual obligations; the drop in international copper prices; and the increase in imports due to the boom in the Chilean economy and to income redistribution. See CORFO [1971a, November 23: 1–2].

61. These included $5.8 million to Kennecott (see subsection 4.2.1, above), $6 million to International Telephone and Telegraph Company, $7.8 million to United States banks, and $4.5 million to the United States Export-Import Bank. For more details, see de Onis [1972b], Vúskovic [1972:544], and Wilcke [1972].

62. The United States held over half of the debt. No other individual country nor all international organizations considered together held as much as a tenth.

Chapter 5

Effective Exchange Rates, Effective Protection Rates, and Domestic Resource Costs

In this chapter, one of the major purposes of this study is carried out: determining the impact of the NER and supporting policies, described in the two previous chapters, on effective rates of protection and exchange and related constructs. The focus of section 5.1 is on the time patterns of import premiums, PLD-EERs, and PLD-EER(PI)s in the years since World War II. In section 5.2, ITR, EPR, and DRC estimates are examined for selected years in the 1960s.

SUMMARY AND CONCLUSIONS

i. Over-all PLD-EERs have been moving secularly downward. PLD-EERs for imported goods, moreover, continued to decline even in the 1965–70 sliding-peg period. Ceteris paribus, this trend implies increasing balance-of-payments pressures.

ii. Import premiums have been quite high and have tended to move inversely to PLD-EERs. During the sliding-peg experience of 1965–70, however, the large expansion in the availability of foreign exchange (primarily from the copper boom generated by the Vietnam War) made it possible to reduce both import premiums and PLD-EERs.

iii. Barriers for imports generally have been quite high and variable.

iv. The dispersion in such barriers has been very substantial among production sectors and subsectors and among end uses. Moreover, policy changes have not been highly correlated in their effect on these categories. Nevertheless, the regimes have generally tended to favor manufacturing over agriculture and agriculture over mining—the traditional "easy" import-substituting industries, which had received high protection since the nineteenth century—over industries producing intermediate goods (at least until the late 1960s); import substitution over export promotion; and goods imports over nongoods international transactions.

v. Such discrepancies in the treatment of sectors of the economy generally declined at the start of liberalization attempts, although not the preference for manufacturing over agriculture. The discrepancies often increased as these efforts faltered. They were reduced most substantially and maintained at a low level for the longest period of time during 1967–70, the last four years of the Frei administration.

vi. In times of foreign-exchange crisis, restrictions have been increased most severely on nongoods transactions and on investment-goods imports. These restrictions have resulted in a clear trade-off between short-run balance-of-payments needs and long-run growth objectives.

vii. Since exports respond to price incentives (see section 7.2), those policies utilized in part because of the export pessimism derived from the Great Depression experience have reinforced that pessimism by strongly discouraging export expansion and diversification.

5.1 TIME PATHS OF IMPORT PREMIUMS, PRICE-LEVEL-DEFLATED EFFECTIVE EXCHANGE RATES, AND PREMIUM-INCLUSIVE PRICE-LEVEL-DEFLATED EFFECTIVE EXCHANGE RATES

Aggregate patterns are described in section 5.1.1; disaggregate patterns, in section 5.1.2.

5.1.1 Time Patterns in Aggregate Import Premiums and Price-Level-Deflated Effective Exchange Rates.

A summary of the aggregate impact of the policies on import premiums and PLD-EERs described in the two previous chapters is shown in Table 5.1; the PLD-EERs are shown for both goods imports and nongoods transactions. The first important characteristic to be noted in the data shown, as well as in the summary statistics shown in Table A.1 and elsewhere, is the secular decline in the PLD-EERs since World War II. These movements have not been monotonic. The PLD-EER for imported goods has increased in seven of the twenty-

TABLE 5.1

Chilean Price-Level-Deflated Effective Exchange Rates for Imported Goods and for Nongoods Transactions and Import Premium Rates, 1946–70

Phase and Year	PLD-EERs: Imported Goods (1)	PLD-EERs: Nongoods Transactions (2)	Ratio: Col. 2 to Col. 1 (3)	Import Premium Rate (4)
II				
1946	5.64	5.30	0.94	76%
1947	4.69	5.68	1.41	79
1948	4.49	6.14	1.37	61
1949	4.11	6.36	1.55	93
1950	4.59	6.51	1.42	68
1951	4.24	5.12	1.21	67
1952	4.01	6.04	1.51	90
1953	3.64	6.74	1.85	112
1954	2.85	6.83	2.40	166
1955	2.90	7.35	2.53	204
III				
1956	3.62	4.61	1.27	132
1957	4.89	4.70	0.96	65
1958	4.37	5.69	1.30	64
IV				
1959	4.61	3.90	0.85	51
1960	4.26	3.53	0.83	60
1961	4.02	3.27	0.81	62
II				
1962	4.00	4.82	1.21	60
1963	4.33	5.68	1.31	46
1964	3.65	4.26	1.17	69
III				
1965	3.85	3.89	1.01	57
1966	3.66	3.80	1.04	56
1967	3.59	3.79	1.06	52
1968	3.70	3.98	1.08	43
1969	3.48	3.83	1.10	46
1970	3.35	3.98	1.19	47
Mean (1946–70)	4.02	5.03	1.25	77

SOURCE: The PLD-EER for imported goods is obtained by deflating the EERs in column 14 of Table A.7 by the Chilean GDP deflator. The PLD-EER for nongoods transactions is the PLD-NER for the black or free market before 1950 and the PLD-NER for the brokers' market thereafter (columns 6 and 12 in Table 3.2) adjusted for the taxes described at the start of section 4.3. The import premium rate is defined in the notes to Table A.1. The PLD-EERs are in 1965 escudos per dollar.

five years shown; the PLD-EER for nongoods transactions, twice as often. Nevertheless, the basic underlying trend is clear: the mean PLD-EER for imported goods over phases and subphases, for example, fell from 8.48 escudos per dollar for 1940–46 to 3.60 for 1965–70, increasing only between 1952 and 1955 and between 1956 and 1958 (line 1.1.7 in Table A.1). The major factor underlying this fall was the drop in PLD-NERs discussed in section 3.2. Ceteris paribus, such a decline would seem to have increased the need for quantitative restrictions to prevent large balance-of-payments deficits.

Second, the import premium rate tended to increase until the end of the quarter-century of Phase II restrictions, in 1955, and tended to decrease secularly thereafter (line 1.1.6 in Table A.1). The latter tendency was possible despite the simultaneous secular decline in the PLD-EERs because of the rapidly expanding command of Chile over foreign exchange from exports and from nonmonetary capital inflows (see Table 8.1).

Third, it should be noted that phase-coincident patterns were superimposed on these secular trends. The PLD-EER for goods increased at the start of each liberalization attempt (1956, 1959, and 1965) because of associated large devaluations. At the same time and for the same reason, the import premium rate declined, its fall reinforced by expanded imports financed from stabilization funds. The PLD-EER for nongoods transactions dropped at the start of each liberalization effort as the government attempted to reduce disparities among various EERs. The ratio of the PLD-EER for nongoods transactions to that for goods transactions was greater in the Phase II periods, as disparities in charges among uses increased with exchange control.

Fourth, in terms of short-run fluctuations, the PLD-EER for imported goods and the import premium rate tended to move *inversely* (the simple correlation coefficient between the two is −0.46), reflecting price responsiveness in import demand or export supply, or both. This point is illustrated in Figure 5.1 by simplified supply-and-demand curves in a foreign-exchange framework. At a price for a unit of foreign exchange of P_0, the available quantity is Q_0, and the import premium rate is $(P_3 - P_0)/P_0$. At a higher price for foreign exchange, P_1, the quantity supplied increases to Q_1, and the import premium rate falls back to $(P_2 - P_1)/P_1$. (In the diagram, the same PLD-EER is assumed to hold for both exports and imports. In reality, a substantial difference has existed, as is discussed below in this chapter.)

Fifth, the PLD-EER for nongoods transactions generally was higher than that for goods. The discrepancy has not been as great, however, as consideration of PLD-NERs alone might suggest (Table 3.2) because other policies have affected exchange costs for goods much more than for nongoods. Nevertheless, policies usually have discriminated against invisible and service imports as opposed to goods imports. Capital inflows, however, have often been

FIGURE 5.1

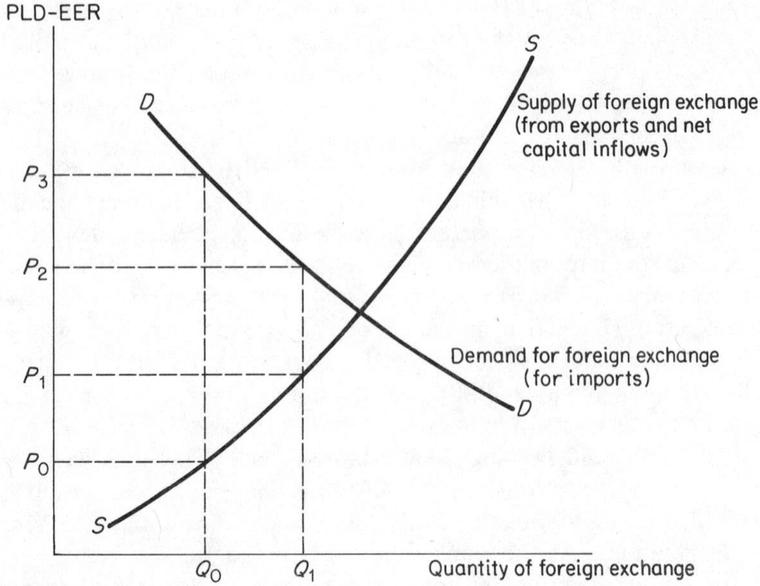

allowed at more favorable PLD-EERs than goods (but vice versa for capital outflows).

The major exception to this situation occurred in the Phase IV years of 1959–61.[1] The unified NER for those years, combined with disparities in the effects of supporting policies, resulted in lower PLD-EERs for nongoods than for goods transactions. As a result, discrepancies between the PLD-EERs for goods and for nongoods were larger than in some periods with a multiple exchange-rate system, e.g., 1965–69.

Sixth, the import premium rate has been quite high, averaging 77 per cent for 1946–70. Import taxes and related policies have absorbed some of the differences between international and domestic prices, but quite substantial returns have been left for importers and for protected industries.

Finally, with regard to the sliding-peg NER policy of 1965–70, it should be noted that despite the government's announced intention to the contrary, the PLD-EER for imported goods declined by 13 per cent during the period. The mean PLD-EER for import goods during the same phase was lower than in all but one (1952–55) of the phases and subphases after 1940 (see line 1.1.7 in Table A.1). The import premium rate declined during the phase and was at the lowest mean level of all post-1945 phases and subphases (see line 1.1.6 in Table A.1) in spite of the low and declining PLD-EER for imported goods. This phenomenon reflected the copper boom generated by the Vietnam War and large net capital inflows that provided foreign exchange to

FIGURE 5.2

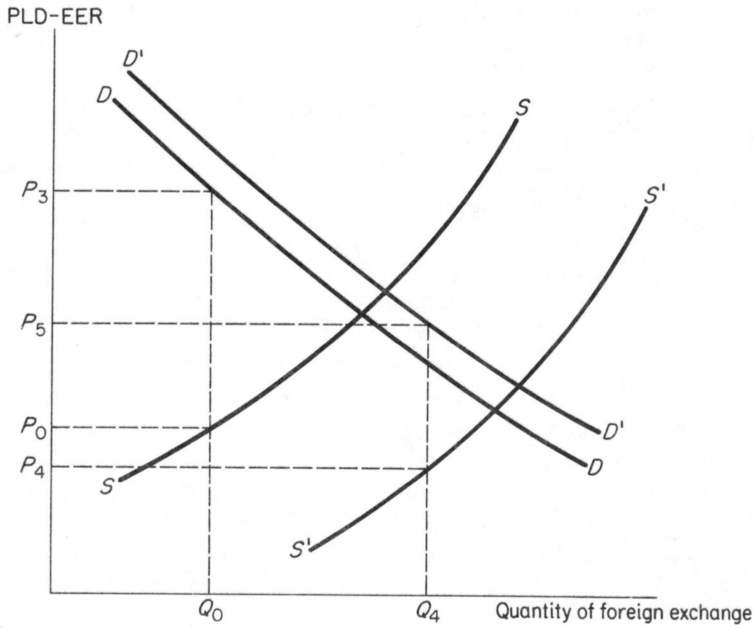

finance substantially increased imports (see Table 8.1). The decline is roughly illustrated in Figure 5.2, which is drawn under the same simple assumptions utilized in Figure 5.1. Before this phase the price of foreign exchange was P_0, the quantity was Q_0, and the premium rate was $(P_3 - P_0)/P_0$. In 1965–70, the demand for foreign exchange may have shifted somewhat to the right to D'. The supply of foreign exchange, expanded as described above, is depicted by S'. As a result the following combination is observed: a reduced price at P_4, an increased quantity at Q_4, and a lowered import premium rate of $(P_5 - P_4)/P_4$.

During 1965–69, the PLD-EERs for goods and nongoods were more nearly identical than in any earlier phase or subphase following the Second World War, except 1946 and 1957. They were also closer than in the years of the unified NER, 1959–61 (Phase IV). The disparity increased year by year during the 1965–70 phase, however, in part because of attempts to limit capital flight during the long political campaign before the 1970 election.

5.1.2 Time Patterns in Disaggregate Premium-Inclusive Price-Level-Deflated Effective Exchange Rates.

Because of the complexities, specificity, and frequent alterations in the foreign-sector regime in recent decades, which was described in the two preceding chapters, determination of disaggregate PLD-EERs and import premiums separately would require resources far beyond those available for this study. Instead, therefore, concentration is on PLD-EER(PI)s for disaggregate analysis. Such measures include the total effect of the international regime on internal prices, that is, on the EERs plus any premium importers receive.[2] Equivalently, these measures represent the total effects of foreign-sector policies on prices paid not by the original importer, but by the second buyer, i.e., the person or firm the original importer sells to.[3]

PLD-EER(PI)s on the individual product level for each of 220 items considered in this study could be presented and examined. Such detail, however, would be overwhelming. Important broad patterns would be difficult to discern. Instead, one would run the risk of being sidetracked by unimportant idiosyncrasies. The focus in this subsection, therefore, is on the intermediate level of aggregation of PLD-EER(PI)s presented in Table A.8: 18 subsectors, three sectors, (agriculture, mining, and manufacturing), and nine demand components. Three other tables contain statistics constructed from the series in Table A.8 to aid in the analysis. Table 5.2 includes ratios of various disaggregate PLD-EER(PI)s; the correlation coefficients among them are shown in Table A.9. Table A.10 contains percentage changes in the PLD-EER(PI)s relative to the national accounts PLD-NER. Six important broad characteristics in the post-World War II patterns of the disaggregate rates may be seen in the data contained in the four tables:

i. Variations in the PLD-EER(PI)s among subsectors, sectors, and demand components have been substantial. The ratio of the highest to the lowest PLD-EER(PI) in each subsector ranged from 2.82 to 12.43, with an average of 5.08 (Table 5.2, column 1). The subsectors with mean PLD-EER(PI)s above the over-all average (in order) are footwear, coal mining, textiles, leather and leather products, nonmetallic mineral products, other manufactures, beverages, food products, and basic metals. Policies since the Second World War, thus, have tended to maintain high barriers for those subsectors which first received protection as "infants" in the nineteenth century!

On the sectoral level of aggregation, barriers have been highest for manufacturing and lowest for mining, with agriculture in between. The ratios of the PLD-EER(PI)s for agriculture to those for manufacturing averaged 0.65 (column 2). The mean PLD-EER(PI) for mining was only half of that for manufacturing (column 3). The impact on sectoral terms of trade, thus, has been considerable. These distortions in incentives probably explain in considerable part the relative stagnation in agriculture and the limited expansion of minerals exports (on responses to price incentives, see Part III, below).

Among demand classifications, barriers have been highest for consumer goods and about the same on the average for both investment and intermediate goods. The mean PLD-EER(PI) for investment goods was 0.64 of that for consumer goods, while that for intermediate goods was 0.62 (columns 4 and 5). These relative values reflect the maintenance of high effective protection to encourage import substitution for consumption products.

The mean PLD-EER(PI) for imports, finally, was 1.53 times that for exports (column 6). This difference reflects the basically inward-looking, import-substituting nature of the post-World War II regimes. The lack of more rapid growth in exports, once again, originates substantially in this discriminatory treatment against them (section 7.2).

ii. If there has been any general secular tendency, it has been a narrowing of differentials among subsectoral PLD-EER(PI)s as well as for agriculture relative to manufacturing, intermediate relative to consumer goods, and imports relative to exports (columns 1, 2, 5, and 6). However, such trends are not very pronounced. That the last phase in the 1946–70 period was more liberal than the first, moreover, may cause phase-coincident changes to be misinterpreted as secular trends.

iii. Shifts to more liberal phases were generally characterized by reductions in differentials. In the first year of each of the three cases of shift, the PLD-EER(PI) for imports declined relative to that for exports (column 6). The range among the subsectors declined (column 1) in the first year in two cases, and so did the relative discrepancy between mining and manufacturing (column 3), with an especially large drop in 1956, the first full year of the *Nuevo Trato* (see subsection 4.2.1 above).

On the other hand, the discrepancies of agriculture relative to manufacturing on two occasions increased in the first year of liberalization attempts (column 2), and in the third case remained unchanged. This apparent anomoly reflects the fact that all three liberalization attempts were part of stabilization programs. In each case considerable effort was expended in trying to moderate agricultural price increases since prices in this sector had large weights in the general price indices. These indices were taken as the most important indicator of the short-run success or failure of the anti-inflationary effort and thus strongly affected short-run inflationary expectations.

The ratio of the PLD-EER(PI) for intermediate goods relative to consumer goods moved toward unity in the first year of only one liberalization attempt (column 5 in Table 5.2). This observation suggests that generally, at least the consumer-good, import-substitution activities were not squeezed by a sharp drop in EPRs at the start of liberalization attempts.

iv. During the more liberal phases, the patterns were somewhat mixed. During the 1956–58 phase, discrepancies tended to decline among subsectors, among demand components, and between mining and manufacturing (columns 1, 3, 4, and 5). Those between imports and exports and, to a lower degree, between agriculture and manufacturing, however, increased substantially as the liberalization attempt faltered (columns 2 and 6).

TABLE 5.2

Chilean Ratios of Disaggregate Price-Level-Deflated Effective Exchange Rates, Premiums Included, 1946–70

Phase and Year	High Subsector to Low Subsector[a] (1)	Agriculture and Forestry to Manufacturing (2)	Mining to Manufacturing (3)	Investment Goods to Consumer Goods (4)	Intermediate Goods to Consumer Goods (5)	Imports to Exports (6)
II						
1946	4.01	0.52	0.47	0.84	0.59	1.85
1947	4.21	0.51	0.52	0.67	0.52	1.72
1948	3.93	0.53	0.55	0.67	0.54	1.73
1949	7.36	0.56	0.48	0.63	0.56	1.79
1950	7.22	0.63	0.54	0.63	0.52	1.68
1951	5.27	0.63	0.54	0.61	0.49	1.54
1952	5.06	0.58	0.51	0.60	0.54	1.44
1953	5.86	0.67	0.54	0.62	0.55	1.37
1954	4.86	0.72	0.50	0.56	0.53	1.52
1955	12.43	0.67	0.39	0.50	0.64	1.35
III						
1956	8.06	0.64	0.47	0.52	0.67	1.34
1957	11.33	0.64	0.50	0.64	0.67	1.74
1958	3.97	0.58	0.56	0.65	0.70	1.90

IV						
1959	4.06	0.58	0.51	0.70	0.70	1.71
1960	3.51	0.65	0.53	0.62	0.69	1.61
1961	3.55	0.68	0.51	0.63	0.65	1.67
II						
1962	3.04	0.71	0.49	0.60	0.63	1.75
1963	3.67	0.71	0.52	0.65	0.65	1.48
1964	4.02	0.72	0.49	0.69	0.65	1.65
III						
1965	3.51	0.65	0.55	0.66	0.64	1.47
1966	2.82	0.68	0.55	0.71	0.65	1.18
1967	3.22	0.74	0.52	0.67	0.66	1.30
1968	3.04	0.70	0.48	0.67	0.68	1.25
1969	3.48	0.78	0.45	0.66	0.71	1.09
1970	5.41	0.74	0.40	0.65	0.70	1.09
Mean (1946–70)	5.08	0.65	0.50	0.64	0.62	1.53

SOURCE: Calculated from data in Table A.8.

a. Based on high and low PLD-EER(PI)s in first nineteen columns of Table A.8. The high subsector is nonmetallic mineral products for 1946–48, coal mining for 1953 and 1955–57, other manufactures for 1970, and footwear for all other years. The low sector is nitrate mining for 1946–48, 1957, and 1961, petroleum and coal products for 1966, and fishing for all other years.

During the 1959–61 phase most discrepancies tended to decline or remain about the same, with the possible exception of those for demand components by use (columns 4 and 5).

In the first four years of the 1965–70 phase almost all relative differences tended to be reduced. Although some increased thereafter, e.g., among subsectors or between mining and manufacturing, important further reductions occurred for agriculture versus manufacturing, intermediate goods versus consumer products, and exports versus imports (columns 2, 5, and 6). In all three cases the relative discrepancy for 1969 was smaller than for any preceding year included in Table 5.2. Liberalization, therefore, increased near the end of the Frei regime to a level which almost merits the characterization of the period as Phase IV.

v. The subsectoral PLD-EER(PI)s were not particularly well correlated. Among the 19 production subsectors, correlation coefficients are positive and significantly nonzero at the 5 per cent level for only 96 of the 171 pairs (Table A.9). In only 55 of these pairs, moreover, was the coefficient of determination 0.50 or higher.

Disaggregation to this level, therefore, usefully points out the disparities not only in the average levels of PLD-EER(PI)s, but also in the changes over time. The latter have arisen for two reasons: First, modification in the regimes, as noted in the two previous chapters, often has been for specific products or small groups of products. Second, unchanged quantitative restrictions have implied import premiums that vary greatly with shifts in demand and supply.[4]

The ratios of the standard deviation to the mean give an index of the relative volatility of the subsectoral PLD-EER(PI)s. On this basis the most volatile subsectors (in decreasing order) have been coal mining, textiles, basic metals, and nonmetallic mineral products (Table A.8). The least subject to such fluctuations (in increasing order) have been other manufacturing, agriculture and forestry, electric machinery, and paper and paper products.

The relative degree of fluctuation among subsectors does not suggest any general cause (intended or otherwise), although the ranking of some of the sectors does have clear explanations. The high value for coal mining, for example, reflects the explicit decision made in the 1950s to reduce the PLD-EER(PI) because of the importance of coal as an input in the new iron and steel industry. The low value for agriculture also may reflect a policy decision (or just good luck) to keep fluctuations relatively low for this politically sensitive subsector.

On the same basis the ranking of fluctuations in PLD-EER(PI)s among demand categories has been (in increasing order) intermediate products, exports, consumer goods, imports, and investment goods. Several aspects of this ranking merit emphasis: (a) The order does not seem to depend upon the extent to which the categories enter into international trade, that is, aggregates made up more substantially of nontraded goods are not necessarily more (or less) volatile than those made up of tradable goods. (b) The level of exports has been discriminated against, not their fluctuations. (c) Variations for intermediate goods have been relatively low. This implies some success of attempts not to disrupt operation of existing capacity through erratic changes in the availability of imported inputs. (d) The high fluctuations for investment goods reflect the decision to postpone machinery and equipment imports at times of foreign-exchange shortages, but to encourage them at other times.

vi. Changes in NERs are poor indicators of variations in EER(PI)s: the ratios of the latter to the former often change quite considerably (Table A.10). Some fairly general consistencies do appear, however, in these ratios. During the last year of phases these ratios generally have increased because of greater restrictiveness in response to foreign-exchange shortages (which often have been an important factor in the decision to shift to another phase).[5] However, for goods actually imported (as opposed to importable), the EER(PI) generally did not fluctuate much relative to the NER. As would be expected, in the first year of liberalized phases, the ratios for imports generally dropped because of reduced restrictiveness,[6] but the export ratios did not because of the attempt to reduce discrimination against them at the start of liberalization efforts.

5.2 IMPLICIT TARIFF RATES, EFFECTIVE PROTECTION RATES, AND DOMESTIC RESOURCE COSTS IN THE 1960s

This section is focused on the implications of relatively careful estimates of ITRs, EPRs, and DRCs, shown in Table 5.3, for 1961, 1967, and 1968 (exports only in the last year) by production subsector.[7]

The implicit tariff rate (ITR) indicates the effect of the international trade regime on the product price. The ITR is defined as the ratio to the c.i.f. price of the difference between the domestic price (net of normal distribution costs) and the c.i.f. price. Chilean ITRs generally cannot be calculated by simply adjusting the c.i.f. prices by legal tariff rates and other legal charges because quantitative restrictions sometimes create substantial import premiums (see line 1.1.6 in Table A.1) and because there are numerous exemptions from the legal rates (see subsections 4.1.5 and 4.1.7). Therefore direct price comparisons [8] are used, as explained in detail in Appendix B.

The effective protection rate (EPR) measures the impact of foreign-sector policies on domestic value added.[9] The EPR is defined as the ratio to the international value added of the difference between domestic value added and international value added. Again, direct price comparisons are used, and the details are presented in Appendix B.

TABLE 5.3

Implicit Tariff Rates, Effective Protection Rates, and Domestic Resource Costs in Chile, 28 Sectors, 1961, 1967, and 1968

(per cent)

	Implicit Tariff Rates (ITRs)			Effective Protection Rates (EPRs)				Domestic Resource Costs (DRCs)	
Tradable Goods Sectors	1961 (1)	1967 (2)	1968[a] (3)	1961 (1)	1961 (2)	1967 (3)	1968[a] (4)	1961 (1)	1968[a] (2)
1 Agriculture and forestry	43	1	19	50	145	−7	15	250	111
2 Fishing	21			25					
3 Coal mining	37			31					
4 Iron mining	2		0	−7			−12		180
5 Copper mining	0		0	−14			−10		60
6 Nitrate mining	1		0	−6			−11		
7 Stone, clay, and sands	66			64					
8 Other mining	46		6	40			−6		82
9 Food products	82	32	27	2,884	217	365	3	253	97
10 Beverages	122	7		609	164	−23		259	
11 Tobacco	106	0		141	1	−13		47	
12 Textiles	182	99		672	462	492		[b]	
13 Footwear and clothing	255	23	29	386	319	16	5	1,916	52

14 Wood and cork	35	0	24	21	30	−4	22	210	161
15 Furniture	129	0	30	209	127	−5	18	241	73
16 Paper and paper products	55	44	27	41	49	95	14	683	164
17 Printing and publishing	72	0		82	77	−15		297	
18 Leather and leather products	161	25	15	714	325	18	−20	2,109	55
19 Rubber products	102	125		109	137	304		77	
20 Chemical products	94	38	24	89	107	64	14	356	75
21 Petroleum and coal products	50	55		45	−26	1,140		47	
22 Nonmetallic mineral products	139	27		227	179	1		b	
23 Basic metals	66	25	28	198	74	35	21	b	380
24 Metallic products	59	80		43	45	92		217	
25 Nonelectrical machinery	84	56	12	85	73	76	−9	150	59
26 Electrical machinery	105	162	26	111	92	449	10	131	50
27 Transport equipment	84	150	21	101	68	271	1	118	56
28 Other manufacturing	125		18	164	129		4	175	41
Equally weighted arithmetic mean	83	48	18	254	133	168	3	419	106
Standard deviation	58	51	11	552	117	282	13	598	86
Range	255	162	30	2,898	488	1,127	42	2,109	339

Notes to Table 5.3

NOTE: Sources and definitions are given in Appendix B. Some analysis of the consistency of the alternative sets of accounts is also presented there. For 1961, two sets of EPRs are given. The first includes more sectors, but the second is more consistent with the 1967 estimates (see Appendix B).

The estimates shown are not adjusted for overvaluation because of the difficulty of establishing the degree of overvaluation. All available indices suggest that the escudo was overvalued by 20 to 70 per cent in the 1960s (see line 1.1.1 in Table A.1 and the source note for column 2.1.3 in Table A.11). If overvaluation were taken account of in the calculations, the real protective barriers for import substitution would not appear to have been so high on average as is implied in the text. In any case, overvaluation did not alter the dispersion of protection among subsectors, which is the point of major interest. To illustrate the possible effect of such adjustments, however, note that Jeanneret [1971: 165] presents overvaluation-adjusted counterparts of ITR1 and EPR1 with respective means of 9 and 111 per cent. Although her adjustment seems to be too large for a 68 per cent overvaluation in 1961, this example is suggestive of the possible order of magnitude of this effect.

a. For subsectoral exports only.

b. Value was negative, indicating that the total foreign-exchange cost per unit exceeds the foreign-exchange final-product price.

The domestic resource cost (DRC) is the value of domestic resources (at opportunity costs) employed in earning or saving a dollar of foreign exchange in the domestic production of a good.[10] As before, the sources and method of construction are presented in Appendix B.

5.2.1 Mean Level of the Rates.

The levels of the ITRs and EPRs for 1961 and 1967 were quite high. The respective mean ITRs were 83 and 48 per cent. For 10 subsectors in 1961 and 3 in 1967 the ITRs exceeded 100 per cent. The respective mean EPRs were 133[11] and 168 per cent. For 11 subsectors in 1961 and 6 in 1967 the EPRs exceeded 100 per cent. The protective barriers created by the trade regimes thus seem to have been quite substantial on the average.[12]

5.2.2 Sectoral and Subsectoral Differences in Relative Protection.

The most important characteristic of the estimates in Table 5.3 is the existence of substantial differentials among sectors and subsectors and between end uses. For all but the 1968 ITR and EPR estimates, which are for exports only, the ranges and standard deviations between subsectors were quite high: for ITR1, a range of 255 per cent and a standard deviation of 58 per cent; ITR2, 162 and 51 per cent; EPR1, 2,898 and 552 per cent; EPR2, 488 and 117 per cent; EPR3, 1,127 and 282 per cent; DRC1, 2,109 and 598 per cent; and DRC2, 339 and 86 per cent. These variations imply substantial cross-sectoral distortions in signals for product usage and in the rates of transformation between domestic and foreign resources. As Nugent [1971] has demonstrated, moreover, the welfare loss due to greater variance in protection among products for a given mean level of protection can be quite considerable.

Ranking of Sectoral Differences.

On the sectoral level, protection has been highest for industry, lowest for mining, and in between for agriculture. However, in 1961 agriculture had a relatively high EPR (EPR2) and DRC. This result raises questions about the widespread assumption that agriculture is a low-DRC sector against which substantial discrimination has occurred.

Ranking of Subsectoral Differences.

In 1961 the ranking (in decreasing order) of subsectors with EPRs (EPR2) of over 100 per cent was textiles, leather and leather products, footwear and clothing, food products, nonmetallic mineral products, beverages, rubber products, other manufactures, furniture, and chemical products.[13] The most protected subsectors near the end of the most liberal phase since the Great Depression thus tended to be the traditional, "easy" import-substitution ones. These industries not only had received conscious protection in most cases since the 1897 tariff law, but most import substitution in them had been made before the Second World War![14] Moreover, the DRCs for many of these subsectors were quite high (see DRC1).

Jeanneret [1971:167] interprets this pattern to mean that those sectors which had relatively high EPRs remained traditional and inefficient in their operation because they had only limited competition from imports. Her interpretation depends upon the assumption that approximately the 1961 EPR structure had prevailed for a number of years. This seems to be a strong assumption, however, given the changes, described earlier, in the international economic regime.

A more plausible interpretation is that in the process of liberalization in 1959–61, protection was lowered less for the more stagnant and more traditional subsectors than for the others, leaving the former relatively protected. This occurred because the vested interests in these industries were very strong politically and because of the desire not to risk too great a disruption in these labor-intensive sectors from a flood of competitive imports. This explanation is consistent with the observed protection patterns in 1961, the general liberalization in the previous years, and the significantly negative correlation between EPR2 and the growth in product over the 1953–61 period (Table A.5).

Import Substitution Versus Export Promotion.

A very important set of discrepancies were those which favored import substitution over export promotion despite the comparative advantage of the latter. The results of discouraging exports included inefficient utilization of resources and reinforcement of already existing export pessimism. At the same time, the authorities evidently failed to appreciate that the limited growth in exports reflected in part a reaction to the policies selected because of the original export pessimism.

Evidence of such differentiation between imports and exports is multi-faceted:

i. The lowest three ITRs and EPRs in 1961 (including the only three negative values for the latter group) were for the export-oriented mining sectors—iron, copper, and nitrates. For these same three sectors in 1961 and for all of the 1968 estimates, which are for exports only, the EPRs were always less than the ITRs.

ii. For the 1968 exports-only estimates the mean ITR was 18 per cent; the mean EPR, 3 per cent. These means were far below those for the other estimates (and significantly so at the 5 per cent level). If a reasonable adjustment were made for overvaluation, moreover, the adjusted means would be negative.[15]

iii. The DRCs for the export-oriented products in each subsector were uniformly below those for total subsectoral production (DRC2 versus DRC1). The mean of the former distribution was significantly below that of the latter.

iv. Table A.5 includes several significant correlations which reflect a bias toward import substitution: the positive association between the 1961 average tariff rate on intermediate inputs and EPR1 and EPR2;[16] the negative correlation between the average tariff rate on intermediate inputs and the exports-only EPR4; the negative correlations between the 1962 ratios of exports to domestic production and ITR1, ITR2, and EPR4; the positive association between the 1962 ratio of imports to domestic production and ITR2; the positive association between the 1962 ratio of imported inputs to domestic production and ITR2 and EPR3;[17] and the negative correlation between the ratio of imported inputs to domestic production and the exports-only ITR3.

v. Bacha and Taylor [1973] present DRCs for a number of new Chilean export-promotion or import-substitution products in the late 1960s. The mean value of the former was over 20 per cent below that of the latter. Selowsky [1970:12] also estimates that the DRC of earning one dollar by exporting in 1969 was two-thirds that of saving a dollar by importing.

Differences Among Final-Use Sectors.

Among final-use categories, some evidence exists to suggest higher protection for the more consumption-oriented sectors. Positive correlations exist between the proportion of sectoral production going to consumption (private or government) and ITR1, ITR3, and EPR4 and between the proportion of sectoral imports going to consumption and ITR1 and ITR2 (Table A.7). These associations again reflect favoritism for the traditional, "easy," and largely consumption-oriented import-substitution industries.[18]

5.2.3 Differences in Relative Protection over Time.

A third general feature of the estimates in Table 5.3 is the indication of important differences between 1961 and 1967. In fact neither the ITRs nor the EPRs are significantly correlated across subsectors for the two years (Table A.4). Given that the 1962–64 Phase II period falls between these two years, the existence of differences is not surprising.

Over-All Differences.

Although the mean level of the ITRs declined from 83 per cent in 1961 to 48 per cent in 1967, the mean level of the EPRs (EPR2) increased from 133 to 168 per cent.[19] The standard deviation and the range for the EPRs increased even more: from 117 to 282 per cent for the former and from 488 to 1,127 per cent for the latter. The barriers protecting various subsectors thus tended to be greater and more dispersed in 1967 than in 1961. This view is consistent with the previous classification of 1961 as being near the end of the most liberal regime since 1930 and of 1967 as being at about the middle of a Phase III regime in which liberalization accelerated during the last years.

Sectoral Differences.

On the sectoral level, protection shifted relatively from agriculture to manufacturing. The EPR for agriculture, in fact, dropped from 145 to −7 per cent. This fall is in sharp contrast to the stated intent of the Frei government to improve the terms of trade for agriculture.[20]

Subsectoral Differences.

Shifts at the subsectoral level were substantial, but were in the direction which the Frei government had indicated it would pursue. The subsectors with EPRs greater than 100 per cent in 1967 (in decreasing order) were petroleum and coal products, textiles, electrical machinery, food products, rubber products, and transport equipment. Even though textiles and food products still were relatively highly protected, a substantial change had been made in the protective structure to favor more import substitution in nontraditional intermediate-goods industries (with lower DRCs, at least in 1961) instead of in the traditional consumption-goods subsectors. The correlation coefficients in Table A.5 provide further support for the foregoing characterization of 1967 protection. The EPRs across subsectors for that year were positively associated with several features of "modern" industries: high ratios of capital to labor, large components of machinery and equipment in the capital stocks, and heavy use of intermediate inputs, especially imported ones.

IMPORT SUBSTITUTION VERSUS EXPORT PROMOTION.

The Frei government also advocated furnishing greater incentives for exports, and introduced some policy changes—such as the expanded drawback program for nontraditional exports—in pursuit of that end (see subsection 4.2.2). The impact of such policies on import substitution versus export promotion, however, was quite limited by 1967. Tables A.5 and A.6 contain no significantly nonzero correlations consistent with either a distribution of EPRs in 1967 or a change in this distribution since 1961 that was relatively favorable to exports.[21] The 1968 exports-only estimates in Table 5.3, as is described above, also do not indicate that any very great success was attained in encouraging export promotion.

DIFFERENCES AMONG FINAL-USE SECTORS.

EPRs shifted away from consumption-oriented subsectors. The ratios of the 1967 to 1961 EPRs, in fact, are significantly negatively correlated with the consumption share in imports (Table A.6).[22] This shift is associated with the fall in relative protection for the traditional, import-substitution industries mentioned above.

It should also be observed that from 1961 to 1967 the ITRs changed from being positively associated with the share of private consumption in imports to being positively associated with the share of investment in imports (Table A.5). This increased discrimination against imported machinery and equipment (for much of which the ITRs are more significant than EPRs, since domestic production is nil) contrasts with the announced intentions of the Central Bank during this phase.

NOTES

1. Isolated exceptions were 1946 and 1957.

2. As is indicated in Appendix A, part of the premium may originate in adjustment lags between domestic and international prices which are independent of the nature of foreign-sector policies.

3. If the original importer uses an import himself then the PLD-EER(PI) represents the effect of the regime on the price which he could have obtained, i.e., on the opportunity cost.

4. Consider how the premium would increase in Figure 5.1, for example, if the demand curve shifted to the right.

5. Another contributing factor was the existence of adjustment lags in highly inflationary conditions, except in 1961 (see section 13.4).

6. Declines in inflation also may have alleviated the shortage of foreign exchange (see the preceding note).

7. For recent discussions of other measures of the effects of the international economic regime on the domestic economy, see Bacha and Taylor [1971], Balassa [1971], Balassa and Schydlowsky [1972], Bhagwati and Srinivasan [1971], Bruno [1972], Cordon [1971], Grubel and Johnson [1971], Hansen [1973], and Krueger [1972a], and the numerous references there.

8. For qualifications to this method occasioned by the presence of market imperfections, see Bhagwati [1970].

9. As Cohen [1971] points out, the notion of effective protection has a long history. Humud [1969] has uncovered references in the Chilean literature dating back to the 1840s. Recent interest in EPRs stems from the studies by Balassa [1965], Cordon [1966], and Johnson [1965].

10. The seminal articles on DRCs are Bruno [1963, 1965] and Krueger [1966]. As Bruno [1972:17] notes, such calculations have a history of practical application at least since the early 1950s in Israel. The problem of determining the appropriate shadow prices in a nonoptimal world is a substantial one, as Balassa and Schydlowsky [1972:66] have stressed. Unless such shadow prices are basically constant, moreover, as Bruno [1972:31–32] has emphasized, DRCs (or, for that matter, EPRs based on shadow prices) cannot be used to infer rankings of projects for ex ante investment decisions, but only to decide whether or not a specific project should be undertaken.

11. For the alternative set of estimates for 1961, i.e., EPR1, the mean was 254 per cent and the EPRs for 13 subsectors exceeded 100 per cent.

12. Since the means for the EPRs exceed the means for the underlying ITRs, both in Tables 5.3 and A.3, it might seem that greater protection is given on average to value added than to product. Under the assumption that the underlying distributions across subsectors are approximately normal, however, none of these differences is significantly nonzero at the 5 per cent level.

13. For the EPR1 estimates for 1961, the ranking differs somewhat in its details, but the basic point is not affected: for either EPR1 or EPR2, reversals in the sense that EPRs were less than ITRs were very rare for the traditional manufacturing subsectors. Instead, cascading predominated.

14. The more traditional industries tended to be subsectors with low ratios of capital to value added and low wages. Therefore the inverse correlations in Table A.5 between each of these two characteristics and EPR2 support the statement in the text. Muñoz [1968] describes the timing of import substitution.

15. Bacha and Taylor [1973], for example, estimate that the escudo was overvalued by 24 per cent in 1968.

16. If final product rates exactly compensated for variances in intermediate import costs, one would expect this correlation coefficient to be nonsignificant. That it is significantly positive suggests overcompensation. The negative one next mentioned likewise implies undercompensation for export-oriented products.

17. The interpretation given in the previous note also holds here.

18. As indicated in Chapter 3, despite the general encouragement of import substitution in consumption industries, certain mass-consumption imports had relatively low EERs. Such imports were concentrated in a few subsectors, however; so the over-all positive association between consumption orientation and protection dominates in the correlation across all subsectors.

19. EPR1 is not comparable to EPR3 because of the different treatment of depreciation. See Appendix B.

20. The figures in column 2 of Table 5.2, however, do indicate some success was achieved in lessening the discrepancy between the PLD-EER(PI)s for agriculture and manufacturing during 1965–70, although the difference at the start of the phase was much greater than that which prevailed in some earlier years (including the preceding phase).

21. As indicated in subsection 4.2.2, however, export-expansion efforts were intensified in the later years of this phase. The suggestion of the figures in column 6 of Table 5.2 is that these intensified efforts were to some extent successful.

22. ITRs may change much differently than EPRs. The ratio of ITRs, in fact, is significantly *positively* correlated with that same variable.

Part III

Impact of Foreign-Sector Regimes

Chapter 6

The Behavior of Merchandise Imports

In Part II of this study, I described the developments in the structure of Chilean foreign-sector regimes since the Great Depression, and I examined the impact of these developments on price- and cost-related measures of rates of exchange and of protection. I did so to lay out the groundwork for investigating a basic subject of this study: the impact of policy on the magnitude and composition of real variables. The price- and cost-related measures are important because they indicate the nature of the signals policies create for real variables and because they transmit many of the effects of policies. In this part, I analyze the real consequences of foreign-sector policies—perhaps as transmitted by price and cost variables—on five major areas of macroeconomic concern: the foreign economic position, economic stability in real and nominal terms, resource allocation and structural change, the distribution of control over income and resources, and economic growth. In the first three chapters of this part, I explore two interrelated general questions: (i) How have the international economic regimes affected the major components of the balance of payments? (ii) Have they succeeded in establishing the long-desired greater national control over the Chilean economic destiny?

SUMMARY AND CONCLUSIONS

i. In a gross sense the post-Depression regimes have clearly succeeded in lessening the level of relative dependence on imports. Imports per capita have never again attained the pre-1931 peak levels. Imports relative to GDP have averaged about a fourth of the 1920s proportion.

ii. This reduction has been accomplished in large part by the use of quantitative restrictions because of pessimism concerning the effectiveness of prices in restraining demand for imports. In respect to total imports, this pessimism was well-founded. General-equilibrium price responses have been very low, partially because of the effects of changed international reserves on domestic prices. The Central Bank has been unable effectively to neutralize such reserve movements.

iii. For some important import categories, nevertheless, price responses were fairly substantial. Therefore, the secularly decreasing PLD-EERs created considerable additional demand for foreign exchange.

iv. Although the gross level of dependence on imports fell, the variance of imports did not. The regimes of recent decades, in fact, in some respects increased fluctuations by maintaining a disequilibrium system with an overvalued exchange rate. When reserves were available from capital inflows or export booms, pressures to utilize them immediately for increased imports were almost irresistible. When a shortfall developed in the supply of foreign exchange, imports quickly had to be cut back.

v. Efforts at changing the composition of imports have met with partial success. The geographical special regimes have at times been quite important. The share of total imports going to the government has fluctuated around an upward trend, with a rapid acceleration under the Allende government.

There have also been some changes in the geographic origin of imports: in the 1960s and 1970s the dominance of the United States declined substantially. Until very recently, however, the share from Latin America did not increase significantly despite considerable rhetoric about the development of regional economic links.

In type of use, the share of capital imports has increased secularly as part of development efforts, and intermediate imports have been subjected less than others to quantitative restrictions in order not to disrupt utilization of already existing capacity. However, announced intentions to favor mass-consumption imports and limit "postponable" durable imports at times of crisis often have not been carried out.

vi. Generalizing about movements to more liberal phases and changes during such phases in terms of total imports or their composition is limited because there have been differences from phase to phase in the availability of foreign exchange and in the government's over-all economic goals. The same is true of movements to more restrictive phases.

vii. Partial-equilibrium estimates of the reaction of the economy to price-related policies or to QRs often are misleading because there have been substantial indirect effects that can be captured only by general-equilibrium analysis.

6.1 IMPORT PATTERNS SINCE 1930

6.1.1 Aggregate Merchandise Imports.

GENERAL CHARACTERISTICS.

The catastrophic impact of the Great Depression on the Chilean economy was discussed in section 1.3. In response to that event, restrictive policies on imports were adopted because they were seen as the most effective means of encouraging domestic industry, reducing dependence on the foreign sector, and conserving scarce foreign exchange. This greater degree of restrictiveness has generally been maintained—albeit with variations—in the four ensuing decades (see sections 1.4 and 4.1 above).

This greater degree of restrictiveness may be seen in a number of indices. For example, the ratio of the black-market to the national accounts exchange rate increased from unity before 1931 to levels considerably above that thereafter (except for 1959–61). Again, although data are not available for the calculation of import premium rates before the Great Depression, they presumably were zero; means for phases and subphases after the Second World War, in contrast, were at least 0.50. Likewise, before the Great Depression, the extent of overinvoicing must have been nil, but it apparently has been extensive in recent decades (see lines 1.1.3, 1.1.6, and 1.2.5.1 in Table A.1).

The aggregate impact on imports of the policy of much greater restrictiveness combined with the changes in international market conditions is clear. Imports declined drastically in the 1930s.[1] The mean ratio of imports to GDP fell from 0.52 in 1908–27 to 0.38 in 1928–30 and to a range of from 0.09 to 0.14 in the subsequent phases and subphases (line 1.2.6.7 in Table A.1). On a per capita basis the pre-Depression import levels have never again been attained, despite the existence of significantly higher real per capita incomes! In a very gross sense, then, the objective was achieved of reducing foreign dependence as measured by the average relative importance of imports.

This relative reduction of imports did not imply complete success in lessening dependence on foreign goods, however, even on this gross level.[2] Another part of that goal was to diminish the vulnerability of the economy to fluctuations in imports. Relative variations in imports were, in fact, not decreased.[3] This failure partially resulted from the attempt to maintain a disequilibrium system with overvalued exchange rates. Whenever a short-run increase in the command over foreign resources occurred, the government found it hard to resist the pressures for increased imports. When the next decrease occurred, the government had to cut back on imports because of the lack of sufficient reserves. In this sense, therefore, the control system itself contributed to rather than reduced import instabilities.

PHASE-COINCIDENT PATTERNS.

Phase-coincident patterns are quite pronounced in the three indices of restrictiveness mentioned above.[4] The mean implicit premium rate for imports dropped for each more liberal phase. The mean ratio of the black-market NER to the national accounts NER, the mean Ffrench-Davis quantitative restrictions index, and mean overinvoicing all declined at every move to a more liberal phase and increased at every move to a more restrictive phase (see lines 1.1.3, 1.1.6, 1.2.5.1, and 1.2.6.2 in Table A.1).

Phase-coincident movements in the constant-dollar value of merchandise imports or in the growth rates of these imports are less clear (Table A.2 and line 1.2 in Table 8.1). The average annual percentage growth rates of imports from the mean of the previous phase or subphase to that of the current one implied by the figures in line 1.2 of Table 8.1, for example, are 1.1 for 1956–58, 6.0 for 1959–61, and 4.6 for 1965–70 (all movements to more liberal phases); 3.0 for 1962–64, and 5.0 for 1971 (both changes to more restrictive phases).[5]

This lack of a clear pattern is not surprising. The explanation is illustrated in Figure 6.1 in a highly simplified supply-and-demand framework for foreign exchange constructed on the assumption that exports and imports face the same PLD-EERs.

Before liberalization the supply and demand curves are *SS* and *DD*, the price of foreign exchange is P_0, the quantity is Q_0, the import premium is $P_5 - P_0$, and the import premium rate is $(P_5 - P_0)/P_0$. If the supply and demand curves do not shift with liberalization, an increase in the price of foreign exchange to P_1 results in an increase in the quantity of foreign exchange to Q_1 and a drop in the import premium to $P_4 - P_1$, and in the import premium rate to $(P_4 - P_1)/P_1$.

At least in the short run, however, the demand for foreign exchange may shift downward because of domestic recession, or inventory dccumulation to reduce levels built up in anticipation of devaluation or because the premium producers receive from import licenses is declining. If *DD* shifts to *D′D′* when P_0 moves to P_1, the new quantity of foreign exchange still becomes Q_1, but the premium and premium rate are lower: $P_3 - P_1$ and $(P_3 - P_1)/P_1$, respectively.

Likewise, the supply curve of foreign exchange may shift to the right, at least in the short run, because of expanded capital inflows resulting from liberalization or previous stockpiling of exportables in anticipation of the devaluation. If *SS* moves rightward to *S′S′* (with *DD* remaining at its original location)

FIGURE 6.1

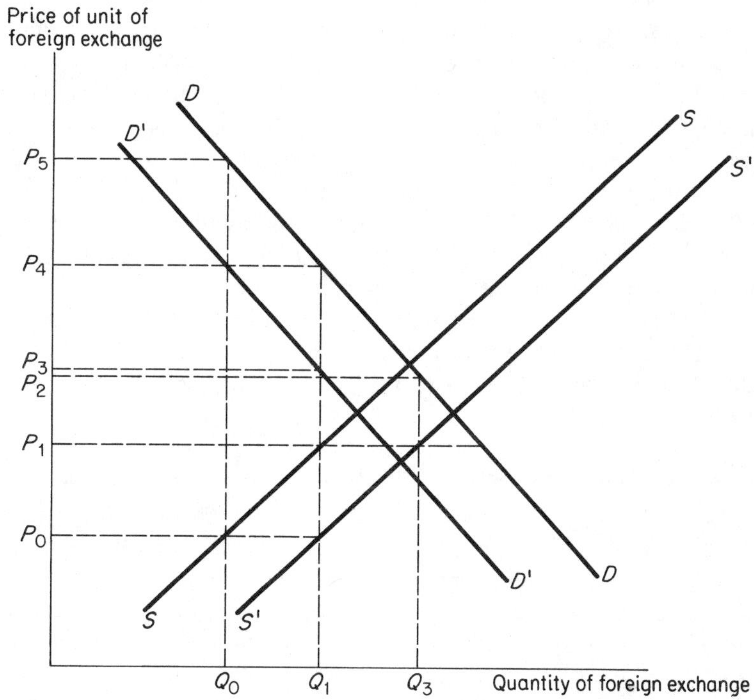

when P_0 increases to P_1, the foreign-exchange supply increases to Q_3, and the premium and the premium rate fall to P_2-P_1 and $(P_2-P_1)/P_1$, respectively.[6]

The supply and demand curves might both shift at the time of liberalization. Also, in the sense that the import premium would decline, liberalization would result if the demand curve shifted to the left or the supply curve shifted to the right even without effective devaluations. (The opposite movements, of course, would imply a higher premium.)

For the 1956–58 liberalization, the mean PLD-EER increased from 3.35 to 4.29 escudos per dollar, the mean import premium rate dropped from 1.43 to 0.83, and mean imports in constant dollars rose very slightly (lines 1.1.6 and 1.1.7 in Table A.1, and line 1.2 in Table 8.1). This configuration of changes suggests that the supply of foreign exchange shifted substantially downward relative to the demand. (In chapters 7 and 8, it is confirmed that this supply curve did indeed shift downward relative to the underlying secular trend.) The data in Table A.1 indicate, for example, that mean net inflows in constant dollars on the current account (exclusive of merchandise imports) fell 15 per cent below the mean for the 1952–55 subphase, largely because of the decline in copper prices.

For the 1959–61 liberalization, the mean PLD-EER remained about the same, the mean import premium fell from 0.87 to 0.58, and mean imports in constant dollars rose substantially. This combination implies a substantial outward shift in the supply curve relative to the demand curve; this implication is confirmed in the next two chapters and in Table 8.1. This time the movement was due largely to expanded exports and net private capital inflows in constant dollars.

Finally, for the 1965–70 liberalization, when the sliding-peg policy was in effect, the mean PLD-EER fell from 4.00 to 3.60 escudos per dollar, the mean import premium dropped from 0.58 to 0.50, and mean imports in constant dollars rose significantly (although not quite as much relatively as in 1959–61). In that case the supply curve shifted far to the right relative to the demand curve primarily because of the copper boom of the late 1960s. Liberalization therefore was possible (at least in the short run) despite the decline in the PLD-EER.

WITHIN-PHASE PATTERNS.

It is particularly noteworthy that in the first year of each of the three liberalization attempts merchandise imports declined in constant-dollar terms even though the four indices mentioned above generally suggest substantial liberalization.[7] The regression for imports in Table A.2 also indicates a significant decline from the secular growth trend in those three years.

For 1965 these falls are understandable in light of the new import approval procedure put into effect in that year, which increased restrictiveness in some respects (subsection 4.1.2).

For 1956 and 1959, the falls in the level of imports are consistent with the analysis of Figure 6.1 and with the declines in the indices of restrictiveness only if the demand curve for foreign exchange shifted far to the left. In fact, a substantial shift may have taken place. Recessions are recorded in both years, with declines in capacity utilization rates and in per capita real GDP. The large decreases in import premiums going to producers also lowered import demand. Furthermore, inventory reductions of importables may have been substituted for current imports (although data do not exist which permit examination of this possibility).

Yet the declines in the value of imports for those two years still remain puzzling—especially for 1959. The downward movements of the demand curve could cause a reduction in the quantity demanded. But if it had moved far enough to do so, the currency would have been undervalued (at least temporarily) unless the supply curve also moved sufficiently to the right. All the available evidence, however, implies that the escudo was overvalued in both those years. Moreover, although the supply curve may have moved to the left in 1956, as is noted above, it clearly moved to the right in 1959.

A second interesting within-phase pattern is the increase in the indices of restrictiveness as the 1956–58 and 1965–70 liberalization attempts faltered. In 1958 imports in constant dollars declined as a result, although they did not do so in 1970. In contrast, at the end of the 1959–61 Phase IV period, there is no indication in most indices that liberalization was reduced before it was entirely abandoned in December 1961. Imports in constant terms also increased until the very end.

Finally, the increase in restrictiveness near the end of the 1965–70 phase, may seem prima facie in conflict with the concurrent reduction in restrictions noted in section 4.1. This apparent paradox is resolved if it is observed that the demand curve for foreign exchange shifted rapidly to the right because of speculative pre-election capital outflows. The result was an increase in restrictiveness as measured, for example, by the premium rate—even though liberalization was continuing in the sense that specific restrictions were reduced.

6.1.2 Disaggregate Merchandise Imports.

Three aspects of goods imports will be discussed: the role of special regimes and of the government, the origin of goods imports, and their end uses.

Role of Special Regimes and of the Government.

The development of a number of special import regimes, which were introduced primarily in the 1950s, was described in section 4.1. Jeanneret [1971:350] reports that by 1960 these regimes affected 41 per cent of Chilean imports, with the regional ones and the regime for CAP being specially significant. Subsequently, the Frei liberalization and rationalization substantially reduced the importance of these regimes. For the entire 1965–70 period they covered only 16 per cent of total import registrations. The relative importance of the regional regimes—especially that for Arica—rose in these years. The Allende government somewhat further decreased the share of special regimes in total imports because the regimes were seen to have negative effects on the distribution of income. Once again, however, the relative importance of those for remote areas increased. Over the past two decades, then, these special import regimes have affected a significant although varying proportion of total imports.

Also considered in section 4.1 was the exclusion of all or part of the trade on government account from the import regimes. As is noted there, such exclusions tended to increase as general restrictiveness intensified and vice versa. Under the Allende government, however, this exclusion became a major factor because of the prior-deposit requirement of 10,000 per cent imposed in 1971. As a result, the government share in registered imports increased from 34 per cent in 1970 to 44 per cent in 1971 and to 65 per cent in the first eight months of 1972. The composition of imports in this respect, thus, changed radically.[8]

GEOGRAPHIC ORIGIN.

Mean percentage shares of Chilean imports by country of origin are shown in Table 6.1 for her most important suppliers for phases and subphases in 1948–70. It is clear from the table that the United States remained the dominant supplier throughout the period, but declined significantly in importance beginning in the 1960s because the dollar was overvalued for most of the period and because the Frei government was promoting diversification among sources as a matter of ideology and to avoid risk. For similar reasons—as well as in response to changes in the geographical distribution of available commercial credit—under the Allende government the relative importance of the United States as a supplier further decreased.[9]

Over the same period, Japan and a number of European countries increased their shares somewhat, but only the Federal Republic of Germany averaged as much as 10 per cent for as long as a decade. Also, despite the formation of LAFTA and of the Andean Group in the 1960s (see subsection 4.1.8), the share of Latin American sources did not increase substantially in this period. Argentina—and only Argentina among LAFTA members—was among the major suppliers. Even for Argentina, moreover, although a steady

TABLE 6.1
Mean Percentage Distribution of Chilean Imports by Country of Origin for Phases and Subphases of 1948–70

Major Trading Partners	1948–51 Phase II	1952–55 Phase II	1956–58 Phase III	1959–61 Phase IV	1962–64 Phase II	1965–70 Phase III
United States	50	47	50	47	37	38
Federal Republic of Germany (West Germany)	2	8	12	12	12	12
Argentina	7	11	5	8	9	10
United Kingdom	8	6	6	7	7	6
France	2	2	2	3	5	3
Italy	1	1	2	2	2	2
Japan	0	0	2	2	2	2
Netherlands	0	1	2	2	1	2
All others	30	24	19	17	25	25

SOURCE: Calculated from data in IMF and IBRD [1949–72]. The countries are listed in order of their mean shares for the entire period.

rise was recorded, there was no evidence of a strong acceleration in the 1960s.

Under the Allende government, however, once again substantial changes occurred. All imports of LAFTA and Andean origin were excluded from the 10,000 per cent prior-deposit requirement in 1971. As a result constant-dollar approved import registrations from LAFTA increased by 61 per cent in 1971 (with an associated increase of from 16 to 21 per cent in the share of total registrations), and those from the Andean Group increased even more.

END USES.

Consistent series are available for 1940–66 for the breakdown of imports: consumption goods were 32 per cent of total imports in 1946–65; investment goods, 29 per cent; intermediate goods, 28 per cent; and services, 11 per cent. Consumption goods are further subdivided into staple goods (22 per cent), durable goods (7 per cent), and secondary goods (4 per cent).[10] Investment goods are disaggregated into machinery and equipment (19 per cent) and transportation-related items (10 per cent). Consumption imports averaged slightly less than 4 per cent of total consumption. Investment imports averaged 28 per cent of total investment.

Trends. In section 1.2 it was noted that at least since the 1830s, the secular shift in the composition of imports had been from consumption goods to intermediate and capital goods because of import-substitution policies. In sections 3.1 and 5.1 a description is given of how these policies were continued until the early 1960s, with increased emphasis over the years on import substitution in intermediate-goods production as well.

As a result of these policies, secular exponential growth rates for 1947–65 for the major components of imports were as follows: transportation-related capital goods, 14 per cent; machinery and equipment, 8.8 per cent; secondary consumer goods, 5.8 per cent; staple consumer goods, 4.5 per cent; durable consumer goods, 4.0 per cent; and intermediate goods, 1.5 per cent (see Table A.2, first column). The secular shift, thus, clearly was from intermediate goods to capital goods, with consumption goods in between. The rapid increase in capital goods imports reflected increasing dependence on foreign machinery and equipment in development programs.[11] In substantial part the emphasis on capital imports was due to the efforts of CORFO.[12]

The moderate increase in consumption goods imports was due to the constraint by the exchange-control system of rapidly rising demands for income-elastic durable and secondary goods, at the same time that foreign products were being substituted for domestic food. The authorities apparently did not lose control of the system, as Huddle [1972a:5] claims happened in Brazil, where low-priority consumer imports expanded more rapidly than equipment imports.

The low rate of growth of intermediate goods imports is surprising. In Table 5.2, the ratios of PLD-EER(PI)s for these goods have a slight secular upward trend. But it is not sufficiently pronounced to imply that such items were in increasingly short supply, nor that protection for them rose greatly during this period. Section 5.2 does contain a suggestion that EPRs for intermediate goods increased, but not before the mid-1960s. In any case, the growth of intermediate imports was much less than expected, given the frequent characterization of import substitution for consumption goods as a device leading to increased dependence on intermediate imports. On the other hand, the slow growth may only reflect the fact, discussed in Chapter 10, that most of such import substitution took place before World War II.

Phase-Coincident Patterns. Mean shares of imports by the three major categories are shown in lines 1.2.1.1–1.2.1.3 of Table A.1. The most immediate feature of the figures shown is that they are not very systematic for movements either to more liberal phases or to more restrictive ones. In the 1956–58 movement toward a more liberal phase, the weight of import shares shifted substantially from intermediate to investment goods; for 1959–61 it shifted somewhat toward consumption goods; for 1965–70, it shifted somewhat toward intermediate imports. In each case the movements differed, depending upon the details of the policies of over-all liberalization plus stabilization (see sections 1.3 and 4.1 and Chapters 5 and 13).

For the movements toward more restrictive phases there is seemingly somewhat more consistency in that in both 1962–64 and 1971 [13] the share of consumption imports increased. However, in 1962–64, the rise in the consumption share of imports was entirely at the expense of intermediate inputs; the proportion of investment-goods imports remained unchanged because the Alessandri government continued to emphasize infrastructural development. In 1971, the share of capital goods plummeted, raising not only the share of consumption, but—even more—that of intermediate inputs.[14] The short-run consumption and capacity-utilization gain was being bought in part at the price of decreased long-run capacity.[15]

In Table A.2 further evidence is provided about phase-coincident changes in the exponential growth rates of various import categories during 1947–65. According to those estimates, phase-coincident deviations of consumption imports were limited. Declines for staple and durable goods are indicated for the Phase II period before 1956 and for durables during the Phase III period of 1956–58, but only the second of these three is significantly nonzero even at the 10 per cent level. Transportation-related investment goods imports have a positive deviation in the 1946–58 Phase III years and a negative one in the 1962–64 Phase II period, but only the latter is significantly nonzero at the 10 per cent level. Intermediate goods has the most significant phase-coincident deviation in growth rates, with negative values for both the Phase II years before 1956 and the 1956–58 Phase III period. These deviations from the secular trend are largely negative and concentrated in the phases before 1959. As is the case for mean shares, however, there is no systematic relation between these deviations and movements to more liberal or more restrictive phases.

Within-Phase Patterns. In the first year of liberalization attempts, the composition of imports tended to shift from capital goods[16] and staple and durable consumer goods toward secondary consumer goods and intermediate goods.[17] Secondary consumption imports gained more relatively because they had been more discriminated against in the preceding Phase II periods. Intermediate goods gained more relatively because of the attempt to avoid production declines occurring in response to the over-all programs of liberalization plus stabilization.

During subsequent liberalization phases, however, the share of intermediate imports declined. These falls reflected policies favoring increased consumption imports intended to stem inflation and increased capital goods imports intended to promote industrial development.

In the last year of both liberalized and restrictive phases, finally, the share in total imports of both consumer and producer durables increased regularly except for transportation-related investment imports in 1958. One possible explanation for the pattern of increase is that demand for durables increased because of uncertainty and the often associated expectations of devaluation generated by the faltering of the prevailing exchange control regime. Because of this same faltering, at least part of the increased ex ante demand was satisfied by imports.

Variations in Trend. As a result of both phase-coincident and within-phase changes, fluctuations in some of the import subdivisions have been considerable. The ratio of the standard deviation from the secular trend of imports in a category to the mean for that category gives an index of the degree of relative variation. The index for intermediate goods is 0.10; machinery and equipment, 0.12; staple consumer goods, 0.20; durable consumer goods, 0.20; secondary consumer goods, 0.28; and transportation-related investment goods, 0.52.

One function of the index is to evaluate the success of the government in restricting particular categories of imports. In times of foreign-exchange shortages, the Chilean government often indicated its intention of restricting "postponable" imports, i.e., primarily consumer and producer durables, but also secondary consumption goods. If the government's intentions are carried out, ceteris paribus, the imports restricted will show relatively large variations. The ordering indicates partial success.[18] Three of the four postponable categories had the three highest indices. However, the indices for consumer durables and for staple consumer goods are identical, and the index for machinery and equipment, moreover, is the second lowest of all.

Another point to notice is that the ranking of subsectors here is the same as the ranking by relative fluctuations in PLD-EER(PI)s given in section 5.1.2 (the subdivisions there, in increasing order, are intermediate goods, consumer goods, and investment goods).[19] This coincidence should not be surprising, since fluctuations in imports were the major source of fluctuations in PLD-EER(PI)s.

Finally, to judge by the index, the government avoided disrupting production in industries using imported intermediate products: this category has the lowest index of variation of the six shown.

Changes in Percentage Shares. The subsectoral mean percentage distribution for consumption, investment goods, and intermediate imports is shown in Table 6.2 for 1960–61, 1962–64, and 1965–68.

Among consumption imports the most striking feature is the substantial and growing relative importance of processed food items. This trend continued in recent years under the Allende government, moreover, as evidenced by a 76 per cent increase in the current-dollar value of approved registrations for food and beverages in 1971. This increasing dependence on imported foodstuffs has preoccupied a number of Chilean economists and government officials for some time. The high EPR long granted to this subsector (Table 5.3), however, has not sufficiently speeded up the growth of domestic production.

A second noteworthy feature is the substantial fall in the share of clothing and footwear. That this fall occurred despite the substantial decline in the EPR for this subsector in the 1960s (Table 5.3) is of considerable interest. Apparently domestic producers were able to meet the competition from cheaper imports; so the latter did not flood the market. If so, this response was especially impressive because this subsector had enjoyed substantial protection for decades.

Finally, the effect of increased restrictiveness in 1962–64 was to cut back the share of vehicle imports below what it was in the preceding or succeeding more liberal phases.

Among investment goods the most notable pattern is a shift from transportation equipment to nonelectrical machinery. Presumably this reflects expanded domestic production of some components of the former.

Among intermediate goods the importance of agricultural and chemical products merit note. The former had a relative phase-related increase in the more restrictive years of 1962–64. The latter increased relatively rapidly throughout this period.

TABLE 6.2

Percentage Composition of Chilean Consumption, Investment, and Intermediate Imports, 1960–61, 1962–64, and 1965–68

	1960–61 Phase IV	1962–64 Phase II	1965–68 Phase III
Consumption goods	100	100	100
Processed foods	32	40	45
Clothing and footwear	14	8	4
Vehicles	12	10	14
Metal-fabricated products	7	6	4
Books and other printed matter	5	8	8
Agricultural products	5	5	7
Rubber products	1	2	5
All other	24	21	13
Nonelectrical machinery	39	49	49
Investment goods	100	100	100
Transportation equipment	35	27	25
Electrical machinery and apparatus	11	11	13
All other	15	13	13
Intermediate goods	100	100	100
Agricultural products	22	25	22
Chemicals	19	22	25
Machinery intermediate imports	10	10	11
Crude petroleum and gas	9	4	5
Basic metals	7	7	6
Petroleum and coal derivatives	5	4	4
Food products	5	6	3
All others	23	22	24

SOURCE: Based on unpublished ODEPLAN data which are consistent with the input-output table in ODEPLAN [1970]. The subsectors are listed in order of their importance in 1960–61.

6.2 EFFECT OF THE REGIMES ON IMPORTS

Up to this point, the focus of this chapter has been on patterns of imports in the decades since 1930, with only general suggestions offered about the nature of responses to different aspects of various regimes. What follows now will be a systematic analysis of these reactions, using specific econometric structural relationships as the framework.

6.2.1 Partial-Equilibrium Responses.

Single-equation estimates of import functions for 1947–1965 are shown in Table 6.3. The disaggregation is the same as the one discussed under end uses in subsection 6.1.2, above. On an over-all level the results in the table seem reasonably satisfactory. The point estimates have the anticipated signs. No undue problems of serial correlation are apparent (but see note a to the table). The corrected coefficients of determination indicate that the hypothesized determinants are consistent with from 83 to 97 per cent of the variance in the dependent variables. Greater consistency is implied for investment goods imports than for consumption and and intermediate imports.

In the basic underlying model current real imports are hypothesized to depend on four factors: relative prices, other demand variables, the degree of policy restrictiveness, and lagged imports.

RELATIVE PRICES.

Relative price terms include the levels (or their inverses) and standard deviations of PLD-NERs, PLD-EERs, and PLD-EER(PI)s.[20] Since these different terms may capture somewhat different features of the regimes, more than one price term is allowed in each relation.

The estimates suggest significant and substantial responses to relative price levels among some imports. For example, the implied elasticities at the point of sample means for a change in the general NER are −0.9 for secondary consumption goods, −1.4 for transportation equipment, and −0.3 for intermediate goods.[21] For these three categories, therefore, price-related policies instead of quantitative restrictions could have been used to control the balance of payments. Such a choice would have been preferable because it would have resulted in more flexibility, less fluctuation in the related PLD-EER(PI)s as supply and demand curves shifted, and less income redistribution toward importers.

For those same three import categories, the secular decline in the over-all PLD-EER caused a secular rise in the demand for imports. The 41 per cent fall in the PLD-EER for imported goods between 1946 and 1970 (column 1 in Table 5.1) and the size of the elasticities listed above, for example, imply respective demand increases of 37, 57, and 12 per cent for the three categories, ceteris paribus. Such intensified demand pressures added substantially to the post-World War II foreign-exchange problems.

For staple and durable consumption goods and for machinery and equipment, in contrast, there is no evidence of a significant real import response to relative prices. For durable consumption goods and machinery and equipment, the extensive use of quantitative restrictions may obscure price responses. However, variables are included in the relations to represent policy restrictiveness

TABLE 6.3

Chilean Real Import Functions[a] for Major Uses of Goods, 1947–65

Type of Import	Relative Prices[b] Level 1	Relative Prices[b] Level 2	Relative Prices[b] Stand. Dev.	Other Demand Factors: Private Consumption	Other Demand Factors: Real Total Credit	Other Demand Factors: Sector-Specific[c]
Consumption goods						
Staple				0.0344[f]	0.0506	−369.0
				(6.0)	(3.4)	(1.7)
				[1.3]	[0.8]	[−1.2][g]
Durable				0.0099[f]	0.0296[f]	
				(6.6)	(5.0)	
				[0.8]	[0.5]	
Secondary	−15.6			0.0019[f]		189.0
	(2.5)			(1.3)[h]		(4.1)
	[−0.9]			[0.7]		[4.7]
Investment goods						
Machinery and equip.			45.0			
			(1.2)[h]			
			[0.1]			
Transport. equip.	182.0	59.0[b]				17.4
	(3.0)	(1.2)[h]				(10.4)
	[1.1]	[0.3]				[1.3]
Intermediate goods	−161.0				0.0182	
	(2.4)				(1.4)[g]	
	[−0.3]				[0.1]	

Type of Import	Policy Restrictiveness: Ffrench-Davis QR Index	Policy Restrictiveness: Export Capacity to Import[d]	Sector-Specific[e]	Lagged Imports	Constant	$\bar{R}^2$ / *SE*	*DW*
Consumption goods							
Staple	−1,207.0				1,324.0	0.88	2.2
	(2.3)				(2.4)	44.6	
	[−3.8]						
Durable			−20.0	−0.532		0.87	2.2
			(4.8)	(2.6)		11.4	
			[−0.2]				
Secondary	−107.0		−13.6	0.418		0.83	1.9
	(2.8)		(1.9)	(2.2)		8.3	
	[−3.5]		[−0.1]				
Investment goods							
Machinery and equip.	−703.0	0.0779		0.678	577.0	0.97	2.4
	(2.6)	(4.6)		(7.6)	(2.2)	23.1	
	[−7.4]	[2.1]					
Transport. equip.	−1,520.0	0.239	−1,891.0		2,988.0	0.94	2.2
	(4.1)	(3.0)	(5.2)		(8.0)	23.8	
	[−9.1]	[−0.0]	[−11.3]				
Intermediate goods		0.113		−0.322	5,549.0	0.86	2.8
		(4.7)		(1.4)[g]	(3.6)	34.0	
		[0.4]					

Notes to Table 6.3

$\bar{R}^2$ = coefficient of multiple determination adjusted for degrees of freedom.

SE = standard error of estimate.

DW = Durbin-Watson statistic.

a. Data sources and estimation techniques are discussed in Chapter 2 and in Appendix A. The figures in parentheses are the absolute values of the *t* statistics. All point estimates are significantly nonzero at the 5 per cent level unless otherwise noted. The figures in brackets are the long-run elasticities at the point of sample means. These elasticities are long run in the sense that all adjustments due to the inclusion of lagged imports are assumed to have occurred. For such relationships in which the lagged import value is included, the Durbin-Watson statistic is biased toward 2.0.

b. The variable used for secondary consumption goods is the corresponding PLD-EER lagged one year, under the assumption that average tax and import deposit cost rates were applicable. For transportation equipment at level 1, the variable is the inverse of the PLD-EER(PI) based on wholesale price indices; at level 2, the inverse of the PLD-EER(PI) lagged one year. The variable used for intermediate investment goods is the ratio of the PLD-NER calculated from unit values of imports to the deflator for inventories; for machinery and equipment, it is the standard deviation of the PLD-NER (see text).

c. The variable used for staple consumption goods is the ratio of current to lagged values of total inventory; for secondary consumption goods, the ratio of wage income to total income; for transportation equipment, a time trend.

d. Nominal value of exports divided by unit value of imports. For transportation equipment, the ratio of net foreign-exchange reserves held by the banking system to the unit value of imports was used with a one-year lag.

e. The variable used for durable consumption goods is the ratio of the black-market NER to the national accounts NER; for secondary consumption goods, a dummy variable with a value of 1.0 in 1962–64 to represent the reversion to a Phase II regime in those years; for transportation equipment, the lagged Ffrench-Davis QR index.

f. Lagged one year.

g. Significantly nonzero at the 10 per cent level.

h. Significantly nonzero at the 15 per cent level.

(see below). Under the assumption that in fact they do so relatively well, significant coefficents for any import price responses should have been obtained even if quantitative restrictions were at times effective.[22]

For the three import categories considered in the previous paragraph, therefore, price-related policies could not have been so easily substituted for quantitative restrictions to enforce balance-of-payments goals. Likewise, the secular decline in the PLD-EER did not generate substantial additional pressures for foreign exchange for use in these categories.[23]

The standard deviation of relative price terms over the past three years is included in the basic model as a proxy for risk associated with future price movements. Table 6.3 includes almost no evidence of a risk-aversion response. Only for machinery and equipment is the relevant coefficient significantly nonzero even at the 15 per cent level. Even for this category the implied extent of hedging against uncertainty by importing more when risks of future price changes are higher is very small.

OTHER DEMAND VARIABLES.

Other demand variables included are selected activity indices (a time trend; the ratio of current to lagged stocks; consumption, for categories of consumption; investment, for categories of investment imports and GDP for intermediate imports),[24] total real credit, and the distribution of income between labor and other factors.

Activity indices have significantly nonzero coefficients for consumption goods and transportation equipment. Total private consumption enters into all three categories of consumption imports. The distribution of elasticities across these categories, however, is somewhat surprising. In contrast to usual Engle-curve patterns, the estimate for staple goods is greater than 1.0 while that for durable goods is less than 1.0. This inversion of the normal ordering may be due to the more extensive use of quantitative restrictions for the latter category. The measure of inventory accumulation (see note d of the table) has a significantly nonzero, inverse relation to the level of imports of staples. Apparently, high inventory accumulation rates lessen the current demand for these imports, but there is no evidence of a significant impact on other categories. Finally, a time trend representing secular shifts in demand is significant for transportation equipment.

Total retail credit is emphasized as an important variable by the Instituto de Economía [1963:73].[25] It has significantly nonzero coefficients for staple and durable consumption goods and for intermediate goods (with implied elasticities descending in the order of presentation). A very direct link, thus, existed between internal monetary policy and international economic flows. Note, however, that there is no evidence of this direct link between monetary policies and investment goods imports. This last result accurately reflects the predominantly short-term nature and use of Chilean bank credit.

Pinto [1962:88] hypothesizes that a shift in the distribution of income from nonlabor factors to labor would reduce Chilean imports. The data in Table 6.3 provide no support for this hypothesis. An income distribution variable is significantly nonzero only for secondary consumption imports. In that case the estimate implies an *increase* in imports as income shifts from nonlabor factors to labor.[26]

POLICY RESTRICTIVENESS.

Policy restrictiveness is represented by five variables: the Ffrench-Davis quantitative restrictions index; the export capacity to import; the net foreign-exchange reserves held by the banking system, deflated by the unit value of imports; the ratio of the black-market NER to the national accounts NER; and phase-specific dummy variables. The first and fourth of these are discussed in

Appendix A. The second and third are included because restrictions were increased when reserves fell.[27] The last makes it possible to explore specific restrictions (or their lack) for various import categories during particular phases.

The results in Table 6.3 indicate that significant and substantial responses to policy restrictiveness occurred for all types of imports: The Ffrench-Davis quantitative restrictions index is significantly nonzero for all but consumption durables and intermediate goods. The export capacity to import has significantly nonzero coefficients for machinery and equipment and intermediate imports. The ratio of net foreign-exchange reserves held by the banking system to the unit value of imports has a significant coefficient for transportation equipment. The ratio of the black-market NER to the national accounts NER has a significantly nonzero coefficient for durable consumption goods. A dummy variable for the reversion to a Phase II regime in 1962–64 has a significantly nonzero coefficient for secondary consumption imports, implying an average reduction of 17 per cent for the three years.

Quantitative restrictions, therefore, had pervasive and substantial impacts. In fact, they apparently were the only effective policy instrument for staple and durable consumption goods and for machinery and equipment imports. Because several different indices of quantitative restrictions are used in the estimates, the relative impact on the various categories of imports cannot be characterized with complete confidence. However, I would suggest that the impact of the QRs was greatest on transportation equipment, followed by machinery and equipment, and then by stable and secondary consumption goods, with the impact on durable consumption goods and intermediate goods not clear. On this basis, QRs can be characterized as favoring consumption goods, at least the nondurable kinds, over investment goods.

LAGGED IMPORTS.

A priori lagged imports may have either positive or negative coefficients. A positive coefficient reflects Houthakker-Taylor [1970] habit formation: more than one year is needed for actual imports to adjust to desired levels.[28] A negative coefficient indicates a Houthakker-Taylor inventory effect: stocks built up from previous imports diminish the demand for current imports.[29]

The estimates in Table 6.3 imply the dominance of the inventory effect for durable consumption goods and intermediate imports. They indicate the dominance of the adjustment or habit formation effects for secondary consumption goods and for machinery and equipment imports. For the other two categories the two effects tend to nullify each other. A priori such a pattern does not seem unreasonable.

One implication of this pattern is that, under liberalization, staple and durable consumption imports, transportation imports, and intermediate imports all adjust rapidly to new levels. Secondary consumption goods and machinery and equipment adjust much more slowly. Ceteris paribus, the result would seem to be more probable relative to increases in EPRs for domestic production of the last two categories than for the others, since in those two, competitive imports adjust more slowly than intermediate imports.

6.2.2 General-Equilibrium Reaction of Imports.

The model described in Chapter 2 provides a tool for examining the general-equilibrium impact of specified changes, ceteris paribus. The resulting elasticities or proportional deviations are shown in Table A.11 for exogenous changes in price-related variables and in QRs.

6.2.2.1 PRICE-RELATED CHANGES.

Simulation 1.2 in Table A.11 involves variations of equal proportion in all import prices and unit values for the first year only. The direct effects of these changes are primarily in imports and various prices.

The total general-equilibrium import elasticity is −0.2 in the first year and −0.3 in the third year. On the basis of these low values, it is questionable whether price-related policies can be effectively used to limit Chilean demand for foreign exchange for imports. Of course it is always possible to hypothesize that radical changes in policies (e.g., elimination of quantitative restrictions) would alter behavior and substantially increase these elasticities. But it is the case that such a hypothesis is very speculative and is not based upon actual Chilean experience.

The underlying composition of imports is altered substantially in this simulation. Shifts reflect the combination of positive first-year elasticities for capital goods and staple consumption goods and fairly large (in absolute value) negative ones for intermediate imports and secondary consumption goods. The indirect effects reinforce the direct effects with the result that the absolute values of the general-equilibrium elasticities exceed those of the partial-equilibrium elasticities for some categories, e.g., intermediate and secondary consumer imports. Examples of the opposite kind also are found, e.g., transportation-related imports. In either case, the possibly misleading nature of partial-equilibrium estimates is illustrated. The other simulations discussed below provide further examples of the same phenomenon.

In simulation 2.1.1 equal proportional changes are assumed in all legal exchange rates in the first year only. This assumption implies direct impacts on exports in addition to those on imports and prices. The general-equilibrium import elasticity is −0.1 for both the first and third year. These estimates are lower in absolute value than those in the previously discussed simulation. The lower values reflect the much more rapid adjustment of domestic prices in this case and the consequent neutralization of much of the relative price effect.

Domestic prices adjust more because of direct links to export prices, changed competition for domestic production from changed exports, and, most important, alterations in the money supply due to larger variations in foreign reserves.

Such results lead to even greater doubt about the effectiveness of devaluation in restraining demand for foreign exchange for imports. They also point to the importance of neutralizing the effects of changes in reserves on the money supply as part of any devaluation effort. Unfortunately, however, at least historically the Central Bank has not had enough control over the money supply to have been very effective in its neutralization attempts (see Chapter 9).

In simulation 2.1.3, the legal exchange rates in all years are represented by the Bacha and Taylor [1973] equilibrium exchange rates. For the first three years this implies respective increases of 45, 35, and 61 per cent above the actual national accounts NER. Devaluations of this magnitude may seem large, but they occurred several times in the sample period and thereafter (see Chapter 3). Given the time required for adjustments, of course, the maintenance of higher exchange rates over the years results in larger effects than does the one-period change of the first two simulations.

This simulation once again reinforces doubts previously expressed concerning import elasticity. For the rather substantial NER devaluations hypothesized, imports decline only 3 per cent in the first year and 5 per cent in the third. The implied elasticities, moveover, are generally smaller in the first year than are those for simulation 2.1.1. Diminishing returns to devaluation, thus, apparently exist.

Simulation 2.2 explores the impact of multiplying the import tax function by 0.9 in the first year only. As expected, given the results of the previous simulations, the effects on imports are quite minor. One interesting feature of this experiment, however, is that over-all government tax revenues in real terms actually increase slightly. The decline of 9 per cent in import taxes is offset by increases in other tax collections. Among the most important is a 4 per cent rise in taxes derived from large-scale mining because of induced additional exports.

6.2.2.2 Changes in Quantitative Restrictions.

Simulation 2.3.1 investigates the results of equal proportional changes in all the QR indices in the first year only. The direct impact of these indices is primarily on various imports and price levels in the model.

Total imports have a substantial inverse initial response to changes in the QR indices. The first-year elasticity is −2.4. By the third year, in contrast, the elasticity is almost zero. QRs thus seem to be quite effective in restraining foreign-exchange demands in the short run.

On a more disaggregate level the first-year responses also are all elastic, except for intermediate imports. The third-year responses are all less in absolute value than the first-year responses, except for secondary consumer imports.[30]

The ordering of the absolute value of the first-year reactions across import categories is transportation-related investment goods, secondary consumer goods, habitual consumer goods, durable consumer goods, machinery and equipment investment goods, and intermediate goods.[31] This ordering is different in some important respects from the ordering suggested by the partial-equilibrium estimates in Table 6.3—especially in the case of machinery and equipment imports.

This ranking provides some basis for evaluating the goals frequently mentioned in regard to the use of quantitative restrictions. The intention has been to use them in periods of foreign-exchange crises to limit luxuries such as vehicle imports, but not to limit the availability of crucial imported intermediate inputs. The high rank of transportation-related imports and the low rank of intermediate imports are consistent with this. Other intentions have been to favor mass-consumption imports in order to limit measured inflationary pressures and to restrict "postponable" durable consumer goods and investment goods imports. The ranking of staple consumer goods ahead of durable consumer goods and machinery and equipment is not consistent with these objectives.

Quantitative restrictions thus appear to have been a powerful tool in restricting short-run demands for foreign exchange. The resulting compositional changes, however, have not always been the ones intended.

NOTES

1. Subsequently, however, the mean rate of growth of imports for subphases and phases generally was positive except in 1962–64 (line 1.2.4.1 in Table A.1). A comparison of relation 1.2 (see section 1.2) with that for total imports in Table A.2, moreover, suggests that the mean exponential secular growth rate for 1940–65 was not less, and was possibly more, than for 1860–1927.

2. As is discussed below, moreover, compositional changes have differed in certain respects from those officially sought.

3. The mean absolute proportional deviation from the level implied by the exponential trend for the constant-dollar value of imports in 1931–55 is 0.19 (with a standard deviation of 0.23). This is not significantly less than the mean value of 0.20 (with a standard deviation of 0.20) reported in section 1.2 for the 1878–1927 phase (under the same assumptions as are indicated in section 1.2).

4. If this statement were not true, of course, serious questions would arise about the delineation of the phases.

5. The fairly large increase in the constant-dollar value of merchandise imports in 1971 may raise the question whether or not in fact the regime became as restrictive

in that year as is claimed. The answer is "yes," despite the large increase in real merchandise imports, for three reasons. First, the regime became much more restrictive during the year, but high rates of imports or import registrations occurred before the new restrictions were announced because of the overvalued exchange rate and uncertainty concerning future import policies. Second, many of the most restrictive changes did not affect merchandise imports as much as invisible imports and capital movements. Third, the direct impact of the new quantitative restrictions altered the composition of imports much more than the level (see below).

6. Whether the premium with a supply shift above is greater than that with a demand shift alone obviously depends upon the magnitude of the shift and the slope of the curves.

7. The only exception is a slight increase in the Ffrench-Davis quantitative restrictions index in 1965. Also, although a slight decline in overinvoicing occurred in 1959, the level still remained relatively high.

8. One rationale for this shift given by the government was that it would have greater bargaining power by dealing as a monopsony with foreign suppliers. Cauas and Corbo [1972:32], however, claim that the uncoordinated purchases of a multitude of state agencies did not permit the government to exploit this power.

9. For example, the source of all mining-related imports, which totaled $36 million for large-scale copper companies alone in the first year of nationalization, was switched from the United States to Europe.

10. Staple goods are essential mass-consumption items (especially food). Secondary goods are nonstaple, nondurable products.

11. Over this same period the ratio of imported to total capital increased at a mean annual rate of 4.6 per cent.

12. CORFO was particularly important in the development of national steel (CAP), electrical (ENDESA), and petroleum (ENAP) enterprises, but also in many other developments which depended heavily on foreign capital goods.

13. According to Allende's annual message to Congress on May 21, 1973, as summarized in CORFO [1973a: June 8, p. VIII], relative price increases for food imports underlay part of the increased consumption share. He stated that the same physical volume of food imports cost $50 million more in 1971 than in 1970 and $120 million more in 1972 than in 1970.

14. Early in 1972, however, according to de Onis [1972a:4], the government began to cut the share of intermediate imports because of foreign-exchange shortage. De Castro [1972:53] also predicted that the rate of growth of intermediate imports in that year would be less than 70 per cent of the over-all import growth rate.

15. In the Phase II years before 1956, a similar pattern favoring the short run also often existed. For example, Mamalakis [1965:133] reports ECLA estimates that in 1953–54 exchange-rate-policy subsidies averaged 44.7 per cent for consumption imports, 41.5 per cent for fuel imports, 37.2 per cent for raw materials imports, and 22.3 per cent for investment goods imports.

16. The only significantly nonzero deviations from the secular growth rates reported in Table A.3 for the first year of liberalization attempts are the negative ones for capital goods imports.

17. There are several exceptions: in 1965 staple consumer imports increased relatively; in 1956, capital goods imports rose, and intermediate imports fell relatively.

18. In contrast, the Instituto de Economía [1963: Table 243] suggests that for the shorter period of their study, i.e., 1950–59, variations in postponable imports exceeded those in nonpostponable imports.

19. If the categories of machinery and equipment and of transportation-related investment goods are combined, the index of variation exceeds a similar one for combined consumption imports.

20. PLD-EERs give the imported price relative to domestic alternatives for the importer if the appropriate domestic price is used as the deflator. Therefore, they are the most appropriate of these relative prices to use in import functions. As is indicated in section 2.2 and chapters 3 and 5, however, PLD-EERs are very costly to estimate for Chilean disaggregates, as are the import premiums—which also would be of interest in these functions. Alternative relative prices, hence, are utilized in some of these functions.

21. These elasticities are based on the assumption that EERs change proportionately to the general NER. For transportation equipment the sign of the elasticity is negative despite the positive coefficients in Table 6.3 because those coefficients are for the inverse of the levels.

22. Multicollinearity with other variables also might make such price responses difficult to identify. It does not appear to be a problem, however, in these cases.

23. The differences in price responses among the six import categories, moreover, point to the difficulties of estimating Chilean import functions on even more aggregate levels, as Corbo [1971:192–196] and Ffrench-Davis [1971:297–314] have attempted. The relatively low price elasticities obtained by the latter apparently in part reflect the aggregation over a wide range of policies and over responses which vary among categories.

24. The inclusion of investment for investment imports might cause problems of interpretation if Mamalakis [1971b] is correct that the level of investment depended on the level of such imports, and not vice versa. This activity index does not have a significantly nonzero coefficient in any case, so it is not included in the results in Table 6.3.

25. Imports in fact are determined simultaneously with total credit. The latter depends partially on the size of foreign-exchange reserves which, in turn, depend partially on imports.

26. The increase in consumption imports which accompanied the redistribution of income in favor of labor under the Allende government also may raise doubts about Pinto's hypothesis. At the same time, however, expectations were altered drastically in a way that might account for the import splurge.

27. Díaz-Alejandro [1974] uses the alternative hypothesis that restrictions were increased when reserves fell below some desired level. The more constant the desired level, the more this hypothesis is like the one in the text for estimation purposes.

28. Another necessary assumption is that the adjustment process is well represented by a geometric distributed lag.

29. The Houthakker-Taylor inventory effect cannot be derived exactly from neoclassical theory. This should be intuitively clear from the lack of an interest rate in their formulation. The added precision obtained by utilizing a theoretically somewhat more satisfactory formulation in this case, however, would be misleading because of the quality of the data. Therefore, the original Houthakker-Taylor form is adopted.

30. For this category the lagged adjustment in Table 6.3 results in a two-year cycle in simulation 2.3.1. Machinery and equipment imports undergo an even slower adjustment in the estimates in Table 6.3, but a cycle is not generated for this category.

31. The largest elasticity recorded, however, is a value of −9.2 in the second year for transportation-related investment imports.

Chapter 7

The Behavior of Merchandise Exports

The focus of this chapter is on merchandise exports. The purpose is to explore the general questions raised at the start of Chapter 6. The organization of the chapter also is parallel to that of Chapter 6: section 7.1 is on patterns of exports since the Great Depression; section 7.2 is on the impact of the foreign trade regimes on exports, and is based on the results of partial- and general-equilibrium analysis.

SUMMARY AND CONCLUSIONS

i. The relative importance of exports in the Chilean economy has been much less since the Great Depression than before. Exports per capita have never again attained their pre-1931 peak levels. Exports relative to GDP have been about a fourth of what they were in 1900–30.

ii. The declines in exports primarily reflect changes in international markets. Chilean policy, however, also has been an important causal factor. Across the board, exports have declined in response to the low and secularly falling PLD-EERs. They have fallen further, moreover, because of the indirect effects of increased quantitative restrictions. Thus, policies originally adopted in part because of export pessimism have in fact lessened the foreign-exchange contribution of exports.

iii. The relative variance of total exports—in contrast to that for imports—has fallen since the Great Depression. The regimes of recent decades at least permitted, if not caused, some of this reduction.

iv. Phase-coincident patterns in exports have been very limited for two reasons: external market conditions, especially for copper, often have been more influential than Chilean policies; and the sharp breaks in policies that delineate phases have been directed much more toward foreign-exchange demands than supplies. In fact, the evidence suggests less that exports responded strongly to changes in phases than that changes in phases were in part a response to fluctuations in real export revenues.

v. Success in promoting nontraditional exports has been very limited even though exports of the nontraditional industries [1] have been more responsive to price-related and quantitative policies than those of any other sector. The problem has been precisely that nontraditional exports have reacted most strongly to the general discrimination against exports. The policies affecting them, moreover, have been altered much more frequently than those for other exports. Attempts to promote these exports, while moving in the right direction, have not been of sufficient magnitude to offset the effects of overvaluation of the escudo.

vi. The record in regard to large-scale copper mining—the dominant traditional export—has been mixed. In its last years, about 1950–56, the fixed NER policy for legal costs of production came closer to maximizing Chilean revenue per unit of copper than to maximizing total revenues, without any other obvious compensating advantages. The price-fixing agreement of the Second World War and the Chilean sales monopoly of 1952–54 also on net apparently worked to Chile's disadvantage. The *Nuevo Trato* of 1955 resulted in an increase in the volume of exports, but a reduction in the value returned to Chile. The longer-run effects are difficult to disentangle, although net investment did increase.

The policy of setting a Chilean producer price and the programs of Chileanization and nationalization have been more successful. They permitted Chile to share substantially in the benefits of the Vietnam War–related copper boom of the late 1960s. The Frei policies of Chileanization and nationalization were followed by substantial capital inflows for expanding industrial capacity. A negative effect of these changes, however, is that Chile apparently now is in the position of being a more marginal supplier in the world copper market—and thus subject to greater fluctuations than before in its copper trade.

vii. Chilean governments have sought greater diversification of export markets for three reasons: to lower the risks of being subjected to market fluctuations; to reduce the possibilities of political and economic dominance; and to increase interchange with other Latin American countries. In recent decades efforts to diversify markets have had some successes. The dominance of the United States, in particular, has dropped considerably. Japan and a number of European countries have increased their shares substantially. Regional outlets, however, have not become very important despite the formation of LAFTA and the Andean Group.

viii. Exports broadly responded to the lessened uncertainty about future PLD-NER developments because of the sliding-peg NER policy of 1965–70. Although all but one export category responded significantly, however, the magnitude of such responses was not very large. In fact, the disincentive to exports because of the generally declining PLD-NER for these years probably more than offset the inducements due to greater certainty.

ix. Partial-equilibrium elasticity estimates for exports—as for imports—are misleading indices of the degree of general-equilibrium responses unless foreign-exchange movements and other indirect effects can be neutralized.

7.1 EXPORT PATTERNS SINCE 1930

7.1.1 Aggregate Merchandise Exports.

GENERAL CHARACTERISTICS.

The catastrophic impact of the Great Depression on the Chilean economy was noted in section 1.3. The evaporation of export markets was a major cause of this disaster. In response, the government adopted the more restrictive international economic policies described in chapters 3 and 4.

An important feature of these subsequent foreign trade regimes has been the maintenance of a substantial discrepancy between the effective return on imports and that on exports. For the 1946–70 period, for example, the ratio of the PLD-EER(PI) of imports to that of exports averaged 1.53 (column 6 in Table 5.2). ITRs and EPRs for the 1960s also reflect this same bias (Table 5.3).

As a result of changed world market conditions *and* the Chilean policy of discrimination against exports, the ratio of exports to GDP since 1930 has been about a fourth of that in the previous three decades (line 1.2.6.8 in Table A.1). As of 1973, 1929 exports per capita still had not been surpassed. The secular exponential growth rate of real exports for 1940–65, moreover, was about a fourth of that for imports (Table A.2).[2]

It is important to emphasize again that this lackluster export performance in part reflects the bias against exports in the trade regimes. Export pessimism, thus, somewhat ironically led to policies that resulted in lower exports than otherwise would have occurred (see section 7.2).

Not only the levels of total real exports but their fluctuations have been a matter of concern. In contrast to imports, relative variations in the constant-dollar value of exports were lower after 1930 than before.[3] In this respect, then, the more restrictive regimes apparently had some success.

PHASE-COINCIDENT PATTERNS.

Phase-coincident patterns for the PLD-EER(PI) ratio of imports to exports are not very clear. The respective means of this ratio for the 1946–55 and 1962–64 Phase II periods were 1.60 and 1.63 (based on column 6 in Table 5.2). For the more liberal phases the means were 1.66 for 1956–58, 1.66 for 1959–61, and 1.26 for 1965–69. Except for the substantial drop during the Frei liberalization attempt of the late 1960s, therefore, average discrimination against exports apparently did not vary significantly among the post-World War II phases. The policies that sharply distinguish these phases from each other affected much more the level and variance of the premium on foreign exchange in domestic use (subsection 5.1.1) than the discrepancy between the average effective returns (premiums included) on imports and exports.

Phase-coincident movements in the constant-dollar value of merchandise exports or in the growth rates of exports are not strong.[4] The data in line 1.1 of Table 8.1, for example, imply average annual percentage growth rates of the mean of the current phase or subphase over that of the previous one of −2.7 for 1956–58, 1.0 for 1959–61, and 13.1 for 1965–70 (all movements to more liberal phases); and 3.2 for 1962–64 and −4.2 for 1971 [5] (both changes to more restrictive phases). The regression for total exports shown in Table A.2 implies significant negative deviations from the 1940–65 secular growth rate both for the Phase II years of 1940–55 and the Phase III years of 1956–58.

The lack of phase-associated patterns reflects both the low correlation, noted above, between the average degree of discrimination against exports and that against imports and the substantial influence of changes in international markets, especially for copper, on movements in the constant-dollar value of exports, an influence that is quite independent of the degree of restrictiveness of Chilean policies.

WITHIN-PHASE PATTERNS.

Within-phase patterns in the ratio of the PLD-EER(PI) for imports to that for exports, as noted in subsection 5.1.2, were distinct for each of the phases. In the first year of each of the three liberalization attempts, for example, this ratio dropped (column 6 in Table 5.2). Subsequently, it increased substantially as the attempt faltered in one case (1956–58), decreased significantly in a second (1965–70), and did not change much in the third (1957–61).

At least two within-phase patterns in the constant-dollar value of exports themselves might be expected to be observed: [6]

i. In anticipation of the devaluation which generally accompanies a new phase, in the last year of each phase there might be increased diversion of exportables from current exports into speculative inventories. The constant-dollar value of merchandise exports, in fact, did drop in the last year of each of the three more liberal phases: by 11.7 per cent in 1958, 8.8 per cent in 1961, and 8.7 per cent in 1970. In contrast, however, it increased in the last year of each of the more restrictive phases: by 18.4 per cent in 1955 and 18.3 per cent in 1964. This over-all pattern suggests an alternative explanation. Given the very limited foreign-exchange reserves, a short-run export boom was an important contributing factor in ending more restrictive phases and vice versa.

ii. If the preceding explanation is correct, it would be expected that increased exports would be drawn out of the speculative stocks in the first year of new phases. Such tendencies would be reinforced in the first year of more liberal phases if competing domestic demands for exportables were lessened due to the recession which would accompany attempts at stabilization combined with liberalization (as in 1956 and 1959). For the first year of three of the last five phases, in fact, the constant-dollar value of exports did increase: by 22.1 per cent in 1959, 7.7 per cent in 1962, and 15.2 per cent in 1965. It decreased by 3.5 and 11.7 per cent respectively, however, in 1956 and 1971. The support for these hypotheses thus seems limited.

7.1.2 Disaggregate Merchandise Exports.

7.1.2.1 Destination of Exports.

Diversity of export markets has long been sought by Chilean governments in order to reduce the political and economic dependence of the nation on any particular foreign country; develop stronger regional economic links; and lessen its susceptibility to cyclical fluctuations abroad.[7] Mean percentage distributions of Chilean exports by destination are presented in Table 7.1 for the country's most important trading partners during phases and subphases in 1948–70. In light of the above aims, three features of the data in this table should be noted.

i. The United States remained the most important market throughout the period, but declined substantially in importance after the mid-1950s.[8] In the first decade after the Second World War, the United States received about half of Chilean exports—more than five times as much as any other country. In the 1965–70 phase it absorbed about a fifth, and four other countries each accounted for about half as much.[9] Under the Allende government this share apparently fell further. This large drop in part reflects success at diversification attempts motivated by the first two reasons stated above. For the late 1960s it also reflects the move from United States copper markets to others because the United States price generally was substantially below that which prevailed elsewhere.[10]

TABLE 7.1
Mean Percentage Distribution of Chilean Exports by Destination for Phases and Subphases of 1948–70

Major Trading Partners	1948–51 Phase II	1952–55 Phase II	1956–58 Phase III	1959–61 Phase IV	1962–64 Phase II	1965–70 Phase III
United States	51	53	42	38	35	21
United Kingdom	7	10	15	16	13	14
Federal Republic of Germany	2	7	14	15	12	10
Netherlands	1	2	7	9	8	12
Argentina	5	9	5	4	3	5
Japan	0	0	1	3	8	12
Italy	4	3	4	3	4	7
France	6	1	2	2	2	5
All others	23	14	10	10	16	15

SOURCE: Calculated from data in IMF and IRBD [1949–72]. The countries are listed in order of their mean shares for the entire period.

ii. Japan and the Netherlands increased their shares quite substantially over this period. Italy and France did so in the late 1960s. The United Kingdom and Germany did so earlier, with peaks during 1959–61. These patterns partially reflect relative growth rates in the importing countries.

As a result of these movements, together with the secular decline of exports to the United States, diversification of destinations among the major trading partners increased greatly. At the same time the importance of the rest of the world excluding the eight countries listed in Table 7.1 dropped substantially through the 1950s. It rose again in the 1960s and probably increased further in the early 1970s because of the Allende government's emphasis on regional contacts and on expanding interchange with socialist nations. By the 1965–70 phase, however, this share still was far below the 1948–51 average of 23 per cent. Thus, concentration on the eight major trading partners vis-à-vis the rest of the world accompanied the diversification among these eight.

iii. One aspect of the concentration on the eight major trading countries is that regional markets did not become significant despite the rhetorical emphasis on LAFTA and the Andean Group. Of all Latin American countries only Argentina was a major buyer for the entire period, and its share fluctuated without any strong upward trend in the 1960s.[11] The failure greatly to expand regional markets reflects the generally limited over-all success of the regional movements and the concentration of Chilean exports on copper, for which demand is highly concentrated in the more industrialized countries. For the latter reason the distribution of exports by destination probably did not change dramatically under the Allende government.

7.1.2.2 Origin of Exports by Sector.

The average share of merchandise exports derived from mining in 1946–71 was 83.3 per cent; from manufacturing, 8.5 per cent; and from agriculture, 8.3 per cent. The secular shift in this composition has been away from agriculture and toward mining and industry (lines 1.2.3.1, 1.2.3.2, and 1.2.3.3 in Table A.1). The estimates in Table A.2, in fact, include a negative secular growth rate for the real value of agricultural exports in 1947–65. The rate for mining also is negative or near zero before 1959, but positive thereafter.[12] The point estimate for industry is the highest for the goods sectors, although it has the largest relative variation.

The only important phase-coincident pattern is seen in the regression for industrial exports in Table A.2, which includes a significantly positive response in the first year of each of the three liberalization periods. For exports from this sector, thus, a short-run boom apparently accompanied liberalization because of previous speculative inventory accumulation and recession associated with the efforts at stabilization plus liberalization.

The absence in tables A.1 and A.2 of any other important phase-coincident regularities is not surprising, since (i) export composition depended heavily on conditions in the world copper market and (ii) policies toward exports and domestic competition for exportables varied substantially among the more liberalized phases (see sections 4.2 and 9.2). It is interesting to note, however, the impact of these factors on fluctuations in various categories of exports. The ratio of the standard deviation from the secular trend of exports in a category to the mean for that category provides an index of the degree of relative variation. The categories in order of increasing values of the ratios for 1946–65 are large-scale mining, 0.13; agriculture, 0.20; small-scale mining, 0.29; and manufacturing, 0.41.

Variations have been smallest relatively in mining, especially large-scale mining, in part because Chile has had some market power over copper, but not over any other exports. Therefore, reduced export quantities of copper may have been offset somewhat by increased prices.[13] Another consideration is that policies toward large-scale copper mining were relatively constant during the two decades following the Second World War except for the Chilean sales monopoly in 1952–53 and the enactment of the *Nuevo Trato* in 1955 (subsection 4.2.1). For other exports, including those derived from small- and medium-scale mining, policies changed with much greater frequency.

Variations in agricultural exports have been relatively small. This result is somewhat surprising because quantitative restrictions have been used more to limit exports from agriculture than from any other sector (subsection 4.2.2).

The largest variations by far have been in manufacturing. Apparently, this result reflects the marginal position of Chile as a supplier of industrial goods in international markets, the relatively great frequency with which policies affecting these products have been changed, and the considerable fluctuation in the competition for domestic use of these exportables.

Finally, the sectoral ordering of relative fluctuations in PLD-EER(PIs), shown in Table A.8, appears to be unrelated to variations in exports.

7.1.2.3 COPPER.

The dominant Chilean export since the Great Depression has been copper. For 1960–70, for example, it accounted for an average of 81 per cent of the value of exports from mining and 70 per cent of the value of total merchandise exports.[14]

The effect of government policy toward large-scale copper mining in the last four decades, discussed in section 4.2.1, has been a secular, although not monotonic, increase in Chilean control over this key export:

i. From the 1930s until the *Nuevo Trato* of 1955 large-scale copper companies faced increasingly discriminatory exchange-rate treatment for local costs of production. Between 1939 and 1955, the PLD-NER for these costs declined by 97 per cent(column 1 in Table 3.2)! Reynolds [1965:378] calculates that this NER treatment, together with tax policies and the Chilean sales monopoly, caused the share of the gross value of large-scale copper mining exports returned to Chile to increase from 28 per cent in 1937 to an average of 93 per cent for 1952–54! Therefore, Chilean terms of trade of copper adjusted for the proportion of total value actually returned to the country increased greatly in the quarter-century after 1930 (and the averages after 1940 exceeded pre-Depression levels). This occurred despite a secular decline in the unadjusted terms of trade (at least until 1952–55) and despite the fact that the highest subphase mean for the unadjusted terms of trade in this quarter-century was only 63 per cent of the 1915–30 average (lines 1.1.5.1 and 1.1.5.2 in Table A.1).

These policies came closer to maximizing Chilean government revenue per unit of large-scale copper mining exports than to maximizing total Chilean revenue from large-scale copper mining exports. To illustrate this point, consider the highly simplified, short-run (i.e., fixed capacity) situation in which the objective of Chile is to maximize its revenue. Revenue is by definition the product of the quantity of copper exports, the world copper price, and the average returned value rate equivalent to the net effects of all relevant government policies. For simplicity, all quantities are assumed to be exported. Assume that copper exports are a function of the price net of returned value (P^*). Relation 7.1 gives the revenue-maximizing average returned value rate ($ARVR$) as a function of the supply elasticity (E_{SP^*}) and the demand elasticity (E_{DP}).

$$ARVR = 1/[1+E_{SP^*}+(E_{SP^*}/E_{DP})] \qquad (7.1)$$

On the basis of the estimates in Table 7.1, E_{SP^*} is about 0.3. On the basis of the Chilean market share and world demand estimates, E_{DP} generally is assumed to be about −4.0. For these values the implied revenue-maximizing returned value rate is 0.82.

Although this rate is quite high, it is still below the actual rate for 1952–54.[15] Considerations regarding capacity expansion, employment of domestic factors, or the nature of the bilateral bargaining process between the Chilean government and the large-scale copper mining companies, moreover, may have resulted in a *lower* optimal rate. But it is hard to reconcile rates as high as those in 1952–54 with stated government objectives.[16] The increases of the rates over the previous decade and a half, furthermore, contributed to the decline in the Chilean share of world copper production from 20.2 per cent in 1934 to 11.2 per cent in 1954.[17]

ii. The 1942–46 agreement between the Chilean and United States governments to fix copper prices resulted in a considerable reduction of returned export value to Chile and a shift of real resources to the United States. Reynolds [1965:240] reports estimates of the loss to Chile as high as $500 million. He characterizes such a figure as "undoubtedly exaggerated," since it is more than 160 per cent of the total returned value for 1941–45. Nevertheless, the cost to Chile clearly was considerable. When the agreement was terminated, at the end of 1946, the price of copper approximately doubled immediately. Full responsibility for the loss, of course, should not fall on the Chilean government. It probably would have found it almost impossible to resist United States pressures for participation in this "wartime effort."

iii. After the decline of active hostilities in Korea, the Chilean sales monopoly found it difficult to find buyers at 35.5 cents per pound. Therefore, sales fell off and inventories accumulated. During the period from 1952 to 1954, when either the monopoly or the Washington Treaty (signed in 1951) was in effect, additions to inventories averaged 14 per cent of production, as contrasted with 4 per cent for the previous four years. By far the largest shortfall from the secular growth rate of total quantities exported implied by the regression in Table A.2, moreover, occurred in 1953.[18] Because of these sales difficulties the monopoly was abandoned in early 1954.

Moran [1970:88–90] explains the failure of this effort partially by shortcomings on the Chilean side. He claims that the Chilean government did not appreciate how thin the wartime copper market was, how limited was its own expertise, how difficult it was to locate new customers, and how closely wartime customers who were looking for marginal purchases had remained tied to their traditional suppliers for their basic purchases. But he also claims that the governments of the traditional producers were opposed to the Chilean policy and apparently caused the International Materials Conference to deduct purchases of Chilean copper from the quotas granted to United Nations allies at the lower ceiling price. He furthermore suggests that Anaconda and Kennecott (the major owners of Chilean large-scale copper mines) searched out potential Chilean customers to sell to at the United States ceiling price in order to disrupt the Chilean effort and protect their own established markets.

iv. The *Nuevo Trato* was signed in 1955. The effect of the new arrangements was to increase the volume of copper production. During 1945–54, Chilean production had dropped by almost 30 per cent. The Chilean share in world production had fallen from 19.7 per cent in 1945 to 11.2 per cent in 1954. In the decade after the signing, production rose steadily to 78 per cent above the 1954 level.[19] The Chilean share in world production increased to as high as 15.1 per cent in 1959.

Despite the increase in the volume of copper production and exports, the short-run impact of the new treatment of large-scale mining probably was to reduce the total value returned to Chile (as opposed to total export value). The short-run (i.e., fixed capacity) impact of the *Nuevo Trato* can be investigated crudely by comparing various characteristics of the 1954 situation with those of 1956–58.[20] Returned value per dollar of sales decreased from 91 per cent to 56 per cent, physical product increased 32.2 per cent, Chile's share of world copper production increased from 12.6 to 13.9 per cent, the price of copper increased 28.8 per cent, and the returned value increased 3.8 per cent. Using the Fisher, Cootner, and Baily [1972] estimate of 0.11 for the Chilean short-run price elasticity, a rough calculation indicates that had the price remained constant the absolute value returned to Chile would have declined by almost 20 per cent.[21] This result only reflects the effect of the *Nuevo Trato* in reducing the average returned value rate substantially below the revenue-maximizing level calculated above.

Longer-run considerations, of course, may have offset the negative short-run impact on Chilean control of foreign resources. A comparison of the 1956–58 values for large-scale copper mining with those for 1952–54 indicates that gross investment increased 146 per cent, gross investment minus amortization rose 129 per cent, the ratio of gross investment to after-tax profits rose from 80 to 90 per cent, and the ratio of gross investment to after-tax profits plus amortization increased from 69 to 73 per cent. A comparison of the decade before the *Nuevo Trato* with that immediately after reveals that the constant-dollar value of gross investment increased by 95 per cent and the constant-dollar value of gross investment minus amortization rose by 50 per cent.[22]

These increases suggest that the longer-run benefits to Chile of the *Nuevo Trato* offset the shorter-run losses. To settle the issue more care would have to be taken to preserve ceteris paribus assumptions, and it would be necessary to identify the time path of additional returns to foreign owners that are due to any further investments. Such an attempt is not made here because of the considerable difficulties involved. However, it is important to note that the results of the *Nuevo Trato* were not so positive as to cause it to be exempt from Chilean criticism. To the contrary, attacks on it intensified over the years.

v. In 1964 the Chilean producer price was made independent of the United States producer price. In 1964 the difference between the two prices was never more than 2.0 cents a pound, and the former averaged 0.6 cents per pound less than the latter and 13.3 cents per pound less than the LME price. In 1965 the Chilean price averaged 0.7 cents per pound above the United States price, but 23.2 cents per pound below the LME price. In 1966 CODELCO broke sharply from the United States price by setting the Chilean price equal to the LME price. Over the next five years, 1966–70, the Chilean price exceeded the steadily increasing United States price by an average of 13.2 cents per pound.

The immediate positive impact of this policy on Chilean control of foreign exchange was considerable. Together with the changes in taxes, surtaxes, and government participation in this phase, it enabled Chile to partake very substantially of the returns from the Vietnam War-related copper market boom.[23] In this respect, the contrast with the Second World War and the early years of the Korean conflict was striking. As a result, ECLA [1970:153] reports, mean annual current-dollar returned earnings in 1965–69 were more than 80 per cent above those of the previous phase. In fact, this increased inflow probably was the single most important factor permitting continuing liberalization during the six years of the Frei administration.[24]

The long-run impact of the new pricing policy is less clearly positive. Moran [1970] hypothesizes that the new pricing policy (together with other changes in the Chilean copper sector, once again) may place Chile in the role of a marginal supplier in the world copper market.[25] In such a position she may reap more from booms, but also be subjected to much greater fluctuations than in the past. That the Chilean price has been below the United States price for much of the time from mid-1970 to the present provides some confirmation of Moran's hypothesis.

vi. The programs of Chileanization and nationalization undertaken by the Frei government in the late 1960s raised the Chilean share of gross profits from large-scale copper mining to about 80 per cent because of direct government participation in addition to direct taxes and surtaxes. The nationalization of July 1971 extended that share to 100 per cent. In a direct sense, ceteris paribus, these measures clearly increased the Chilean short-run command over foreign resources.

The Frei programs also caused a substantial rise in net foreign investment in large-scale mining. These flows had been negative in the previous two phases (line 10.1 in Table 8.1) and averaged −$36.1 million in 1965–66.[26] After the agreements of 1967, however, they reversed to a mean level of $19.6 million in 1967–69. The Chileanization program also resulted in a mean increase of $40.8 million in other private long-term capital inflows between these two subphases and probably in additional increases in net capital inflows to the Chilean government (lines 12 and 13.1 in Table 8.1). Gross investment in large-scale copper mining in 1967–69, moreover, exceeded by more than 10 per cent the total at any time since the *Nuevo Trato*. The goal of these investments was to expand capacity to 23 per cent above the 1964–69 level by 1970 and to 71 per cent by 1972. Until the end of the Frei administration the necessary investment appeared to be occurring almost on schedule, although some lags were evident.

In several areas, therefore, the Frei programs seemed to have been successful. In a bilateral monopoly situation, however, it is usually possible to quibble with the terms of the solution and hypothesize that the Chilean government could have done better. In fact, the Chilean leftist Radomiro Tomic (the Christian Democratic candidate for president in 1970) and others did so.[27] Moreover, the Chileanization and nationalization programs combined with the pricing policy may have made Chile a more marginal supplier in the world market (see above).

Under the Allende government copper did not provide the hoped for expansion of foreign exchange. Part of the explanation for the shortfall lay in lower world copper prices. The average Chilean price for 1971–72, for example, was 22 per cent below that for 1970, a decline which more than offset the 8.2 per cent increase in the volume of Chilean copper production in the same year.

A more important factor, however, was that copper production did not expand nearly as rapidly as had been planned for. The 1971 quantity, for example, was less than 80 per cent of that predicted in the 1971 ODEPLAN [1971b:17] plan. Two new mines (Exótica and Andina) commenced production at annual rates of 50,000 metric tons in that year, but output in the three previously existing major mines fell by 9 per cent, offsetting almost half of the increment from the new sources.

It is not clear to what extent realized production was lower than anticipated because of government policy. Government officials and sympathetic observers suggested that the causes of the delayed expansion included technical problems,[28] flooding and power shortages resulting from severe weather, shortages of equipment and parts due to a lack of cooperation from United States suppliers, and maltreatment of the physical plant by former owners in anticipation of nationalization. On the other hand, a wide range of observers, including Allende and other members of his government, pointed to problems in large-scale mining which arose partially from changes in the international or over-all economic policy regimes: the exodus of several hundred skilled engineers and other technicians whose real wages were reduced because of the shift from dollar to escudo remunerations or who were charged with being "politically unreliable" by political splinter groups; political squabbles among labor groups identified with political parties both within and outside of the governing coalition; assignment of positions not on the basis of merit but on the basis of political identification; and substantial increases in costs because of bad management, lack of labor discipline, strikes (including, in May 1972 at Chuquicamata, the first general strike since 1966), and the failure of the copper workers (Chile's labor aristocracy) to make the sacrifices required to achieve the objectives of socialism.[29]

Because of the coup of September 1973, future over-all developments in the Chilean economy are very uncertain at the time of this writing. The possibilities of substantially expanded foreign-exchange earnings from copper, however, seem to be good. World copper prices have increased from the relatively low levels of 1971 and 1972 and are likely to remain in a somewhat higher range for the near future.[30] The realization of large production increments at a relatively small marginal cost seems quite possible because of the as yet unrealized potential from the investment program initiated in 1967.

7.1.2.4 Nontraditional Exports.

There has been increasing policy emphasis on nontraditional exports in recent phases, especially during the Frei government, under which the sliding-peg NER, special credit programs, expanded drawbacks, and inducements for related investments were instituted (see subsection 4.2.2).

Comparisons of export values before and after the major development of policies favoring nontraditional exports in 1967 does not indicate great success for these programs. For a few products large positive shifts were recorded. The mean annual value of paper, cellulose, and related exports, for example, rose from $9.8 million in 1963–66 to $25.8 million in 1967–70 (and averaged 27 per cent of industrial exports in the latter period).[31] In a number of cases, however, the current-dollar values of affected exports actually fell.[32] For some other items (largely agricultural), Jul [1969:143] notes that the increment in export value was less than the change in drawbacks paid. Total industrial exports in constant dollars declined 3 per cent from 1963–66 to 1967–70, and agricultural exports fell 9 per cent.[33]

Why did nontraditional exports perform so poorly? A large part of the answer is that policy continued to discriminate against them.[34] Any advantage granted by drawbacks and special credits was more than offset by substantial overvaluation. The export-related ITRs and EPRs were significantly less than those for imports and were negatively associated with the importance of exports in subsectoral product.[35] Only for a few products for a short period of time did the drawbacks offset the overvaluation as estimated by Bacha and Taylor [1973].[36] The export-promotion program in essence offered a small reduction in discrimination against exports—and that reduction was probably widely perceived as transitory. The decreasing PLD-NER for 1968–70 (column 13 in Table 3.2) provides support for that perception.

7.2 ECONOMETRIC MEASURES OF THE RESPONSES OF EXPORTS TO THE REGIMES

In the remainder of this chapter, I attempt to determine the nature of export responses to recent regimes within the framework of specific structural relationships: partial-equilibrium analysis in subsection 7.2.1, general-equilibrium analysis in subsection 7.2.2.

7.2.1 Partial-Equilibrium Responses.

Table 7.2 contains single-equation estimates for exports from the goods-producing sectors for 1947–65. Mining is subdivided into large scale and small and medium scale because the two parts are treated differently.

On an over-all level these results appear to be reasonably satisfactory. The point estimates generally are of the anticipated sign, and problems of serial correlation are not apparent (but see note a). The corrected coefficients of determination ($\bar{R}^2$) indicate that variations in the hypothesized determinants are consistent with from 74 to 96 per cent of the variations in sectoral real exports. Small- and medium-scale mining has the highest $\bar{R}^2$ followed by large-scale mining alternative a, agriculture, large-scale mining alternative b, and industry. The weak suggestion of this pattern is that the underlying model may be more consistent with variations in real exports from traditional than from nontraditional sectors.[37]

The basic model hypothesizes that current real sectoral exports depend on relative price factors, quantitative supply factors, quantitative demand factors, and lagged real sectoral exports.

Relative price terms include both levels and standard deviations. The latter is justified as a crude proxy for uncertainty. The underlying price ratios themselves are of three types: (i) the ratio of the product of the external price

TABLE 7.2

Sectoral Real Export Functions[a] for Chile, 1947–65

Sector	Relative Prices: Level 1	Relative Prices: Level 2	Relative Prices: Level 3	Relative Prices: Stand. Dev.	Quantitative Supply Factors 1	Quantitative Supply Factors 2	Quantitative Demand Factors 1	Quantitative Demand Factors 2	Lagged Exports	Constant	$\bar{R}^2$ / *SE* / *DW*
Agriculture	39.2[b]	6.72[c]		−17.5[b]	49.8[d]	0.0531[e]	42.6[f]			−103.0	0.87
	(9.1)	(2.6)		(1.6)	(1.4)[g]	(2.3)	(5.5)			(2.1)	11.5
	[0.5]	[0.1]		[−0.0]	[0.4]	[0.6]	[0.2]				1.6
Mining											
Large-scale (a)	6.83[h]	1.34[i]		−306.0[j]	−190.0[k]	−1,454.0[l]			−0.379	2,737.0	0.91
	(7.8)	(6.2)		(4.1)	(3.6)	(5.0)			(3.8)	(9.4)	46.9
	[0.2]	[0.1]		[−0.1]	[−0.0]	[−1.0]					1.8
Large-scale (b)	7.99[h]	1.58[i]		−332.0[j]	−218.0[k]				−0.557	1,363.0	0.75
	(5.6)	(4.4)		(2.7)	(2.4)				(3.5)	(8.6)	78.9
	[0.2]	[0.1]		[−0.1]	[−0.0]						2.9
Small- and medium-scale	0.992[m]	25.1[n]			0.106[o]		7.14[p]	11.5[p]		−1,083.0	0.96
	(5.8)	(1.5)[g]			(1.7)[g]		(3.2)	(4.5)		(11.2)	31.9
	[0.4]	[0.4]			[0.0]		[2.1]	[3.2]			2.7
Industry	5,271.0[q]	117.1[n]	40.8[r]	48.8[c]	0.137[e]	−273.0[s]			0.363	−706.0	0.74
	(2.8)	(4.2)	(5.1)	(2.6)	(5.8)	(1.9)			(2.3)	(2.8)	27.7
	[1.0]	[1.9]	[4.4]	[−0.2]	[2.0]	[−1.3]					2.2

Notes to Table 7.2

$\bar{R}^2$ = coefficient of multiple determination adjusted for degrees of freedom.

SE = standard error of estimate.

DW = Durbin-Watson statistic.

a. Data sources and estimation techniques are discussed in Chapter 2 and in Appendix A. The figures in parentheses are the absolute values of the t statistics. All point estimates are significantly nonzero at the 5 per cent level unless otherwise noted. The figures in brackets are the long-run elasticities at the point of sample means. These elasticities are long run in the sense that all adjustments due to the inclusion of lagged imports are assumed to have occurred. For such relationships in which the lagged import value is included, the Durbin-Watson statistic is biased toward 2.0.

b. Ratio of unit value of sectoral exports multiplied by the exchange rate to the sectoral labor price including employer social security contributions.

c. Black-market PLD-NER minus national accounts PLD-NER.

d. Sectoral output relative to sectoral output lagged.

e. Sectoral GDP.

f. Dummy variable for LAFTA (value of 1.0 in 1961 and thereafter).

g. Significantly nonzero at the 10 per cent level.

h. Ratio of United States producer price for copper adjusted for direct tax rate on mining to index of intermediate prices for mining adjusted for the NER for large-scale mining.

i. Ratio of United States producer price for copper adjusted for direct tax rate on mining to price of labor in mining including employer social security contributions.

j. PLD-NER.

k. Post-Korean War Chilean sales monopoly dummy variable with value of 1.0 in 1953.

l. Ratio of total GDP lagged one year to total GDP lagged two years.

m. Same as i, but lagged one year.

n. PLD-NER lagged one year.

o. First difference of sectoral GDP.

p. Factor 1 is an index of industrial activity in the United States. Factor 2 is the same index lagged one year.

q. Ratio of unit value of sectoral exports multiplied by the exchange rate to domestic sectoral product price.

r. Same as c, but lagged one year.

s. Sectoral capacity utilization.

(or unit value) and the NER (adjusted for unit direct tax rates in the case of mining) to factor costs (intermediate or labor costs, the latter adjusted for employers' social security taxes); (ii) the ratio of the product of the external price and the NER to the domestic market price; and (iii) ratios relating to various PLD-NERs. The last group of ratios may be thought to be redundant because it is incorporated in the others. This third group, however, does seem to provide information about the most volatile element in the other ratios. In the cases in which the black-market NER is involved, moreover, it provides a measure of an added incentive for exporting (perhaps accompanied by some such action as underinvoicing) beyond that captured by the other two types of ratios. Thus more than one type of relative price ratio is allowed in the estimates.

The estimates in Table 7.2 suggest that significant responses to both price levels and standard deviations are widespread. All three types of price ratio mentioned above are relevant. The implied elasticities are fairly substantial for some sectors. For example, the elasticities with respect to the general NER are 2.9 for industry, 0.8 for small- and medium-scale mining, 0.5 for agriculture, and 0.3 for large-scale mining.[38]

In general, price reactions were more pervasive for exports than for imports (subsection 6.2.1). The estimates indicate that the secular decline in the PLD-NER caused substantial foreign-exchange losses through reduced exports.[39] Ceteris paribus, the foregoing elasticities and the 63 per cent drop in the over-all PLD-NER between 1946 and 1972, for example, imply complete elimination of exports from industry; and drops of 50 per cent from small- and medium-scale mining; 32 per cent from agriculture; and 19 per cent from large-scale mining.

The nontraditional industrial exports were particularly responsive to price. The maintenance of a disequilibrium exchange-rate system with an overvalued exchange rate, therefore, especially discouraged these exports.[40] In this manner the effect of the post-World War II regimes has been to increase relative dependence on the traditional exports even though one persistent underlying motive supposedly was to reduce their dominance. As is noted above, the export-promotion programs started in the 1960s were not very effective because they only partially compensated for overvaluation.

The price response of large-scale mining exports, in contrast, was relatively small. The result is consistent with an earlier contention that the benefits to Chile of the more favorable treatment of this subsector initiated by the *Nuevo Trato* of 1955 probably were quite limited.

For all export sources except small- and medium-scale mining, the estimates suggest a significant negative response to the standard deviation term. A policy to reduce uncertainty regarding future real returns from exports thus would have a widespread payoff in the form of increased exports. The sliding-peg NER of 1965–70 was such a policy. Although the payoff was widespread across sectors, however, the elasticities imply that it was limited in magnitude.

Quantitative supply factors include levels and indices of marginal changes of real sectoral outputs (to find out whether the availability of sectoral real product affected sectoral exports); sectoral capacity-utilization rates and measures of over-all aggregate demand (to find out whether in sectors with low demand—and thus low sectoral capacity utilization—there were increased attempts to sell to external markets); the Ffrench-Davis quantitative restrictions index (to find out whether QRs either on imported inputs or on particular exports limited the levels of aggregate sectoral exports); and dummy variables such as one for the period of the Chilean sales monopoly in mining after the Korean War.

The results support the claim that there were important reactions to these quantitative supply factors. Marginal changes in output caused significant and, in most cases, substantial responses in exports from agriculture, small- and medium-scale mining, and industry. The state of capacity utilization reinforced this effect in industry. The continuance of the Chilean copper sales monopoly in the face of declining demand after the end of the Korean War was associated with a fall of approximately 20 per cent in the real value of large-scale mining exports.

Large-scale mining exports also seem to have been significantly and strongly negatively related to the lagged rate of growth in over-all GDP. This relation can be interpreted in several ways: (i) In periods of general stagnation inputs were more readily available for this subsector than was otherwise the case. (ii) In recessions the government more vigorously pursued policies to induce an expansion of exports from large-scale mining in order to increase aggregate demand generally and in order to obtain income to offset reduced tax revenues from the rest of the economy. (iii) In cyclical downturns the rate of inflation was less, ceteris paribus; so the PLD-EER for such exports was more favorable. (iv) At those times competing demands for domestic uses were less; so a higher proportion of production was exported.[41]

All of these rationales have some merit—although, in some cases, only if the hypothesized effect is not really better represented by some other variable included in the regression which a priori would seem more logical (e.g., for iii, the price ratios). That the total effect of such factors was as large as is implied by the data in Table 7.2, however, is somewhat doubtful. Therefore, this table also contains an alternative relationship which is identical except for the exclusion of this one variable.

Despite widespread evidence regarding the importance of supply considerations, finally, no significant response to quantitative restrictions is reported. This lack of statistical evidence does not definitely indicate that QRs had no impact on exports. For example, since QRs were applied to only a few specific products, their effect may be obscured by aggregation. Variations in the QR index, moreover, might not well represent possible negative effects on the competitiveness of Chilean exports. Inefficiencies may have been fostered by the generally high protective barriers, but may have varied quite slowly in response to changing QRs.

Quantitative demand factors include a dummy variable for the impact of LAFTA and indices of demand in the most important destination countries.[42] The results indicate that only agricultural exports increased with the formation of LAFTA, but they rose by 20 per cent of the mean real export value for the entire sample period.

The structuralist school (e.g., Sierra [1969:62]) has placed considerable emphasis on the role of fluctuations in the importing countries. Statistical support for this hypothesis is observed only for small- and medium-scale mining. The explanation for this result may be that this subsector was relatively a marginal supplier in the markets in which it participated and thus was more subject to demand fluctuations. Small- and medium-scale mining was a marginal supplier because it lacked the intracorporate ties of large-scale mining and because it expanded its productive capabilities relatively quickly and had to find new buyers.

Lagged exports are included to represent either the distributed lag adjustment of actual to desired real sectoral exports over several periods due to adjustment costs or an inventory effect (in the sense that large real sectoral exports one year result in inventory depletion and smaller exports in the subsequent year, ceteris paribus). The a priori expected signs of the two effects are opposite; so they may cancel each other out partially or completely.[43] No attempt is made to identify these effects separately, however, in this study.

The estimates suggest that the inventory effect was dominant in large-scale mining; and the adjustment effect, in industry. In small- and medium-scale mining and in agriculture, the two effects neutralized each other.

7.2.2 General-Equilibrium Responses.

The model described in Chapter 2 once again is used to examine the general-equilibrium impact of specified changes, ceteris paribus. Table A.11 contains the resulting elasticities or proportional deviations. Exogenous price-related changes are analyzed first and then exogenous QR changes.

7.2.2.1 PRICE-RELATED CHANGES.

Simulation 1.1 involves equal proportional variations in all export prices and unit values for the first year of the simulation only. The direct impact of such changes is primarily on exports.

The total general-equilibrium export elasticity is only 0.1 in the first year and 0.2 in the third year. The fairly pervasive partial-equilibrium price responses in Table 7.2—as in the case of imports (subsection 6.2.1.1)—are almost swamped by indirect effects on domestic prices. In the case of exports, however, the problem is clearly not a lack of general price responsiveness. The results in Table 7.2 suggest widespread and, in some cases, substantial reactions to prices. The limited general-equilibrium responsiveness, instead, lies in the inability of the banking system to neutralize the effects of changes in international reserves.

In simulation 2.1.1 equal proportional changes are assumed for all legal exchange rates in the first year of the simulation only. Direct impacts on imports and prices are involved, in addition to those on exports.

The first-year total elasticity—0.2—is somewhat higher than in simulation 1.1, although the third-year response is lower. These differences are marginal, however. The basic thrust of this simulation is to reinforce the view that exports respond hardly at all to changes in NERs, i.e., in this general-equilibrium analysis, exports are inelastic with respect to the hypothesized foreign-trade regime.

In simulation 2.1.3 actual NERs are replaced by the Bacha and Taylor [1973] equilibrium exchange rates—45, 35, and 61 per cent above the national accounts NER for the first three years of the model run. The results again reinforce the findings of general-equilibrium export inelasticity. Despite the quite substantial hypothetical devaluations, exports increase by only 4 per cent in the first year and 6 per cent in the third year. As for imports, moreover, there are apparently diminishing returns to devaluation since the implied aggregate first-year elasticity is less than that for simulation 2.1.1.

On the disaggregate level, also, it is diminishing returns that are generally found. One important exception is industrial exports, for which the first-year elasticity is higher in this simulation than in simulation 2.1.1. In addition, the price responsiveness of the export sectors in the two simulations—industry first, followed by agriculture, and then by large-scale mining—bears out the partial-equilibrium conclusion that the disequilibrium regimes with their overvalued exchange rates discouraged most particularly the industrial exports whose expansion the government supposedly desired.

In simulation 2.5, the question of the price responsiveness of nonmining exports is further pursued by positing a subsidy for agricultural and industrial exports equal to a 10 per cent increase in world prices for these products in the first year of the simulation only. Most of the nontraditional exports and most of the products receiving drawbacks are included in these two sectors (see subsection 4.2.2).

The impact of such a policy is to increase total exports by 0.01 in the first year due to a 0.04 increase in agricultural exports and a 0.18 increase in industrial exports. Note that this implies that in escudo terms the subsidy to agriculture is 2.5 times the increment in exports since all exports (not just marginal ones) are subsidized. This result is consistent with the above-mentioned Chilean experience for a number of products in the late 1960s.[44]

The reactions of other exports and imports are generally quite small. As a result the surplus on current account, net international banking reserves, and Central Bank reserves all rise, and the GDP deflator increases by 0.01. However, in a longer-run sense, control of foreign resources may not be expanded because the enlarged government deficit (due to the subsidies) financed abroad exceeds the increment in the current account.[45] The subsidization of nontraditional exports, thus, would immediately increase control of foreign resources from exports, but the associated greater government deficit would result in greater inflationary pressures or foreign-debt obligations, or both.

Simulation 2.6.1 explores the general-equilibrium price sensitivity of traditional exports by altering the NER for large-scale mining. The elasticity of total exports with respect to this change is 0.2 in both the first and third years. For large-scale mining the elasticities for the two years are 0.3 and 0.2. Interestingly enough, in the third year, as the result of indirect effects related to the over-all increase in economic activity, the elasticities for both agricultural and industrial exports are larger than the elasticity for large-scale mining.

The net responses in the surplus on current account and in net banking system reserves are positive. The responses in government deficit and in government deficit financed abroad also are positive because the government's revenue has risen as a result of the favorable differential on foreign exchange which it purchases from large-scale mining enterprises and then resells.

The indirect effects of altering the NER for large-scale mining have some significant consequences in other major policy areas. Real capacity utilization reacts with an elasticity of 0.1 in the third year. The GDP deflator has an elasticity of 0.2 in the first year owing primarily to the increased international reserves (augmented by the impact of the altered NER on internal large-scale-mining–related prices). Long-run capacity among the goods sectors responds relatively positively in mining, and short-run real product responds more positively in industry and in agriculture. In the income distribution area the most noticeable response is the strong first-year inverse reaction in net factor income from abroad, but inverse reactions also occur for both years in labor income. Among the aggregate growth-related variables some of the responses are positive, although small.

Substantial costs, thus, were incurred by maintaining a fixed NER for large-scale mining for long periods of time (see section 3.2). The gains in lessening inflationary pressures, reducing factor payments abroad, and increasing the labor share of income do not seem to have been sufficient to warrant these costs.

Simulation 2.6.2 further explores the sensitivity of traditional exports to price-related policies by positing that the average direct tax function for large-scale mining is multiplied by 0.9 in the first year only. In response to this tax reduction total exports increase by about 0.01 because of an increase of the same relative value in large-scale mining exports, a somewhat larger proportional increase in industrial exports, and a somewhat smaller proportional increase in agricultural exports. The net impact on the balance on current account is positive, although the reduction in direct large-scale mining taxes (which are paid in dollars) about offsets increased gross dollar export earnings in the first year, with the result that banking system and Central Bank international reserves do not change substantially. Also, because of this tax reduction, the government deficit and the government deficit financed abroad increase slightly.

The effects of this tax reduction on most other major areas of concern are quite small. Some shift in real product toward mining occurs in the first year and toward industry in the third year. A shift in income distribution toward foreigners takes place in the first year. An increase in gross domestic savings is found in the first year. Such effects do not seem to be very substantial (and are not all positive) which reinforces the earlier analyses of the tax reduction in the *Nuevo Trato* (see subsection 7.1.2.3).

7.2.2.2 CHANGES IN QUANTITATIVE RESTRICTIONS.

Simulation 2.3.1 investigates the consequences of equal proportional changes in all the QR indices in the first year only. As is discussed in subsection 7.2.1, there is not statistical evidence of direct export responses to quantitative restrictions. The indirect effects, however, are fairly large. In the first year of the simulation, the total general-equilibrium export elasticity is −0.7. Industrial exports are particularly affected: they have a first-year elasticity of −8.9. Increases in quantitative restrictions prompted by foreign-exchange shortages, thus, exacerbate the situation by causing reductions in foreign-exchange earnings from exports. The exports most affected, moreover, are once again the industrial exports whose expansion supposedly has been most desired by the government.

NOTES

1. Not all nontraditional exports are from industry, but many of the most important ones are.

2. If the time period is extended to include the late 1960s (with the Vietnam War–related copper market boom), however, this discrepancy is much less (see lines 1.1 and 1.2 in Table 8.1).

The data in line 1.2.4.2 of Table A.1 and the growth rate presented in Table A.2 differ in three ways: the 1930s are excluded from the Table A.2 figures; geometric growth rates over the previous year are used in Table A.1 and exponential growth rates are used in Table A.2; and, most important, the Table A.1 data are deflated by the United States GNP deflator, and the Table A.2 data, by a Chilean export price deflator that is dominated by the price of copper. As a result of the last-mentioned difference, the data in Table A.1 are a better measure of the real purchasing power of exports, and the data in Table A.2 better approximate the physical quantity of exports.

3. For example, the mean absolute proportional deviation from the level implied by the exponential trend for the constant-dollar value of exports for 1931–55 is 0.14 (with a standard deviation of 0.14). This is significantly less at the 20 per cent level than the mean of 0.19 (with a standard deviation of 0.24) reported above in section 1.2 for the 1878–1927 phase (under the same assumption as is made there).

4. Phase-coincident patterns are also not obvious in the extent of underinvoicing as measured by the ratio of exports recorded by Chile to imports recorded by destination countries (line 1.2.5.2. in Table A.1). This ratio has its highest and lowest values for Phase II regimes, with those for the more liberal periods falling in between.

5. Banco Central [1972b:310] reports an ODEPLAN estimate that exports in constant escudos increased by 5.7 per cent in 1971. The difference between the constant-

escudo and the constant-dollar estimates is due to the difference between the decline in copper prices and the over-all increase in international prices. For the first three quarters of 1972, Banco Central [1973b:33] reports an increase of 1.5 per cent in the current-dollar value of exports, which implies a fall of about 1.5 per cent in the constant-dollar value.

6. An important qualification of the following analysis is that ceteris paribus conditions are not maintained. Other changes, such as in the terms of trade, might be obscuring the underlying relationships.

7. The assumption has been that such fluctuations are not perfectly correlated among countries; so diversification of destinations results in less fluctuation in exports.

8. The fall in the share of the United States in exports was somewhat greater than the fall in the share in imports noted above in subsection 6.1.2.

9. On an annual basis this decline is even more striking—from 64 per cent in 1953 to 14 per cent in 1970.

10. The ratio of the United States to the London Metal Exchange price averaged 1.04 for 1956–58, 1.03 for 1959–61, 0.93 for 1962–64 (but 1.03 for 1962–63), 0.66 for 1965–70, and 1.04 for 1971.

11. The Brazilian share grew rapidly in the 1960s, but still was less than 2 per cent in 1970. This proportion placed it behind the eight countries in Table 7.1, as well as behind Belgium and Sweden.

12. The late 1960s are not included in these estimates because of problems of data consistency. If they were included, however, the secular trend for mining might exceed that for industry because of the copper-market boom of those years.

13. The price elasticity of demand for Chilean copper is generally assumed to be about −4.

14. In the same period, the share in total merchandise exports of nitrates, the dominant export from 1880 to 1930, was 5 per cent. Within mining this proportion was exceeded not only by copper, but also by iron ore, which had 9 per cent of total gross exports.

15. The elasticity estimates, of course, are subject to statistical error. If E_{SP*} were really as low as 0.1 or E_{DP} as low as 1.3, the actual rate would have been optimal for short-run revenue maximization. The possibility that E_{SP*} was in fact that low is hard to evaluate. The probability that E_{DP} was that low must be quite small since such a value would imply considerably more market power than anyone claims Chile had.

16. One can conceive of objectives with which these rates might have been consistent, e.g., to conserve copper resources for future uses or to drive the companies out of business. Such objectives, however, were not the stated ones of the Chilean government in the early 1950s.

17. For evidence of responses to such policies see subsection 7.2.1 below and Behrman [1972b and 1973a].

The statements in this subsection on Chilean copper production, market shares, investments, etc., are based primarily on Senado, Oficina de Informaciones [1970].

18. For 1953 the proportional deviation from the level (not the logarithm) was −0.20. In the 1940–65 period, the mean absolute deviation was 0.063 (with a standard deviation of 0.049). In only four years—1941, 1948, 1949, and 1951—were absolute proportional deviations even half as large as the deviation for 1953. On the other hand, on the basis of an exponential growth rate for total exports in constant dollars for the entire 1931–55 period, the proportional deviation for 1953 was 0.03. Thus, in that year, although the sales monopoly may have resulted in a fall in export quantities, it apparently did not result in a fall in the constant-dollar purchasing power of exports.

19. Steady increases occurred even though copper prices peaked in 1955 and 1956 at levels which were not exceeded until 1964. The LME price averaged 44.3 cents per pound in 1955, 41.4 cents per pound in 1956, and not above 31.1 cents per pound in 1957–63. The United States producer price averaged 37.5 cents per pound in 1955, 41.8 cents per pound in 1956, and not above 32.1 cents per pound in 1957–64.

20. The year 1954 is used instead of 1955 because the *Nuevo Trato* was enacted in the latter year; 1952 and 1953 are not included with 1954 because of the very special conditions in those years due to the operation of the sales monopoly discussed in the text. Because of the lumpiness of investment, however, in the long-run comparison below the 1952–54 period is used as the base. Sources for the data used in this calculation are Reynolds [1965:378], Senado, Oficina de Informaciones [1971:22], and Behrman [1974].

21. In this calculation it is assumed that the returned value rate would have been the same as it actually was in 1956–58 if production had been lowered due to a lower price. In fact, it probably would have increased somewhat in such circumstances because of the tax structure and because some of the legal costs of production were fixed.

22. A 10 per cent discount rate is used in these calculations. Moran [1970:102] made comparisons in current dollars with a zero discount rate. He then concluded that the long-run impact was negative since by his calculations the dollar value of gross investment minus amortization fell by 33 per cent.

23. Because of the copper boom the United States price in 1965–70 averaged 39 per cent above that in 1962–64, and the LME price averaged 77 per cent higher. Chilean terms of trade therefore increased considerably (line 1.1.5.1 in Table A.1).

24. Ffrench-Davis and Carrasco [1969] suggest instead that the sliding-peg NER policy created sufficient surpluses to permit continued liberalization. They seem to overstate the relative benefits from this NER policy, however, because they assume a "normal" copper price of 40 cents per pound as compared to an average actual price of only 30.7 cents per pound for 1957–64. They also are much more optimistic about the absolute magnitudes of Chilean trade elasticities than seems warranted on the basis of the results reported in sections 6.2 and 7.2. Finally, they ignore the fact that the PLD-NER was quite low (and decreasing in later years) under the sliding-peg NER policy (Table 3.1).

25. The world copper market is segmented because of the pricing policies of United States producers and the existence of a large scrap market. The LME price reflects conditions in a relatively small part of the total market and therefore fluctuates considerably more than the United States price. For more details see Behrman [1970], Fisher, Cootner, and Baily [1972], and McNicol [1972].

26. All the figures cited in this paragraph are in 1958 dollars.

27. Griffin [1969] calculated the present discounted value of net income to the Chilean government resulting from the 1967 Chileanization alone. Although his results probably are biased downward because his estimate of world copper prices is too low, they suggest that from the point of view of control over resources this program was more beneficial than would have been a continuation of previous policies. Nevertheless, he claims that Chile could have done better.

28. Examples included excessive accumulation of sediment at Chuquicamata, adjustment problems for local minerals at El Teniente, geological problems at El Salvador, and an unexpected composition of copper from Exótica which requires more sulfuric acid than the Chuquicamata plant can provide.

29. According to de Onis [1971c] Alejandro Halles, minister of mining in the Frei government, estimated that the production cost of a pound of copper increased from 29 cents in June 1970 to 76 cents in June 1971 primarily because of bad management. Although Halles is referring to the year before the complete nationalization of July 11,

1971, much of the cost increase he cites apparently arose from higher labor costs because of state pressure to expand the labor force and to increase real wage rates (or because of union pressure which the companies felt that they could not resist owing to the known very strong labor sympathies of the government). Note that this cost rise *may* bring into question the charge that in this period the companies were maximizing short-run profits by mining rich ores and ignoring maintenance operations. However, Halles's estimate is not consistent with the statement in October 1971 by Allende that costs per pound had risen to an average of 47 cents since May 1971, which also was reported by de Onis [1971c]. Reconciliation of these estimates is not easy, especially since CODELCO considers all copper cost estimates to be secret information.

Chilean sales in this period were constrained by supply problems. On the demand side, Kennecott's attempts to impound Chilean shipments to Europe were somewhat troublesome. The signing of contracts for substantial shipments to various socialist nations, however, probably basically compensated for any demand difficulties in the traditional markets.

30. For forecasts of developments in the copper market, see Behrman [1970], Fisher, Cootner, and Baily [1972], and Sutulov [1972].

31. The years 1963–66 were not ones during which Chile had a great boom in nontraditional exports; so this comparison is biased against finding a favorable impact of those policies. For 1963–66 as compared to 1950–53, in fact, Balassa and associates [1971:41–42] report that Chile's competitive position (as measured by market shares) deteriorated for minor exports.

32. A few examples include nitrate and iodine products (from a mean of $109.4 million in 1964–66 to one of $79.1 million in 1967–68), molybdenum (from $39.7 million to $34.4 million), fish flour (from $50.1 million to $49.6 million), and semi-elaborated copper (from $126.6 million to $24.4 million).

33. Declines continued under the Allende government in part because of increased domestic competition for these goods. In 1971 the government increased drawbacks by 50 per cent in constant-escudo terms, but the constant-dollar value of embarkations declined for all exports except fresh fruit, fish flour, possibly chemical and metal products, and some minor mining products (but neither copper nor iron). In the first nine months of 1972, the current-dollar value of agricultural and industrial exports, respectively, fell 29 and 14 per cent. The exchange-rate realignment of August 1972, however, was supposed to favor nontraditional exports with high NERs (although data are not yet available with which to evaluate this policy).

34. In section 7.2 evidence is presented of substantial responsiveness of nontraditional exports (especially from industry) to government policies. Baerresen [1966:5–6, 12] gives further evidence for gold and wine in the 1950s. The large fall in the constant-dollar value of nonmonetary gold exports after 1955 (line 2 in Table 8.1) also apparently originated in such a reaction.

35. Changes in ITRs and EPRs between 1961 and 1967 also were not significantly associated with the degree of concentration of production destined for exports (Table A.6).

36. Ffrench-Davis [1971:95] also suggests that the drawback program encouraged inefficiency by giving larger drawbacks to more costly operations. If the drawback rates in fact were based on tax incidence, the basis for this claim is not clear. However, if the establishment of rate levels reflected in part political pressures (such as Jul [1969] claims for many of the category-B products) then Ffrench-Davis may be right.

De Castro and de la Cuadro [1972] also criticize the drawback program for discouraging efficient production because of disparities in the rates among different commodities and for being more uncertain than devaluation because the former policy could be changed at any time (although in Chile, exchange-rate policy also seems to be subject to sudden changes).

37. This interpretation is valid if nontraditional exports are defined to be well-represented by industrial exports and if alternative a for large-scale mining is acceptable. However, industrial exports include traditional exports at least in the sense that many industrial commodities have been exported for decades (see Chapter 1); nontraditional exports certainly include some agricultural commodities and (depending on the definition used) perhaps some mining products; and the acceptability of estimate a for large-scale mining is somewhat questionable. Therefore, the distinction made here between traditional and nontraditional exports is weak.

38. These elasticities refer only to changes in the ratios. It is assumed that the standard deviation and the difference between the PLD-NER for the black-market and the national accounts rate remain unchanged.

39. For most export categories the PLD-EER has moved closely with the PLD-NER.

40. Sierra [1969:85] also emphasizes this point.

41. In that case the variable might better be reclassified as representing quantitative demand.

42. Incorporation of quantitative demand factors makes the results in Table 7.2 for some sources more reduced-form market-clearing relationships than export-supply functions.

43. The two effects have opposite implications for short- and long-run elasticities. If the inventory effect is dominant, the short-run elasticity exceeds the long-run elasticity. The opposite is the case if the adjustment effect is dominant.

44. If the escudo is sufficiently overvalued and the subsidies are given in escudos, the subsidy could be less than the incremental value of exports measured in escudos of equilibrium value.

45. If, alternatively, the increased government deficit were financed internally, the domestic price impact would be greater.

Chapter 8

Other Components of the Balance of Payments

The stress of the two previous chapters was on the effects of recent Chilean international economic regimes on her goods trade. In this chapter, the stress is shifted to the impact of the regimes on, first, services and transfers and then, capital and gold flows.

SUMMARY AND CONCLUSIONS

i. The net balance from aggregate services was quite responsive to changes in the regimes. In reaction to the systematic changes in the PLD-EERs for nongoods transactions, noted earlier, this balance declined substantially during more liberal periods and rose in more restrictive ones.

ii. Variations in service imports accounted for most of these reactions. In part this was because that import category was relatively responsive to policy changes. The partial-equilibrium price and QR elasticities for service imports, for example, were higher than those for two-thirds of the imported goods categories. That service imports were subjected to relatively great variations in policies was another factor. As a result, the relative variations in service imports were high in comparison with those for goods imports and for service exports.

iii. The partial-equilibrium price responsiveness of service imports implies, ceteris paribus, that the demand for such imports increased 50 per cent in 1955–72 because of the secular fall of the PLD-EER. Thus, the exchange-rate policy added to balance-of-payments pressures.

iv. Within a general-equilibrium framework, on the other hand, the direct price responsiveness was almost swamped by the indirect effects. Quantitative restrictions were much more effective for constraining short-run balance-of-payments deficits than were price policies, given that exchange movements were not neutralized.

v. Patterns were less clear for service imports on a more disaggregate level. However, liberalization tended to increase deficits due to net outflows for freight, transportation, and income on direct investments. Increases were allowed in the last category even near the end of phases when other items were restricted because of foreign-exchange shortages. In a sense, then, policies favored foreign over domestic interests.

vi. Unilateral tranfers increased during liberalization attempts, primarily because of enlarged inflows to the government. Such net inflows aided the liberalization efforts, but never averaged as much as a quarter of the deficit on the goods and services account.

vii. The totals of capital and gold inflows reveal that Chile was consistently a debtor nation. Fluctuations in these totals, however, were not closely phase-associated.

viii. The aggregate capital inflows to nonmonetary sectors, in contrast, reflected the degree of liberalization. They increased in more liberal phases and fell in more restrictive ones. The causes of this phase association included direct investment responses to specific policies and to the general economic climate and private short-term capital movements due to these same factors and to speculation. Net long-term private capital flows and net flows to the government, on the other hand, were not closely phase-related; they were dominated instead by the Alliance for Progress, political attitudes of the donor governments, and repayment requirements.

ix. Net direct-investment inflows increased relative to net outflows from income on such investments during the first two liberal phases and fell during more restrictive periods. For the quarter-century following the Second World War, however, the inflows averaged but 30 per cent of the outflows. Such figures caused many Chileans to question the appropriateness of the distribution of benefits from direct investment.

x. Compensatory capital movements of considerable magnitude were required to sustain the first two liberalization programs. The resulting exhaustion of reserves and of bank credit abroad led to their termination. The overvalued NER could not be maintained for very long.

In the third liberalization attempt, in contrast, these movements were in the opposite direction. The world copper market boom of the late 1960s was the primary cause of this difference. The accumulated reserves, however, were quickly exhausted under the Allende government because net capital outflows from traditional private and public sources were only partially offset by new sources.

TABLE 8.1

Chilean Balance of International Payments, Annual Averages for Phases and Subphases, 1947–71

(millions of 1958 United States dollars)

	1947–51	1952–55	1956–58	1959–61	1962–64	1965–69	1970	1971
A. Goods and services	−50.1	−5.6	−81.7	−163.0	−179.9	−79.2	−66.2	−139.7
1. Merchandise[a]	20.7	56.3	−5.6	−71.0	−74.4	100.0	88.0	−56.0
1.1 Exports	392.2	475.2	429.8	442.8	485.1	757.7	836.0	738.0
1.2 Imports	−371.5	−418.9	−434.9	−513.8	−559.5	−657.7	−748.0	−794.0
2. Nonmonetary gold	5.4	5.3	2.7	1.8	1.8	0.3	—	—
3. Freight and other transportation	3.6	9.0	6.4	4.0	3.5	14.2	—	—
4. Travel	0.6	−0.8	−7.8	−21.5	−8.8	−1.3	—	—
5. Investment income	−77.1	−67.8	−71.4	−67.1	−89.0	−170.5	−95.2	−63.4
5.1 On direct investment	−66.3	−53.7	−57.2	−45.7	−52.5	−83.0	—	—
6. Govt., n.i.e.	0.9	−4.2	−9.1	−6.0	−2.9	−5.6	−11.4	—
7. Other services	−4.1	−3.3	2.6	−3.2	−10.1	−16.3	—	—
B. Unrequited transfers	1.1	−0.1	19.6	38.2	9.6	14.4	23.7	—
8. Private	0.9	−1.4	5.3	10.1	5.0	5.0	—	—
9. Central govt.	0.2	1.3	14.3	28.2	4.6	9.4	—	—
Net total (lines 1–9)	−49.0	−5.6	−62.1	−124.7	−170.3	−64.8	−32.5	—
C. Capital and monetary gold	46.0	10.9	70.1	129.1	168.9	79.0	42.7	139.2
Nonmonetary sectors	39.9	18.6	37.4	82.6	143.9	153.1	110.0[b]	−78.8[b]
10. Direct investment	22.0	16.8	42.8	43.7	−2.4	1.0	—	—
10.1 Large-scale mining	13.0	9.2	20.7	−2.9	−18.7	−2.6	—	—
11. Other private long term	−0.3	−0.3	8.8	23.5	48.5	51.3	—	—
12. Other private short term	1.1	−1.2	−8.6	16.0	6.6	18.6	—	—
13. Central government, n.i.e.	17.0	3.4	−5.4	−0.6	91.3	82.1	—	—

13.1 Loans received	29.1	6.8	−5.8	7.7	93.2	86.8	—	—
13.2 Chilean govt. securities	0.0	0.0	0.0	−2.8	−4.5	−4.7	—	—
13.3 U.S. govt. escudo holdings	0.0	1.3	3.4	1.1	4.8	5.5	—	—
13.4 Subscriptions to IDA and IDB	0.0	0.0	−0.1	−4.8	−3.7	−4.0	—	—
13.5 Other short term capital	−12.1	−4.8	−2.8	−1.8	1.6	−1.6	—	—
Monetary sectors	6.1	−5.6	32.7	46.4	24.9	−74.2	−67.3[c]	218.0[c]
14. Commercial banks	2.6	−0.9	2.6	13.4	14.0	−14.4	—	—
15. Central institutions: liabilities	16.8	−1.1	22.1	53.2	15.6	−17.8	—	—
15.1 Use of IMF credit	13.5	1.0	9.9	27.0	11.5	−7.3	—	—
15.2 Loans received	1.9	−2.2	15.6	23.3	6.4	−12.2	—	—
15.3 Payments agreements	1.7	0.1	−0.4	4.4	−3.4	−0.5	—	—
15.4 IDA and IDB escudo holdings	0.0	0.0	0.0	1.4	1.8	2.2	—	—
16. Central institutions: assets	−13.2	−7.0	8.0	−20.2	−4.6	−42.0	—	—
16.1 Changes in IMF reserve position	0.0	0.0	0.0	−16.2	0.0	0.0	—	—
16.2 Payments agreements	−0.8	−2.2	−0.6	4.2	0.0	−0.5	—	—
16.3 Other claims	−5.6	−4.9	7.1	−5.7	−6.1	−40.8	—	—
16.4 Monetary gold	4.6	0.1	1.5	−2.5	1.5	−0.7	—	—
Net errors and omissions	3.0	−5.2	−8.0	−4.3	1.5	−14.6	−10.2	—

SOURCE: Annual data in current dollars are from International Monetary Fund [1950a–1969a] for 1947–69 and from Banco Central [1972b:263] and unpublished Central Bank data for 1970 and 1971. The United States GNP deflator was used to convert the data into constant dollars. The data for 1970 and 1971 are not strictly comparable to the data for earlier years; so 1970 is presented separately rather than in combination with the rest of the 1965–70 phase. Also because of problems of making the data for the earlier years compatible with those for later years, not all the subtotals for 1947–51 sum to the final totals shown.

a. Exports f.o.b., imports c.i.f.

b. Called "autonomous capital movements" in the source.

c. Called "compensatory capital movements" in the source.

8.1 SERVICES AND TRANSFERS

In this section an attempt is made to answer three questions about services and transfers after the Second World War. What were the patterns in constant-dollar mean values for phases? Were there any within-phase regularities? Within a structural model how responsive were services to various policies?

8.1.1 Mean Values for Phases.

Average constant-dollar values of all of the major components of the Chilean balance of payments for phases and subphases in 1947–71 are presented in Table 8.1. The data in this table, together with others elsewhere in the study, suggest, first, that in each of the three more liberal phases (i.e., 1956–58, 1959–61, 1965–70), the mean net constant-dollar balance from all services (Table 8.1, line A less line A1) declined from the level of the previous phase. In two of the three more restrictive phases or subphases, the opposite was true. The systematic reductions in discrimination against nongoods transactions that accompanied liberalization (and vice versa) noted above (column 3 in Table 5.1),[1] thus, generally caused increased movements in the net balance from services. More careful examination of the data underlying Table 8.1 indicates that most of this variation was in the imports of services.[2] Policy changes affected the value of such imports much more strongly than they did goods imports or goods or nongoods exports.[3]

The secular growth rate in 1947–65 for total services was the highest by far among export categories and second only to transportation-related capital goods among imports (column 1 in Table A.2). The value of these transactions increased relatively rapidly over time, therefore, despite the fluctuations due to phase changes. The only significant (at the 20 per cent level) phase-coincident deviation from the secular growth rate is a decline for the 1962–64 Phase II years.

On a more disaggregate level, the relations between phases and mean values are less consistent. In the 1956–58 liberalization, mean net flows fell for every category except other services. In 1959–61 they fell for all but investment income and government. For 1965–70 they fell for all but travel, freight, and other transportation.[4]

The pattern of outflows for investment income merits some comment. These returns were largely from large-scale copper mining. For the phase immediately after the *Nuevo Trato* of 1955, they increased somewhat. During the liberalization of 1959–61 they fell by 6 per cent. In the 1965–70 liberalization, however, their absolute value increased tremendously. The copper boom of the late 1960s was a major factor in this bulge. The foreign owners reaped substantial returns from this boom despite the increase in Chilean participation (see subsection 7.1.2.3).

For net flows from unrequited transfers, a phase-related pattern also prevailed. On the average these inflows rose substantially in each of the three more liberal periods. These increases originated primarily in enlarged transfers to the central government. Changes in transfers to the private sector also were important in 1956–58 and 1959–61. Such inflows helped facilitate the liberalization efforts, although in none of these three attempts did they cover as much as a quarter of the mean deficit on the goods and services account.

8.1.2 Within-Phase Patterns.

Careful examination of the annual data underlying Table 8.1 reveals some systematic patterns within phases. The aggregate deficit from net services rose at the start of each of the liberalization episodes. These increases originated predominately in higher freight and transportation payments resulting from increased exports and in larger investment income outflows. Credits from travel usually grew enough, on the other hand, to offset increased deficits in this category.

In the last year of the first two more liberal phases, the deficit from aggregate net services continued to grow. The primary contributing factor was the rising outflow for income on investment. The incentives for such outflows were strong because of impending foreign-exchange crises. Despite the growing foreign-exchange scarcities, however, the government did not effectively restrict these returns to foreigners. Instead it limited other items such as expenditures on travel. In fact greater stringency—together with reduced goods exports—generally caused increases in net credits in the other categories. The expanded outflow of investment income to foreigners, thus, was probably offset by net reductions in other categories. In a sense, therefore, foreign interests were favored over domestic ones.

Comparable data are not available for the last year of the third liberalization attempt. The lack of an immediate foreign-exchange shortage, however, probably resulted in different patterns. Expenditures on travel, for example, apparently rose throughout most of 1970. Less because of policy stringency than because of the ending of the worldwide boom in the copper market, outflows of investment income also fell.

At both the beginning and end of the more restrictive 1962–64 phase net debits for aggregate services declined. This again emphasizes the relative impact of greater restrictiveness on the service categories. Despite the over-all greater stringency, however, once again foreign investors were favored by allowing larger outflows.

Enlarged net credits from unilateral transfers (especially to the central government) helped facilitate liberalization at the start of the first two attempts. In the first case they continued to grow throughout the phase, but in the last year of the second effort they fell off. In 1965, in contrast, such transfers dropped. Subsequently they grew somewhat and then leveled off in 1968. Under the Frei government, however, these inflows were definitely smaller than during the two previous liberalization attempts, reflecting a worldwide shift in the form of aid flows from grants to loans.

8.1.3 Partial-Equilibrium Responses of Services.

SERVICE IMPORTS.

Relation 8.1 is for service imports (M_s). The underlying model is the same as is used for other imports in subsection 6.2.1:

$$M_s = \underset{\substack{(2.5)\\[-0.8]}}{-43.7\ PLD\text{-}NER} + \underset{\substack{(1.2)\\[0.3]}}{48.0\ (PLD\text{-}NER^{BM}/PLD\text{-}NER^{BM}_{-1})} \quad (8.1)$$

$$+ \underset{\substack{(11.7)\\[1.9]}}{0.105(X+M)} - \underset{\substack{(3.4)\\[-7.6]}}{1{,}503\ QR} + \underset{(3.1)}{1{,}366}$$

$$\bar{R}^2 = 0.92;\ SE = 30.4;\ DW = 2.5;\ \text{years covered, 1947–65}$$

Each of the same four sets of determinants is considered in turn.

The response to relative prices is fairly large. The elasticity with respect to the PLD-NER is −0.8, which is greater than four of the six imported-goods categories included in Table 6.3.[5] Ceteris paribus, this value implies that the 62 per cent fall in the brokers' PLD-NER between 1955 and 1972 induced an expansion of almost 50 per cent in desired service imports. The attempt to maintain increasingly overvalued exchange rates thus generated strong inducements for imports in this category. On the other hand, such price responsiveness also suggests that price-related tools rather than QRs could have been used to limit these imports.

The second term in relation 8.1 is the ratio of the current to the lagged PLD-NER for the black market. It represents speculative pressures. The estimate provides some evidence of a response in service imports to such pressures, but the relevant coefficient is significantly nonzero only at the 15 per cent level. The existence of a reaction to risk (as measured by the standard deviation of relative prices), in contrast, is not supported even at the 25 per cent level of significance.

The only important nonprice demand factor is the activity index for total trade $(X+M)$, which is included because imports of certain services (e.g., freight and insurance) depend upon it. The elasticity estimate of 1.9 implies that such services are quite sensitive to the level of total trade. In contrast to some of the consumer and intermediate goods categories, however, banking system credit does not seem to have affected service imports directly.

On the other hand, the reaction to quantitative restrictions (*QR*, the Ffrench-Davis index) is significant and large. The elasticity of −7.6 implies a greater response than for all but investment goods among the import categories in Table 6.3. This supports the hypothesis made several times above (e.g., section 5.1, subsection 8.1.1) that changes in the stringency of quantitative policies affected services relatively strongly. Great use of QRs to curb service imports was required to offset the previously mentioned price response to the overvalued NER.

Finally, dominance of neither the habit-adjustment nor inventory effects, as represented by lagged dependent variables, is supported by the results.

SERVICE EXPORTS.

Relation 8.2 is for service exports (X_s):

$$X_s = \underset{\substack{(5.1)\\[0.2]}}{23.3}\ PLD\text{-}NER_{-1} + \underset{\substack{(4.9)\\[0.0]}}{11.5}\ \Delta PLD\text{-}NER + \underset{\substack{(2.7)\\[0.3]}}{0.0261}\ (X+M) \quad (8.2)$$

$$+\underset{\substack{(4.1)\\[0.6]}}{0.0567}\ (X+M)_{-1} + \underset{\substack{(4.1)\\[0.7]}}{0.233}\ GDP^{AR}$$

$$+\underset{\substack{(3.9)\\[0.1]}}{65.2}\ LAFTA - \underset{(5.2)}{0.600}\ X_{s_{-1}} - \underset{(7.6)}{266}$$

$\bar{R}^2 = 0.99$; $SE = 9.1$; $DW = 1.4$; years covered, 1947–65

The basic underlying model is the same as that used in subsection 7.2.1 for other exports.

i. Although the response of exports of services to price policies is statistically significant, the price elasticity is substantially smaller than that for imports of services, and it is also smaller than the price elasticities for other exports (Table 6.2). The relatively limited reaction of service exports to price policies is illustrated by the fact that this estimate implies only a 12 per cent reduction in response to the 62 per cent decline in the relevant PLD-NER for the 1956–72 period—in contrast to the almost 50 per cent increase in desired service imports noted above. The combination of these two elasticities, of course, still implies a considerable net response in services. If service exports and imports were in balance initially, for example, such a drop in the PLD-NER would cause a deficit of over 60 per cent of the original level of imports, ceteris paribus.

For both service exports and imports, no evidence exists of a significant response to risks concerning future relative price movements. However, the reaction to a Harberger [1963] accelerator term—the first difference of the PLD-NER—is significant and large. This term represents (naive) anticipations regarding future changes in the PLD-NER.

ii. In contrast to all the other export categories included in Table 7.2, quantitative supply factors have not directly limited service exports. This result reflects the vagueness in capacity definitions for the service sector in general, even though some components (e.g., tourist hotels) may have specific capacity constraints.

iii. Three significant quantitative demand factors are incorporated in the regression. One is over-all trade $(X+M)$, which represents the demand for the Chilean provision of certain services analogously to the situation for the import of services. A second is Argentinian product (GDP^{AR}), pertinent because more tourists visiting Chile have come from neighboring Argentina than anywhere else and that tourism is income sensitive. A third is the LAFTA dummy variable, which suggests that the formation of that organization resulted in increased regional tourism in the early 1960s.

iv. The significant coefficient of the lagged dependent variable implies the dominance of an inventory effect for services. Although the existence of an inventory effect for service exports such as for tourists from neighboring countries does not seem unreasonable, the absolute magnitude of this coefficient is surprisingly large. The explanation probably is that the series for the dependent variable better reflects the payment for services (for which an inventory effect makes more sense) than the provision of services. Lags in payments also underlie the significance of the lagged trade term $(X+M)_{-1}$ in addition to the current one.

CHILEAN NET FACTOR INCOME FROM ABROAD.

Relation 8.3 is for Chilean net factor income from abroad in constant terms $(NFIAB/PGDP)$, where $PGDP$ denotes the GDP deflator:

$$\frac{NFIAB}{PGDP} = \underset{\substack{(2.1)\\ [-0.8]}}{26.5V_1} - \underset{\substack{(2.2)\\ [0.4]}}{0.840V_2} - \underset{\substack{(3.0)\\ [0.4]}}{0.116V_3} + \underset{\substack{(1.8)\\ [-0.7]}}{0.377V_4} - \underset{(5.6)}{376} \tag{8.3}$$

$\bar{R}^2 = 0.81$; $SE = 31.4$; $DW = 1.7$; years covered, 1947–65 where

V_1 = real wage rate in mining including employers' social security tax contributions;
V_2 = dollar value of mining exports after adjustment for direct tax on large-scale mining relative to dollar cost of intermediate mining inputs at special NER for large-scale mining;
V_3 = export value after adjustment for direct tax on large-scale mining relative to intermediate input index for mining with adjustment for ratio of national accounts to large-scale mining NERs (with all components lagged one year);
V_4 = real value of legal cost of production for large-scale mining at large-scale mining NER (with all components lagged one year).

Chilean net factor income from abroad (*NFIAB*) is composed primarily of outflows from mining. The primary determinants of this flow are variables related to that sector: the prices of mining inputs (labor and intermediate), the real level of total or of mining exports, the price of mining products (or of copper in particular), the legal cost of production in large-scale mining, the employers' social security tax rate and the direct tax rate on large-scale mining, the NER for large-scale mining, and possibly quantitative restrictions. This relationship is a somewhat ad hoc attempt to estimate the determinants of real factor income from abroad in response to composite variables constructed on the basis of such considerations.

These factors are consistent with a considerable portion of the variance in the dependent variable. The coefficients are of the anticipated signs. Judging from the *t* statistics and the elasticities, government policies regarding the NER, the legal cost of production, and the tax rates for large-scale mining played particularly important direct roles in determining variations in net factor payments from abroad.

Quantitative restrictions,[6] on the other hand, were not important because the Chilean government never limited the freedom of the large-scale mining companies to repatriate after-tax earnings as they saw fit. In fact, the companies were not required either to return such earnings to Chile or to convert them into escudos.

Finally, relation 8.3 supports the observation that the Chilean governments wished to limit factor payments abroad and were reluctant, therefore, to increase the PLD-NER for large-scale mining. The export estimate for large-scale mining in Table 7.2, however, implies that the limiting of foreign factor payments from this subsector was purchased at the price of reduced national control over foreign exchange from exports. It is not clear that the government was always aware of this trade-off.

8.1.4 General-Equilibrium Responses of Services.

The model introduced in Chapter 2 and the simulations summarized in Table A.11 once again provide the basis for commentary on the responses of services within a general-equilibrium framework.

The general-equilibrium responses of service imports and exports to exchange-rate variations show the same basic characteristic as do most other exports and imports (subsections 6.2.2 and 7.2.2). Most of the large partial-equilibrium reactions are swamped by indirect effects resulting especially from domestic price responses to changes in international reserves. As a result, the relevant first-year elasticities are about 0.1 in absolute value (simulation 2.1.1). Note that the elasticity for service exports is about the same in absolute magnitude as for service imports despite the partial-equilibrium differences observed in the previous subsection.[7] Pessimism about the effectiveness of exchange-rate policy thus seems appropriate for the service categories as well as for the goods categories.

The response of net factor income from abroad to changes in the over-all exchange rate is inverse and elastic in the first year, with a fairly substantial re-action occurring during the next several years (simulations 2.1.1 and 2.1.3).[8] The first-year elasticity for a change in the NER for large-scale mining alone is −0.9 (simulation 2.7.1). The general-equilibrium results thus reinforce the partial-equilibrium conclusion that the low NER for domestic purchases of large-scale mining significantly reduced foreign-factor earnings.

The general-equilibrium responses of services to changes in quantitative restrictions are quite large (simulation 2.3.1). The first-year elasticity of −0.9 for service exports is greater in absolute value than those for all but one other export category. The first-year elasticity of −4.6 for service imports is the largest in absolute value among all import categories.[9] The first-year elasticity for net factor income from abroad is −4.0, and the third-year one is −5.8.

These results suggest that quantitative restrictions affect service imports more strongly than any other category; for balance-of-payments constraint of services, quantitative restrictions are more effective than price-related measures unless the impact on domestic prices of the latter can be largely neutralized; QRs are also quite effective in restraining factor payments abroad despite the lack of evidence of any significant partial-equilibrium response (subsection 8.1.3).

8.2 CAPITAL AND GOLD FLOWS

The sum of movements in the merchandise, service, and transfer accounts, of course, were offset by flows in the capital and gold accounts (except for the relatively small error and omissions item). The mean net inflows on the capital and gold accounts were positive in all the post-World War II phases and subphases (line C in Table 8.1).[10] Thus Chile was consistently a debtor nation.[11]

Variations in these means were not obviously primarily associated with degrees of liberalization or of restrictiveness. They rose in the more liberal phases of 1956–58 and 1959–61 and also in the more restrictive phases of 1962–64 and 1971–73. They fell in the more liberal phase of 1965–70 and the more restrictive subphase of 1952–55. Although these patterns in some ways directly reflected the nature of the regime (see below), of much greater importance was the situation in the world copper market and the general availability of foreign loans.

8.2.1 Net Capital Flows to the Nonmonetary Sectors.

Total net capital inflows to the nonmonetary sectors, in contrast to those to all sectors, clearly have been associated with the degree of liberalization. Means increased for each of the three more liberal phases and decreased for more restrictive phases and subphases (with the single exception of 1962–64). The ratio of these flows to all capital and monetary-gold movements rose in each more liberal phase and fell in each more restrictive one (although not in the 1952–55 subphase). Consideration of the four major components of the net capital flows to nonmonetary sectors facilitates understanding of these patterns.

Long-Term Investment Flows.

The most striking phase associations were in *net direct investment* (Table 8.1, line 10), which increased in each more liberal phase and decreased in each more restrictive one. The lags in these changes, moreover, were quite small; so the indicated movement generally was reached in the first year of each phase.[12]

This association of net direct investment inflows with phases partially reflects a similar pattern for the substantial share of these inflows going to large-scale mining. As is discussed in subsection 7.1.2.3, the *Nuevo Trato* of 1955 and the Frei Chileanization and nationalization programs of 1967–69 shaped much of the latter flow.[13]

In recent phases major total net direct investment inflows have been going to subsectors other than large-scale mining (line 10 less line 10.1). These flows, too, responded to specific policies which eased or restricted capital entry and subsequent repatriation (subsection 4.3.2). Of even more importance than such specific policies, however, apparently was the perception of a "favorable investment climate" caused by the over-all program of stabilization plus liberalization.

Larger net direct investment inflows by themselves did not guarantee that the total direct impact of liberalization policies was to increase the net short-term command over foreign exchange related to direct investment.[14] Such policy changes also generally allowed larger net outflows of income from direct investments (Table 8.1, line 5.1). In fact, however, for all but one of the recent phases, the short-term command over foreign exchange rose in liberalization and fell in more restrictive periods even when both of these flows are taken into account.

The single exception was the Frei liberalization. For those years the mean net outflow with both factors taken into account rose more than 50 per cent over that of the previous phase. Most of this increased net outflow, however, only reflected the sharp shift in the composition of capital inflows to large-scale mining from direct investment to long-term loans, which was caused by the Chileanization and nationalization programs.

The ratio between net direct investment inflows and net income on direct investment outflows is also revealing. This ratio increased in each liberalization phase (including the Frei one) and fell in each more restrictive phase. Only during the 1956–58 and 1959–61 liberalizations in fact did this ratio exceed one-half (the values were 0.75 and 0.96, respectively). The implied large excess of outflows over inflows related to direct investment, of course, does not prove that Chile did not gain significantly from these investments. That this ratio averaged only 0.30 for 1947–69, however, caused many Chileans to question the appropriateness of the distribution of the gains from direct foreign investment.

The Allende government therefore attempted to establish a more desirable distribution of the benefits from direct foreign investment and greater Chilean control over operations.[15] A number of existing foreign firms and some new ones agreed to continue or expand production, often with minority participation in mixed enterprises and with state-guaranteed minimum rates of net return of 5 per cent (e.g., RCA International, General Tire, FEMSA, General Electric, Gillette, Standard Oil of New Jersey, Pfizer, Renault, Citroen, Pegasso, and Fiat). Others, however, terminated their Chilean operations on terms apparently more or less satisfactory to the foreign owners, at least given their expectations about future developments there (e.g., the Bank of America, Northern Indiana Brass, Purina, First National City Bank, Dow Chemical, and du Pont). A few, the largest of which were International Telephone and Telegraph and Ford, had acrimonious interactions with the Chilean government concerning operations and compensation.[16] The over-all result was a large net direct investment outflow. This contrasted with most earlier phases (although not with 1962–64) and contributed to the drop of $188.8 million in autonomous capital movements between 1970 and 1971.

Other private long-term investment movements were not particularly phase-associated (Table 8.1, line 11). Mean net inflows rose in each of the phases for which data are available (but they almost certainly declined in the 1971–73 Phase II period, for which data are not yet available).[17] The largest absolute positive increment, on the other hand, also was for a Phase II period (1962–64).

Due to the secular increase (at least until the end of the 1960s), net flows from this source became substantially more important in the over-all net inflow of capital and nonmonetary gold. In the 1950s, for example, this source averaged 11 per cent of the total net inflow of capital and nonmonetary gold. In the 1960s it accounted for 37 per cent.

This level of aggregation, however, does conceal one important change which occurred in the late 1960s. Because of the Frei Chileanization and nationalization programs for large-scale mining, substantial long-term private loans were made to that subsector starting in 1967. Such inflows accounted for 80 per cent of net other long-term private capital movements in 1965–69, although they had been insignificant earlier because capital inflows to this subsector previously had been in the form of direct investment. Thus, underlying the aggregate increase in this phase was a substantial drop in net inflows other than to large-scale mining. Therefore, this liberalization really resulted more in a shift in composition than an increase in total private long-term capital inflows.

For both these other long-term capital inflows and for direct investment, outflows for income also must be considered in evaluating the total direct impact on the balance of payments. The available data, unfortunately, do not distinguish income on these other private long-term capital movements from that on private short-term capital movements. However, a comparison can be made between total other private inflows (Table 8.1, line 11 + line 12) and the resulting outflows for income (line 5 less variable 5.1). In such a comparison two features stand out:

i. The mean ratio of the former to the latter for 1947–69 is 0.89, which is much higher than the comparable ratio for direct investment. Differences in timing of the flows account for only a part of this discrepancy.[18] Apparently the more important factor was that direct investments were much more profitable from the point of view of foreigners than were these other inflows.

ii. The over-all short-run impact of these other private capital movements, in contrast to those for direct investments, was not increased control of foreign exchange in periods of liberalization and vice versa in restrictive periods. In fact, for all recent phases for which data are available, except the 1959–61 liberalization, the pattern is the opposite.

Short-term Investment Flows

Other private short-term capital flows may be very volatile in a country with a history of inflation and foreign-sector policy like Chile's. The repeated pattern of maintaining the NER fixed and then devaluing substantially to a new fixed level was a strong inducement for speculative short-term capital movements. The real rates of interest as seen by foreigners and by nationals often diverged by large amounts, and both rates also varied greatly over time. After a devaluation and while the NER remained unchanged, for example, the real interest rate for foreigners was equal to the nominal rate. The latter, in turn, was quite high because of internal inflation. As a result, the real return on foreign loans probably exceeded their real product.

Mean net other private short-term capital inflows reflected the degree of liberalization (Table 8.1, line 12). For each more liberal phase except 1956–58 they increased.[19] For each more restrictive phase or subphase they fell.

In the 1959–61 liberalization effort the special repatriation arrangements and the establishment of dollar accounts induced part of the expanded inflow. In the 1965–70 attempt, the sliding-peg NER apparently had the same effect by reducing uncertainty about future PLD-NER variations and encouraging investment in export industries (but see note 19). In both of these phases revised expectations about the over-all performance of the economy resulting from the program of stabilization plus liberalization probably also contributed. The gains in short-run control over foreign exchange helped to extend these liberalization attempts. In neither case, of course, did such inflows offset the effects of overvaluation. In the first case, moreover, the increasing real interest rates for foreigners resulting from inflation in combination with the fixed NER meant that the real return on such loans probably exceeded their real product.

Under the Allende government short-term capital inflows dropped considerably (although data comparable to those in Table 8.1 are not available). This fall reflected speculation about NER movements, capital flight to avoid nationalization and redistribution policies, and the cutting off of short-term credits by many traditional suppliers in retaliation for the compensation decision for large-scale copper mining.[20] This decline exacerbated an already difficult foreign-exchange situation.

The annual data underlying Table 8.1 provide further information about speculative movements of short-term capital. If speculation were successful enlarged outflows would be expected in the last year of phases in anticipation of devaluation. Countermovements in the first year of liberalization attempts would reverse the process.

Only limited support for such patterns is found in the annual data for short-term capital inflows. They decreased in half of the last years of phases and increased in only one-third of the first years of liberalization. If errors and omissions are also considered because they include unrecorded short-term capital movements, however, the patterns were more consistent with those hypothesized. In three-fourths of the last years of all phases, drops were reported and in two-thirds of the first years of liberalizations increases were recorded. If such a phenomenon prevailed, therefore, it operated largely through unrecorded movements.[21]

CAPITAL FLOWS TO THE CENTRAL GOVERNMENT

Net capital movements to the central government were not highly associated with the degree of liberalization (Table 8.1, line 13). Mean ratios decreased for two of the three liberalization efforts and rose very sharply in the 1962–64 Phase II period. Annual ratios fell in the first year of two of three liberalization attempts and increased in 1962.

Loans to the central government were the most important component of total net capital movements to the government (Table 8.1, lines 13.1–13.5). The pattern of the latter largely reflected movements in the former. The net balance for these loans, in turn, reflected both supply and demand considerations.

On the supply side the most dominant single factor was the Alliance for Progress. In the 1960s the United States considered Chile to be an important alternative to Castroism and militarism in Latin America. Therefore, the United States made available substantial capital funds. As a result, net loans received by the central government expanded enormously in the early 1960s and remained at almost as high a level under the Frei regime.[22] After Allende was elected, however, that support from the United States dried up quickly, although it was partially replaced by new sources.[23]

Other fairly important supply factors were increased funds made available in response to major earthquakes in 1939 and 1960 and in support of the three stabilization efforts. The impact of these inflows, however, was much less than that of those mentioned in the previous paragraph.

Demand factors included, first of all, the need for repayment of previous debts. Owing to such repayments, for example, in 1956–58 outflows exceeded inflows despite foreign support for the program of liberalization and stabilization. A second factor was the attempt to facilitate price stabilization by financing government deficits abroad during the stabilization programs. In each case the plan was to utilize such measures only until the government deficit was eliminated, but that plan was not realized.

Together these supply and demand factors resulted in great command over foreign exchange from capital received by the government in the late 1940s and the 1960s. The net impact in the 1950s and early 1970s, however, was small or negative because of repayment requirements and the political views of potential donors.

8.2.2 Net Capital and Gold Flows to the Monetary Sectors.

Net credits resulting from flows to and from the monetary sectors followed two patterns. Before 1965 the total and most of the components rose on the average for each liberalization effort and fell in each more restrictive phase or subphase. During 1956–58 and 1959–61, for example, large increases in net loans from stabilization funds and in the use of IMF credit offset the greater deficits on the goods and services account (Table 8.1, lines A, 15.1, and 15.2). These credits were critical for these liberalization efforts.[24]

But because of such credits, together with ones in the nonmonetary sectors, foreign debts grew and foreign reserves shrank. During the 1956–58 phase total public-sector foreign debt increased 56 per cent to a level of $392 million, and net foreign reserves held by the banking system fell from $88.6 million to −$13.4 million. During the 1959–61 period total public-sector foreign debt increased 101 per cent to a level of $788 million, total Chilean debt in foreign currency [25] rose 82 per cent to a level of $954 million, and net foreign-exchange reserves held by the banking system plummeted to −$164.8 million. The foreign debt in 1961 was equal to 183 per cent of exports or 22 per cent of GDP. These liberalization attempts with an overvalued NER thus had a definite cost in terms of the longer-run command over foreign exchange.

For the 1965–70 Phase III years and the Phase II period thereafter, the previous pattern was in some important respects reversed. During 1965–70, foreign exchange for expanded imports was available from enlarged export revenues and capital inflows to the nonmonetary sectors. As a result, net credit from monetary sectors fell from $24.9 million to −$74.2 million. Net international reserves held by the banking system increased from $238.7 million at the end of 1964 to over $300 million at the end of 1970. Foreign debt, however, grew from $1,896 million at the end of 1964 to over $3,000 million at the end of 1970. At the end of the period this debt equaled about two and a half years of exports and over a quarter of annual GDP.

In 1971, the Allende government introduced a more restrictive regime. The enlarged deficit on current account and the sharp drop in credits from the nonmonetary sectors nevertheless implied that compensatory capital movements had to increase substantially. Between 1970 and 1971, in fact, they rose by over $285 million. Additional credits from international organizations were very limited, in part because of United States pressure. The net international reserves of the banking system that had been accumulated in the previous phase were quickly depleted. In addition large debt payments were due, in part because of debt rescheduling in 1965. The combination of a decline in the world copper price, the inability to exploit the expanded copper capacity, the unavailability of capital from traditional sources, the inability to obtain sufficient capital from new sources (e.g., the Socialist nations), and the large foreign debt all led to a foreign-exchange crisis. As is described in subsection 4.3.3, at the end of 1971 Chile stopped payment on her foreign debt and asked for renegotiation of these obligations. In 1972 some relief was provided by the debtors, but the foreign-exchange shortage continued to pinch the economy. When the Allende government fell, in September 1973, discussion about further relief was scheduled.

NOTES

1. Given that the black market has been used more for nongoods than for goods transactions, the changes in the mean PLD-NER for that market provides further evidence of this pattern (line 1.1.3 in Table A.1).

2. Some of the variance originated in exports of services. For example, in 1972 exports of services to visitors rose substantially because of attractive bargains for tourists dealing in the black market and because UNCTAD III was held in Santiago in April.

3. The coefficient of variation (i.e., the ratio of the standard deviation to the mean) of the secular time trend for service imports for 1947–65 was 0.30; for service exports, it was 0.20. Among all import categories a higher ratio was reached only for transportation-related investment goods. Among all export categories, in contrast, higher ratios than those for service exports were experienced in all cases except for large-scale mining.

4. The estimates in Table A.2 suggest that the rate of growth of both exports and imports of services declined in the first year of liberalization attempts and that the former declined more than the latter. This result probably reflects the extensive dependence of service exports on total imports, which also fell significantly in the first year of liberalization efforts.

5. For the sample period the PLD-EER and PLD-NER for services are almost identical. For 1956–70 the former fell 46 per cent and the latter, 52 per cent (column 12 in Table 3.2 and column 2 in Table 5.1).

6. That is, quantitative restrictions beyond those which limited large-scale mining to a special NER for currency to pay for domestic inputs.

7. For the larger deviations to the Bacha-Taylor equilibrium values (simulation 2.1.3), however, the absolute value of the first-year deviation is larger for imports than for exports, although the discrepancy still is not as great as the partial-equilibrium estimate might suggest.

8. The relatively large elasticities, however, may reflect in part the fact that this variable is the difference between two flows. See note a to Table A.11.

9. By the third year, however, the response to a one-time change reverses in sign.

10. They were positive, in fact, in all but three years (1954, 1955, and 1969) when copper-export booms were unusually important.

11. The data line of 1.2.6.5 of Table A.1 suggest that Chile also was a substantial debtor nation during the decades before the Great Depression. In most years external public foreign debt exceeded ordinary government income or total export value.

Data consistent with those in Table 8.1 are not available for the 1930s. The piecemeal evidence extant, however, indicates that capital movements plummeted to almost nothing in the early 1930s and recovered slowly thereafter. Baerresen [1966:2], for example, reports that the foreign investment inflow was $232 million in 1930, $16 million in 1931, and effectively zero in 1932. Marshall [1957:51] claims that foreign loans contracted to the government in the same three years were $85 million, $3 million, and zero. According to Senado, Oficina de Informaciones [1971:48, 54], finally, in no year in the 1931–46 period did direct gross investment in large-scale mining (the dominant destination for foreign investment in the previous two decades) exceed amortization charges.

12. The only exception was in the 1965–70 liberalization phase, when an increase did not occur until the second year of the phase.

13. Somewhat earlier, the introduction of more favorable NERs for the domestic cost of investment in large-scale mining in 1948 and 1950 also coincided with substantial expansion in capacity at Chuquicamata, Chile's largest copper mine. However, Mikesell [1971:370–371] maintains that this investment would have occurred without this policy change because Anaconda long had been concerned about maintaining its 13–14 per cent long-run share of world copper production—and 70 per cent of Anaconda's output came from its Chilean mine.

14. In addition to that direct impact, of course, direct investment caused other changes in the balance of payments indirectly through effects on imports and exports.

15. This paragraph is focused on foreign investments other than in large-scale mining (on the latter, see subsection 7.1.2.3, above). Szulc [1970:2] reports that such investments from the United States totaled over $400 million at the time of Allende's election. According to Picks' [1965:121], six years earlier direct investments of other foreigners totaled more than $300 million.

16. In 1967 ITT agreed to sell up to 49 per cent of its common stock in its Chilean Telephone subsidiary to Chileans and to the Chilean government with the added stipulation that Chile could purchase the entire system in 1980. By early 1971, 30 per cent control of the subsidiary lay in Chilean hands, but the government wished to include this operation in the state area of control; long negotiations for nationalization were therefore initiated. On September 15, 1971, ITT was informed that it would be nationalized, but discussions continued over the terms of compensation for what ITT claimed was a $153 million investment. In March 1972 relations between ITT and the Chilean government were severely strained by the charge of Jack Anderson in his syndicated column that ITT had been attempting to prevent the inauguration of President-elect Allende in the fall of 1970. As one result ITT was not compensated for its former Chilean holdings. For details as reported in United States newspapers, see Anderson [1972a, 1972b], de Onis [1971d, 1972e], Hammer [1972], Jensen [1971], New York *Times* [1972a, 1972b], Philadelphia *Evening Bulletin* [1972], Szulc [1972], and Welles [1972b].

17. Regular patterns of a type did occur, however, within phases. In every case (except for 1956) during the first year of a phase net other long-term capital inflows fell. In every phase they also rose in the last year.

18. The other inflows were relatively concentrated near the end of the period, thereby increasing this ratio, ceteris paribus.

19. Errors and omissions may consist primarily of unrecorded short-term movements. Net errors and omissions plus recorded net short-term capital movements rose in 1956–58, but not in 1965–69.

20. For example, according to a speech of July 1972 by Minister of Finance Orlando Millas, short-term credit lines from United States banks had been reduced from $220 million to $32 million, a decline which had been only partially offset by increased short-term credit from Japan and from European banks. The Chilean government claimed that this drop reflected implementation of a policy of financial blockade imposed by the United States. Anibal Palma, the Chilean Under Secretary of Foreign Affairs, so described United States actions and pressures on the IBRD and IDB in his address of April 14, 1972, before the General Assembly of the Organization of American States in Washington, as did Allende in his address to UNCTAD III in Santiago the previous day and also in his subsequent 1972 May Day address. Also see Welles [1972a].

21. Picks' [1955:59; 1965:121; and 1970:129] gives evidence of quite large capital movements which he speculates occurred in substantial part through black markets. The

PLD-NER for this market also reflects strong phase associations (line 1.1.3 of Table A.1).

22. Contrary to widespread impressions, United States [1960–70] reports that mean annual aid flows from the United States did not increase during the Frei period, but instead dropped by 20 per cent as compared to the previous phase. The average terms of such loans also became somewhat less favorable.

23. The United States long had used credits and loans to attempt to shape Chilean policies. For example, Cohen [1960:15] suggests that credits from the Export-Import Bank and the Institute of Inter-American Affairs were used by the United States to put pressure on Chile to break relations with Germany during the Second World War. Also Moran [1970:58–59, 65–69] relates the following events: Early in his term President Gonzalez sent the Pedregal Mission to Washington to renegotiate the Chilean foreign debt and to arrange new credits. The mission met with less than complete success, however, and was advised that Chile should treat the United States–owned large mining companies better. Subsequently, in 1948, after the passage of the Law for the Defense of Democracy which banned the Chilean Communist party (three members of which had been in the first cabinet of President Gonzalez, a situation about which the United States had expressed open concern), Export-Import Bank credits were increased substantially. As a result net loans to the central government for 1947–51 also rose to a level that was exceeded only in the 1960s.

24. It is interesting to note that the large increase in the use of these credits came not in the first year of the liberalization attempt, but thereafter. This suggests that they were not used to counter initial speculation about the seriousness of the liberalization attempt. Instead, they prolonged the maintenance of the overvalued NERs.

25. This figure does not include direct private credits or deferred payment import credits because data are not available for these items.

Chapter 9

Short-Run Stability in Nominal and Real Terms

In the previous three chapters an examination was made of the impact of Chilean international economic regimes on her balance of payments. In the remainder of Part III, the effects in other major areas of concern of macro-economic policy are explored. This chapter is focused on short-run stability. Short-run fluctuations are of considerable importance because they frequently have undermined Chilean attempts to liberalize, to transform the structure of the economy, to redistribute economic power, and to develop more rapidly. Price stability is taken up in section 9.1, and variations in real output and in the utilization of primary factors are explored in section 9.2.

SUMMARY AND CONCLUSIONS

i. Prima facie, inflation rates seem to have been inversely related to the degree of liberalization. Such an association does not reflect causality. Instead it reflects the fact that the liberalization efforts were part of the briefly succesful stabilization programs.

ii. At times, inflation may have been imported from abroad owing to price increases in world markets. On the average, however, Chilean price increases have far outpaced those in the relevant world markets.

iii. The impact of devaluation and liberalization on prices is quite complex because of many simultaneous indirect effects, especially through the nexus of monetary system, prices, wages and anticipated inflation. Devaluation alone leads to fairly considerable short-run price increases: the impact elasticity of price with respect to the NER is 0.6. This result in isolation validates a widespread Chilean fear of the inflationary effect of devaluation.

Reductions in quantitative restrictions, however, work in the opposite direction. This last fact has often been ignored in discussions of the inflationary impact of liberalization and devaluation. Such a policy package, therefore, would be less inflationary than is often hypothesized.

iv. Prima facie, short-run fluctuations in capacity utilization do not seem to have been related to the degree of liberalization. This lack of association is not surprising given the importance of domestic factors in determining output and given that many of the important foreign-sector factors have been beyond Chilean control and thus not affected by her international economic regime.

However, Chilean policies have exacerbated the sensitivity of her capacity utilization to international market fluctuations beyond her control by discouraging risk reduction through diversification of exports and by increasing the probability of balance-of-payments crises with their attendant shortages of imported inputs through negative inducements for exports and positive ones for imports.

v. The short-run impact of devaluation and liberalization on output is negative. Reduced quantitative restrictions lower output immediately through increased competition more than they increase it by higher imports of intermediate inputs. These results reinforce the frequent Chilean pessimism about the short-run real impact of liberalization and devaluation. They contrast sharply, moreover, with the Taylor and Black [1973] estimate of an employment elasticity with respect to devaluation of 0.9. The Taylor and Black result appears to be misleading because of the assumed exogenism of nominal wages, the money supply, and anticipated inflation.

vi. The instruments at the Chilean government's disposal for improving the trade-off between unused capacity and inflation are limited indeed. Monetary policy has exogenous elements, but the monetary base and the monetary multiplier both respond substantially to foreign-sector changes. The development of more effective monetary tools would increase the possibility of avoiding some of the negative short-run effects of devaluation. However, the trade-off would remain unless there was a fairly substantial drop in inflationary expectations. Because of the long history of inflation in Chile, inducing such a change in anticipations is quite difficult.

9.1 NOMINAL STABILITY

In previous chapters it was repeatedly emphasized that Chile has a long history of considerable inflation. Since World War II, for example, the rate of increase of the GDP deflator has averaged over 35 per cent per year!

In this section three questions are taken up concerning the impact of the foreign sector on domestic price changes: [1] (i) Has there been a relation between the rate of inflation and the degree of liberalization? (ii) To what extent have international price increases contributed to the Chilean inflation? (iii) What have been the implications of liberalization for Chilean prices?

9.1.1 Relation of Inflation to Exchange Control Phases.

In every more liberal phase since the Great Depression, the mean rate of inflation fell (line 2.1 in Table A.1). In every more restrictive one, it increased.[2] With no further information one *might* be tempted to posit some inverse causal relation between liberalization and inflation. The real explanation, however, is that the three major liberalization attempts were each part of a stabilization program which met with some initial success.[3] Instead of reducing inflation, in fact, liberalization itself ceteris paribus probably intensified inflationary pressures (see subsection 9.1.3, below).

9.1.2 Contribution of International Price Increases to Chilean Inflation.

Examination of the annual rates of change of foreign trade unit values reveals that in many instances, external price changes undoubtedly fed the Chilean inflation. The percentage increase in the unit value of imports (measured in U.S. dollars) averaged 15.2 in 1940–46, 23.6 in 1947, and 16.8 in 1951. The percentage increase in the unit value of exports (measured in U.S. dollars) was 16.2 in 1946, 31.4 in 1947, 26.5 in 1951, 15.4 in 1952, 14.4 in 1956, and 11.4 in 1959. For both imports and exports, moreover, increases in external prices were relatively high in the late 1960s and early 1970s.

On the average, however, internal price rises far outpaced external ones. For the 1945–65 period, for which consistent data are available, for example, the mean percentage increase in the unit value of imports was only 2.1 and that for exports was 5.1. The mean percentage rate of growth in the GDP deflator, in contrast, was 29.6. Although international price movements at times contributed significantly to Chilean inflation, therefore, generally they were not a dominant factor.

9.1.3 Price Impact of Liberalizations.

Much of the Chilean reluctance to liberalize and reduce the extent of overvaluation is rooted in fears of the inflationary consequences of such actions.

9.1.3.1 Partial-Equilibrium Analysis.

In a long-run, perfectly competitive equilibrium with no quantitative restrictions and no water in the tariff, the domestic producer price of internationally traded commodities would equal the c.i.f. price of the same commodities adjusted for price-related factors in the international economic regime. In such a situation the exchange rate and the prices of nontraded commodities also would have adjusted so that equilibrium existed in international payments and so that the domestic demand for real monetary balances equaled the supply.

Actual Chilean prices, of course, are not at long-run, perfectly competitive equilibrium levels. Instead, they are constantly adjusting in response to substantial shocks, especially in monetary policy and in the international economic regime including varying degrees of use of quantitative restrictions. Thus, to estimate price determinants, sector-specific characteristics of the impact of relevant domestic and international variables and the sector-specific adjustment to those characteristics must be included.

The general specification adopted here is a somewhat eclectic quasi-reduced form with the rate of change of sectoral product prices dependent on both domestic- and foreign-sector factors, some general and some sector-specific. A quasi-reduced form is necessary because the lack of sectoral demand and inventory data precludes direct estimation of structural relations. The rate of change rather than the level of prices is used because the high Chilean inflation rates in the sample period cause so much multicollinearity if levels are utilized that it is not possible to distinguish among competing hypotheses.[4]

Table 9.1 contains estimates of the determinants of the rate of change of Chilean sectoral prices for 1945–65. From an over-all viewpoint these estimates appear quite satisfactory. The corrected coefficients of determination indicate that the specification is consistent with from 0.90 to 0.98 of the variance in the dependent variable over the sample period. No serious problems of serial correlation are obvious. The estimated coefficients generally have the anticipated signs.

Much of the explanatory power lies in the domestic-sector variables. General domestic factors include a dummy variable for the initiation of stabilization programs and rates of change in the monetary supply, real GDP, an NBER-type index of current activity, the total inventory level relative to total GDP, and the distribution of factoral income and sectoral product. Sector-specific domestic factors include the rates of change in total real sectoral demand (including exports) relative to real sectoral output, sectoral capacity utilization, intermediate-input prices (by means of which the influence of monetary changes may be transmitted partially or totally in some sectors),[5] real sectoral unit labor costs (including employers' social security tax contributions), and real sectoral average labor productivity. An extensive discussion of these factors is given in Behrman [1974].[6] However, it should be emphasized that a substantial indirect impact of the international economic regime may be trans-

TABLE 9.1

Determinants of the Rates of Change of Chilean Sectoral Prices,[a] 1945–65

Dependent Variable: Rates of Change of Sectoral Product Prices	Rates of Change in Domestic Variables												
	Money Supply[b]			Real Product[c]		Economic Activity[d]				Unit Real Labor Costs[e]			
	Order of Polynomial					Current Indicator Index	Alternative 1	Alternative 2	Interm. Input Prices	No Lag	1-Yr. Lag	Av. Real Labor Productivity	Sector-Specific[f]
	1	2	3	1	2								
Agriculture							0.417	−0.715	0.890				
							(2.2)	(2.2)	(10.0)				
Mining							0.217			0.160			
							(2.4)			(3.9)			
Construction	−0.648[k]	0.187	−0.0167[k]				1.21	0.378				−1.37	−0.515
	(4.2)	(3.3)	(3.0)				(3.0)	(3.1)				(3.8)	(5.1)
Industry	−1.24	0.433	−0.0414	0.250					0.478	0.191			−0.146
	(8.0)	(7.3)	(6.9)	(2.9)					(7.6)	(2.9)			(4.6)
Transportation						0.634		−1.05	0.357	0.0623	0.0891	−0.870	
						(4.5)		(2.7)	(2.4)	(1.3)[l]	(1.5)[m]	(6.6)	
Utilities	−0.621	0.163	−0.0128	0.566		0.338			0.298[n]	0.145	0.298		
	(3.2)	(2.2)	(1.7)	(3.7)		(2.1)			(3.1)	(3.5)	(3.1)		
Housing	−0.0465			1.814	−0.236						0.125		1.12
	(5.9)			(4.0)	(3.6)						(3.5)		(5.1)
Services	−0.111[k]	0.0128[k]							1.03	0.272		−0.776	−0.509
	(2.2)	(2.2)							(8.7)	(4.3)		(4.8)	(6.0)

(*continued*)

TABLE 9.1 (*concluded*)

Dependent Variable: Rates of Change of Sectoral Product Prices	Rates of Change in Foreign-Sector Variables							
	Exchange Rate[g]							
	Order of Polynomial		Relative EER for Interm. Inputs[h]	Import Defla-tor	Ffrench-Davis QR Index[i]	Prior Deposits[j] or Sector-Specific	Constant	$\overline{R}^2$ *SE* *DW*
	1	2						
Agriculture	−45.2 (1.5)[m]	5.43 (1.5)[m]	0.283 (2.9)					0.93 0.050 2.0
Mining				0.0854[n] (2.8)		0.749 (15.6)		0.98 0.040 2.3
Construction			0.191 (2.0)		−0.903 (1.8)	−1.04 (2.0)	0.0599 (1.8)	0.93 0.039 2.1
Industry						−0.0091 (2.9)	0.128 (1.4)[m]	0.98 0.033 2.6
Transportation			0.492 (3.8)	0.470 (3.5)	0.992 (1.6)[m]	−0.0015 (2.4)	−0.295 (3.8)	0.94 0.047 2.3
Utilities					0.204 (3.8)		0.232 (1.8)	0.97 0.036 2.6
Housing			−0.234 (1.9)		−0.325 (2.4)			0.90 0.062 2.3
Services					−1.66 (2.7)	−0.0041 (1.4)[m]	0.0467 (1.5)[m]	0.98 0.036 3.0

Notes to Table 9.1

$\bar{R}^2$ = coefficient of multiple determination adjusted for degrees of freedom.

SE = standard error of estimate.

DW = Durbin-Watson statistic.

a. The figures in parentheses are the absolute values of the t statistics, each of which is significantly nonzero at the 5 per cent level unless otherwise noted. Since the variables are in the form of rates of change, the point estimates are elasticities. In those cases in which the lagged dependent variable is included, the Durbin-Watson statistic is biased toward 2.0. For data sources, see Behrman [1974].

b. The Hall-Sutch [1969] polynomial method (without a tail) is used over a six-year period. The implied lag patterns are as follows:

	Lag (no. of years)					
Sector	0	1	2	3	4	5
Construction	.770	.290	.088	.056	.098	.113
Industry	.819	−.034	−.270	−.136	.119	.247
Utilities	.642	.171	−.052	−.103	−.060	−.000
Housing	.279	.232	.186	.139	.093	.046
Services	.203	.105	.033	−.014	−.035	−.030

c. The Hall-Sutch [1969] polynomial method (without a tail) is used over a six-year period. The implied lag patterns are as follows:

	Lag (no. of years)					
Sector	0	1	2	3	4	5
Industry	−1.50	−1.25	−1.00	−0.75	−0.50	−0.25
Utilities	−3.40	−2.83	−2.26	−1.70	−1.13	−0.57
Housing	−2.37	−0.797	0.308	0.940	1.10	0.786

d. The NBER-type indicator of current economic activity is unlagged, as are the variables used in alternative 1. The variable for agriculture and mining is the ratio of total real sectoral demand to total real sectoral output; for construction, sectoral capacity utilization. The alternative-2 variables are taken with a one-year lag. For agriculture, the variable is the ratio of total current inventory to total GDP; for construction, sectoral capacity utilization; and for transportation, the ratio of total inventory to total GDP.

e. Includes employers' share of social security tax.

f. For construction and services, the dependent variable is lagged. The underlying variable for industry is a stabilization dummy with a value of 1.0 in 1956, 1957, 1960, 1961, and 1965, and 0.0 otherwise. For housing, the variable is the share of GDP originating in agriculture.

g. The Hall-Sutch [1969] polynomial method (without a tail) is used over a six-year period. The implied lag pattern for the sector is as follows: no lag, 0.0763; one year, 0.0364; two years, 0.0073; three years, −0.0104; four years, −0.0181; five years, −0.0145.

h. For agriculture, the underlying variable is the ratio of the domestic price index for agricultural products to the U.S. wholesale price index, the whole as a ratio to the national accounts EER. For construction and for housing, the variable is lagged one year.

i. For utilities, the underlying variable is the ratio of the black-market NER to the national accounts NER; for housing, it is the ratio of the domestic GDP deflator to the U.S. GDP deflator adjusted for the average import-tax rate and the average prior-deposit rate.

j. For mining, the underlying variable is the unit value of mining exports multiplied by the national accounts NER; for construction, the QR index is lagged one year. Note that the prior-deposit variable used is the change in the cost of prior deposits, not the rate of change in the cost.

k. The underlying variable is the ratio of the money supply to real GDP.

l. Significantly nonzero at the 15 per cent level.

m. Significantly nonzero at the 10 per cent level.

n. This variable is lagged one year for this sector.

---

mitted through some of these variables, especially through the money supply, real product, intermediate-input prices, and sectoral demands.

Some element of the international economic regime apparently is a significantly nonzero direct determinant of the rate of change of prices in every sector:

Price-related factors have a significantly nonzero impact in five of the eight sectors. These factors include expectational effects of exchange-rate changes,[7] cost-push factors related to imported intermediate inputs,[8] and international prices.[9] The estimates imply the highest relative responses to devaluation in the export-oriented mining sector and in the relatively import-dependent transportation sector.

Quantitative restrictions have significantly nonzero effects on price changes in five of the eight sectors.[10] The largest positive response is in transportation, which seems consistent with the relatively large impact of quantitative restrictions on transportation imports that is discussed in subsection 6.2.1 above. However, negative responses are suggested for three sectors having nontradable output: construction, housing, and services. This might be rationalized as reflecting an inverse relationship between quantitative restrictions and the availability of inputs and credit to these sectors, but such an explanation seems somewhat forced.

For industry, transportation, and services, finally, evidence exists of one further significantly nonzero direct link between the international economic policy regime and price changes. In these three sectors especially, when prior import deposit requirements are increased, part of the banking system credit is absorbed and inflationary pressure is reduced.

The partial-equilibrium estimates, then, suggest that the most important direct determinants of sectoral price changes are domestic ones, especially the money supply. The impact of the foreign sector, nevertheless, is significant for a number of sectors, even if the questionable inverse responses in the nontradable sectors are ignored.[11] Devaluation would be accompanied by increased direct inflationary pressure, particularly for mining, transportation, and agricultural products.

9.1.3.2 General-Equilibrium Analysis.

Domestic factors are more important than foreign ones in the partial-equilibrium analysis of price determination. Within a general-equilibrium context, however, international factors may be much more important than in the partial analysis if they have an impact through some of the domestic variables. The nature of the general-equilibrium impact, of course, depends upon what kind of macro model is appropriate for the analysis.

In a classical world with price flexibility and an exogenous money supply and no quantitative restrictions, devaluation leads to changes in relative prices but not in the over-all price level. Such assumptions have little relation, however, to recent Chilean experience. Product and factor prices have not been flexible because of conditions resembling "unlimited supply of labor" in the traditional sector, strong unionization and administered prices in parts of the modern sector, and government minimum-wage and price-ceiling legislation. Quantitative restrictions have been used extensively (see Part II, above).[12] Determination of the money supply has not been entirely exogenous. Therefore the economy has not been at full employment as in a classical model. Instead, during the two post-World War II decades, forgone output due to underutilization of capacity equaled almost a year and a half of actual output![13]

A Keynesian-like model is much more appropriate for short-run analysis of the Chilean economy because of the presence of price rigidities and underutilized capacity.[14] A simple Keynesian model is given in Appendix C which can be used to explore the price impact of devaluation and of changing quantitative restrictions.

A Keynesian National Income Determination Model. Consider the situation in which anticipated inflation, nominal wages, and the money supply are all assumed to be exogenous. Relationship C.15′ in Appendix C gives the total differential of prices under these assumptions. Devaluation and increased quantitative restrictions both probably increase the price level. Both work to increase aggregate demand. Both will have greater price impact the larger the absolute value of the marginal propensity to consume out of disposable income, the interest rate response of the demand for real monetary balances, the second derivative of production with respect to labor, and the sensitivity of the marginal product of capital to changes in the size of the employed labor force.[15] Both will have greater price impact the smaller the absolute value of the marginal tax rate, the marginal propensity to import out of income, the consumption response to real interest rates, the sensitivity of desired real monetary balance to income, the marginal product of labor, the sensitivity of investment to discrepancies between the marginal product of capital and the cost of capital, and the responsiveness of import demand to the domestic price level. Devaluation will increase prices more the larger the responses of exports and imports to the exchange rate and of taxes to imports and the smaller the sensitivity of taxes to exports. Increases in quantitative restrictions will increase prices more the larger the marginal propensity to consume, the sensitivity of taxes to imports, and the response of imports to quantitative restrictions.

For reasonable values of the parameters in relationships C.15′, the inflationary impact of devaluation or of increased quantitative restrictions may be quite substantial. But that is not the whole story. The effect of three variables—anticipated inflation, nominal wages, and the money supply—which were assumed to be exogenous to obtain C.15′, apparently has been to increase the inflationary impact of devaluations.[16] Anticipated inflation has been related to exchange-rate policy in at least two ways:

i. Several Chilean governments—most notably under Alessandri in the stabilization attempt of 1959–61 and under Allende in 1970–71—explicitly used a fixed NER as a symbol of their quest for price stability. When devaluation finally was forced because of foreign-exchange crises, inflationary expectations soared. At other times, the NER has not been an official symbol of price stability, but it has been a widely known unofficial indicator of probable price movements.

ii. Under the more restrictive trade regimes the government often has favored the importation of items with large weights in the domestic price indices. The hope has been that such expanded supplies would lessen price increases for these items, lower measured inflation, and thus reduce inflationary expectations. To the extent that liberalization has resulted in more unified exchange rates, of course, this phenomenon has been reversed.[17]

Nominal wages have not been exogenous, but have responded to price expectations which, in part, directly and indirectly reflected exchange-rate movements.[18]

The money supply has reflected foreign-sector policies in a number of respects:

i. The monetary base has varied substantially in its dependence on foreign exchange and gold. Before the Great Depression and in its early stages this direct dependence was almost complete. This led to very deflationary monetary policies at the start of the 1930s. Owing to the fall in the Central Bank's reserves of more than 58 per cent between the end of 1929 and mid-1931 and to a misguided stubbornness in maintaining the gold standard, for example, the money supply declined by 38 per cent, the real rate of interest was allowed to increase by 50 per cent (in hopes of lessening gold outflows), and the wholesale price index dropped by 16 per cent. In mid-1931, after an abrupt change in the foreign trade regime and the resignation of President Ibañez, a cheap-money policy was adopted.

In subsequent years, according to estimates by Luders [1970:15], there was much less direct dependence of total monetary emissions on Central Bank foreign exchange and gold operations. They were less than a fifth of the total monetary base in the 1931–39 subphase, somewhat over a third in 1940–46, and often less than that in the post-World War II phases and subphases. Nevertheless, changes in foreign-exchange reserves due to variations in the balance-of-payments surplus have had substantial effects on the monetary base. The Central Bank usually has not been able to neutralize more than a limited part of these changes because of the limited effectiveness of its policy instruments. As a result, both devaluation and increased quantitative restrictions have caused additional indirect inflationary pressure through their impact on foreign-exchange reserves and on the monetary base (see the discussion of C.10′ in Appendix C).

ii. The monetary base has also depended indirectly on the foreign sector through the impact of the international economic policy regime on the magnitude of the government deficit financed internally. Much of the impact has been on the revenue side. Important foreign-sector-related direct revenue sources have included import taxes, export taxes, direct taxes on large-scale mining, participation in profits of large-scale mining, and net revenues from exchange-rate differentials.[19] There has been a secular reduction in the relative direct dependence of the government on the foreign sector for tax revenues. Taxes related to foreign trade averaged 83 per cent of total taxes in 1908–27, 34 per cent in 1940–55, and about 21 per cent in 1956–70 (line 1.2.6.6 in Table A.1).[20] This decline partially originated in the conscious development of alternative domestic sources of revenue in order to reduce dependence on the foreign sector. It also has reflected the indirect and not clearly intended impact of some of the policies discussed in Part II above. These policies have discouraged exports and created the need to restrain imports, both of which have lowered trade-related tax revenues.

The impact of devaluation on the real value of tax revenues depends on the magnitude of increased revenues from expanded production and exports in comparison to probable reduced revenues from imports[21] and from reactions to increased anticipated inflation (relations C.5′, C.6′, C.9′, C.14′, and C.15′ in Appendix C).[22] The net effect probably is to increase government revenues. The impact of increased quantitative restrictions on real tax revenues depends on the magnitude of increased taxes from domestic production relative to that of reduced taxes from imports (relations C.5′, C.9′, and C.14′).[23] A one-sector model obscures, however, one interesting additional result of quantitative restrictions. The intensification of these restrictions often has favored mass-consumption items over other categories for income-distribution purposes and as part of the attempt to moderate inflationary expectations (see above). For the same reasons, these items generally have had relatively low import tax rates. Therefore, the intensification of quantitative restrictions at times reduced government tax revenues by lowering the average import tax rate because it not merely reduced total imports but changed their composition as well.[24] The net effect of all of these factors probably has been to reduce government revenues when restrictions increased.

The major direct impact of the international economic regime on government expenditure included the direct financial costs to the government of operating the regime and subsidies associated with the regime. No attempt is made in this study to present econometric estimates for the first of these costs, but evidence for other countries indicates that they may have been rather substantial.[25] Explicit subsidies associated with the international economic regime during the 1945–64 period were very limited, although subsequently they were increased as part of the expanded export-promotion programs under Frei and Allende (see subsection 4.2.2). Substantial implicit subsidies were made by use of favorable exchange rates and special regimes for various commodities (see Chapter 3 and sections 4.1 and 6.1). Furthermore, the foreign sector apparently affected government expenditure by substitution between net foreign savings and government savings (see subsection 12.2.3.2). Unless the last effect was quite strong, however, the net impact of devaluation and liberalization probably has been to reduce government expenditures.

Beyond the question of how foreign-sector policy has affected government revenues and expenditures is the question of determining what proportion of the government deficit has been financed externally. To the extent that such deficits have been financed externally *and* that the increased foreign exchange has been used to raise the flow of imports, the monetary base has not been increased.

As is noted in the previous chapter, sources for external financing of the government deficit dried up completely with the Great Depression. In the 1940s and early 1950s they increased somewhat, but still were not of major importance. As part of the stabilization and liberalization efforts of 1956–58 and 1959–61, however, government deficits were financed mainly abroad. The aim was to reduce inflationary pressures.[26] In addition to some short-run attainment of this goal, one result was a considerable addition to Chile's foreign debt.

iii. The foreign sector has not only affected the monetary base, but also has altered the money multiplier. Behrman [1974] gives estimates of behavioral relations which determine the money multiplier. These estimates together with the results presented in Appendix C suggest that devaluation has increased the money multiplier by reducing the currency-to-money ratio (owing to higher interest rates and higher income), the reserve-to-deposit ratio (owing to higher interest rates and higher anticipated inflation), and the ratio of time deposits to money (owing to higher anticipated inflation). They imply some counteracting tendencies of devaluation to reduce the money multiplier by increasing the ratio of time deposits to money (owing to higher interest rates and a higher PLD-NER, which affects expectations) and the currency-to-deposit ratio (owing to the higher PLD-NER).[27] The net effect on the monetary multiplier probably has been expansionary.

iv. Several additional relations between foreign-sector policy and the money supply merit mention in passing. Increases in prior-deposit requirements on imports have had the deflationary effect of absorbing part of the money supply (especially after such deposits were switched from the banking system to the Treasury in the 1960s). Devaluation also has had an additional deflationary effect not mentioned above, since at least a portion of the premiums previously received by importers has been transferred to the government. Given that imports generally have exceeded exports, devaluation has had a further deflationary effect, since more domestic currency has been required after a devaluation to finance the same dollar value of deficit as before.

General-Equilibrium Implications. The model in Chapter 2 provides a framework for evaluating the empirical magnitude of general-equilibrium price responses to changes in NERs and quantitative restrictions. This model roughly parallels the one in Appendix C on a multisector level, with the incorporation of inflationary anticipations, wages, and the money supply as endogenous variables.

For simulation 2.1.1 in Table A.11, equal proportional changes are assumed in all NERs, ceteris paribus, in the first year only (1962). The first-year price elasticity is 0.6, and the third-year elasticity is 0.3.[28] This quite positive price response partially reflects a response in the money supply due to increased international reserves, reduced net free reserves, and the changed composition of money demand. Also of importance are the direct price and price expectational links and a positive relation to the ratio of net demand to net supply as the foreign trade flows change (see subsection 9.1.3.1).

The widespread reluctance of Chileans to devalue because of an anticipated negative short-run inflationary impact, then, is well-founded. Such price increases, moreover, undo much of the potential positive effects of devaluation on the balance of payments (see subsections 6.2.2.1 and 7.2.2.1). Unless much more powerful monetary tools are developed, however, Chile cannot avoid the intensification of inflationary pressures from devaluation.

For simulation 2.3 in Table A.11, equal proportional changes are assumed in all quantitative restrictions, ceteris paribus, in the first year only. The general-equilibrium elasticities of price are quite high, 1.6 in the first year and 1.5 in the third. These sizable responses primarily reflect the impact of quantitative restrictions on the money supply through changes in international reserves. Such results lead to more optimism about the short-run impact of liberalization than does consideration of simulation 2.1.1 in isolation. If liberalization accompanies devaluation, the price effects of the former will at best partially offset the inflationary consequences of the latter. This counteracting tendency has been too often ignored in discussions of the short-run consequences of devaluation and liberalization in the Chilean economy.

9.2 REAL FLUCTUATIONS

Variations in real output are a second short-run concern. A frequently encountered criticism of Chilean liberalization efforts is that they have caused losses in real output and employment. In this section, three questions regarding this charge are taken up: (i) Have there been phase-associated fluctuations in capacity utilization?[29] (ii) Have capacity-utilization rates been sensitive to foreign-sector changes on a partial-equilibrium basis? (iii) What has been the general-equilibrium response of capacity utilization to changes in the international economic regime, ceteris paribus?

9.2.1 Associations of Capacity-Utilization Rates with Exchange Control Phases.

A simple association between the mean capacity-utilization rates for phases and subphases and the degree of liberalization is not evident (line 2.2 in Table A.1).[30] The highest means are for the Phase II periods of 1962–64 and 1971–73.[31] Next is that for the Phase III years of 1965–70,[32] followed by that for the type-II subphase of the Second World War.[33] The lowest average by far was for 1931–39 and was due to the impact of the Great Depression (see section 1.3). Next lowest were those for the Phase II years of 1947–51 and Phase III years of 1956–58.[34] The mean rose from that of the previous period for the 1959–61 Phase IV liberalization, but fell for the two Phase III liberalizations.

That lack of a simple association is not surprising: capacity utilization is largely determined by domestic factors rather than foreign ones (see subsection 9.2.2). Much of the importance of the foreign sector in the determination of capacity utilization, moreover, has been due to wars and export-market fluctuations. These phenomena are beyond Chilean control. They clearly are not caused by any changes Chile might make in her international economic policy regimes.

On the other hand, Chilean policy probably somewhat exacerbated short-run instability in real terms. Overvaluation effectively discouraged greater diversification in exports, which would have reduced vulnerability to international fluctuations (see Chapter 7) and led to restrictions on imported inputs at times of balance-of-payments crisis.

9.2.2 Partial-Equilibrium Determinants of Capacity Utilization.

Table 9.2 contains regression estimates of the determinants of capacity utilization for eight Chilean sectors in 1945–65. In the underlying model real

TABLE 9.2

Determinants of Chilean Sectoral Capacity Utilization,[a] 1947–65

Dependent Variable: Sectoral Real GDP	Domestic Determinants: Price Ratio: Product to Labor Input, No Lag	Price Ratio: Product to Labor Input, 2-Yr. Lag	Economic Activity Indicator	Ratio: Credit to GDP[b]	1960 Earthquake Dummy	Sector-Specific	Constant	Foreign-Sector Determinants: Ratio: Imports to Product[c]	Ffrench-Davis QR Index	NER Ratio: Black-Market to Nat. Accts.	Constant	R^2 / *SE* / *DW*
Agriculture			0.190			0.302[d]	0.913	−1.10				0.96
			(3.9)			(3.9)	(32.8)	(6.5)				47.4
			[0.1]			[0.1]	[1.0]	[−0.2]				1.8
Mining	0.0042[e]	0.0305		1.58			1.59	11.8	−1.76			0.95
	(4.3)	(2.6)		(2.9)			(2.6)	(3.1)	(2.8)			57.9
	[0.3]	[0.2]		[0.1]			[1.8]	[0.5]	[−2.0]			2.0
Construction					−0.119	1.48[f]			0.882		−25.8	0.98
					(2.4)	(1.5)[g]			(5.6)		(1.2)[h]	23.9
					[−0.1]	[0.1]			[0.9]			1.9
Industry			0.305				0.574		0.0966[i]	0.0367	222.1	0.97
			(5.0)				(7.5)		(2.0)	(2.6)	(1.4)[g]	100.0
			[0.2]				[0.6]		[0.1]	[0.1]		2.0
Transportation		0.231[j]	−4.08[k]			−12.9[l]	3.25			−0.098		0.96
		(1.9)	(7.0)			(5.7)	(7.6)			(3.7)		59.4
		[0.2]	[−1.4]			[−1.3]	[3.7]			[−0.2]		2.5
Utilities	0.00318[e]	0.00119[e]	0.367			0.0357[m]	0.234[n]		0.135[l]		−26.9	0.98
	(6.2)	(3.6)	(6.2)			(6.9)	(3.0)		(2.7)		(2.6)	6.4
	[0.4]	[0.2]	[0.3]			[0.2]			[0.2]			2.6
Housing			0.216	4.53	0.176	−5.35[l]		−1.50	1.47		−590.	0.98
			(2.1)	(4.8)	(4.3)	(4.3)		(1.3)[h]	(9.4)		(4.1)	47.4
			[0.1]	[0.5]	[0.0]	[−0.5]		[−0.2]	[1.6]			2.6
Services		0.00922[o]		1.45					0.715		−941.	0.94
		(2.3)		(4.0)					(5.6)		(2.2)	286.0
		[0.2]		[0.2]					[0.7]			2.0

Notes to Table 9.2

$\bar{R}^2$ = coefficient of multiple determination adjusted for degrees of freedom.

SE = standard error of estimate.

DW = Durbin-Watson statistic.

a. Each independent variable is multiplied by the sectoral capacity of real GDP. Except as indicated in the notes, the variables are not lagged. The figures in parentheses below the point estimates are the absolute values of the *t* statistics. All point estimates are significantly nonzero at the 5 per cent level unless otherwise noted. The figures in brackets are the elasticities at the point of sample means. Behrman [1974] gives data sources and further details.

b. Public credit only for mining; private credit only for housing; public plus private credit for services.

c. Ratio of imports of staple consumer goods to agricultural capacity for agriculture; ratio of intermediate imports to total GDP for mining; and ratio of lagged total imports to lagged total GDP for housing.

d. Sum of value of real government direct and indirect investment, depreciated at rate of 3 per cent through past year, as ratio to total real GDP.

e. Ratio of product price, adjusted for direct and indirect taxes, to unit labor costs including employers' social security contributions.

f. Ratio of noninventory investment to GDP.

g. Significantly nonzero at the 10 per cent level.

h. Significantly nonzero at the 15 per cent level.

i. Ratio of domestic GDP deflator to United States GDP deflator adjusted for the average import tax rate and the average prior-deposit rate.

j. Ratio of product price, adjusted for direct and indirect taxes, to material input price index.

k. Ratio of total inventory level to GDP.

l. Average indirect tax rate.

m. Rate of change of GDP deflator.

n. Lagged dependent variable (*not* multiplied by sectoral capacity). For this sector the Durbin-Watson statistic is biased toward 2.0.

o. Ratio of product price, adjusted for direct and indirect taxes, to wages adjusted for employers' social security contribution.

---

sectoral GDP [35] adjusts toward a level determined by the desired capacity-utilization rate and actual real sectoral capacity.[36]

On an over-all level these estimates appear to be quite satisfactory. The corrected coefficients of determination imply that the results are consistent with from 94 to 98 per cent of the variance in the dependent variable over the sample period. Evidence of considerable problems of autocorrelation does not appear. The signs of the significantly nonzero coefficient estimates generally are those anticipated a priori.

Variations in sectoral real capacities underlie much of the fluctuation in real product, but the variations in the desired sectoral capacity-utilization rates also are quite important. Among the domestic determinants of the desired utilization rates, significantly nonzero coefficients are obtained in at least three sectors for price ratios of product to labor input, indices of the change in current economic activity, and relative availability of credit. In addition, there are several significant sector-specific coefficients. A proxy for public infrastructure development affects agriculture. The level of over-all investment influences utilization in construction. The 1960 earthquake reduced utilization in construction and increased it in housing. Indirect taxes discouraged production particularly in transportation and housing. Anticipated inflation has induced higher production in utilities.

Space limitations preclude discussion of these factors here. Some of them, however, have important roles in the indirect transmission of the impact of foreign-policy changes which are included in the general-equilibrium analysis of the next subsection.[37]

For every sector there is evidence of some direct significantly nonzero impact of the international economic regime on the level of desired capacity utilization. The ratio of competing imports to domestic product is inversely related to real product in agriculture and housing. For the former sector the frequent policies of increasing food imports as part of the anti-inflationary strategy (e.g., through Public Law 480), therefore, may have had a direct negative feedback on subsequent domestic production. The ratio of intermediate imports to product has a significant impact in mining, but not in other sectors. At least for industry the lack of significance of intermediate imports may be somewhat surprising given the hypothesized increasing dependence of that sector on imported inputs.[38] Indices of quantitative restrictions (including the ratio of the black-market to the national accounts NERs) have significantly nonzero coefficients for every sector except agriculture. For mining and for transportation these coefficients are negative, which suggests that the restraining effect on production due to limitations on imported inputs together with the association between the use of quantitative restrictions and an overvalued exchange rate which penalizes mining exports are dominant. For other sectors, however, apparently any restraining effects of quantitative restrictions due to imported input shortages are more than offset by increased demand due to shortages of competing imports. For services, furthermore, the significantly positive coefficient of the quantitative restrictions index presumably also reflects the direct use of increased numbers of people to administer the QR regulations.

The direct effects of foreign-sector policies on capacity utilization, thus, have been widespread. They have sometimes, however, been partially offsetting. Indirect effects, moreover, may have been reinforcing or offsetting. To discern the net impact of changes in the international economic regime on capacity utilization, therefore, a general-equilibrium framework must be used.

9.2.3 Impact of Foreign-Sector Policies on Capacity Utilization Within a General-Equilibrium Framework.

The model of national income determination in Appendix C gives an insight into the impact on production of changes in NERs and quantitative restrictions. If price anticipations, nominal wages, and the money supply are exogenous, relationship C.14′ gives the comparative static effects of such changes on production. Both devaluation and intensified quantitative restrictions probably increase aggregate demand and therefore production. The effects of changed marginal propensities and productivities on the size of these increases generally are the same as is discussed in subsection 9.1.3.2, above. However, the impact is greater the higher the marginal product of labor and the lower the second derivative of production with respect to labor, instead of vice versa.

The arguments presented in subsection 9.1.3.2 for the endogenism of price anticipations, nominal wages, and the money supply again hold for devaluation and also, in the case of the money supply, for changes in quantitative restrictions. Induced increases in anticipated inflation and in the money supply both probably increase aggregate demand and production. Therefore, they reinforce the effects noted in the previous paragraph. Induced rises in the nominal wage, however, have the opposite effect because the aggregate supply curve moves up owing to higher labor costs (relation C.12′) and the aggregate demand curve moves down owing to reductions in the incentive to export because of higher labor costs (relations C.6′ and C.14′).

The model in Chapter 2 again provides a framework for evaluating the empirical magnitude of general-equilibrium production responses to changes in NERs and quantitative restrictions. In this model sectoral capacity-utilization rates are determined by the estimates in Table 9.2. Therefore, direct effects of quantitative restrictions on production are incorporated, in contrast to the more simplified model of Appendix C.

Simulation 2.1.1 in Table A.11 explores the impact of equal percentage changes in all NERs, ceteris paribus, for the first year only of the simulation. The first-year response is inverse, although quite small in absolute value. The positive responses in most other sectors almost offset the negative responses in industry, services, and housing. The third-year elasticity is positive, although still quite small at 0.1.[39]

Under the assumption that employment rates are highly correlated with capacity-utilization rates, these results prima facie contradict the Taylor and Black [1973] estimates of an employment elasticity of 0.9.[40] This discrepancy reflects the consequences of three different sets of assumptions in the two models: (i) Taylor and Black posit immediate adjustment in the labor market and no adjustment in the capital stock, while the model used here has lagged adjustments for both labor and capital; (ii) Taylor and Black maintain the nominal wage constant when they change the exchange rate, but considerable wage adjustment occurs in simulation 2.1.1;[41] (iii) Taylor and Black exclude a number of indirect effects that are passed through the monetary system but which are incorporated here.

Although the labor-adjustment mechanism in the present study may be somewhat too slow and, therefore, the true value of the first-year employment elasticity may be positive, a general-equilibrium value approaching that presented by Taylor and Black seems quite unlikely. More probable is a conclusion consistent with the results presented in Table A.11. The first-year employment-capacity utilization impact is likely to be very small—and possibly inverse. The medium-run impact is likely to be positive, although still not very large.[42] These results support the conventional Chilean wisdom that devaluation has a very limited and possibly negative short-run impact on production.[43]

Simulation 2.3 in Table A.11 investigates the effects of equal proportional changes in all quantitative restrictions, ceteris paribus, in the first year only. The protective effects of quantitative restrictions on competing final goods apparently dominate effects on imported input supplies. The elasticity of real capacity utilization is 0.1 in the first year and 0.2 in the third year.

The total implications of these two simulations are not very encouraging for liberalization programs. They imply that devaluations together with reductions in quantitative restrictions almost certainly will cause a drop in capacity utilization rates. Offsetting expansionary fiscal and monetary policies might be called for. However, such policies would feed the already considerable inflation unless spiraling inflationary expectations were radically lowered. Such a readjustment of price anticipations may be possible only with substantial short-run political or economic dislocations or both—a topic far beyond the subject of this book.

NOTES

1. The related question of how price changes affected the international economic policy regimes is considered in Chapter 13.

2. In Table A.1 only 1971 is included for the Phase II Allende period. In 1972 the inflation rate exceeded 160 per cent, and in 1973 it rose to an even higher level.

3. During the Phase III 1965–69 period, however, much of the liberalization occurred after the abandonment of price stabilization attempts.

4. The adjustment processes are represented by the Hall-Sutch [1969] polynomial method (without a tail) over a six-year period for the rates of change of the money supply and real GDP and for expectations regarding the rate of change of the NER. Other adjustments are represented by the possibility of a geometric process for the dependent variable or by simple lags for other variables.

5. Intermediate-input prices include the price of imported components and, thus, the direct impact of the international economic regime.

6. Alternative estimates are in Behrman [1973c], Corbo [1971:198–201], García [1964], Harberger [1963], and Yver [1970].

7. The NER changes also may represent a cost-push factor in that the local-currency cost of external indebtedness increases as the NER increases.

8. The results suggest that the rate of growth of the price of services declines relatively when these imported inputs increase relatively in price.

9. For no sector is there evidence of a significant response to rates of change of import unit values multiplied by the EER or to sectoral imports relative to domestic absorption.

10. To the extent that changes in quantitative restrictions only changed the premiums going to traders with import licenses, of course, these changes did not affect sectoral prices.

11. Behrman [1974] includes estimates for the determination of the rate of change of deflators of final demand components that suggest similar conclusions. Among that group devaluation would have the strongest direct impact on exports, imports, and investment. Quantitative restrictions have a fairly pervasive direct impact, including an inverse relationship for the export deflator, apparently because use of such restrictions makes possible continuance of an overvalued NER.

12. Sohmen [1958:271–273] demonstrates that prices must decline after devaluation if economic welfare increases when quantitative restrictions, import taxes, etc., are used. However, he assumes that money national income is kept constant due to monetary and fiscal policies and that full employment is maintained. Such assumptions are not appropriate for recent Chilean history.

13. This estimate is from Behrman [1973b:256]. It is very conservative because it is based on a trend-through-the-peaks capacity definition which refers to shortfalls from actually attained rather than potential production levels.

14. A Keynesian model is much more appropriate in the Chilean case than for most developing economies because the nonmonetized sector is quite small, saving and investment decisions often are separated, and there is some evidence of a significant role for interest rates (see Behrman [1972b]). On the other hand, comparative statics analysis with a Keynesian model has many of the same limitations in the Chilean case as in the case of more developed economies. Probably most important is the focus on equilibrium solutions rather than disequilibrium adjustments. Despite the burgeoning recent literature on disequilibrium, however, at this time the state of the art does not permit satisfactory analysis of disequilibrium behavior except under very particular ad hoc assumptions.

The term "Keynesian model" is *not* used here to mean a case in which all focus is on aggregate demand, and supply considerations are ignored. To the contrary, an aggregate production function is explicitly included (see Appendix C).

15. If the sign of any dependent term cited here or subsequently is ambiguous, but one sign is much more likely than the other, given the available empirical evidence or a priori expectations or both, no qualifications are made, both because of limitations of space and because of the complexity of the explanation.

Space limitations also preclude a detailed explanation of why these dependencies are of the indicated sign (e.g., the more sensitive the marginal product of capital to the number of laborers, the greater is the inducement to invest in response to the expanded aggregate demand which occurs because of foreign trade responses to devaluation). Careful consideration of Appendix C, however, should generally provide any necessary clarification.

16. For changes in quantitative restrictions, the behavior of the money supply has not been exogenous.

17. In the 1956–58 effort at stabilization plus liberalization, for example, the imported component of the wholesale price index rose quite substantially (about 30 per cent) relative to the over-all index. The relative unification of NERs resulted in rather large effective devaluations for some of the "essential" imports (e.g., sugar, coffee, Para-

guayan tea) which previously had been more favored and which had disproportionately large weights in the price indices. Likewise the changes in the regime caused relatively large increases for export and mining-related price indices owing to the reduction of discrimination against key products included there.

18. For evidence see Behrman [1971a,1974] and Behrman and García [1973].

19. Not all of these sources are independent. The tax function estimates in Behrman [1974], for example, imply a direct trade-off between government revenues from NER discrimination for the legal cost of production of large-scale mining and government revenues from direct taxes on large-scale mining. For every escudo increase in the legal cost of production due to the former, revenues from direct taxes decreased by 0.41 escudos (after the *Nuevo Trato*).

20. The 18 per cent figure for 1965–70 in Table A.1 is misleading in a sense because government participation replaced some direct taxes in large-scale mining.

21. Imports decline if the price and exchange-rate effects in relation C.5′ outweigh the income effect.

22. For evidence of an inverse relation between taxes and expected inflation in Chile see Behrman [1974]. This reaction reflects the incentive to postpone tax payments when expected inflation is high because the nominal penalties for late payment do not offset the expected capital gains from postponement until prices have increased.

23. It is assumed that the quantitative restrictions in fact do reduce imports despite the increase in import demand due to over-all expanded aggregate demand.

24. A regression of the logarithm of nominal import taxes (TXM) on the logarithm of the nominal value of imports (M), a secular time trend ($TIME$), an anticipated inflation variable to represent tax avoidence (π), and an index of quantitative restrictions (QR) provides some weak support for this hypothesis:

$$\underset{}{TXM} = \underset{(6.3)}{0.610\, M} + \underset{(3.7)}{0.116\, TIME} - \underset{(2.0)}{0.0029\, \pi} - \underset{(1.7)}{2.71\, QR} + \underset{(1.0)}{1.63}$$

$$\bar{R}^2 = 0.997;\ SE = 0.101;\ DW = 2.0;\ \text{years covered, 1945–65}$$

25. See Bhagwati and Srinivasan [1975] and Krueger [1972b] for examples.

26. The external financing was supposed to be an interim measure while fiscal reforms were enacted.

27. The institution of dollar deposits in 1959–61 also lowered the money multiplier by increasing the ratio of time deposits to money.

28. For a sustained devaluation, such as in simulation 2.1.3, the third-year price impact is much larger than in this case due to the cumulative effects. For both simulations 2.1.1 and 2.1.3 the first-year estimates are quite comparable to the range of 0.48 to 0.69 which Harberger [1964] presents for a model based in substantial part on his Chilean experience. Harberger assumes a constant nominal money wage rate and complete adjustment to a sustained devaluation. The effect of the first of these assumptions should be to lower his estimate relative to that of the present model, but the effect of the second should be to increase it relatively.

29. A trend-through-the-peak capacity definition is used throughout this section. This definition measures output against attainable capacity (not rated capacity) and therefore gives relatively high utilization rates. Behrman [1973b] and others he cites there discuss the advantages and limitations of this definition.

30. For recent years the Santiago unemployment rate provides supplementary information about the utilization of productive resources (line 2.3 in Table A.1). The movements in this variable reinforce the characterization of short-run developments based on the capacity-utilization measure alone.

31. Table A.1 includes only 1971, but the scanty available evidence suggests that high capacity utilization continued at least into 1972. For example, for January–April 1972 as compared to the same period for 1971, CORFO [1972a,1/8/72:1–3] reports increases of over 15 per cent for industrial production, industrial use of electrical power, cement production, and shipments of iron and steel products. Also the unemployment rate of the Greater Santiago area on March 1972 was 0.048 as compared to 0.082 a year earlier. The only negative figure concerning the use of real capacity was a decline of 4.4 per cent in kilometer-tons of freight transported by the railroads.

32. As liberalization accelerated later in this phase, however, utilization rates tended to decline.

33. Note that capacity utilization in 1908–27 averaged as high as during the relatively prosperous World War II subphase. This observation raises questions about the structuralists' characterization of Chilean capacity utilization as being very vulnerable to fluctuations emanating from the foreign sector in the period of relatively liberal foreign economic policies before the Great Depression.

34. Critics of the Ibañez-Klein-Saks stabilization program of 1956–58 have focused on this decline, although they have tended to overstate its magnitude.

35. Given capacity, variations in product directly determine variations in capacity-utilization rates.

36. The adjustment process is a geometric distributed lag, but only for utilities do the results suggest significant adjustment extending beyond one year.

37. For further consideration of these results see Behrman [1974]. For an earlier attempt to estimate Chilean capacity-utilization determinants see Behrman [1973b].

38. Anne Krueger has suggested that this impact may be represented by the quantitative restrictions variable. The effect of such restrictions on intermediate imports was explored in section 6.2.

39. By the third year, however, changes in capacity occur. Therefore, the production elasticity no longer is the same as the utilization-rate elasticity.

40. Taylor and Black obtain this estimate when they use the same elasticities of substitution between capital and labor that are utilized in this study. Under the assumption of elasticities of substitution between capital and labor of 1.0, they obtain an elasticity of employment with respect to the NER of 1.7.

41. Taylor and Black acknowledge that a constant nominal wage is not at all probable under exchange-rate adjustments.

42. Within a partial-equilibrium framework de Castro and de la Cuadra [1971:12–13, 20–21] reach the same conclusion for the immediate impact on employment in Chilean industry (although their specification of time periods is not clear). They maintain that for given industrial capacity, the subsectoral increases in the demand for labor originating in exchange-rate alterations would offset approximately the subsectoral decreases.

43. If devaluation induces substantial decumulation of speculative inventories built up in anticipation of the devaluation, the results may not be more deflationary than is suggested by the present model.

Chapter 10

Resource Allocation and Structural Change

The foreign sector long has been important in Chilean resource allocation among sectors and subsectors. Before the Great Depression, substantial resource movements accompanied the rise and fall of nitrates and the decline and resurgence of copper, to cite but two examples. In that era the government also consciously used the international economic regime to promote industrial import substitution (see section 1.2).

The catastrophic impact of the Great Depression greatly strengthened export pessimism (sections 1.3 and 1.4). The nation turned inward. The government utilized numerous foreign-sector policy tools to try to induce resource shifts into industry (Chapters 3 and 4). The impact of those policies on PLD-EERs, ITRs, EPRs, and DRCs after the Second World War was analyzed in Chapter 5. A major characteristic of these price-related measures is the substantial variation in their applicability to different production sectors and subsectors and different end uses. Trade barriers have been highest for manufacturing and lowest for mining, with agriculture in between. Within industry they have been greatest for the traditional "easy" consumer-oriented subsectors (at least until the late 1960s). They also have been higher for consumer products than for intermediate or investment goods. Finally, the price-related measures generally have favored import substitution over export expansion.

The general patterns noted in the previous paragraph have persisted throughout recent decades. Distortions in the signals for product use and in the rate of transformation between domestic and foreign resources, therefore, also have persisted. The degree of discrimination among categories, however, has varied significantly. Liberalization has tended to reduce discrepancies [1] and vice versa.

These patterns and variations in the price-related measures raise several questions: (i) What have been the long-run trends and phase-related movements in resource allocation? (ii) What has been the relation between ratios of the prices of final product to intermediate inputs and resource allocation? (iii) What have been the costs of the attempts to alter resource allocation by using the international economic regime to create differential incentives?

SUMMARY AND CONCLUSIONS

i. Secular trends in the composition of output have included declines in the shares of agriculture and mining, increases in industry until the early 1950s, and increases in all other sectors. Discriminatory aspects of the international economic regimes have contributed to the declines in the first two sectors and to the initial rise in industry. The lack of correlation between import-substitution coefficients and industrial subsectoral growth, however, suggest that in manufacturing, foreign-sector policies may have been less important than is often claimed. Overvaluation has helped to induce the shift from goods to services, although increased quantitative restrictions have tended to work in the other direction.

ii. The secular declines in agriculture and mining have increased pressure on the balance of payments. In this respect the industrialization strategy has added to foreign-sector difficulties.

iii. Phase-associated responses have been quite considerable. The response to liberalizations in agriculture and in the manufacturing subsectors that are more modern and oriented more toward intermediate-goods production has been particularly positive. The more traditional and consumer-oriented manufacturing subsectors, in contrast, have been unable to meet the increased competition associated with liberalization. This failure is all the more striking since protection for many of the latter subsectors dates back to the nineteenth century.

iv. The responses described in the preceding paragraph create somewhat of a dilemma for the government, given industrialization as one of its objectives. Although manufacturing grew considerably in the early years of restrictiveness following the Great Depression, it has stagnated in recent decades and has declined in its share of product and of labor-force absorption. Further restrictiveness does not promise future development. Liberalization, on the other hand, involves considerable short- and medium-run costs until greater efficiency is induced in traditional industries or resources are turned aside from them. For the transitional period some direct subsidization might be necessary.

Given the fiscal problems of the government, however, this alternative can be used only with great care.

v. There is little empirical support for a relationship between subsectoral resource allocation and EPRs or for other price ratios of final to intermediate product partially because factors other than price ratios are important in capacity-utilization and capacity-creation decisions. The poor correlation may also reflect erratic changes in the price-related measures occasioned by the use of quantitative restrictions.

vi. The international economic regimes have had significant implications for resource allocation. Nevertheless, care must be taken not to exaggerate the expected gains from policy improvements in foreign sectors as compared with those in the domestic area.

10.1 LONG-RUN TRENDS AND PHASE-RELATED PATTERNS IN RESOURCE ALLOCATION

Table A.1 contains the mean composition of value added by sector for phases and subphases between 1908 and 1971 (lines 3.1.1.1–3.1.1.3). The sub-sectoral breakdown of value added and of total value of manufacturing in 1957, 1962, and 1967 is given in Table 10.1.

10.1.1 Industrial Production by Sector.

AGRICULTURE.

The secular trend in the share of agriculture in production clearly has been downward (line 3.1.1.1 in Table A.1).[2] The same trend exists for the agricultural percentage share of the labor force: 36.2 in 1920, 34.8 in 1945, and 28.2 in 1965. In part these declines reflect an Engel-curve phenomenon. The income elasticity of the demand for domestic agricultural goods is smaller than the income elasticity for all goods.

The falling share of agriculture is not due to relative income elasticities alone, however. It also reflects the response of capacity and capacity utilization to the disincentives for production created by recent international economic regimes (Table 5.2, column 2, and tables 9.1 and 12.1). Numerous policies have had the intent of shifting resources into industry and of mitigating inflationary pressures by keeping agricultural prices low. Partially because of such policies not only has the agricultural share of product steadily fallen, but Chile has changed from a major agricultural exporter in the nineteenth century to a net importer of basic agricultural commodities. One unintended result of these

TABLE 10.1
Pattern of Chilean Industrial Production, by Subsectors, 1957, 1962, and 1967

Subsectors	Proportion of Manufacturing Value Added			Proportion of Manufacturing Total Value			Proportion of 1962 Total	
	1957	1962	1967	1957	1962	1967	Value Added	Total Value
Agriculture							.100	.090
Fishing							.003	.004
Mining							.085	.065
Manufacturing	1.00	1.00	1.00	1.00	1.00	1.00	.283	.412
Food	0.175	0.120	0.163	0.268	0.232	0.224		
Beverages	0.045	0.062	0.051	0.036	0.082	0.048		
Tobacco	0.054	0.028	0.026	0.026	0.014	0.016		
Textiles	0.128	0.086	0.101	0.120	0.074	0.087		
Clothing and footwear	0.078	0.156	0.047	0.080	0.139	0.048		
Wood and cork	0.032	0.029	0.029	0.029	0.033	0.027		
Furniture	0.016	0.046	0.010	0.012	0.037	0.008		
Paper and paper products	0.018	0.022	0.021	0.030	0.019	0.019		
Printing, publishing	0.037	0.021	0.027	0.027	0.016	0.020		
Leather, leather products	0.012	0.012	0.011	0.016	0.014	0.012		
Rubber products	0.012	0.014	0.016	0.013	0.010	0.012		
Chemicals	0.078	0.050	0.088	0.078	0.054	0.072		
Petroleum and coal products	0.032	0.058	0.018	0.037	0.046	0.031		
Nonmetallic minerals	0.057	0.054	0.032	0.045	0.036	0.026		
Basic metals	0.109	0.044	0.165	0.093	0.040	0.229		
Metal products	0.041	0.045	0.046	0.035	0.036	0.039		
Nonelectrical machinery	0.017	0.031	0.044	0.013	0.027	0.031		
Electrical machinery	0.017	0.034	0.033	0.012	0.027	0.028		
Transportation equipment	0.023	0.060	0.062	0.018	0.041	0.044		
Misc. manufacturing	0.012	0.030	0.011	0.010	0.028	0.048		
Construction							.053	.056
Utilities							.013	.013
Commerce							.232	.179
Housing							.057	.040
Transportation, communications							.053	.049
Services							.120	.093

SOURCE: Calculated from data in DEC [1960a], INE [1970], and ODEPLAN [1970].

policies, thus, has been to add to balance-of-payment pressures by increasing the need for basic imported foodstuffs.[3]

The agricultural share of production also has responded to medium-term fluctuations in the degree of liberalization. For two of the three liberalization attempts it increased on the average (line 3.1.1.1 in Table A.1).[4] The estimates in Table A.2, moreover, indicate significantly positive liberalization-associated increments in the exponential growth rate of agricultural GDP—and significantly negative ones for total GDP. The greater the degree of liberalization, thus, the greater the apparent extent of both short- and long-run resource flows into this sector, ceteris paribus.

Mining.

The secular trend for the share of mining in total GDP also has been downward (line 3.1.1.2 in Table A.1).[5] The same downward movement again is found for the percentage share of mining in the labor force: 5.1 in 1930, 5.4 in 1945, and 4.2 in 1965. Engel curves do not aid much in explaining this decline. The response of capacity and capacity utilization to policies which generally discriminated against mining and in favor of manufacturing, however, again was important (Tables 9.1 and 12.1). Such policies, in fact, were even less favorable toward mining than toward agriculture (columns 2 and 3 in Table 5.2), and their impact on the balance of payments again was negative—this time by reducing exports (see Chapter 7).

Both the mean shares of GDP for phases (line 3.1.1.2 in Table A.1) and the estimated deviation from the secular exponential growth rates (Table A.2) suggest a negative impact of liberalization on GDP in mining! This result, prima facie, is quite surprising given the lessening of discrimination against this sector at the start of liberalization attempts (column 3 in Table 5.2). In fact, however, it largely reflects coincidental relative price movements. In the 1956–58 liberalization, for example, the volume of copper production increased significantly, and copper was the dominant mining product.[6] But the copper price fell so much that the relative contribution of mining to GDP dropped despite the expansion of production in quantity terms. For this sector—and for this sector alone—fluctuations in the shares of GDP may be quite misleading indices of variations in real product.

Manufacturing.

The secular trend for the share of manufacturing in GDP was fairly strongly upward until the early 1950s, but has been downward ever since (line 3.1.1.3 in Table A.1).[7] The percentage share of manufacturing in the total work force reflects the same pattern: 15.2 in 1920 (including construction), 18.4 in 1945, 19.7 in 1952, and 18.0 in 1960.

The increased protection given manufacturing import substitution in the

1930s was an important factor in the early relative surge of industry.[8] According to Muñoz's [1968:82] careful estimates, the share of import substitution in real industrial growth in the period from 1927 to 1937–38 was 0.73, as compared with a Chenery normal value of 0.17 (see Table 10.3, below). However, for 1937–38 to 1952–53, Muñoz's estimate of the coefficient of import substitution is only 0.15, as compared to a Chenery normal value of 0.19.[9] For 1952–53 to 1963–64 his estimates imply very little net additional industrial import substitution.

From a longer-run viewpoint, then, the protectionist policies generally utilized after the Great Depression have been unsuccessful in a number of their direct objectives regarding manufacturing. Since the Second World War, import substitution has been quite limited. Since the early 1950s industrial growth has been lower than over-all growth. At the same time this sector has declined relatively in its labor absorption, thereby adding to the unemployment and underemployment problems of the 1960s and 1970s.[10]

From a shorter-run perspective, nevertheless, there appears to have been an inverse association between the degree of liberalization and the relative importance of industry in resource utilization and in production. During the past two decades, for example, the mean share of industry in GDP has fallen or remained constant with each liberalization effort and has risen or remained constant with each more restrictive phase or subphase (line 3.1.1.3 in Table A.1).[11] This phase association reflects a definite response in industrial capacity utilization to the reduced favoritism that has accompanied liberalization, and vice versa (see Tables 6.2 and 9.1). Many of the industries that developed behind high protective barriers have not been able to compete very well when those barriers have been lowered. Rather than make their production more efficient or allow resource shifts to other subsectors, moreover, they have found it more effective to push for the reinstitution of higher barriers for competing products.

The combination of short-run and long-run considerations thus leaves a policy dilemma. Highly protectionist policies have realized sharply diminishing returns in Chilean industrialization efforts. Yet the inflow of competing products accompanying a liberalization causes a reduction in the utilization of existing industrial capacity. To make Chilean manufacturing efficient might require a prolonged period of liberalization so that expectations of a return to higher barriers for competing products would be dissipated. But such an approach entails substantial short-term economic and political costs.

All Other Sectors

For all other sectors—mostly services, but including construction—the secular trend in the share of resources absorbed has been positive. The mean percentage of total GDP originating in these sectors has increased steadily: 57

for 1908–51, 61 for 1952–61, and 64 for 1962–71 (based on lines 3.1.1.1–3.1.1.3 in Table A.1). The same trend is evident in the percentage of the labor force absorbed by these sectors: 41.4 in 1945, 44.2 in 1952, and 47.7 in 1960. Numerous Chilean observers have been preoccupied for some time by the large size of the service sector and by this shift from goods to services.

The causes of this shift are quite complex and hard to identify because the service sector has so many heterogeneous components. In the context of the present study, however, one hypothesis merits mention. Higher quantitative restrictions tend to raise the share of services per unit of foreign trade because they increase the paper work required by traders for each unit of trade; they cause a substantial increase in the expected private returns from lobbying for exceptions to the regime or for reclassification of traded goods; and they require a substantial government bureaucracy for monitoring and enforcing the restrictions. Thus, unless such increased services per unit of trade are offset by reductions in trade, intensified quantitative restrictions would contribute to the shift from goods to services.

A very crude test of this hypothesis from a long-run viewpoint is to examine the secular path of the share of GDP service production to see if it rose substantially in periods during which quantitative restrictions intensified significantly. The percentage shares of GDP cited above do not provide support for this hypothesis. The largest increment in the share of nonmerchandise production occurred not in the 1930s, when quantitative restrictions increased the most, but in the 1950s and 1960s, when three liberalization efforts were made. This test is very weak, however, because ceteris paribus conditions are not maintained.

Taken over a shorter run, the same test leads to ambiguous results. The mean share of services increased in the more restrictive years of 1952–55 and 1962–64, but fell in 1971.[12] It fell in the quite liberal 1959–61 period, but rose during the 1956–58 and 1965–70 liberalizations. For annual data simple regressions of the ratios of major components of the service sector to the merchandise sector, moreover, generally do not indicate a significant role for various indices of quantitative restrictions.[13]

The general-equilibrium model of Chapter 2 provides a much more satisfactory tool for examining this hypothesis. Under the assumption that the model captures the structure of the Chilean economy, an intensification of quantitative restrictions results in a substantial short- and medium-run shift from services to goods! The first-year elasticity of the goods-to-services ratio with respect to quantitative restrictions is 0.8, and that for the third-year is 1.4 (line 3.5.4 for simulation 2.3.1 in Table A.11). The expansion of agricultural and industrial production induced by greater quantitative restrictions outweighs the hypothesized effects on services.

However, the results of the general-equilibrium model also indicate that overvaluation has contributed to the shift from goods to services. Devaluation, ceteris paribus, reverses that shift—especially if the NER for large-scale mining is devalued (simulations 2.1.1–2.1.3 and 2.6.1). This impact would at least partially offset that of reduced quantitative restrictions in a program combining liberalization with devaluation.

10.1.2 Manufacturing Subsectors.

The manufacturing sector is of particular interest since industrialization per se has long been an objective of Chilean policy. Systematic analysis of the impact of international economic regimes on subsectors of manufacturing is beyond the scope of this study because of the difficulties of maintaining ceteris paribus conditions. Nevertheless, the examination of long-run trends and short-run phase associations in the composition of manufacturing may be suggestive.

From a long-run viewpoint, it is worth noting, first, subsectoral growth rates in real industrial production before and after the Great Depression (columns 1 and 2 in Table 10.2) and, second, Muñoz's [1968:82] estimates of import-substitution coefficients for 1914–15 to 1963–64 and for various subperiods (Table 10.3).

TABLE 10.2
Chilean Mean Percentage Growth Rates of Manufacturing Subsectors for Selected Years, 1914–65, and for First Year of Three Periods of Liberalization

Subsectors	1914–27 (1)	1937–65 (2)	1952–55 Phase II (3)	1956–58 Phase III (4)	1959–61 Phase IV (5)	1962–64 Phase II (6)	1956, 1959, 1965 (7)
Food	3.2	3.6	4.5	−2.4	11.3	5.2	−0.7
Beverages	2.3	5.9	4.9	9.6	15.8	1.4	9.6
Tobacco	6.5	−0.1	8.4	0.7	−4.0	0.8	9.5
Textiles	4.3	4.9	3.4	0.6	11.9	8.7	7.3
Clothing and footwear	5.3	1.2	0.1	−0.8	−1.5	1.6	2.5
Furniture and wood products	1.0	2.1	3.0	−3.2	8.6	6.4	−3.8
Paper, paper products, and printing	4.0	5.6	2.1	20.4	15.6	2.2	9.9
Leather and rubber products	3.6	3.9	0.9	0.1	16.5	5.0	5.1
Chemicals	4.8	8.9	5.4	18.5	12.7	3.0	1.5
Nonmetallic minerals	3.9	6.1	−3.4	9.4	15.4	6.8	11.4
Metal products	9.7	7.9	3.6	1.8	6.1	11.8	9.8

SOURCE: Calculated from data in Muñoz [1968:160–161].

The manufacturing subsectors in order of the degree to which the mean growth rate in the more restrictive period, 1937–65, exceeded that for 1914–27 are chemicals, beverages, nonmetallic minerals, paper and printing, furniture and wood products, textiles, food, leather and rubber products, metal products, clothing and footwear, and tobacco (column 2 less column 1 in Table 10.2). With a few obvious exceptions (e.g., beverages and metal products) this ordering suggests a shift from traditional, consumption-oriented subsectors to more modern, intermediate-goods industries. Such a change is consistent with stated government priorities.

That more restrictive international economic regimes caused this shift, however, is questionable. The Muñoz import-substitution coefficients (Table 10.3) indicate that most import substitution took place *before* 1937. Thus, import substitution was not a major determinant of growth in the 1937–65 period. Another way of making the same point is to note that the correlation between growth rates and import-substitution coefficients by industrial subsector is not significantly nonzero.[14]

From a shorter-run viewpoint the question arises of the extent to which changes in industrial composition have been phase associated. Table 10.1 provides some data pertinent to this question: 1957 and 1967 were in Phase III periods and 1962 was in a more restrictive Phase II regime. Industries that were relatively flourishing under liberalization, therefore, might be expected to have had a larger share of manufacturing value added in 1957 and 1967 than in 1962. However, the breakdown obtained by classifying sectors on this basis does not suggest any interesting patterns.

The mean growth rates over phases also provides information about medium-run compositional changes (columns 3–6 in Table 10.2). Among the 11 manufacturing subsectors included in the table, mean growth rates for the more liberal phases exceed those for the more restrictive phases by at least 5 per cent in five cases (in order)—paper products and printing, chemicals, nonmetallic minerals, beverages, and leather and rubber products (columns 4 plus 5 less the sum of columns 3 and 6). The opposite is true for two subsectors—tobacco and metal products. These patterns suggest, first, that mean growth rates for industrial subsectors were higher in the more liberal years 1956–61 than in the Phase II periods immediately preceding and following. This occurred even though all but four subsectors experienced relatively low rates of growth during the 1956–58 Ibañez-Klein-Saks attempt at stabilization plus liberalization. For the first year of the three liberalization attempts, moreover, a comparison of columns 7 and 2 indicates that the average growth rates exceeded the secular trend for all but three of the industrial subsectors (food, furniture and wood products, and chemicals). The frequent charge that liberalization implied widespread slowdowns in the manufacturing sector, thus, is not supported by these data.

TABLE 10.3

Chilean Import-Substitution Coefficients, by Manufacturing Subsectors, 1914–64

Subsectors	1914–15, 1927	1927, 1937–38	1937–38, 1952–53	1952–53, 1963–64	1914–15, 1963–64
Food, beverages, and tobacco	0.388	0.455	−0.145	−0.017	0.154
	(0.029)	(0.025)	(0.030)	(0.035)	(0.051)
Textiles	(0.482)	0.788	0.570	0.120	(0.586)
	0.333	(0.396)	(0.362)	(0.270)	0.623
Clothing and footwear	(0.145)	2.261	0.105	0.540	(0.188)
		(0.106)	(0.089)	(0.067)	
Wood products	1.314	0.043	0.101	−0.038	0.336
	(0.109)	(0.092)	(0.094)	(0.082)	(0.176)
Paper and publishing	−0.235	0.385	−0.168	0.327	0.328
	(0.271)	(0.221)	(0.215)	(0.169)	(0.393)
Leather and rubber products	−0.715	0.869	−0.521	0.714	0.116
	(0.356)	(0.288)	(0.259)	(0.197)	(0.462)
Chemicals	1.636	0.644	0.248	0.330	0.885
	(0.388)	(0.348)	(0.341)	(0.302)	(0.550)
Nonmetallic minerals	0.817	0.955	0.269	0.077	0.821
	(0.192)	(0.145)	(0.134)	(0.082)	(0.251)
Metal products	0.470	0.907	0.529	0.216	0.774
	(0.585)	(0.522)	(0.493)	(0.360)	(0.753)
Total	0.431	0.730	0.150	0.145	0.410
	(0.194)	(0.171)	(0.184)	(0.153)	(0.297)

SOURCE: Muñoz [1968:82]. The import-substitution coefficient is defined as $(u_0 - u_1) Z_1/(X_1 - X_0)$, where u is the ratio of imports to total supply, Z is total supply, X is the gross internal product, and the subscripts refer to the endpoints of the period in question. The values in parentheses are the "normal" values based on Chenery [1960].

Second, the subsectors with higher growth rates in the more liberal phase relative to less liberal ones tended to be more modern and oriented more toward production of intermediate goods. The long-protected consumer-oriented subsectors tended to perform relatively less well under liberalization. These patterns point to the failure of many "infant" industries in the latter group to gain sufficient maturity to compete successfully in the world market.

10.2 RELATIONS BETWEEN RESOURCE ALLOCATION AND PRICE RATIOS OF FINAL TO INTERMEDIATE PRODUCT

In the past decade there has been considerable debate over the extent to which EPRs and related price ratios of final to intermediate product might indicate incentives for resource allocation (see Appendix B for references to this literature). By the early 1970s it had been established that these measures did not provide theoretically reliable indicators under a wide set of apparently reasonable assumptions. Nevertheless, the question remains whether or not such measures have actually been associated with resource movements.

Evidence bearing on this question is presented below. For the most part, it requires strong ceteris paribus assumptions. Taken together, it lends very little empirical support for the relations sometimes hypothesized between price-related measures of the ratio of final to intermediate product (such as EPRs) and resource allocation.[15] In part, this reflects the impact of a number of other important factors that simultaneously interact within the economic system. In addition, it may reflect the effect of frequent and often bizarre changes in the EPRs resulting from the widespread use of quantitative restrictions.[16]

i. Compositional changes in manufacturing value added do not appear to have been associated with subsectoral EPR levels or changes.

ii. Hachette [1966] provides data for 1959–61 from which the average change in customs barriers and the standard deviation in the annual values of those changes can be calculated. However, neither of these variables was found to be significantly correlated with industrial subsectoral growth over the same period.

iii. Sectoral ITRs for 1967 and changes in ITRs between 1957 and 1967 are significantly correlated with the increase in value added between 1957 and 1967 (Tables A.5 and A.6). Changes in ITRs also are significantly correlated with additions to capacity in terms of horsepower in the same decade. Neither the levels nor the changes in EPRs, however, are significantly correlated with any index of relative growth in output or in resource allocation.

iv. Using the general-equilibrium model of Chapter 2, it is possible to explore the effect on sectoral resource allocation when price ratios of final to intermediate product vary (lines 3.1.1–3.1.3 in Table A.11). Changes in resource allocation are indicated by changes in the allocation of the labor force (lines 3.2.1–3.2.3), capital stock (lines 3.3.1–3.3.3), production capacity (lines 3.4.1–3.4.3), and GDP (lines 3.5.1–3.5.4). Examination of the simulation results leads to a striking finding: in a large number of cases relative changes in the price ratios of final to intermediate product are in different directions than short-run or longer-run movements, or both, in resource allocation (e.g., simulations 1.1, 1.2, 2.1.1, 2.1.3, 2.2, and 2.3.1)! Upon reflection, of course, such a result should not seem surprising, since many determinants besides relative prices enter into capacity-utilization and capacity-creation decisions (see subsections 9.2.2, 9.2.3, and 12.2.3.1).

10.3 COSTS OF ATTEMPTS TO ALTER RESOURCE ALLOCATION THROUGH DIFFERENTIAL INCENTIVES CREATED BY THE INTERNATIONAL ECONOMIC REGIMES

The implication of the previous section is *not* that foreign-sector regimes have not affected resource allocation but only that EPRs and related measures do not provide very good indications of the direction of such effects.

The general-equilibrium model of Chapter 2, in fact, suggests that foreign-sector policies have had substantial impact on resource allocation among sectors. In the short and medium run, for example, higher quantitative restrictions result in shifts primarily into industry, secondarily into agriculture, and away from mining and services (lines 3.4.1–3.4.3 and 3.5.1–3.5.4 for simulation 2.3.1 in Table A.11). Below-equilibrium NERs, similarly, cause shifts primarily into industry, but also into agriculture relative to mining (simulation 2.1.3).

The costs of such shifts, of course, include the extent to which their occurrence reduced the degree of attainment of all other objectives. Without a social welfare function such trade-offs cannot be evaluated. Evaluation of costs normally focuses, therefore, on the amount of forgone output. Output apparently was lost by the shift in resources from mining to industry.[17] Under the strong assumption that wages have been proportional to marginal product, for example, the mean marginal product in mining averaged over 20 per cent above that for industry in the quarter century from 1945 to 1969. Within industries, moreover, the range of DRCs shown in Table 5.3 suggests that the international economic regimes caused some shifts into inefficient production.[18]

Balassa [1971:82] calculates the over-all static cost of Chilean protection to have been 1.4 per cent of national income on the basis of Jeanneret's 1961 EPR estimates (EPR1 in Table 5.3). He also estimates that the total net cost of protection in that year was a substantially larger 6.2 per cent. To obtain this figure he adds to the static effect 9.6 per cent for dynamic cost and 0.6 per cent for the consumption effect.[19] These are partially offset by additions of −3.5 per cent for a terms-of-trade effect and −1.9 per cent for the cost of increased exports under free trade.

To most neoclassical economists these costs—especially the static ones alone—would be regarded as surprisingly small, given the degree of distortion indicated in Table 5.3, if it were not for a number of other similar estimates made over the past fifteen years. Furthermore, on the basis of conservative estimates in Behrman [1973b], the mean forgone output in underutilized capacity due primarily to domestic policies has been greater—even if Balassa's dynamic costs are included. Some significant output gains thus may be possible from a more liberalized trade policy. But improvements in other policies—such as anticyclical ones—may have higher benefits. The potential gains in output from resource allocation due to changes in the international economic regime should not be exaggerated.[20]

NOTES

1. The extent to which manufacturing has been favored relative to agriculture is one important exception (see subsection 5.1.2).

2. For 1940–65 the secular growth rate for real agricultural GDP was 0.02 as compared to 0.038 for total real GDP (Table A.2).

3. For some countries increased imports of basic foodstuffs would be suggested by comparative-advantage considerations. A large number of agricultural economists, however, have agreed that Chile has a comparative advantage in the production of many basic foodstuffs (for example, see Schultz [1968]).

4. During the third attempt (1965–70) it decreased slightly, but this may be part of the secular trend and not a fluctuation due to a change in the foreign-sector regime. In general, the increases occurred despite the first-year drops in the PLD-EER(PI)s for agriculture relative to industry, that are described in section 5.2, above. For the 1956–58 liberalization, Crosson [1970] explains that the price ratio of agricultural output to input rose even though the price ratio of agriculture to total manufacturing fell. Therefore, there were price incentives for expanding agricultural production.

5. For 1940–65 the secular growth rate for mining was 0.018 as compared with 0.038 for total real GDP (Table A.2).

6. See the discussion of the impact of the *Nuevo Trato* in subsection 7.1.2.3.

7. The estimates in Table A.2 suggest that for the entire 1940–65 period the mean exponential growth rate for real industrial GDP has been the same as for total product —0.038.

8. Domestic policies also at times played important roles in the structure of incentives for import substitution. For example, the shift from production to sales taxes, enacted in Law 11575 of August 14, 1954, implied an increase in EPRs because the production tax had been basically on goods produced by domestic industries.

9. The Instituto de Economía [1963:2, 9] suggests that during World War II substantial import substitution occurred because of shortages of imported supplies. A finding that considerable import substitution may have occurred then and in the subsequent subphases in an *absolute* sense would not be inconsistent with the *relative* estimates of Muñoz, given that the rate of growth of industrial product was two to three times as high in the three subphases after 1940 as in 1931–39 (line 5.2 in Table A.1).

10. For these reasons Mamalakis [1971:214–217, 370–371] also has serious doubts about the structuralists' characterization of Chilean industrialization as being relatively successful.

11. Table A.2 provides further support for this characterization. The only significantly positive deviation from the exponential growth rate for industrial GDP in 1940–65 is for the 1940–55 Phase II period, and the only significantly negative one is for the 1959–61 Phase IV years.

12. The mean share of services is given by 1.0 minus the sum of lines 3.1.1.1–3.1.1.3 in Table A.1.

13. Only in the regression of the ratio of the size of government to industrial production is a significantly nonzero coefficient of the Ffrench-Davis QR index obtained.

The significantly nonzero deviations from the exponential growth rates for GDP in Table A.2 also are ambiguous. Construction had a negative deviation for the Phase II 1940–55 period. Services had a negative deviation for the 1956–1958 liberalization. Government had a positive deviation for the 1940–55 Phase II years, but a negative one for the 1962–64 Phase II period.

14. In fact if the coefficient of determination between these two series is corrected for degrees of freedom, it becomes negative.

15. Taylor and Black [1973] also find that EPR measures often are poor indicators of the magnitude and sometimes of the sign of resource shifts among Chilean subsectors owing to reductions in import taxes.

16. In the real world, not only does domestic policy keep changing, but it takes time for adjustments to these changes to work themselves out.

17. Restriction of mining output might have been an optimal strategy had Chile been able to exploit her limited market power in copper without retaliation. Until the late 1960s, however, she was not able to do so because of the foreign locus of decision-making in large-scale mining.

18. An extreme case of inefficiency due to the international economic regime was the restriction of the automobile industry to Arica in northern Chile by the special regime for that area. Johnson [1967] describes the state of this industry as of 1965. He notes the considerable problems of seasonality due to the difficulties of obtaining both domestic and foreign imputs as well as the pressure to produce before the end of each calendar year so that the annually increasing national-component requirements could be met. He estimates that the trade-off between local resources used and the dollars saved was as high as 4 to 1 at the official NER or 2.4 to 1 at the black-market NER (although he suggests that the elimination of extraordinary rents might lower these estimates somewhat).

19. The relatively large dynamic effect is based on the assumption that those industries which continued after a switch to free trade would do so with production costs which declined to competitive levels. This dynamic effect, however, does not include some important possible benefits of openness, such as greater exposure to technical progress and innovation. Thus, it may understate the true benefits of liberalization. For more details concerning this and other calculations see Balassa [1971:80–82].

20. In Chapter 12 I return to the question of the beneficial effects of liberalization on economic growth.

Chapter 11

The Distribution of Control over Income and Resources

In the past decade, there has been a general resurgence of interest in the impact of policies in developing nations on the distribution of control over income and resources. In Chile, too, there has been a rising interest in distributional questions, although in that country such issues have not been far from center stage for some time.[1]

The primary focus in those discussions has been on the distribution of income by classes or by factors. A number of other dimensions of the distribution of control over income and resources, however, also have been important: private versus public shares in output, domestic versus international shares, the distribution among sectors, regional concerns, and the interests of the present generation versus those of future generations.

In this chapter the impact of the international economic regime on some of those dimensions will be explored.[2] The focus is on three questions: (i) What have been the distributional objectives? (ii) What have been the effects of foreign-sector policy on distribution? (iii) Were there alternative means of achieving the same objectives at lower cost?

In most of these dimensions generalizations about the objectives are very difficult. Various governments at various times and different groups in society at particular times have not agreed on distributional priorities. More often than not recent governments have tended to state as their preferences decentralization and redistribution in favor of lower-income classes and labor, the public sector, manufacturing, and future generations. Only in the domestic-foreign dimension, however, has there been widespread agreement. In that case the consensus has been growing for some time that a reduction of foreign control is desirable.

The distributional consequences of the international economic regimes have been manifold and sometimes contradictory. For example, consider the impact on the labor share. Overvaluation has led to higher real wages and higher employment in the short run. Even in the short run, however, more intensive quantitative restrictions have led to lower real wages, especially because of the considerable protection given to some important mass-consumption subsectors. In the longer run, moreover, the international economic policies have created inducements for substitution of capital for labor. In some sectors the negative effects on the demand for labor have been considerable. Protective barriers, furthermore, have precluded competition from the world market and, thus, competitive pressures for greater efficiency and productivity.

Consideration of the labor share also provides illustrations of some trade-offs which are pervasive in considerations of distributional questions. One quandary is provided by the difference between short-run and long-run results. Keeping food prices low, for example, increases real labor income in the short run, but discourages agricultural production in the long run. More generally, devaluation and liberalization might create more jobs in the long run, but tend to cause immediate unemployment.

Trade-offs among the distributional objectives also are important. Protection has resulted in redistribution toward industry, for example, as has been widely desired. The high protection for some of the traditional consumption-oriented subsectors, however, has lessened real wages of labor because of the effects on prices of consumer goods used by wage earners.

Finally, the distributional consequences of the international economic regime are often very hard to reverse because of the establishment of strong vested interests. In the Chilean case the prime example is provided by the traditional consumer-goods subsectors. These industries have received protection at least since the 1897 tariff law. To lower the implicit subsidies they receive because of the foreign-sector regime would be very difficult, however, because of the strong political forces which have grown up as a result of that protection.

Neoclassical analysis can almost always devise more efficient ways than QRs to redistribute control over income and over resources. Sometimes the neoclassical prescriptions suffer, however, from unrealistic assumptions about the ease of tax-transfer mechanisms. Nevertheless, the greater use of price-related mechanisms would make it possible to pursue distributional objectives with fewer distortions in inducements. The use of explicit subsidies instead of implicit ones, furthermore, would make the nature of the resources transfer clearer and thus subject to more conscious examination through the political process.

11.1 DISTRIBUTION BY INCOME CLASS

Recent Chilean governments, especially those under presidents Frei and Allende, have had as one proclaimed important objective the reduction of disparities in the distribution of income. This objective has shaped the international economic regime in a number of respects. For example, Chilean governments often have been reluctant to devalue the currency in part because of perceived regressive income-distributional effects of that action.[3]

Chilean society, however, has not been monolithic in its objectives. A number of competing groups have attempted to maintain or extend their shares of income. In reference to foreign-sector policy, the narrow interests of some of these groups have prevailed over the more diffuse interests of the general public and of consumers. The existence of these and other strong pressure groups has limited the success of redistributional measures even under the most progressive governments.[4] Under governments with a lower priority for redistribution or none, the influence of these special-interest groups has dominated.

The nature of past international economic regimes, moreover, has significantly strengthened the relative position of some of these groups. To be more explicit, the maintenance of high industrial protection by means of restrictive regimes has encouraged the development of strong vested interests among the factor owners in the more protected industries, the importers who receive the import premiums, and the bureaucrats who run the system.

Redistributional efforts have involved many policies other than those in the foreign sector. Minimum wages, price ceilings, human-capital investments, agrarian reform, and changing control and ownership in industrial and service sectors all have been utilized. However, foreign-sector policies also have had considerable effects.[5] The available evidence is somewhat fragmentary, but does permit some analysis of these effects on one of the special-interest groups[6] and on the factoral division of income.

11.1.1 Import Premiums and Distribution.

An important special-interest group comprises the importers themselves. The mean import premium rate for 1946–70 was 0.77 (column 4 in Table 5.1). Although at times import licenses have been allocated directly to producers, generally traders have been the recipients. Therefore, traders also have received substantial income increments due to the restrictive regimes.

The relative magnitude of the import premiums has varied inversely with the degree of liberalization and the degree of overvaluation. As is noted in subsection 5.1.1, the correlation coefficient between the import premium rate and the PLD-EER was −0.46 for the quarter-century after the Second World War. Movements in the imported component relative to other components in price indices also are suggestive in this regard. In 1956, for example, the imported component decreased relatively substantially despite a devaluation of about 25 per cent which accompanied the initiation of the Alessandri effort at stabilization plus liberalization. The Instituto de Economía [1963:25] claims that this fall primarily reflected the reduction of oligopolistic returns to the previously more limited number of importers.

Even without devaluation, of course, the government could mop up the import premiums going to traders without affecting production substantially by utilizing exchange auctions or increasing import taxes. This probably would be desirable given apparent Chilean objectives.[7] An alternative possibility, which the Allende government explored, was to replace private traders by government trading companies. Such a tactic clearly decreased the import premiums going to private traders. It also expanded substantially another interest group, namely, the government bureaucracy. Available data do not permit rigorous analysis of the efficiency of this alternative operation.

11.1.2 Real Wages and the International Economic Regime

More information is available about the impact of the international economic regimes on the factoral shares of real income. The mean shares of labor in GDP for phases and subphases since 1940 do not have a strong phase association (line 4.2 in Table A.1).[8] The largest decline was recorded in the Phase IV period of 1957–61, but the only other fall was for Phase II of 1952–55.[9] Otherwise, an upward secular trend dominated. The same secular trend also predominated in the average real wage—again with little indication of phase-associated fluctuations (line 4.1 in Table A.1).

Despite the foregoing suggestions of very limited phase associations, other data reveal that the foreign-sector regime has had substantial impact on real wages and employment.[10] Four types of empirical approach are used here to explore the relation of real wages to the international economic regime.[11]

i. Cross-sectional data is used to determine whether there are significant associations between the variance in protection across subsectors and wages. Tables A.5 and A.6 contain all the significantly nonzero correlation coefficients among levels and rates of change of ITRs and EPRs and levels and rates of change of wages and wage shares. Significantly negative correlations are found between both ITRs and EPRs and both wages and wage shares. The changes in wages and wage shares between 1957 and 1967 are significantly positively correlated with ITRs and with the change both in ITRs and in EPRs between 1961 and 1967. The nominal and effective structures of protection created by the international economic regimes, thus, were associated with low but relatively rapidly increasing wages. These increases, moreover, were associated positively with the changes in protection.

Cross-sectional evidence also sheds some light on the impact of foreign-sector regimes on consumption-goods prices wage earners have had to face. As is mentioned several times above, the government has often tried to lessen price increases for certain mass-consumption items by instituting favorable import provisions. The ITRs in Table 5.3 suggest that it succeeded in keeping the relative price increases due to trade barriers fairly small for the most important single mass-consumption category, food products.[12] At least in 1961, however, such barriers were quite high for some other important mass-consumption sectors, especially footwear and clothing, textiles, and beverages. Unless the level of aggregation is obscuring the impact, therefore, it must be concluded that this attempt by the government was not completely successful.

ii. Time series for subsectoral PLD-EER(PI)s in Table A.8 provide further information about the success of the government in using the foreign-sector regime to keep mass-consumption items relatively cheap. Food products did have a low mean PLD-EER(PI) in comparison to other mass-consumption items such as beverages, textiles, and footwear. However, the mean for food products was above that for at least eight other manufacturing subsectors, to say nothing of agriculture and mining. Moreover, discriminatory policies favoring cheap food imports presumably would have caused the PLD-EER(PI) for food products to become relatively low in more restrictive periods, but it did not. Subject again to the caveat about aggregation, this evidence reinforces the doubts raised in the previous paragraph about the success of the government in its attempt to keep mass-consumption items cheap through discriminatory trade policies.

iii. Partial-equilibrium time-series regression analyses of the determinants of the rates of change of sectoral wages are presented in Behrman [1971 and 1974]. The only significant direct impact of the international economic regime is through the price-expectational effect of changes in NERs. Estimates in Behrman [1974] of the determinants of the rate of change of the consumer deflator indicate a much stronger reaction to foreign-sector changes, including variations in NERs. The net direct result of devaluation, thus, would be a decline in real wages.

iv. The general-equilibrium model of Chapter 2 provides further insight about the impact of changes in foreign-sector policies on real wages. For the reasons suggested in the previous paragraph, the impact elasticity of real wages with respect to the NER is negative, amounting to −0.4 (line 4.1.1 for simulation 2.1.1 in Table A.11). Thus, this result supports the reluctance to devalue because of the perceived negative effects on real wages and on total labor income.[13] Because wages also adjust more slowly than product prices to changes in quantitative restrictions, however, the elasticity of real wages with respect to such restrictions also is inverse and rather sizable: −1.1 (simulation 2.3.1).[14] Liberalization at the same time as devaluation, therefore, would tend to offset the negative consequences for real wages of the latter.[15]

11.1.3 Employment and the International Economic Regime.

The above approaches also provide insight into the impact of the international economic regime on the other component of real labor income—employment:

i. Cross-sectional data are used to determine whether there are significant associations between the variance in protection across subsectors and factor-to-factor or factor-to-output ratios (Tables A.5 and A.6). Protection was positively correlated with the capital-labor ratio (EPR3) and growth in horsepower capacity between 1957 and 1967 (ITR2). The same associations hold for changes in protection between 1957 and 1967. These results suggest that the structure of protection may have encouraged the use of capital-intensive technology despite the abundance of labor. If so, the international economic regimes may have added significantly to unemployment problems.

ii. Time series for PLD-EER(PI)s provide supporting information. The mean PLD-EER(PI) ratio of investment goods to consumer goods for the quarter-century following the Second World War was 0.64 (column 4 in Table 5.2). Foreign-sector policy thus encouraged the use of capital-intensive technologies by keeping the price of foreign capital goods relatively low. Mamalakis [1971:565–587] reports, moreover, that CORFO loan procedures further reduced the cost of capital.[16] Loans to enterprises made in domestic currency but backed by hard currency were repaid in domestic currency at less than their original value because of negative real interest rates.[17] The effect of such CORFO policies on employment is illustrated by the decrease in the relative share of the labor force after 1945 in the most rapidly growing industrial subsector, basic metals, because of the capital-intensive nature of the CORFO-financed CAP operations.

iii. The partial-equilibrium time-series analysis in Behrman [1972a] further corroborates this conclusion. The estimated sectoral elasticities of substitution between capital and labor generally are significantly nonzero. The technical possibility of substituting subsidized capital for labor therefore existed.

These estimates of the elasticity of substitution make it possible to illustrate the employment impact of some specific foreign-sector policies. Labor demand in large-scale mining, for example, was more affected by the international economic regime than demand in any other sector. Large-scale mining enterprises could purchase imported capital equipment directly with the foreign-exchange proceeds earned by their exports. They paid much of their domestic labor, however, in domestic currency which had to be purchased at an often quite disadvantageous NER (see section 3.2 and column 1 in Table 3.2).[18]

The employment impact of this discriminatory exchange-rate policy can be seen under the following assumptions: the production function for large-scale mining is a CES type with an elasticity of substitution of 0.51 as estimated for all of mining in Behrman [1972a], output and prices are given, and tendencies for labor demands to adjust to marginal productivities prevail in the long run. Relation 11.1 then gives the ratio of labor that would have been employed in large-scale mining in long-run equilibrium (L') at different labor prices (PL') to those actually employed in long-run equilibrium (L) at actual prices (PL).

$$L'/L = (PL/PL')^{0.51} \qquad (11.1)$$

Reynolds [1965:284] gives an implicit estimate for PL/PL' of 2.03. This value, together with the above assumptions, implies that the long-run demand for labor in large-scale mining would have been 44 per cent larger had exchange-rate discrimination not affected the dollar cost of labor. If PL/PL' is assumed to have been the ratio of the bank spot NER to the special NER in 1954 (although the former clearly was undervalued) and other assumptions are maintained as before, the long-run equilibrium labor demand in large-scale mining would have been 590 per cent larger! With the option of increasing output, the demand for labor would have been even greater.[19] Such calculations should not be taken literally, but they do suggest that the employment effects of the discriminatory NER policy may have been quite considerable.

iv. The general-equilibrium impact of the international economic regime on the economywide demand for labor in the short and medium run is given in Table A.11 under the assumption that such demand is highly correlated with the capacity-utilization rate. As is discussed in section 9.2 above, devaluation and liberalization both have immediate negative impacts on the utilization rate variable (line 2.1 for simulations 2.1.1 and 2.3.1).

This result poses a trade-off between the longer-run employment gains discussed above and the short-run loss. Policies to moderate this trade-off by facilitating labor mobility, by increasing aggregate demand, and by gradually reducing protection in the weaker subsectors may be necessary for a successful liberalization program. On the other hand, moderate policies may not work because they may encourage the maintenance of expectations of a return to the previous situation.

11.2 PRIVATE VERSUS GOVERNMENT CONTROL OVER OUTPUT

The objective of the government with regard to the division between private and government control over output has fluctuated over the years. Some governments—for example, Alessandri's in 1958–64—have favored a larger role for the private sector because of a belief in the greater efficiency of the private sector and because of a desire to protect or to promote certain private interest groups. Other governments—for example, Allende's in 1970–73—have seen a need to expand substantially the government's role in order to make necessary reforms and to restructure society despite the opposition of strong vested interests. Even though the governments themselves have maintained a range of positions on this spectrum, moreover, a large portion of the government bureaucracy always has found the expansion of government activity to be in its own self-interest.

The desirability of relative expansion of government control over resources thus has been a matter of dispute among various groups in Chilean society and among different administrations. Most of the assertions that are made pro and con are very difficult to test. To attempt to do so, moreover, would be beyond the scope of the present study. However, some indication of the relationship between the type of international regime and the relative role of the government can be made.

More restrictive regimes have shifted resources to the government in at least two important ways: [20] First, government imports have been given high priority at substantially overvalued EERs (subsection 4.1.7). In 1971, for example, the government share of imports increased to 45 per cent mainly because government imports were exempted from the 10,000 per cent prior import deposit requirement introduced in May of that year. Second, the government netted substantial revenues from its operation of the multiple exchange-rate system because of the large differential (especially before the *Nuevo Trato* of 1955) between the escudo price it paid to large-scale mining enterprises for dollars and the price at which it sold such dollars (compare columns 1 and 13 in Table 3.2).

On the other hand, greater restrictiveness has also worked in the opposite direction: First, it reduced the quantity of foreign trade, a relatively convenient source of tax revenue (see sections 6.2 and 7.2). Partly as a result of this decline, tax revenues related to foreign trade as a proportion of total taxes have dropped secularly from a mean of 0.83 in 1908–27 [21] to a mean of 0.18 in 1965–70 (line 1.2.6.6 in Table A.1).[22] Second, at times it lowered the effective average import tax rates since restrictions usually were applied more stringently to commodities with higher legal tax rates.[23] The intensity of restrictions also has had some relation to the availability of loans to the government from foreign sources (see Chapter 8).

Partially as a result of these counterbalancing effects, the share of the government in GNP, savings, and investment does not indicate any strong phase association (see lines 3.1.2.3 and 3.3.1–3.3.4 in Table A.1).[24] Within the framework of the general-equilibrium model of Chapter 2, however, the net consequences can be identified: [25] devaluation leads to an immediate drop in government revenues as the reduced taxes from imports offset increased revenues from large-scale mining (lines 4.4.1, 4.4.1.1, and 4.4.1.2, for simulation 2.1.1 in Table A.11). Reductions in quantitative restrictions, however, have the opposite effect (simulation 2.3.1). Tax revenues increase because of large increments from imports and large-scale mining. Government consumption also increases. Devaluation apparently has a negative effect on government revenues because of inflationary pressures, but an appropriate degree of liberalization could offset this effect.

11.3 DOMESTIC VERSUS FOREIGN SHARES

Before the Great Depression, net outflows to the foreign owners of Chile's nitrates were quite substantial (see section 1.2). Since then, the division between domestic and foreign income has been determined primarily by the government's treatment of large-scale copper mining.

Policies toward large-scale copper mining are discussed in some detail in sections 4.2.1 and 7.2. Their dominant feature has been a strong secular trend toward increased Chilean control, which culminated in the nationalizations of 1971. Superimposed on this trend were some fluctuations associated with the extent of liberalization. The more restrictive regimes usually tended to increase the Chilean share relative to the foreign share of returns from mining. However, at times, they did so at the expense of the absolute magnitude of the Chilean share (subsection 7.1.2.3).

One important component of the division between domestic and foreign factor shares is the size of net factor payments from abroad. The effect of devaluation and liberalization on this flow can be examined within the framework of the general-equilibrium model of Chapter 2. The first-year elasticity of net factor income from abroad with respect to all NERs is −1.8 and that with respect to quantitative restrictions is −4.0 (line 4.2.1 for simulations 2.1.1 and 2.3.1 in Table A.11).[26] Devaluation, then, would increase foreign income because there would be higher exports from large-scale mining and reduced unit dollar costs for domestic factors utilized in mining. This increase in foreign income, however, does not imply a reduction in Chilean control of foreign resources. To the contrary, the surplus on current account and international reserves both rise (lines 1.3.1 and 1.3.3). Although maintenance of overvalued NERs would reduce factor payments to foreigners, therefore, it would be at the expense of Chilean control of foreign resources.

Liberalization, too, would increase factor payments abroad because of the expansion of exports (Table A.11, line 1.1).[27] But imports would increase even more than exports; so in this case Chilean control of foreign exchange would fall (Table A.11, lines 1.2, 1.3.1, and 1.3.2). If sufficient devaluation accompanied the liberalization, of course, this negative feature could be offset.

Another important factor in the division between domestic and foreign shares is the size of capital movements. Increased quantitative restrictions discourage net inflows, but they also restrict outflows. The net effect is not a priori obvious (for detailed discussion of these movements, see section 8.2). Positive associations of these movements with the degree of liberalization do seem to have prevailed for direct investment and private short-term capital movements. For other components, however, there is no evidence of such a correlation.

11.4 SECTORAL AND REGIONAL DISTRIBUTION OF INCOME AND RESOURCES

Mamalakis [1965,1971b] has characterized the distributional conflict in Chile as having been essentially one of "sectoral clashes." He portrays a process in which the manufacturing sector gained the upper hand in terms of policy formation in the 1930s at the expense of agriculture and mining.

Whether or not one agrees with Mamalakis's emphasis on the importance of conflicts between sectors, there is no doubt but that foreign-sector policy has had significant implications for sectoral shares. The effect of the more restrictive regimes has been to shift income and resources toward government, manufacturing, and services (see Chapter 10). In manufacturing, at least until very recently, foreign-sector policy has favored the same traditional subsectors for which in many cases explicit protection dates back to the 1897 tariff.

A pertinent question I wish to raise at this point is the extent to which patterns of protection reflect the degree of political power. One index of relative political power of the various subsectors is the degree of industrial concentration. The greater the concentration, the greater is at least the potential for organized political pressure from a subsector. Tables A.5 and A.6 contain all significantly nonzero correlation coefficients between the degree of concentration in 1957 (the only year for which the data are readily available) and levels and rates of change of ITRs and EPRs.

ITRs for 1967 and the change in ITRs between 1961 and 1967 are positively correlated with the degree of concentration. Under the above assumption and subject to the usual ceteris paribus qualifications, thus, these correlations support the hypothesis that levels and changes in product protection reflected the degree of political clout. Because of such political power, moreover, reducing protection in certain subsectors is very difficult. Some long-protected infants may never grow up, but they may maintain enough political power to induce the general public to continue to transfer resources to them behind trade barriers. Such a characterization fits a number of Chilean manufacturing subsectors all too well.

In the Chilean case, questions of regional distribution are tied quite closely to sectoral ones. Increased quantitative restrictions generally have caused shifts from the north (mining) and south (agriculture) to the center (manufacturing, commerce, and government). Most government revenues have been spent in the center, most imports are made to the center, and most expenses of operating the regime have been incurred in the center. The attempts to offset these movements, such as the operation of special regimes for the extreme ends of the country (subsection 4.1.5.1), have only partially balanced the flows to the center induced by the other aspects of foreign-sector policy.

NOTES

1. Chileans may have been more sensitive to distributional questions than citizens of many other countries because of the high inflation rates (line 2.1 in Table A.1). With product and factor prices changing so much there has been much more potential for relative-price changes than in most countries. Under such conditions the income distribution might change substantially quite quickly. Therefore, it has been privately useful for numerous interest groups to devote considerable resources to defending their share of income. The private returns from such activities have been quite high in comparison to the returns from increasing real productivity.

2. Since some of these subjects are discussed fully in other parts of this book, they are covered here in only a limited way (e.g., sectoral distributions, which are explored in Chapter 10) or not at all (e.g., the generational trade-off, which is taken up in Chapter 12).

3. The sliding-peg NER policy of 1965–70 was one exception to this situation. Even in that period, however, the PLD-NER and PLD-EER declined (see column 13 in Table 3.2 and column 1 in Table 5.1).

4. The existence of trade-offs between the accomplishment of redistributional objectives and other objectives of the government also has limited success in the attainment of redistributional goals.

5. The government has seemed to be conscious of some of the redistributional implications of foreign-sector policies, but not of others. An example of the latter is the decision to use only fiscal bonds for prior import deposits in 1962–64 (see subsection 4.1.4). The intent of this shift was to limit imports. One regressive result, however, was to create very high scarcity rents for the relatively wealthy bond owners.

6. A second important special-interest group, the highly protected sectors or sub-

sectors, is briefly considered in section 11.4, below. The bureaucracy to run and cope with the exchange-control system is yet another interest group. Some aspects of the impact of the degree of restrictiveness on government expenditures—in part to support this bureaucracy—are taken up in section 11.2.

7. It clearly would not be desirable from the point of view of the traders. It also *might* not be desirable from a social point of view. If growth were the overwhelmingly dominant objective, if a shortage of domestic savings were a critical bottleneck restraining growth, if traders had a higher marginal propensity to save than the government, and if traders did not illegally transfer too much of these savings abroad, for example, this transfer of the import premiums might not be socially desirable.

8. If the information were readily available the division of labor into blue- and white-collar groups would be useful and might reveal differential results since social legislation earlier favored the latter group. For the 1940–50 period for which the data exist, however, Marshall [1957:190–192] reports that changes in income distribution between these two groups were not statistically significant.

9. Contrary to the claims of Ffrench-Davis [1971:20], Instituto de Economía [1963: 71], and Sierra [1969:51], the mean real wage and mean wage share for the 1956–58 attempt at stabilization plus liberalization were at least as high as in the previous subphase. This point is important because these and other commentators have made such claims part of their criticism of the Ibañez-Klein-Saks effort.

10. Only developments since the Great Depression, and primarily since the Second World War, are considered in this section. Information for the years before the Great Depression is very scanty. However, the expansion of mining production for export did provide a climate conducive to the development of the first strong Chilean labor movements and did provide new loci of political power which supported the election of Arturo Alessandri in 1920 and the subsequent passage of extensive white-collar labor legislation in 1924. For details see Mamalakis [1971:92–118], Muñoz [1968:197], Pinto [1962:100], and Reynolds [1965:228–229].

11. One important point is not discussed below because it is hard to quantify with available data. Restrictive systems tended to discriminate against labor because the large private gains which could be attained by obtaining special exemptions from the regime generally were not captured by the laboring class. Luxury imports through the special regional regimes, especially in Arica, were one example.

Another possibly important point which cannot be quantified is that labor productivities and therefore wages may have been lower because of protection from competitive pressures for efficiency from the international market.

12. Agricultural production, however, may have been discouraged by this policy; so there may have been a long-run direct cost in terms of domestic food production (section 9.2).

13. Hachette [1966] concludes that overvaluation affects the different income quartiles about identically, but benefits the lower-income groups slightly more. If labor income is concentrated in the lower-income groups, the present results are consistent with the direction of relative benefit indicated by Hachette, although the magnitude of the benefits indicated by the present results probably is greater.

Some commentators have pointed to the increasing proportion of indirect taxes in total taxes during liberalization attempts and have concluded that such a shift also was regressive. For example, Ffrench-Davis [1971:36] and Sierra [1969:89] make such a claim because of the increase in indirect taxes from 44.4 to 49.1 per cent of the total during 1959–61. However, most of this increase occurred in import taxes in such a manner that the burden probably was borne largely by middle- and upper-income classes.

14. To the extent that movements in the consumer deflator overstate movements in the prices paid by laborers because of the differential impact of quantitative restrictions on imports which favor wage goods, the elasticities in Table A.11 overstate the impact on real wages and on the labor share in income. However, it seems unlikely that such a consideration would alter substantially the results reported there.

15. Note that liberalization would raise average real wages, but increase the disparity between low agricultural wages and much higher mining and manufacturing wages (lines 4.1.1.1–4.1.1.3 for simulation 2.3.1 in Table A.11).

16. In a neoclassical world with an elasticity of substitution less than 1, a reduction in the cost of capital services would increase the labor share in output. This result is not certain in the real world of Chile, however, because of adjustment problems, unemployed factors, and nonprice determinants of capacity utilization.

17. The central government provided the necessary subsidies to CORFO.

18. Some of the more skilled Chilean workers and technicians were paid in dollars before 1971. This procedure meant that inducements existed for substituting more skilled for less skilled labor, as well as capital for labor.

The termination of this practice by the Allende government lowered those recipients' real incomes substantially because they previously had converted part of their dollars into escudos at the favorable black-market NER. Part of the problem in realizing the programmed expansion of large-scale copper mining in the early 1970s, in fact, is reputed to have originated in the exodus of Chilean and foreign technicians because of this change (see subsections 4.2.1 and 7.1.2.3).

19. With changes of this size, however, the adjustment of copper prices and the price of labor probably would have somewhat offsetting effects on the demand for labor.

20. The Chileanization and nationalization of copper, the major export, also led to a large movement of resources to the government. This action, however, was part of a long secular trend and was not particularly phase related (see subsection 4.2.1).

21. It is emphasized in section 1.2 that government revenue depended on the foreign sector before the Great Depression. Total government revenues increased at an annual exponential rate of 0.044 between 1844 and 1928 due to expansion of foreign trade and despite the reduction of revenues from other sources.

22. Not all of this drop was due to the discouragement of exports by Chilean policy. Part of it reflected a conscious effort to develop domestic sources. Part of it also reflected a decline in exports for reasons beyond Chile's control.

23. The very restrictive 1952–55 subphase is one example. At other times, however, this pattern did not always hold (line 1.2.6.9 in Table A.1).

24. Likewise, the only two significant deviations from the secular growth rate for government GDP and for real government direct and financial investment in 1940–65 do not indicate a clear pattern. They both are for Phase II periods, but are opposite in sign (Table A.2).

25. Within this model, however, the extent of government access to foreign financing is held constant.

26. Four points about these simulations should be kept in mind: (i) The pre-1967 share of foreign ownership in large-scale copper mining is assumed. (ii) The estimates in Behrman [1974] indicate no direct (or partial-equilibrium) effect of quantitative restrictions on net factor payments from abroad. All the impact is indirect, primarily through variables relating to large-scale mining activity and profits. (iii) The elasticities are so large because the variable of interest is the difference between two flows (see note a to Table A.11). (iv) Capital movements are held fixed exogenously.

27. Calculations from data in Moran [1970:383] suggest no phase-associated pattern

in mean profit rates (i.e., the ratio of net profits to book value) for the two largest Chilean copper mines.

Mine	*1945–55*	*1956–58*	*1959–61*	*1962–64*
Chuquicamata				
Book value with disputed 1913 claim	.115	.120	.101	.104
Book value without disputed 1913 claim	.337	.193	.156	.150
El Teniente	.284	.366	.283	.153

The lack of a phase association is not surprising given the importance of world copper prices in determining profit rates. For the simulation discussed in the text, world copper prices are held constant.

Chapter 12

Economic Growth

In Chile, as elsewhere in the developing world, growth has been a high-priority objective. The focus of this chapter, therefore, is on questions such as the following: To what extent has growth been associated with the degree of liberalization? How has it been affected by devaluation and liberalization? How have foreign-sector policies affected each of these factors?

Exploration of these questions leads to the identification of a number of associations between the Chilean international economic regimes and growth factors. More restrictive regimes, for example, have tended to lessen growth by encouraging inefficient shifts of primary factors among subsectors, inducing technology too capital-intensive for the Chilean economy with its large numbers of unskilled workers, reducing domestic savings, increasing marginal capital-output ratios, limiting the importation of embodied technology, prohibiting the importation of second-hand equipment, discouraging the expansion of command over foreign resources through increased exports, discriminating against the development of linkages, and encouraging plants of less than optimal scale. There have been some counterbalancing effects, but they appear to have been much smaller in magnitude. No evidence was found, moreover, that productivity has increased relatively in the more protected industries. The net impact of restrictionism on growth, thus, appears to have been negative.

At the same time, it is important to emphasize that the absolute size of this growth effect has not been very large insofar as a judgment can be made based on a statistical analysis of Chilean experience. In part, the smallness of the effect reflects the canceling out of opposing responses. In part it may also be an effect of basing the analysis on a historical period of disequilibrium in which expectations that any liberalizing attempt would fail were soon fulfilled. Under such conditions, adjustments related to growth might be quite slow. Perhaps much larger responses would occur if expectations of a longer-run liberalization could be created. But this is very speculative. And to do so would be very difficult given the repeated failures of the past.

12.1 OVER-ALL GROWTH RATES

In this section time-series and cross-sectional evidence are brought to bear on the question of the association between foreign-sector policy and economic growth. Then the effects of devaluation and liberalization within the structural general-equilibrium model are considered.

12.1.1 Time-Series Evidence.

The mean growth rates of real GDP per capita for phases and subphases are given in Table A.1 (line 5.1). The highest values are for recent phases (6.0 per cent for 1971, 2.5 per cent for 1965–70, and 1.6 per cent for 1962–64) and the Second World War subphase (2.2 per cent). This pattern suggests a positive secular trend, with fluctuations depending in part on the state of world markets. The pre-Great Depression average (1.5 per cent for 1908–27), however, is higher than those of all subsequent phases and subphases except for the four mentioned above. On the face of it, therefore, the historical record does not support the claim of the structuralists that restrictionism leads to higher growth rates.

Focusing on the more recent phases reinforces this last point. The Phase II periods following the Second World War had the highest (6.0 per cent for 1971[1]) and the lowest (0.9 per cent for 1952–55) mean growth rates in real per capita GDP. For the more liberal periods the mean values have been in between: 1.4 per cent for 1956–58, 1.2 per cent for 1959–61, and 2.5 per cent for 1965–70.[2] The increase in the mean growth rate for 1956–58 to the highest level between the Second World War and 1962–64 is of particular interest because one of the major criticisms of the structuralist school has been that the Ibañez-Klein-Saks stabilization efforts caused stagnation.[3] Therefore, Ffrench-Davis [1971:245] suggests that the 1957 national accounts must be overestimates because they imply a growth of real GDP per capita of 5.2 per cent. Unfortunately, he is not specific in his evidence, nor is he clear as to whether he thinks the rate of growth also is underestimated in the national accounts in 1956 or 1958 or in some other year because of what he considers to be an error. Without specific evidence to the contrary, however, it seems reasonable to conclude that significant real growth did occur in this period despite the claims of many critics of the stabilization program. But it is also relevant to note that as a result of such growth, the level of per capita real GDP only returned to about the 1953 level.

In the first years after the Second World War, a number of economists in Chile and elsewhere in Latin America placed great emphasis upon the role of deteriorating terms of trade in the retardation of growth. The question naturally arises, therefore, whether or not there is any evidence of a positive association between Chile's terms of trade and her rate of growth. Examination of the data in lines 1.1.5.1 and 5.1 in Table A.1 prima facie leads to some skepticism about this hypothesis. In only three of the seven phases and subphases between 1931 and 1964 were movements in the mean terms of trade in the same direction as changes in the mean per capita growth rate (but see subsection 12.1.3, below).

Deviations from the secular growth rates for real GDP and for capacity provide further insight into the relation between growth and phases of restrictionism in the foreign-sector regime (Table A.2). For real GDP significantly negative deviations occurred for 1956–58 and 1959–61. For capacity a significantly negative deviation (but only at the 40 per cent level) results for 1959–61. These deviations do *not* imply that growth was lower in those two more liberalized periods than in the previous Phase II years. To the contrary, as noted above, on the average growth was higher. What they do imply is that growth tended to decline during those two more liberal phases. Those decelerations undoubtedly contributed to the failure of the efforts at stabilization plus liberalization.

12.1.2 Cross-Sectional Evidence.

The subsectoral estimates of protection and DRCs in Table 5.3 can be used to explore the extent of association between the price structures created by the international economic regimes and sectoral growth. Table A.5 contains all significantly nonzero correlations between ITR, EPR, and DRC measures and each of the following sets of measures of growth: (i) rates of growth of product between 1953 and 1961; (ii) rates of growth of gross product and of value added between 1957 and 1962; (iii) rates of growth of gross product, value added, total capital, and capacity in horsepower terms between 1957 and 1967; and (iv) rates of growth of gross product and of value added between 1962 and 1967. Table A.6 contains all significantly nonzero correlations between changes in ITRs and EPRs in 1961–67 and the same sets of growth measures.

The resultant data lend some support to the hypothesis of a positive relation between protection levels or changes and growth.[4] ITRs for 1967 are positively correlated with growth in value added and in horsepower capacity between 1957 and 1967. The changes in ITRs between 1961 and 1967 are positively associated with the same two variables, as well as with growth in product between 1953 and 1961. These results may be somewhat puzzling because it is hard to understand why within a neoclassical model ITRs (as opposed to EPRs) should be related to relative growth. Perhaps they served as signals, however, of the government's intentions to favor particular subsectors.

For the EPRs, and for DRC1, however, there is no evidence of a positive association with growth. The only significantly nonzero correlation coefficient, in fact, is a negative one between EPR2 and the growth in product between 1953 and 1961. The available empirical evidence thus suggests that ITRs may have been positively associated with capacity allocation—but not EPRs.[5]

12.1.3 General-Equilibrium Analysis.

The analyses in the two previous subsections are limited because no means is provided for guaranteeing the maintenance of ceteris paribus assumptions. This lack is filled by the general-equilibrium model of Chapter 2.

For the investigation of growth effects, however, one important reservation concerning use of this model must be made clear: [6] the behavioral relations in the model were estimated from a sample period during which overvaluation and fluctuations of policy were substantial. Perhaps such a history created expectations of failure for any liberalization efforts and thus greatly limited growth-related responses. If disequilibrium were eliminated in a credible way, a substantial change might result in the relevant parameters. The Chilean experience does not provide data to test such a hypothesis. However, Bhagwati [1975] and Krueger [1975] explore this possibility in the summary volumes for this project by comparing experiences in various countries. For Brazil in particular, the work of Fishlow [1975] suggests support for this hypothesis. If this hypothesis is true for Chile, the present model underestimates growth responses. To make any attempt at stabilization plus liberalization sufficiently credible in Chile, however, would be very difficult indeed because of the failure of four stabilization efforts and three liberalization attempts in less than two decades. A radical break with past policies and some important short-run successes might be required to establish credibility.

Subject to this qualification, several conclusions based on selected simulations in Table A.11 can be drawn:

Simulation 1.1 gives the impact of an increase in the terms of trade due to a proportional increase in all export prices and unit values in the first year only. After some time for adjustment (i.e., in the third year) the elasticity of capacity is not significantly different from zero, but that of GDP is 0.1 (lines 5.3 and 5.1). The response of investment in the third year (line 5.3.1) does cause an increase in capacity by the fourth year. Under ceteris paribus conditions, therefore, changes in the terms of trade do have a significant impact on growth.

Contrast this result with the lack of apparent association noted in subsection 12.1.1 above.

In *simulation 2.1.1,* it is assumed that there are equal proportional devaluations in all legal NERs in the first year only. In *simulation 2.1.3* the Bacha-Taylor equilibrium NER is assumed for all years. In both cases even the third-year elasticity of capacity is not large. In the first case the third-year elasticity of GDP is 0.1. In the second case, this translates into a 4 per cent increase in GDP. Whether such a product increase is large or small is a matter of definition. Given the required devaluations for the Bacha-Taylor equilibrium rates (i.e., 45, 35, and 61 per cent), the growth gain is smaller than many advocates of devaluation seem to suggest. On the other hand, such an increment clearly is significant and is desirable, ceteris paribus.

Simulation 2.3.1 gives the consequences of a change in quantitative restrictions in the first year only. The third-year elasticities indicate that liberalization would have an insignificant impact on capacity, but a negative effect on GDP. As in a number of cases discussed in previous chapters, therefore, liberalization tends to offset some of the effects of devaluation.

Thus, the impact of changes in the foreign sector on GDP may be significant. Subject to the qualifications made above, however, the response of capacity is quite small. The impact on GDP is primarily due to variations in capacity utilization. Even these reactions, moreover, require several years to work out. Unless a liberalization program did indeed change some of the parameters of the system, therefore, the growth consequences would only begin to appear after a couple of years. Unless the government had some successes in regard to other macro objectives, history suggests that it would be difficult to maintain momentum until the growth effects became evident.

12.2 AN AGGREGATE PRODUCTION FUNCTION

In this section, the effect of foreign-sector policies on major growth factors is examined within the framework provided by an aggregate production function. Consider capacity to be determined by the quantity and quality of labor, the quantity and quality of capital, the quantity of natural resources, and the quantity of foreign factors available.

The designation of these factors as separate inputs depends upon the limited substitution among them. Limited substitution is not the same as no substitution, however. The empirical evidence summarized in Behrman [1972a and 1972b] suggests that considerable substitution may be technically possible among some of these factors. To the extent that considerable substitution is possible, no single factor will, strictly speaking, be an absolute bottleneck within reasonable policy horizons.

The rate of growth of output within this framework is the weighted sum of the rates of growth of those factors. The weight for each factor is the elasticity of output with respect to that factor. If there are constant returns to scale and factors are paid their marginal products, the weights are the factor shares in total income.

12.2.1 Quantity of Labor.

If factor shares even roughly approximate the weights described above for the determination of growth, changes in the effective labor force are of substantial importance.[7]

Foreign-sector policies have significantly influenced the quantity of labor utilized through their impact on capacity utilization and on factor proportions (see sections 9.2 and 11.1). There probably also has been an effect on labor participation, perhaps transmitted through the unemployment rate. The discussion in previous chapters suggests that, in the long run, liberalization and devaluation might increase the size of the labor input.[8] Because of adjustment problems, however, the short-run consequences probably would be in the opposite direction.

The importation and exportation of labor services have not been very important in purely numerical terms. Chile long has provided some professionals for work elsewhere and has utilized professionals and technicians from other countries in her own economy. In comparison to the total work force, the numbers involved have always been quite small.

12.2.2 Quality of Labor

Harberger and Selowsky [1966] present a Denison-like calculation of the source of Chilean growth. For the postwar period they attribute a substantial proportion of total growth to improvements in Chilean human capital. Selowsky and Taylor [1973] estimate that the return to investment in nutrition for Chilean infants is very high. These results suggest that the quality of labor is quite important in Chilean development. Extensive attempts to utilize the Harberger and Selowsky human capital series in econometric estimates for the Chilean economy, however, do not result in significant statistical support for the importance of this factor, perhaps because of problems of aggregation or because in generating their series, they arbitrarily attribute all wage differentials to education.

Despite the lack of success in finding statistical support for the role of the quality of the labor force in Chilean development, this factor probably has been important in the growth process and has been affected by international economic regimes in at least five important ways.

i. The effect of more restrictive regimes generally has been to encourage or require importation or training of skilled labor or both for some of the industries which have developed behind trade barriers.

ii. The Allende foreign trade regime, however, had the opposite effect in the short run. Many skilled professionals and technicians, both Chilean and foreign in nationality, left the country in part because of changes in economic policy. To be more specific, the nationalization of some foreign industries and limitations on the extent to which wages and salaries could be paid in dollars both caused net outflows of highly skilled individuals. The latter change may have been an important factor, in fact, in the failure of copper production to expand as rapidly as programmed (see subsections 4.2.1 and 7.1.2.3).

iii. Foreign-sector policies encouraged some sectoral and subsectoral shifts of labor which were socially inefficient. While strictly speaking the quality of labor is not diminished by these shifts, in the aggregate the effect appears to be the same as a lessening of quality. The most obvious example of this has been the utilization of skilled labor by the government to maintain restrictive regimes and by the private sector to attempt to circumvent them. Restrictive regimes also have encouraged shifts from mining to industry (see subsection 10.1.1), which apparently have been from a high to a lower marginal labor productivity sector.[9]

iv. Some advocates of more restrictive regimes claim that these barriers will permit development of native entrepreneurs and increases in labor productivities through learning by doing. Evidence to support these claims is difficult to find. The relatively low and stagnant productivities in the traditional import-substitution subsectors alluded to in Chapter 10, for example, if anything suggest the opposite conclusion.[10] Restrictive barriers may have primarily lessened pressures for increased efficiency and productivity that the international market otherwise would have provided.

v. To the extent that foreign-sector policy affects nutrition in the lower income classes by altering the income distribution, the Selowsky and Taylor [1973] results suggest the possibility of considerable impact on the quality of labor in the long run. If an upward shift in the labor share of income is highly correlated with an increase in lower-class income,[11] then, as was suggested in section 11.1, in the short and medium run restrictionism has a positive effect on the quality of labor through this mechanism. It is implied in that same section, however, that the results may be in the opposite direction in the longer run.

12.2.3 Quantity of Capital.

Research of the past decade has raised strong doubts about earlier claims for the almost absolute primacy of capital bottlenecks in the growth process.[12] Nevertheless, additions to the effective capital stock remain a major factor in the growth of capacity. If factor shares roughly approximate the appropriate weights in the growth accounting mentioned at the start of this section, for example, changes in the effective capital stock are weighted second only to those of the effective labor force in over-all growth.[13] On a per capita basis, the growth of the effective capital stock has the highest weight of any factor.

12.2.3.1 INVESTMENT.

Since World War II, slightly more than 10 per cent of GDP has been accounted for by investment (Table A.1, line 3.1.2.2).[14] The secular growth rate of investment has been higher than that for GDP, but not enough substantially to alter this ratio.[15] No significant phase associations are evident in either the share of investment in product or the secular growth rate of investment.[16]

A significant relation between the foreign sector and real investment nevertheless seems likely. It is emphasized in subsection 5.1.2 that, on the average, international economic regimes have favored investment-goods imports over consumption goods.[17] This favoritism contrasts sharply with the experience of Chile's neighbor, Argentina. For that country Díaz [1965] estimates that because of the high protection given domestic capital goods producers, a 25 per cent savings rate results in investment of only 14 per cent of GNP when evaluated at world prices. For Chile the change is in the opposite direction because the protection given domestic capital goods producers is relatively low. The share of investment in GNP for 1947–71 is 11 per cent at domestic prices, and 17 per cent at world prices.[18] In the late 1960s, however, as is concluded in section 5.2, protection did increase relatively for domestic capital goods production.

In subsection 5.1.2, it is also suggested that even though on average investment imports were favored over other import categories, at times of crisis this import category was the one must severely restricted because investment was deemed relatively postponable. The result was that relative fluctuations in the PLD-EER(PI) for this category exceeded those in any other category.

In subsection 6.1.2 and section 6.2 a detailed examination is made of the impact of the PLD-EER(PI) for capital goods on imports of such goods. Their share increased secularly, but responded substantially to variations in quantitative restrictions. The relative size of the imported component of investment, thus, also tended to increase over time, but with substantial variations (line 1.2.2.2 in Table A.1). The very size of the imported share of investment, from about 20 to 40 per cent even in domestic prices, also points to the importance of the foreign sector in the investment process.

Statistical Evidence About the Foreign Sector and Investment. Tables A.5 and A.6 include all significantly nonzero correlations between the levels and rates of change of the subsectoral measures of protection shown in Table 5.3, on the one hand, and various measures of capital intensity, on the other.

EPRs in 1967 were significantly higher for the industries which a decade earlier had been relatively capital-intensive and in which machinery and equipment had dominated in the composition of capital (but less so over time). The rise in EPRs between 1961 and 1967 also was significantly higher in the industries which in 1957 were more capital-intensive, but in which the importance of machinery and equipment in the composition of capital had declined.[19]

Both the levels and the rates of rise of EPRs, thus, were correlated with earlier capital intensities. However, the direction of causality is not completely clear. The capital intensities may have been higher because of long-ongoing protection, in which case protection restricted economic growth by encouraging utilization of too much scarce capital in the highly protected industries (also see section 9.1). The more capital-intensive industries, moreover, may have been able to assure increasing EPRs over time because of the political power they were able to wield on the strength of their large holdings of assets.

ITRs in 1967 and the increase in ITRs between 1961 and 1967 both were associated with the increase in horsepower capacity between 1957 and 1967. These patterns provide some further support for the associations between capital intensity and protection which are discussed in the previous paragraph. In 1961 ITRs were positively correlated with the importance of consumer goods in inputs, but in 1967 they were positively associated with the shares of investment goods. This change reflects the movement toward greater protection of investment goods in the 1960s (see section 5.2).

Table 12.1 contains partial-equilibrium time-series estimates of investment functions for six sectors. The underlying model assumes a response to replacement needs and to changes in the desired capital stock. Relationship 12.1 presents a similar estimate for a residual category which includes construction, services and government.

$$\underset{}{GDIR} = \underset{(3.8)}{0.487\, GDIR_{-1}} + \underset{(1.8)}{0.0969\, \Delta\, (GDPR_{-1})} \tag{12.1}$$

$$- \underset{(3.5)}{526\, R[PGDP]} - \underset{(6.9)}{504.\, DUMMY}$$

$$+ \underset{(1.9)}{0.216\, MK_{-1}} - \underset{(3.5)}{3{,}885.\, QRFD} + \underset{(3.5)}{3{,}609.}$$

$\bar{R}^2 = 0.84$; $SE = 80.2$; $DW = 2.4$; years covered, 1950–65 where

$GDIR$ = real gross domestic investment in physical capital in the residual sectors;
$GDPR$ = real GDP in the residual sectors;
$R[PGDP]$ = rate of growth of GDP deflator;
$DUMMY$ = dummy variable for data definition problems in 1954 and 1959;
MK = real capital goods imports;
$QRFD$ = Ffrench-Davis quantitative restrictions index.

Examination of the results in Table 12.1 and in relationship 12.1 suggests that on an over-all level the model is satisfactory. There is no evidence of serious problems of serial correlation, the coefficients generally have the a priori anticipated signs (although in some cases the estimated lag structure includes some unexpected signs, especially at endpoints), and the values for the corrected coefficients of determination indicate that the specification is quite consistent with variations in the dependent variable for utilities, agriculture, transportation, and the residual sectors, but less so for industry and housing, and least so for mining. The quite limited success in mining probably reflects the special characteristics of that sector mentioned above in subsections 4.2.1 and 7.1.2.3. The relatively limited success in housing probably also reflects the existence of special determinants in this sector and particularly serious problems with the price indices for housing because of rent control.

Replacement investment is related to the level of real capacity and the state of technology. Responses to replacement factors are significant in agriculture, industry, transportation, and the residual category. The foreign sector does not affect replacement needs substantially, although it may have some impact on the state of available technology.

The desired capital stock depends on the neoclassical term derived from the sectoral CES production functions in Behrman [1972c]. The strict neoclassical term is modified by considerations relating to the degree of historical capacity utilization and to uncertainty as represented by the standard deviation of relative prices over three years.[20] Responses to the neoclassical term are significant in agriculture, mining, industry, utilities, and the residual category. Capacity utilization is important in mining and housing. Uncertainty affects investment decisions in agriculture, mining, industry, and transportation. All three factors are directly affected by events in the foreign sector.

i. The price of investment goods in the neoclassical term depends heavily on foreign prices and on the international economic regime because of the substantial importance of imports in the composition of investment. Increases in

TABLE 12.1
Sectoral Investment Functions for Chilean Real Physical Capital,[a] 1945–65

				Change in Desired				
	Elasticity of Substitution	Replacement Investment[b]		Neoclassical Term			Capacity Utilization	
Sector		1	2	1	2	3	1	2
Agriculture	.0[c]	140.0	−29.0	−12.8				
		(3.6)	(3.6)	(1.9)				
Mining	.51			191.0	−94.6	12.1	−2.06	0.349
				(1.9)	(1.6)[e]	(1.3)[d]	(1.9)	(1.5)[e]
Industry	.76	−461.0	89.6	−13.3		0.573		
		(1.9)	(1.9)	(1.5)[e]		(1.2)[d]		
Transportation	.0	−93.9						
		(2.6)						
Utilities	.32				64.9	−15.4		
					(2.1)	(2.2)		
Housing	.0						5.38	−0.296
							(3.5)	(3.5)

$\bar{R}^2$ = coefficient of multiple determination adjusted for degrees of freedom.
SE = standard error of estimate.
DW = Durbin-Watson statistic.

a. The figures in parentheses are the absolute values of the *t* statistics, each of which is significantly nonzero at the 5 per cent level unless otherwise noted. The figures in brackets are the long-run elasticities at the point of sample means.

b. The Hall-Sutch [1969] polynomial method with the tail constrained to zero is used for replacement investment and for change in the desired capital stock variables; the numbers in the column heads refer to the degree of the relevant polynomials. The implied lag patterns are shown on the following page.

c. An elasticity of substitution of 0.31 was actually used, but in exploration of a putty-clay type of hypothesis the neoclassical term was split into quantity and price components. Since the coefficients of the latter were not significantly nonzero even at the 25 per cent level the price component was dropped. With only a quantity component the model reduced to what it would be with an elasticity of substitution of zero.

d. Significantly nonzero at the 15 per cent level.

e. Significantly nonzero at the 10 per cent level.

f. Current value for 1960 and after; included because of change in data definition for government direct and indirect real investment.

Capital Stock[b] Standard Dev. of Relative Prices			Govt. Direct and Indirect Real Investment		Imported Investment Goods			
1	2	3	No Lag	1-Yr. Lag	No Lag	1-Yr. Lag	Constant	$\overline{R}^2$ *SE* *DW*
0.875			0.0511	0.0269	0.0404		−75.2	0.95
(3.1)			(3.9)	(1.9)	(1.1)[d]		(1.8)	8.7
			[0.7]		[0.2]			2.9
6.21		−0.448					63.5	0.42
(2.7)		(3.2)					(8.6)	33.0
								1.4
3.94			0.224				−279.0	0.60
(1.6)[e]			(1.4)[e]				(1.9)	75.0
			[0.5]					2.2
−10.9	2.76		0.0966	0.152[f]			−700.0	0.92
(2.9)	(3.3)		(1.2)[d]	(2.3)			(2.2)	42.0
			[0.3]					2.4
			0.0681	0.148[f]		0.0498	25.0	0.97
			(4.2)	(9.8)		(1.8)	(2.8)	12.0
			[0.5]			[0.1]		1.6
			0.138[f]				491.0	0.54
			(2.7)				(22.8)	78.0
			[0.1]					1.9

Note b concluded

	Lag (no. of years) 0	1	2	3	Σ
Agriculture					
Replacement	−0.0964	0.0147	0.0677	0.0629	0.0489
Neoclassical term	0.0512	0.0384	0.0256	0.0128	0.128
Standard deviation	−3.50	−2.63	−1.75	−0.875	−8.75
Mining					
Neoclassical term	−0.0248	0.0841	0.0762	0.0241	0.160
Capacity utilization	265.0	94.2	−6.9	−38.3	0.314
Standard deviation	381.0	957.0	1,265.0	1,035.0	3,637.0
Industry					
Replacement	0.410	0.039	−0.153	−0.166	0.129
Neoclassical term	0.0167	0.0039	−0.0054	−0.0079	0.0072
Standard deviation	−15.8	−11.8	−7.89	−3.94	−39.4
Transportation					
Replacement	0.378	0.282	0.188	0.094	0.939
Standard deviation	−0.68	−80.81	−11.4	−8.47	−29.4
Utilities					
Neoclassical term	−0.0513	−0.0019	0.0848	0.116	0.148
Housing					
Capacity utilization	−258.0	251.0	532.0	557.0	1,132.0

the PLD-EER for investment goods or in the premium received by the importers of such goods, therefore, significantly reduce real investment.

ii. The capacity-utilization term indirectly reflects foreign-sector policies. In the short and medium term, aggregate capacity utilization tends to decline with devaluations and reductions in restrictiveness (section 9.2). This negative short-run effect of liberalization, thus, would have negative longer-run consequences.

iii. Uncertainty about relative prices also tends to depress real investment. Much of the variation in these prices originates in changing foreign-sector policies. As noted above, the government has considered investment goods to be postponable at times of foreign-exchange crises. The relative variance of the PLD-EER(PI) for this category, therefore, exceeded that for all other groups, with a negative effect on investment.

In addition to the terms for replacement and for change in the desired stock of capital, the a priori specification of investment behavior includes two other factors. The availability of government financial investment (largely through CORFO) and the availability of imported machinery and equipment both may affect the desired level of real capital stock or the speed of adjustment toward the desired level.[21] Mamalakis [1971b] in particular has emphasized the importance of the latter.

The results suggest that government direct and indirect investment has significantly nonzero and rather substantial effects in the infrastructure sectors of transportation, utilities, and housing, and in the goods-producing sectors of agriculture and industry. The implied distribution of government investment across sectors, with over-all emphasis mostly on industry but with increased relative emphasis on infrastructure under Alessandri in the early 1960s, also seems consistent with the historical patterns of such investment.

Imported investment goods and the QR index have significantly nonzero coefficients for the residual sectors and for utilities and agriculture, but only at the 15 per cent level for the last of these. The evidence for a strong *direct* impact of the foreign sector on real physical capital investment in Chile through imports, as hypothesized by Mamalakis, thus seems weak.[22] The indirect effects through the price system and through capacity-utilization rates apparently have been more important.

Because of the existence of these indirect effects, the general-equilibrium consequences of changes in the international economic regime for investment are of interest. The results of simulations 2.1.1 and 2.1.3 suggest that devaluations have almost no net general-equilibrium investment impact (line 5.3.1 in Table A.11). Responses to higher capital costs and lower utilization rates just about neutralize possible inducements. The implication of simulation 2.3.1 is that liberalization has a much more substantial effect, but the response changes from positive in the short run to negative in the medium run.

In consideration of the investment response to both devaluation and liberalization, the reservation stated in section 12.1 above must be repeated. Perhaps expectations could be changed sufficiently so that this response would be much greater than indicated by the historical data. Studies of other countries may provide support for such a possibility. Unless such changes occurred, however, large positive investment responses to efforts at devaluation plus liberalization should not be expected.

12.2.3.2 Savings.

The availability of resources for capital accumulation is determined by savings. If the government could costlessly use fiscal policy to alter savings rates or if unlimited foreign savings were available, the amount of available domestic savings would not be a constraint on investment. Such conditions, however, have not predominated in recent Chilean history. The impact of the foreign sector on savings thus is of some interest.

The available data permit the estimation of time-series savings-consumption functions for households and nonprofit institutions,[23] business, and the government. Alternatives for each of these categories are presented in Table 12.2. The model utilized hypothesizes that savings-consumption decisions depend basically on an appropriate income variable, with modifications due to a number of factors discussed below.

The degree of consistency of the relations in Table 12.2 with variations in the dependent variables seems reasonably satisfactory nor are there any apparent problems of serial correlation. However, substantial multicollinearity exists among a set of variables that includes per capita real monetary balances, the black-market PLD-NER, the inverse of the GDP deflator, net foreign savings, and the standard deviation of the PLD-EER. Therefore, in all three cases alternatives are presented with various subsets of those values deleted: (i) the combination of variables that maximizes the degree of consistency with the variance in the dependent variable; (ii) the combination that maximizes the degree of consistency with the variance in the dependent variable subject to the inclusion of real net foreign savings; and (iii) for households and nonprofit institutions, the combination for which the degree of consistency with the variance in the dependent variable is almost as great as in the first alternative, but in which per capita real monetary balances are included instead of the black-market PLD-NER. The coefficient of the variables among which there is multicollinearity must of course be interpreted with care.

The major determinant of real savings in each case is the net income variable: for households, real disposable income; for business, real after-tax nonwage income; and for government, real government revenues. The marginal savings propensities for these three groups vary substantially. After complete adjustment,[24] the point estimates range from 0.04 to 0.38 for households and

TABLE 12.2

Real Consumption-Savings Functions for Chilean Households and Nonprofit Institutions, Business, and the Government,[a] 1945–65

Dependent Var.	Per Capita Real Disposable Income (Z1[b]) (1)	Rate of Inflation Z1[b] (2)	Rate of Inflation Z2[b] (3)	Per Capita Real Monetary Balances (Z1[b]) (4)	Black-Market PLD-NER (5)	Inverse of GDP Deflator (6)
Real per capita private consumption						
I	−0.623	2.24	−0.418		13.6	−1.04
	(6.5)	(6.9)	(6.2)		(2.9)	(4.9)
	[0.6]	[−0.0]			[0.0]	[−0.0]
II	−0.674	2.32	−0.439	−9,128.0		−1.11
	(5.8)	(5.4)	(4.8)	(2.0)		(4.6)
	[0.6]	[−0.0]		[1.2]		[−0.0]
III	−0.961	1.94	−0.371		15.0	
	(24.6)	(4.7)	(4.4)		(2.3)	
	[0.9]	[−0.0]			[0.1]	
	Real After Tax Non-wage Income	PLD-EER Z1[b]	PLD-EER Z2[b]	Real Monetary Balances		
Real business savings						
I	0.633	26.0		−0.627		4.55
	(13.4)	(5.5)		(5.1)		(4.7)
	[0.3]	[−0.2]		[−1.5]		[0.4]
II	0.554	108.9	−18.9	−0.767		
	(10.9)	(2.4)	(2.1)	(4.4)		
	[0.3]	[−0.2]		[−1.9]		
	Real Govt. Revenues					
Real government consumption						
I	0.331					−0.667
	(11.0)					(1.1)[e]
	[0.6]					[−0.0]
II	0.275					1.25
	(7.0)					(1.2)
	[0.5]					[0.0]

Real Foreign Savings (7)	Standard Deviation: Rate of Inflation (8)	Standard Deviation: PLD-EER (9)	Income Ratio: Nonwage to Total (10)	Ratio: Agric. to Total GDP (11)	Constant (12)	$\bar{R}^2$ *SE* *DW* (13)
	3.65 (3.7) [0.0]	−61.9 (1.6)[c] [−0.0]	508.0 (4.0) [0.1]	−2,083.0 (4.0) [−0.2]	798.0 (3.8)	0.98 18.5 2.4
	4.75 (3.6) [0.0]	−72.0 (1.5)[c] [−0.0]	512.0 (3.5) [0.1]	−1,841.0 (3.0) [−0.1]	572.0 (2.0)	0.98 20.9 2.5
0.837[d] (4.3) [0.0]	2.0 (1.6)[c] [0.0]		790.0 (4.7) [0.1]	−591.0 (1.1)[e] [−0.0]		0.96 26.9 2.4
					644.0 (2.5)	0.94 89.9 2.1
−0.178 (1.6)[c] [−0.0]					650.0 (2.0)	0.91 110.0 2.4
Real Foreign Savings: Z1[b]	Z2[b]	Z3[b]			516.0 (4.9)	0.94 94.5 1.7
0.400 (1.5) [0.1]	−0.252 (1.6)	0.0372 (1.4)			758.0 (4.8)	0.96 80.0 2.2

Notes to Table 12.2

$\bar{R}^2$ = coefficient of multiple determination adjusted for degrees of freedom.

SE = standard error of estimate.

DW = Durbin-Watson statistic.

a. The figures in parentheses are the absolute values of the *t* statistics, each of which is significantly nonzero at the 5 per cent level unless otherwise noted. The figures in brackets are the long-run elasticities at the point of sample means.

b. The Hall-Sutch [1969] polynomial method with the tail constrained to zero is used for this variable. Zi ($i = 1$ or 2) is the order of the polynomial. The implied lag patterns are as follows:

	Lag (no. of years)				
	0	1	2	3	Σ
Real per capita private consumption					
I Income	0.249	0.187	0.125	0.063	0.623
Rate of inflation	−227.0	−44.5	53.9	68.8	−148.0
II Income	0.270	0.202	0.135	0.067	0.674
Rate of inflation	−225.0	−37.4	62.9	75.4	−125.0
Monetary balances	0.3651	0.2738	0.1826	0.093	0.9128
III Income	0.385	0.288	0.192	0.096	0.961
Rate of inflation	−183.0	−25.7	−57.0	65.6	−85.8
Real business savings: real cost of foreign exchange adjusted for import taxes					
I	−10.4	−7.80	−5.20	−2.60	−26.0
II	−13.3	−42.9	9.3	23.6	−23.3
Real government consumption: real net foreign savings					
III	0.065	0.250	0.153	0.004	0.465

c. Significantly nonzero at the 10 per cent level.

d. Estimates of per capita real savings of households and nonprofit institutions.

e. Significantly nonzero at the 15 per cent level.

nonprofit institutions, 0.55 to 0.63 for business, and 0.67 to 0.73 for the government. Income shifts within the private sector from households to business and income shifts from the private sector to the government, then, would tend to increase real savings.[25] As is discussed in subsection 11.2, overvaluation led to the latter shift and thus increased total domestic savings in the short run. Increased restrictiveness, however, tended to work in the opposite direction.[26]

For households and nonprofit institutions there is further evidence of a distributional impact on savings. The data in columns 11 and 12 indicate that shifts from nonwage to wage income and from the rest of the economy to agriculture would both increase savings. The former result in particular may be somewhat surprising.[27] If the inference is valid, the Chilean world is clearly not Kaldorian, and savings could not be increased by shifting income away from labor. In the short and medium run, these results imply that reducing quantitative restrictions would increase savings by increasing both the labor and agricultural shares. Devaluation, on the other hand, would have the counteracting effects of increasing the share of agriculture but reducing that of labor (see sections 11.1 and 11.4).

For the private sector, real monetary balances in excess of desired levels might induce expenditures and therefore reduce savings. Desired real balances are not directly observable, but presumably depend on the level of after-tax real income and the cost of holding real balances. The major component of this cost is the expected rate of inflation.[28]

Under the assumption that the expected rate of inflation might be represented by a distributed lag of past price changes or by a distributed lag of PLD-EERs, the estimates in Table 12.2 provide some support for the view that the role of excess real monetary balances in the savings process is inverse. Consistent with this hypothesis, for both households and business the point estimates imply an elastic inverse response of savings to the level of actual balances, an inverse response to price expectations as represented by patterns of PLD-EERs, and a positive response to after-tax real income.[29] On net, as is suggested in subsection 9.1.3, both devaluation and increased restrictiveness would reduce savings by increasing real balances.

The positive sign for the response of household saving to the distributed lag of the rate of change of prices, in contrast, is not consistent with the real-balance hypothesis. However, the sign of this response probably only reflects the relative inability of households to defend their share of command over goods in the face of high inflation rates. Thus they end up with some forced savings.

Weisskopf [1972], among others, has hypothesized that foreign savings are at least partially substituted for domestic savings (Papanek [1972, 1973] presents a critique of this view).[30] The last alternative for each of the three groups provides some support for this hypothesis. In one sense, in fact, the support is too strong because the total of the relevant coefficients implies that a permanent increase in real net foreign savings of one unit ceteris paribus results in a decrease in real net domestic savings of at least the same order of magnitude. If it were not for the problem of multicollinearity, therefore, one might conclude that in the Chilean case there is support for a rather extreme version of the hypothesis. However, given that the relevant coefficient estimates for the real private domestic savings functions are probably biased upward in absolute value because part of the effects of price and possibly of real monetary balances are incorporated, any deduction about at least the size of the substitution must be qualified. Nevertheless, the conclusion seems warranted that the impact of net real foreign savings on Chilean real domestic savings may be quite significant.

There is some evidence of statistically significant responses for uncertainty, which is the final determinant of real savings behavior.[31] For household savings the point estimates suggest an inverse response to increased uncertainty about inflation but a direct response to increased uncertainty about PLD-EERs. Neither of these effects, however, is very large.

All the evidence of the impact of the foreign sector on domestic savings discussed up to this point is based on partial-equilibrium analysis. The model of Chapter 2 again provides insight into what happens within a general-equilibrium context. In respect to savings there is no trade-off on the aggregate level between the effects of devaluation and of liberalization. For both actions, the net aggregate consequence of all the reactions discussed above is to increase savings (line 5.2 for simulations 2.1.1 and 2.3.1 in Table A.11). To the extent that savings have been a constraint on growth, therefore, the prevalent international economic regimes of recent decades have reduced economic expansion.[32]

12.2.4 Quality of Capital.

It can be hypothesized that in a number of respects international economic regimes affect the quality of capital—or at least what appears to be the quality of capital—as it would be specified in an aggregate production function. Comprehensive evidence bearing on this hypothesis often is hard to come by. Some fragments of evidence, however, are available.

i. The aggregate marginal capital-output ratio reflects counteracting tendencies related to the effects of foreign-sector policies. First, the ratios reflect the degree of capacity utilization. Utilization rates might decline with greater restrictiveness because of shortages of key imported inputs. It is suggested in section 9.2, however, that liberalization and devaluation cause a net reduction in these rates because of competition from imports and a number of indirect effects.

The ratios also reflect the size of inventories. Under restrictive regimes, *desired* inventories would be higher, ceteris paribus, because of the need to hedge against future supply shortages. At the same time, however, *actual* inventories might be lower because of limited past and current supplies.

In addition, changes in the geographic sources of investment goods are reflected in the ratios. If restrictions limit capital goods imports, the origin of investment goods may shift toward domestic sources (especially in the case of construction materials).[33] The mean ratios of imported investment goods to total investment provides some support for this view (line 1.2.1.2 in Table A.1).

Finally, the foreign-sector regime also might alter the aggregate capital-output ratio through changes in the allocation of investment by destination among production sectors with different capital intensities. In subsection 12.2.3.1, above, in fact, evidence is reported of more restrictive regimes leading to greater investment in more capital-intensive subsectors.

The net effect of all these considerations on the aggregate marginal capital-output ratio was to lower it in the more liberal phases (line 5.5 in Table A.1). The lowest mean value of this ratio in the post-World War II period was for the 1965–70 Phase III years, followed by the 1956–58 Phase III years, and the 1959–61 Phase IV years.[34] In this sense, therefore, liberalization was associated with greater quality of capital. In fact, however, this aspect of quality primarily reflects capacity-utilization rates and different dimensions of compositional change.

ii. Imported capital equipment generally is higher in quality than are domestically produced goods because of the limited development of Chilean industries producing machinery and equipment.[35] It is emphasized in subsectors 6.1.2 and 12.2.3.1 that liberalization generally increased the availability of imported capital equipment. It thus also increased the quality of Chilean capital.

iii. At times, under more restrictive Chilean international economic regimes, the importation of second-hand machinery and equipment was prohibited in order to limit capital flight through overinvoicing. In many instances such equipment might have been economically more efficient than new goods.[36]

iv. If the protective structure created by the international economic regime were positively associated with DRCs, it might be concluded that capital and other factors were allocated inefficiently. In the aggregate this would be the same as a lower quality of capital. In Table A.4, there is some evidence that the higher-DRC subsectors in 1961 had higher ITRs and EPRs.

These bits of evidence, thus, all seem to point in the same direction. The degree of restrictiveness has been inversely associated with the aggregate "quality" of capital. In this respect the prevalent restrictive nature of recent Chilean foreign-sector policies have had a cost in terms of growth.

12.2.5 Quantity of Natural Resources.

Foreign-sector policy affects the effective quantity of natural resources as specified in an aggregate production function in two important respects. First, some important raw materials, e.g., petroleum, must be imported at least in part. Second, most of Chile's mineral wealth is in fact wealth only if it can be exported. Chileans could not have utilized more than a small fraction of the nitrates mined between 1870 and 1930 or of the copper mined since 1920.

In subsections 6.1.2 and 7.1.2.3 it is suggested that the contribution of natural resources in either of these respects has tended to be greater the more liberal the regime. However, in more restrictive periods natural resource imports have been relatively unconstrained. Moreover, the division of returns from mining exports was less advantageous to Chile than it might have been in certain more liberal periods (see section 1.2 and subsections 4.2.1 and 8.1.1).

12.2.6 Quantity of Foreign Factors.

If substitution is very low between some imports and domestic factors, command over foreign-exchange resources is itself a separate input in the aggregate production function.[37] Sources of foreign exchange include exports of goods and services and net capital inflows. For a given level of foreign exchange the government also can attempt to shape its composition so that critical needs are serviced first.

In chapters 3 through 8, the impact of Chilean international economic regimes on the command over foreign-exchange resources is considered in great detail. To be sure, in the short run the more restrictive regimes generally have allowed continued inflows of foreign inputs despite very limited foreign-exchange resources. However, at such times, they generally have discriminated strongly against capital-goods inputs. Moreover, they have increased the long-run vulnerability of the economy to such crises by discouraging expansion of exports. From this point of view, the net effect of the general atmosphere of restrictiveness on growth has probably been negative.

12.2.7 Miscellaneous Sources of Growth.

The literature on development emphasizes a number of other sources of growth: research and development leading to improvements in the quality of labor or the quality of capital, or both, economies of scale, motivation (N-achievement), linkage effects, externalities, infrastructure development, to name a few.

For most of these factors it is extremely difficult to obtain data that permits satisfactory testing of the relation between their contribution to growth and foreign-sector policies. In at least two cases, however, these policies probably have had detrimental effects: (i) They have discouraged linkages between the export sector and the rest of the economy. The discriminatory NER policy for large-scale mining, for example, strongly discouraged the use of domestic labor and other inputs (see sections 3.2 and 11.1 and subsections 4.2.1, 5.1.2, and 7.2.1). (ii) They have encouraged the development of plants at far below optimal scale. In the early 1960s, for example, eleven different plants were involved in the manufacture of fewer than 4,000 automobiles per year.

NOTES

1. Because of lags in data availability, only 1971 is included for the Allende period. The high growth rate in that year was due more to increased capacity utilization than to growth. In fact, total real investment fell 7.7 per cent and imports of machinery and equipment fell 16.8 per cent.

2. For the 1965–70 period, however, much of this growth was in the first two years, before the acceleration of liberalization attempts. In 1967 and 1970 per capita product declined, and in 1968 and 1969 it increased moderately.

3. For example, see Edel [1969:86], Instituto de Economía [1963:75] and Ffrench-Davis [1971:245]. Sierra [1969:64] is an exception. He criticizes the stabilization program from a structuralist viewpoint, but concludes that growth occurred. On the other hand, Mamalakis [1971b:164] generally opposes the structuralist analysis, but agrees that 1956–58 was a quite stagnant period.

4. The significantly nonzero correlation coefficients for the 1968 export-oriented measures are not discussed here because of doubts about how well the over-all subsectoral characteristics relate to the few products within each subsector for which these ITRs, EPRs, and DRCs are constructed.

5. For references to discussions of the theoretical reasons why EPRs would not be expected to be related to relative growth see Appendix B.

6. This qualification is much more important for growth concerns than for others because the gestation period is relatively long for many changes related to growth.

7. The wage share has averaged at least 60 per cent in recent phases (line 4.2 in Table A.1).

8. In the long run there might also be an impact on population. If population responds, GDP per capita probably is a better indicator of the degree of success in attaining growth-related goals than is total GDP.

9. Under the assumption of sectoral CES production functions with constant returns to scale, the marginal product of labor (*MPL*) is related to the average product of labor (*APL*) as follows: $MPL = (b \cdot APL)^{1/\sigma}$, where σ is the elasticity of substitution and b depends on the state of the technology and other parameters of the production function. On the basis of estimates of the sectoral elasticities of substitution and other relevant parameters presented for agriculture, mining, and industry in Behrman [1972a] marginal labor productivity was highest for mining, followed by industry and agriculture. This calculation must be viewed with a certain amount of caution, however, since it depends on the magnitude of the constant term in the original estimates.

10. No significantly positive correlation coefficients were found, moreover, between rates of protection and labor productivity levels or changes (Table A.5).

11. That the correlation is high is not obvious. Many individuals in the lowest income class may be made worse off by measures which benefit organized labor and increase only its share.

12. In the Chilean case, for example, see Behrman [1972c and 1973b] and Harberger and Selowsky [1966].

13. Most of the nonlabor share of product (i.e., 1.0 minus line 4.2 in Table A.1) is the capital share.

14. This proportion is in domestic prices. As is discussed below, the share of investment is higher in terms of world prices. Comparable data for the pre-war period are not available. According to ECLA estimates reported by Mamalakis [1971b:121] the share of investment in national product fell from 20 per cent for 1925–30 to 4 per cent in 1933 and then rose to 10–15 per cent in 1935–40. The direction of changes in this pattern seems reasonable, but it is doubtful that the share of investment for 1935–40 averaged above the means for postwar periods. In particular, the decline in GDP per capita in the 1930s in contrast to increases on the average after the war create doubts about the level of the ECLA proportions relative to those in the national accounts (lines 3.1.2.2 and 5.1 in Table A.1).

15. In Table A.2, the secular exponential growth rates in 1940–65 are 3.8 per cent

for GDP and 6.0 per cent for investment. The discrepancy between these two rates, however, is misleading for the post-World War II period because of the very low share of investment in GDP during the war (line 3.1.2.2 in Table A.1).

16. A slight decline in the growth rate of investment for the first year of each of the three liberalization attempts, however, is significant in Table A.2. This fall is emphasized by critics of these efforts. During the most liberalized episode, moreover, Hirschman [1963:219] claims that investment sagged further in the second year (i.e., 1960), laying open the government to further criticisms from the left and from the structuralists. But the national accounts indicate there was a record 29.5 per cent increase in real investment in 1960.

17. CORFO also helped to establish a favorable investment climate, focused attention on the importance of imported machinery and equipment, made possible more systematic analysis of the Chilean economy by its data collection and processing efforts, probably increased foreign capital inflows, and made possible large-scale investment projects under Chilean control. This activity was somewhat phase related. Mamalakis [1971b:565–587] suggests, however, that it may have in large part resulted more in a shift in investment than a net addition because of other scarcities (e.g., skilled labor and foreign exchange) and because of deterioration in the capital market due in part to deficit financing of CORFO.

18. Based on line 3.1.2.2 in Table A.1 and the mean value of 0.64 for the ratio of PLD-EER(PI)s of investment to consumption goods in column 4 of Table 5.2.

19. Correlations with ITR3 and EPR4 are not included in the discussion because they are for subsectoral exports only and are not representative of the entire subsector.

20. The first component of the desired capital stock is in putty-putty form in that the response to expected price and quantity terms is symmetric. For an examination of the relative merits of the putty-putty and putty-clay hypotheses in the Chilean context see Behrman [1972b].

21. However, some preliminary nonlinear maximum-likelihood estimates in which these considerations are hypothesized to affect the adjustment processes directly are not very promising.

22. The evidence seems surprisingly weak given that the sectoral investment series are based in part on data for imported investment goods. Investment in mining, of course, has depended much more directly on the foreign sector than investment in other production sectors. See subsections 4.2.1, 7.1.2.3, and 8.2.1.

23. For households and nonprofit institutions, the national accounts indicate a negative savings rate for every year from 1960 to 1971. This characteristic presumably is more an artifact due to the residual nature of savings and a systematic overvaluation of depreciation than a reflection of reality. The estimates below are made under the assumption that such a measurement error is independent of the included variables. For further discussion of the negative savings estimates in the Chilean accounts, see Mamalakis [1967b] and ODEPLAN [1970a].

24. For households there is an adjustment for permanent income. For the first year, the point estimates of the marginal propensity to save for households range from 0.61 to 0.75. Therefore, they are as high as for any other group if only the immediate impact is considered. This range also implies that impact multipliers are not very large because of the considerable leakage into savings.

25. Under Allende, however, it is not clear that the government remained a relatively high marginal saver. In 1971, for example, real savings fell (and became negative, in fact), although real revenues rose.

26. Unless the marginal propensity to save out of the import premiums was as high

as the marginal propensity to save of the government, these results overstate the gain in savings from restrictiveness because the aggregation obscures the effect of changes in the premiums.

27. This result may reflect the use here of a very broad definition of labor, i.e., returns to self-employed proprietors are included in the wage share.

28. Real interest rates a priori would seem to be much less important because of their small magnitude in comparison to expected inflation. No statistical evidence of their significance could be found.

29. The effect of real income on desired real balances, however, cannot be disentangled from its direct impact on savings.

30. The two-gap model posits a different relation between domestic and foreign savings. Because of a lack of foreign exchange, savings may be frustrated at the margin.

31. Actually Table 12.2 also includes the inverse of the GDP deflator (column 6). This variable is included because the functions were originally specified in nominal terms, but then deflated in order to lessen multicollinearity and heteroscedasticity.

32. One point that is not touched upon in this subsection is that in sheltered foreign markets added savings might be induced for financing attractive investment. Evidence for exploring this possibility is very difficult to obtain. In a related vein, however, Mamalakis [1971b:565–587] claims that CORFO investment largely replaced rather than supplemented other investment due to shortages of skilled labor and foreign exchange and the deterioration of local capital markets once inflation became high. The more important the shortages of other factors, the less likely it is that restrictive regimes induced additional savings through this mechanism.

33. In the 1956–58 liberalization, for example, housing investment fell an average of 21 per cent per year. This drop partially reflected tight credit conditions, but also was due to the end of a building boom in the previous phase that had been inspired by near hyperinflation and very severe restrictions on imports.

34. Several qualifications should be kept in mind: First, the mean for the 1952–55 Phase II subperiod was not significantly higher than that for 1959–61. Secondly, the absence of data precludes inclusion of the Allende years during which time the aggregate marginal capital-output ratio probably was very low owing to the high utilization ratio and very limited investment. Finally, and for the same reasons, the mean during the Second World War was relatively low.

35. If production possibilities ex ante have fixed coefficients and the factor proportions associated with imported equipment differ strongly from those domestically available, in a very important sense imported capital may not be of "high quality." This possibility does not seem to have offset other quality advantages of imported capital goods in the Chilean experience.

36. The most outstanding single example of distortions introduced by the prohibition of second-hand inputs, however, may have been for automobiles. See subsection 10.1.2 for a brief description of this subsector.

37. The two-gap model usually is based on the extreme assumption of no substitutibility between domestic and foreign inputs. For a critique of this model and references to some of its most prominent uses, see Behrman [1971b].

Part IV

Three Liberalization Episodes

Chapter 13

Recent Liberalization Episodes

In section 1.4 the major features of three recent attempts at stabilization plus liberalization were outlined: the Ibañez-Klein program of 1956–58, the Alessandri program of 1959–61, and the Frei program of 1965–70. Details of each program were given in Part II of this book, and the impact of each on price-related measures was analyzed there. In Part III the consequences of the programs were explored for five major areas of macroeconomic policy.

In this final part, the three liberalization episodes are taken up again, with the focus of the analysis on four questions: Why were the liberalization efforts made? What was done? What were the short-run effects? Why did they fail?

Four major conclusions are drawn from this analysis.

i. The central objective in each case was not liberalization of the foreign sector. The change in the international economic regime was but part of an over-all stabilization effort. The primary objectives were to arrest inflation and end stagnation. The international economic situation was an important contributing factor, but less significant than the domestic issues.

ii. The limited degree of short-run success in regard to these and other concerns substantially weakened the foreign-sector liberalization attempts. Without such success, political momentum could not be maintained sufficiently long to reap the potential long-run advantages noted in Part III above.

iii. In all three efforts, even under the sliding-peg exchange-rate policy, the PLD-EER was kept substantially below equilibrium and was allowed to decline. The boom in the copper market in the late 1960s enabled the Frei government to follow such a NER policy without encountering major foreign-exchange shortages. The two earlier programs were not so successful in relation to the world copper market. The attempt to maintain a below-equilibrium and declining price for foreign exchange, therefore, resulted in severe foreign-exchange shortages.

iv. A gradual approach to stabilization and liberalization has the advantage of not strongly disrupting the economic-political system. Some short-run successes may be scored in order to maintain momentum.

For Chile, the last point is highly pertinent. Given the failure of four major stabilization efforts and three major liberalization attempts in less than two decades, however, a gradual approach is not likely to be very credible there.[1] If it is not credible, changes will not occur to enable Chile to reap longer-run advantages. Instead, resources will be devoted to protecting vested interests from the transitory lessening of restrictions. Under such conditions it would be very hard to have enough short-run successes to maintain political momentum for a gradual approach even though long-run changes are not evident.

The best hope for gaining the long-run benefits from liberalization, therefore, may be by an abrupt transformation of policy.[2] The short-run costs may be large (and may be mitigated in part by appropriate policies). But only such an attempt may make the whole effort credible and thus change expectations sufficiently quickly so that the long-run advantages begin to appear before all political momentum is lost.

13.1 MOTIVATIONS FOR LIBERALIZATION EFFORTS

Both external and internal factors entered into the decisions to initiate liberalization programs. Table 13.1 includes some indicators of these factors for the year immediately preceding each program as well as for its first and last year of operation.

13.1.1 External Factors.

Three aspects of the external situation are of primary interest: the role of pressure from the IMF and from donor and creditor countries; the extent to which the immediate foreign-exchange position was unusually precarious; and the significance of perceptions of inefficiencies due to foreign-sector policies.

IMF PRESSURE.

The IMF in particular repeatedly has advocated reform and liberalization of Chilean international economic regimes. The policies prescribed by the IMF comprise what is known as the "monetarist" position in the "structuralist-

TABLE 13.1

Selected Indicators of External and Internal Chilean Economic Conditions in Years Preceding Liberalization Attempts and in First and Last Years of Liberalization Episodes, 1955–70

		Ibañez Period		Alessandri Period			Frei Period	
	1955 (1)	1956 (2)	1958 (3)	1959 (4)	1961 (5)	1964 (6)	1965 (7)	1970 (8)
External								
1. PLD-EER for goods imports	2.90	3.62	4.37	4.61	4.02	3.65	3.85	3.35
2. PLD-EER transactions ratio: nongoods to goods	2.53	1.27	1.30	0.85	0.81	1.17	1.01	1.19
3. NER ratio: black market to national accounts	3.12	1.50	1.54	1.01	1.01	1.96	1.65	1.93
4. Ratio of high to low subsectoral PLD-EER(PI)s	12.43	8.06	3.97	4.06	3.55	4.02	3.51	5.41
5. PLD-EER(PI) ratio: imports to exports	1.35	1.34	1.90	1.71	1.67	1.65	1.47	1.09
6. Average import premium rate	2.04	1.32	0.64	0.51	0.62	0.69	0.57	0.47
7. Ratios of Chilean trade statistics to those of major trading partners								
7.1 Imports recorded by Chile to exports recorded by others	1.44	1.05	1.36	1.35	1.06	1.27	0.98	1.17
7.2 Exports recorded by Chile to imports recorded by others	0.99	1.02	0.96	0.96	0.95	0.92	0.90	0.99
8. Net balance of payments (mill. 1958 dol.)								
8.1 Goods and services	27.0	−25.9	−107.1	−42.2	−288.6	−131.4	−46.9	−66.2
8.2 Ratio: capital to nonmonetary sectors	−0.8	21.8	34.3	42.6	163.4	135.0	81.2	110.0
8.3 Ratio: capital and gold to monetary sectors	−35.0	2.6	22.3	−28.2	124.5	−20.2	−49.6	−67.3
9. Net foreign reserves held by banking system (mill. dol.)	100.6	88.6	−13.4	12.0	−164.8	−238.7	−182.9	300.0
Internal								
10. Rate of change of GDP deflator (per cent)	75.6	58.3	26.2	40.6	7.9	47.2	28.2	34.3
11. Capacity utilization rate for GDP	0.89	0.88	0.91	0.90	0.93	0.90	0.93	0.96
12. Ratio: government deficit to GDP	0.02	0.02	0.03	0.03	0.04	0.04	0.04	0.00
13. Average wage/consumption deflator (1965 = 1.0)	0.74	0.78	0.80	0.72	0.84	0.96	1.00	1.09
14. Wage share of GDP	0.63	0.66	0.63	0.57	0.63	0.65	0.65	0.66
15. Rate of growth of real GDP per capita	−1.1	−1.3	0.2	−2.0	0.8	0.4	4.8	−0.9

SOURCE: Lines 1, 2, and 6 are from Table 5.1. Lines 3, 4, and 5 are from Table 5.2. The source for lines 8.1–8.3 is the same as for Table 8.1. The sources for all the other data are given in Table A.1. The series and means in the earlier tables provide points of comparison for the annual observations here.

monetarist" debate referred to a number of times above. Pinto [1960] and others have criticized the 1956–58 attempt because they claim it followed the IMF prescription, with the result being "neither stability, nor development."

Pressure from the IMF and donor and creditor countries apparently was considerable in the mid-1950s. For the 1952–55 subphase net capital inflows to the central government and net IMF credit both dropped substantially in comparison with the previous subphase (lines 13 and 15.1 in Table 8.1). Before the 1965–70 attempt, significant pressures, at least implicitly, were applied from abroad because Chile sought foreign cooperation in the debt rescheduling of 1965. The decline in the net credit from the IMF in the years immediately before the Frei liberalization also may indicate more direct pressure (line 15.1 in Table 8.1).

For the first and, to a smaller extent, the third liberalization episodes, therefore, outside official pressure provided an impetus for liberalization. Before the second attempt, there is no evidence of unusual foreign pressure, nor of a decline in net inflows from official sources (lines 13 and 15.1 in Table 8.1). Even before the third effort, moreover, a large increase in the net inflow to the government much more than offset the above-mentioned fall in IMF credit. Thus, the importance of foreign official pressure in the initiation of these liberalization attempts should not be overemphasized.

It should be pointed out, nevertheless, that the identification of the 1956–58 attempt in particular with foreign interests discredited this program in the eyes of many Chileans. In part the identification was with official foreign agencies, especially the IMF. Much more of this identification, however, was associated with Klein-Saks, a Washington-based private consulting firm hired by the Ibañez government. Hirschman [1963] claims that the presence of the Klein-Saks mission probably facilitated the rapid acceptance of policies largely suggested previously by the Central Bank and former ministers of finance Felipe Herrera and Jorge Pratt. He also maintains, however, that the intermediary role employed by this mission enabled the major political groups in Chile to avoid direct confrontation over the basic issues. Fundamental problems were covered up, but not resolved. Subsequent criticisms of the over-all program, moreover, have been directed in large part toward Klein-Saks. The net result has been an overemphasis on the role this mission actually played, and further avoidance of the basic underlying issues.[3]

FOREIGN-EXCHANGE SHORTAGES.

Before the second and third attempts, the immediate foreign-exchange shortages were severe. The deficits on current account were quite large, and net foreign reserves were very low (columns 3 and 6 for lines 8.1 and 9 in Table 13.1). Capital flight through overinvoicing of imports apparently was extensive (line 7.1 in Table 13.1). In the third case, moreover, the previously noted large debt repayment obligations added further claims on the limited supply of foreign exchange. For both of these efforts, therefore, a substantial immediate foreign-exchange crisis added to the pressure for a change in the international economic regime.

Before the first attempt, in contrast, the role of an immediate foreign-exchange crisis was much less. True, substantial capital flight was occurring (column 1 for lines 3 and 7.1 in Table 13.1). But the surplus on current account actually was quite large and net foreign reserves were relatively high (lines 8.1 and 9).

In the third episode, moreover, the immediate reaction to the initial foreign-exchange crisis included some increase in restrictions, e.g., the import application rejection procedure of 1965 described in subsection 4.1.2. In that case, in fact, foreign-sector liberalization accelerated over the phase. One factor in this intensification was the concentration of the efforts of a number of talented individuals in the Central Bank on reforming the foreign sector after hopes for the reforms in other areas had been frustrated. Of very substantial importance, however, was the improvement in Chile's foreign-exchange position over the phase, which was largely due to the booming international copper market.

Thus, immediate foreign-exchange crises were a motivating factor in the second and third liberalization efforts, but not in the first. Once the liberalization program commenced, subsequent intraphase changes generally reflected a direct rather than an inverse association between liberalization and the availability of foreign exchange.

INEFFICIENCIES OF FOREIGN-SECTOR POLICIES.

Many of the distortions and income effects of restrictive Chilean international economic regimes are analyzed in Chapters 5, 10, and 11. Although it is very difficult to specify the exact importance of the regimes, apparently the perception of a number of their negative effects on certain areas of the economy partially underlay the desire for liberalization among an important group of Chilean technicians and businessmen. Specific perceived shortcomings included extreme instability, large windfall gains, corruption, disincentives for investment and for exports, whose foreign-exchange proceeds paid for imported investment goods, inefficient resource allocation, preferences in import quotas granted to large firms, overdependence on imported inputs, delays, arbitrariness of operation, and large personal economic rewards—not for increasing productivity, but for obtaining better NERs, larger quotas, or correctly anticipating massive devaluations.

13.1.2 Internal Factors.

The external situation had some importance in the motivation for each of the three liberalization episodes. Of much greater significance, however, was the internal situation, two of its characteristics in particular:

i. In all three cases liberalization of the foreign sector was *not* the dominant goal in itself. Instead it was but one component of an over-all stabilization program. The primary motives were to reduce inflation and to increase capacity utilization. In the year immediately preceding the commencement of each of the efforts the rates of inflation were, respectively, 76, 26, and 47 per cent (line 10 in Table 13.1). In each case inflation was accelerating.[4] Capacity-utilization rates also were low, although less so in the second case (line 11 in Table 13.1). These internal concerns predominated among the motives for the three efforts.

ii. In an immediate sense, all three efforts also were the result of new programs that followed substantial political shifts.[5] In the first case, the internal political and economic conditions had deteriorated so much that complete breakdown of the political and economic systems seemed imminent. That threat induced the formation of an informal coalition among Ibañistas, Conservatives, and Liberals with the help and guidance of the new finance minister, Oscar Herrera (not to be confused with Felipe Herrera, mentioned earlier), and the Klein-Saks mission. This new grouping broke a long-existing parliamentary stalemate and legislated the 1956–58 program of stabilization with liberalization.

In the other two cases the nature of the political shift was more obvious. Presidential elections caused changes in the government. In late 1958 Alessandri won the election, and in late 1964 Frei was elected to succeed him. In both cases the new governments, counting somewhat on their initial political momentum, soon tried to initiate major programs of stabilization with liberalization.

At times discussions of liberalization of the foreign sector are written as if all internal motives and policies were but adjuncts to the primary concern with the international sector. Such a view does not reflect the reality of the Chilean political economy. The basic causes of liberalization efforts generally have been internal factors. Foreign repayment obligations, speculation against the currency, capital flight, and donor- and creditor-country pressures have all been significant, but less important than internal concerns. Foreign-sector policy generally has been much more an appendage of domestic policy, albeit an important appendage, rather than vice versa.

13.2 WHAT WAS DONE

Details of the changes in the components of the international economic regime included in the liberalization packages were given in Chapters 3 and 4. Here four major characteristics of the programs are summarized: the net or effective devaluation, the changes in import premiums and in EERs for the different categories, related monetary and fiscal policies, and the size and impact of official foreign credits.

13.2.1 Net Devaluations.

The liberalization packages all included substantial initial nominal devaluations. In the first year the weighted average of all NERs changed, respectively, by 94, 47, and 34 per cent (line 13 in Table A.7). Prima facie, these appear to be large devaluations. However, two factors are not taken account of in these figures. First, given the extent and duration of the Chilean inflation, some deflation of the NERs is necessary. In the first year of each episode, the respective changes in the PLD-NERs were only 22.5, 4.3, and 4.4 per cent (column 13 in Table 3.2). Second, at the same time that the nominal devaluations occurred, other changes were being made in the international economic regime. The net impact of these other changes was to lessen price and quantitative trade barriers. The PLD-EERs changed by 24.8, 5.5, and 5.5 per cent (column 1 in Table 5.1 or line 1 in Table 13.1). Therefore, the initial net devaluations were somewhat larger than an examination of PLD-NERs alone would indicate, but much smaller than examination of NERs or EERs alone would suggest.

After the first year, the patterns of changes in the PLD-EERs varied substantially in the three liberalization attempts (column 1 in Table 5.1). In the first episode, the weighted average rose 35 per cent in the second year, but fell 11 per cent in the third year. In the second attempt a constant NER was maintained as a symbol of price stability. Therefore, the PLD-EER dropped 7.6 and 5.6 per cent, respectively, in the second and third years. In the third program a sliding-peg NER policy was adopted. Nevertheless, the PLD-EER fell in four of the five subsequent years of the program by from 1.9 to 4.9 per cent. The exception was a 3.0 per cent rise in 1968. The general tendency, therefore, was for the PLD-EER to decline after the initial large devaluation. In only two of the nine relevant years did it increase instead.

In all three cases, however, the really major problem with NER policy was not the tendency to let PLD-EERs decline during the phase. The major problem was that initial devaluations were not sufficient to achieve equilibrium (see Bacha and Taylor [1973:144] and line 1.1.1 in Table A.1 for two indices of the extent of disequilibrium). The tendency for the PLD-EERs to fall only exacerbated the situation. Given the responses of various items in the balance of payments (see sections 6.2 and 7.2 and Chapter 8), the continued maintenance of below-equilibrium PLD-EERs guaranteed an eventual foreign-exchange crisis or pressure to increase trade barriers in order to avert such a crisis.

13.2.2 Changes in Import Premiums and in Discrepancies in Effective Exchange Rates.

The import premium rate fell substantially in the first year of the three liberalizations—by 34, 20, and 17 per cent respectively (column 6 in Table 13.1 or column 4 in Table 5.1). There was a considerable immediate shift in income per unit of imports, therefore, from the former recipients of import privileges. During both the first and the third episodes, moreover, further declines were recorded. In a few years, these subsequent decreases were quite large—51 per cent in 1957 and 17 per cent in 1968 (although increases of 9 per cent in the next two years partially offset the latter). During the second effort, however, the premium increased 24 per cent after the first year with the result that in the last year it was not significantly less than before the commencement of that phase.

As is indicated by the data in Table 13.1, lines 2, 3, 4, and 5; Table 5.1, column 3; and Table 5.2, columns 1 and 6, discrepancies among the EERs for different categories of transactions also generally fell significantly with the initiation of liberalization compared to the year preceding the effort. Quite generally, therefore, distortions and differential incentives were cut—often substantially—by the initiation of the liberalization efforts, with one important exception, however, which was pointed out in subsection 5.1.2: discrimination against agriculture increased in two of the cases and remained the same in the third because the government tried to damp inflationary expectations by keeping the rate of increase of food prices down.

After the first year of liberalization, many of these discrepancies widened again. In 1956–58 this was true for the nonmerchandise-to-merchandise ratio, the black-market to national accounts NERs, and (most strongly) the imports-to-exports ratio. In 1959–61 differences grew for the nonmerchandise-to-merchandise raito. In 1965–70 the same occurred for the first two indices but not for the imports-to-exports ratio. As the liberalizations lost their initial momentum, therefore, differential incentives and distortions commonly grew, especially in the two cases in which the import premium rate tended to fall.

13.2.3 Related Fiscal and Monetary Policies.

As is emphasized in section 13.1, fiscal and monetary policies were not basically subsidiary components of the foreign-sector liberalization programs. To the contrary, the liberalization of the foreign sector was but one aspect of the over-all stabilization effort. The major concern of the government in all three stabilization episodes was to reduce inflationary pressures. In 1956–58 restrictive monetary policy reduced the rate of growth of the money supply from 62 per cent in 1955 to 44, 35, and 28 per cent respectively in each of the next three years. In the first year of the next effort, 1959–61, it increased somewhat to 30 per cent, but thereafter fell to 23 and then to 26 per cent. In the first year of the 1965–70 phase it increased to 54 per cent (as compared to 40 per cent in 1964). In the next two years it declined to 46 and then to 22 per cent respectively, but thereafter increased to 36 per cent in 1968, to 42 per cent in 1969, and to 66 per cent in 1970. Except in the first attempt, then, monetary policy was initially not all that restrictive. In the last two efforts it subsequently became tighter, but then loosened near the end of each phase.

In all three stabilization programs the government announced its intention to reduce the size of the government deficit (line 12 in Table 13.1). In the first year of the Ibañez-Klein-Saks program a cut of 15 per cent in real terms was achieved. In the next two years and continuing through the Alessandri program, however, the size of the real government deficit increased steadily, with annual increases of 53, 14, 26, 29, and 1 per cent. These governments were able neither to reduce expenditures significantly nor to reform the tax system to make it more effective.

In the first year of the Frei period, once again the real government deficit increased—this time by 18 per cent. Thereafter, however, it fell to a much lower level. It dropped 23 per cent in 1966 and another 45 per cent in 1967, and fluctuated around the resulting new lower levels for the rest of the phase. The reasons for this change are twofold: the Frei government was much more successful than its predecessors in implementing some effective internal tax reforms; and the copper boom greatly increased real revenues from mining and exports, in part because of the relatively high degree of participation of the Chilean government in the returns (see subsection 4.2.1).

Not only the size of the government deficit is important. If aggregate demand has a role in the determination of output, the level of government expenditure for a given deficit also is significant. In the first year of the Ibañez-Klein-Saks program real government current expenditures were cut 3.7 per cent as part of the stabilization effort. In the last two years of that program and in all three years of the Alessandri effort expenditures increased (by 6.7, 11.1, 1.6, 6.1, and 1.4 per cent, respectively). They rose 16.6 per cent in the first year of the Frei phase and 8.6 per cent in the second. In the third year they declined imperceptibly, and therafter increased at moderate rates.

Except for the first year of the 1956–58 phase and the last two years of the Frei program, thus, fiscal policy was fairly expansionary during the three stabilization-liberalization episodes. The maintenance of expansionary policies in the midst of anti-inflationary programs was due to difficulties in obtaining and implementing fiscal reforms on the one hand and to the desire to limit recessions on the other.

The over-all impact of monetary, fiscal, and other policies on inflation had the same general pattern in each of the three episodes (line 10 in Table 13.1 and line 2.1 in Table A.1). The annual rate of change of the GDP deflator dropped substantially in the initial stages of the program. As political momentum tailed off, however, discipline faltered and inflationary pressures once again grew.

The total impact of such policies on capacity utilization and growth differed somewhat in the three episodes (lines 11 and 15 in Table 13.1 and lines 2.2 and 5.1 in Table A.1). The first two programs were characterized by an initial drop in both capacity utilization and over-all growth, followed by an increase and then a decline as the effort fizzled out. The Frei period had high capacity-utilization rates and growth in the first two years (e.g., per capita GDP increased by 4.8 and 9.0 per cent respectively in 1965 and 1966), followed by relative stagnation.

13.2.4 Size and Impact of Official Foreign Credits.

Average annual net inflows to the central government and central institutions in millions of 1958 dollars increased from 2.3 in 1952–55 to 16.7 in 1956–58 and to 52.6 in 1959–61 (line 13 plus line 15 in Table 8.1). In the first two liberalizations the increased supplies from imports made possible by these larger net inflows aided substantially in the reduction of inflationary pressures. These increases did not occur, however, in the first year of these programs. Instead, they were recorded in the second and third years as the government attempted to salvage the effort by using enlarged foreign debt to provide purchasing power. When additional foreign credits became difficult to obtain—especially in late 1961—the programs collapsed.

For the Frei attempt the pattern was reversed. The net inflow in millions of 1958 dollars increased from 81.8 in 1964 to 135.3 in 1965, but the average annual level declined from 106.9 in 1962–64 to 64.3 in 1965–69. As is noted in section 8.2, the drop in the mean inflow primarily reflected a drop in foreign-exchange needs because of enlarged revenues generated by the copper boom of the late 1960s.

In all three cases, then, net inflows of official foreign credits played important short-run roles. In the first two programs they allowed the liberalization efforts to be prolonged. In the third they helped it to get started. In no case, however, did they lead to long-run success. In the long run, in fact, they may have been dysfunctional by obscuring the fact that the exchange rate remained well below equilibrium.

13.3 SHORT-RUN EFFECTS OF LIBERALIZATION

The long-run advantages of liberalization as they relate to four areas of Chilean macroeconomic policy—foreign-exchange position, resource allocation, income distribution, and development—were taken up in earlier chapters. But whether or not a liberalization prevails long enough for those advantages to be realized depends in considerable part on the short-run impact of those policies. Consequently, the latter question, also, has been taken up in detail, and the issues are summarized in this section.

13.3.1 Foreign-Exchange Position.

A wide variety of responses of components of the balance of payments to liberalization and devaluation are detailed in chapters 6, 7, and 8. Speculative inventory holding and capital flight fell. Extralegal flows declined. Exports, especially of a nontraditional nature, and net direct investment inflows increased. Desired imports tended to drop due to higher PLD-EERs, but actual imports tended to rise significantly because there were fewer quantitative restrictions. (The latter situation particularly characterized capital goods imports.)

On a general-equilibrium level many substantial partial-equilibrium direct responses were largely offset by indirect effects, especially those transmitted through the nexus of foreign exchange, money, and prices. The general-equilibrium response to a devaluation alone, therefore, was not large. Moreover, since devaluation was not sufficient to reach equilibrium levels and since the PLD-EERS tended to decline during the more liberal phases, pressure on foreign exchange was increased. In addition, the import responses to reduced quantitative restrictions were substantial.

The net result of all of these factors included rather substantial deficits on current account in all three attempts (line 8.1 in Table 13.1 and line A in Table 8.1). In the first two efforts the mean annual deficit in constant dollars rose significantly over that for the previous phase. In all three cases these deficits tended to increase during the phase—in part because of the declining PLD-EERs for imports (line 1 in Table 13.1 or column 1 in Table 5.1).[6] Increasing differentials between the PLD-EERs for imports and for exports exacerbated the problem in the 1956–58 and 1959–61 phases (line 5 in Table 13.1).

The pressure on foreign exchange, therefore, was great and growing. In 1965–70 the copper boom and the large net capital inflows relieved this pressure. In the earlier attempts the net official inflows provided transitory relief (see subsection 13.2.4). When funds from these sources became less readily available or dried up, the government had to alter the international economic regimes. It chose to abandon the liberalization attempt, gradually in the first case and quite abruptly in the second. In neither case did it first increase the PLD-EER for imports or reduce the discrimination against exports. In 1958 the Ibañez government did not consider such alternatives because the whole political situation had so disintegrated that only piecemeal, ad hoc measures could be applied. In 1961 the Alessandri government did not pursue them because a fixed NER was an important symbol, if not the cornerstone, of the price stabilization effort.

13.3.2 Cyclical Fluctuations in Nominal and Real Terms.

Within a general-equilibrium context, devaluation alone led to substantial immediate inflationary pressure. This part of the stabilization-liberalization package thus worked strongly against initial price stability. Reduction in quantitative restrictions, however, had the opposite effect. As long as sufficient foreign exchange was available to finance increased imports, reductions in restrictions led to increased supplies and lower inflationary pressure.

In the 1959–61 program, this method was used to reduce inflation to the lowest level since the Second World War. The GDP deflator increased only 9.5 per cent in 1960 and 7.9 per cent in 1961. A fixed NER, as is noted above, also was utilized as a symbol of stability in order to damp inflationary expectations. Shortly after the foreign-exchange crisis of late 1961, quantitative restrictions were intensified and the fixed NER was abandoned. Inflation accelerated rapidly.

The short-run impact of both devaluation and liberalization on output was negative. Increased competition from imports more than offset the greater availability of imported inputs. This effect could have been lessened by lowering trade barriers immediately on noncompetitive imports and only more slowly on competitive imports. To do so, however, would have left many inefficient industries with even greater effective protection. It also might have made the whole liberalization attempt seem less credible.

Another possibility would have been to use fiscal and monetary policy to offset the contractionary impetus of liberalization. This was done in 1965 and 1966. The obvious problem is that such a strategy increases inflationary pressures. In the Frei program the government tried to increase capacity utilization and growth by expansionary fiscal and monetary policy limited by a programmed decline in the rate of inflation. The latter, it was hoped, would reduce inflationary expectations despite the booming economy. There was initial success, but momentum could not be maintained for more than a year or two. Thereafter, both inflation and stagnation again became more troublesome.

13.3.3 Resource Allocation and Structural Change.

The effect of liberalization on resource allocation among sectors and subsectors is detailed in Chapter 10. Agriculture and the more modern and intermediate-goods-oriented manufacturing subsectors were particularly responsive to liberalizations. Mining also responded positively. The more traditional and consumer-oriented manufacturing subsectors, in contrast, generally were unable to meet the increased competition of the liberalized flow of imports.

The pattern of response poses a dilemma for the government. On the one hand, the short- and medium-run costs of diverting resources from some of the long-protected traditional industries are quite high. These costs are not only economic but political as well, because some of these subsectors have acquired considerable political power. On the other hand, in the absence of foreign competition the same industries have shown little tendency to become efficient. Continued protection apparently would entail incurring a number of the costs described earlier without promoting substantial development. Moreover, it would further reinforce those who already have vested interests in a restrictive system.

Perhaps some gradual reduction in protection with interim aid in reallocating resources would provide a solution. Given past experience, however, any proposal for gradual adjustment might not be credible. Rather than cooperate, the affected industries might see their own interests to be in intensive lobbying for reinstitution of high EPRs.

13.3.4 Distribution of Control over Income and Resources.

As detailed in Chapter 11, the consequences of liberalization for the various elements of control over income and resources have been complex and often dependent upon the time period under consideration. In the short run, liberalization and devaluation had a negative impact on the income going to labor,[7] traders who received the import premium, the owners of factors in heavily protected industrial subsectors, the bureaucrats who ran the system, and domestic, as opposed to foreign, factor owners. The effect on the split between public and private control over resources depended on the relative weight of devaluation versus a reduction in restrictions, with the government being favored the more there were reductions in restrictions.

Some very strong or very important groups, thus, were adversely affected in the short run by liberalization. One can always conceive of partial liberalizations or subsidies which would mitigate these effects. Too much emphasis on the former would hamstring the whole effort. Adoption of explicit subsidies would lessen distortions and make the transfers more explicit and, it would be hoped, more responsive to the general political will. Given the problems in fiscal reforms, however, subsidies, also, involve significant costs.

13.3.5 Economic Growth.

The impact of liberalizations on economic growth is detailed in Chapter 12. In the short run, of course, there was very little effect on the over-all capacity of the economy. Because of induced changes in capacity utilization, however, measured real GDP per capita changed. That it declined by −1.3 and −2.0 per cent, respectively, in the first year of the first two stabilization-liberalization programs caused critics to cry out in alarm (line 15 in Table 13.1). At the start of the Frei program, therefore, the government followed more expansionary policies to avoid the same outcome. The effort was rewarded by a growth rate of real per capita GDP of 4.8 per cent in 1965, followed by a rate almost twice as high in 1966.

13.4 WHY LIBERALIZATION FAILED

All three of the liberalization efforts failed. The same general factors underlay the lack of success, but with different relative weights in different episodes.

The end of the Ibañez-Klein-Saks effort formally was signaled by the presidential election of late 1958. Effectively, however, this program had faltered long before the election. The basic problem was a lack of sufficient short-run success in the over-all stabilization program to allow the maintenance of political momentum. Inflation had been reduced significantly, but still was quite high and was accelerating again in 1958. Significant positive growth in real per capita income had been obtained only in one year of the program, and the growth rate was declining in 1958. Parliament refused to pass basic tax reform legislation. Rumors of graft and corruption increased, especially regarding the operation of the special regime in the department of Arica. Students demonstrating against increases in bus fares clashed with troops, and 18 deaths and over 500 injuries resulted in April 1957. In the same year, a poor harvest caused relatively rapid increases in food prices. Government fiscal-deficit problems were not solved. By the time of the 1958 departure of Klein-Saks, the government had lost control of the situation.

The failure of foreign-sector liberalization accompanied the failure of stabilization. The foreign-sector situation was exacerbated, moreover, by growing foreign-exchange shortages. These shortages, in turn, partially originated in excess demand due to the falling PLD-EER. Government reluctance after mid-1957 to keep up with the internal inflation had its toll. The drop in the world price of copper after 1956 further aggravated the foreign-exchange shortage.

The end of the Alessandri liberalization also reflected insufficient short-run success. The rate of increase in the GDP deflator had fallen to the lowest level since the end of the Second World War, but the average rate of growth of real product also had dropped to the lowest level since 1955. Despite some success in fiscal reform, the government deficit increased to all-time highs.

In an immediate sense, however, the termination of this phase was almost entirely due to a balance-of-payments crisis. Foreign-exchange reserves and the national foreign credit standing were exhausted because of failure to control the government deficit and because a substantially overvalued NER, with its overvaluation steadily increasing, was being maintained side by side with a liberal trade regime. The public-sector debt in foreign currency had increased 101 per cent to a level of \$788 million by the end of the phase. Total Chilean debt in foreign currency (not including direct private credits or deferred payment import credits for which data are unavailable) increased 81.7 per cent to a level of \$954 million, equal to 183 per cent of exports or 22 per cent of GDP (at the official exchange rate) in 1961. Net international reserves held by the banking system plummeted to a new low of −\$164 million at the end of 1961. In December 1961 the Central Bank liquid reserves were down to the equivalent of approximately ten days of imports. A considerable number of import applications were still pending. The Central Bank could not borrow further from abroad because of the substantial foreign debt. On December 27, 1961, the Central Bank revoked all authority to deal in foreign exchange and established prohibitive 10,000 per cent prior deposits on all imports. Thus, the Phase IV period and the internal stabilization program ended.[8]

The Frei government had the advantage of hindsight about the two previous failures. Therefore, it adopted a strategy with two major components: a programmed decline in the inflation rate over several years so that inflationary expectations could be lowered but a recession averted and a sliding-peg NER policy in which the PLD-EER would be increased over time to its equilibrium value.

In 1965 and 1966 success was fairly general. Inflation was cut significantly, and growth was quite high. The PLD-EER declined, however, despite the intent of the sliding-peg policy.

In 1967 considerable internal political cohesion was dissipated in an abortive attempt to introduce a compulsory savings plan for 1968 wage increases exceeding 10 per cent and to suspend the right to strike. In reaction to these proposals a general strike was called in December 1967, the political parties of the left coalesced against the government, and political support from the right also declined in opposition to the features of the program which would limit the freedom of business and in opposition to other government programs such as agrarian reform. Several ministers of finance resigned in succession, and the government proposal was defeated after months of acrimonious debate. With that failure, stabilization efforts faltered considerably. In this instance, however, foreign-sector liberalization was not abandoned. If anything, it was intensified.[9] The reasons for this were twofold. (i) The copper boom of the late 1960s led to an immediate relaxation of the foreign-exchange constraint. Because of this boom the mean United States producer price for copper exceeded that in the previous phase by 39 per cent, the mean IME copper price exceeded that in the previous phase by 77 per cent, and the Chilean terms of trade improved substantially. (ii) A number of skilled Chilean economists in the government, once their efforts at internal reform had petered out, turned their attention to reforming the international economic regime.

Despite the expanded emphasis on liberalization of the foreign sector, the PLD-EER was very low and declining (except for a slight rise in 1968). Nevertheless, revenues from copper were sufficient to avert an immediate foreign-exchange crisis.[10] This phase was brought to an end, instead, by the election of the Allende government in late 1970. The earlier failure of stabilization, of course, probably was an important factor in the election outcome.

Thus, Chile has had at least one abrupt stabilization-liberalization effort which failed because the short-run success of the effort was insufficient to maintain political momentum. It also has had one gradual attempt which failed in part because the short-run success could not be maintained for a long enough time to generate stability. It has always attempted to liberalize with a below-equilibrium and often declining PLD-EER.

To increase the probability of reaping the long-run benefits of successful liberalization, one obvious prescription is to draw the PLD-EER much closer to its equilibrium level and prevent it from declining under the pressure of inflation. When sufficient political momentum exists to attempt another liberalization, moreover, an abrupt change would seem preferable to a more gradual one. The sudden alteration would have short-run costs, some of which could be mitigated by transitory subsidies. But it might make it possible to change underlying expectations before political momentum was lost, so that some of the longer-run benefits would begin to appear. Given three liberalization and four stabilization failures in less than two decades, cynicism about the probability of success of any gradual attempt is liable to kill it before longer-run benefits appear.

NOTES

1. This point is not in conflict with the second point above. The latter refers to past efforts, while this one refers to any future attempts, given the past failures.

2. As is discussed in Chapter 12 and other segments of Part III, however, the empirical foundation which the Chilean experience provides for expectations of large long-run benefits is weak. To argue strongly for these long-run benefits one must rely on analogies with the experience of other countries, such as Brazil.

3. The existence of foreign scapegoats, in other words, allowed a superficial consensus without a basic agreement on the sacrifices required of the type which Sturc [1967:216] has emphasized.

4. The 1958 rate of inflation was below that for 1957, but it accelerated during 1958.

5. It is always possible to ask whether or not economic conditions caused the political shifts. In fact, their contribution seems to have been considerable. But in an immediate sense these political changes were important in themselves.

6. The PLD-EER for 1958 exceeded that for 1956, but was less than that for 1957.

7. The wage share of GDP rose in the first year of the Ibañez-Klein-Saks program, but fell during the phase. It fell substantially in the first year of the Alessandri effort and recovered only partially during the phase. It remained the same in the first year of the Frei episode and increased slowly thereafter (line 14 in Table 13.1). This share, of course, was affected by all policies—not only foreign-sector ones.

8. Although anticipated in some quarters, these events were not foreseen by all observers. For example, apparently late in 1961 Hirschman [1963:220] approved the appointment of Luis Escobar (a representative of the structuralist school who had been dean of the Faculty of Economics at the University of Chile) as Minister of Economics in August 1961. He also noted that the government had a majority in both houses and had the assurance of long-run assistance from the Alliance for Progress. He concluded: "Hence, the chances for improving the performance of the Chilean economy in various structural ways while keeping the traditional scourge [i.e., inflation] under control looked more promising than they had for a long time."

9. Rather extensive plans to further liberalize the tariff and the whole trade system in order to encourage more domestic efficiency were later discussed in Banco Central [1970b:463–467], but because of the subsequent political events these plans were never carried out.

10. At the end of this phase the banking system had the highest level of net international reserves in more than two decades. At the same time, the foreign debt totaled close to $3 billion. As a proportion of annual export value it had fallen somewhat to 248 per cent. Relative to GDP it had dropped to 27.2 per cent. Nevertheless, these debt obligations remained very large and constrained the new Allende government.

Appendixes

Appendix A

Statistical Tables

TABLE A.1
Arithmetic Means for Major Economic Variables During Phases and Subphases of the Chilean Exchange Control Regime, 1908–71

Line No.	Variables	1908–27	1928–30
	PHASE	III–IV	IV
1.	Foreign sector		
1.1	Prices		
1.1.1	PLD-NER (1/27/59=1.00)		1.64
1.1.2	1960 U.S. $ per escudo	304	200
1.1.3	Free or black-market rate/NA rate		1.00
1.1.4	EER/NA rate		
1.1.4.1	Consumption goods (1965=100)		
1.1.4.2	Investment goods (1965=100)		
1.1.5	Terms of trade		
1.1.5.1	Export unit value/import unit value (1965=1.00)	1.44[a]	1.46
1.1.5.2	Copper returns: export unit value/import unit value	1.16[c]	1.06
1.1.6	Import premium rate		
1.1.7	PLD-EER		
1.2	Quantities		
1.2.1	Import goods		
1.2.1.1	Consumption		
1.2.1.2	Investment		
1.2.1.3	Intermediate		
1.2.2	Imports/total supply		
1.2.2.1	Consumption		
1.2.2.2	Investment		
1.2.3	Export goods		
1.2.3.1	Agriculture		
1.2.3.2	Mining		
1.2.3.3	Industry		
1.2.4	Rates of growth (%)		
1.2.4.1	Import value (constant U.S. $)	2.5	−4.1
1.2.4.2	Export value (constant U.S. $)	3.5	−11.7
1.2.5	Trade statistics: Chile's major trading partners		
1.2.5.1	Imports recorded by Chile/exports recorded by others		
1.2.5.2	Exports recorded by Chile/imports recorded by others		

1931–39	1940–46	1947–51	1952–55	1956–58	1959–61	1962–64	1965–70	1971
I–II	II	II	II	III	IV	II	III	II
2.54	1.53	0.79	0.61	0.79	0.77	0.73	0.69	0.57
66.0	31.0	14.7	4.78	1.44	0.95	0.58	0.15	0.05
1.25	1.11	1.70	2.66	1.44	1.01	1.70	1.55	4.06
	0.99	1.27	1.49	1.06	0.99	1.03	0.96	
	1.25	1.24	1.30	0.96	0.97	1.01	0.96	
0.90	0.66	0.68	0.91	0.89	0.86	0.94	1.18[b]	
0.96	1.39	1.93	2.65	1.93				
	0.76[d]	0.73	1.43	0.87	0.58	0.58	0.50	
	8.48	4.42	3.35	4.29	4.30	4.00	3.60	
	0.35	0.31	0.30	0.30	0.33	0.35	{0.32 0.16}	0.19
	0.15	0.24	0.27	0.37	0.35	0.35	{0.33 0.36}	0.22
	0.50	0.45	0.43	0.34	0.32	0.30	{0.34 0.44}	0.59
	0.04	0.03	0.03	0.03	0.04	0.05	{0.04 0.02}	0.03
	0.16	0.19	0.24	0.32	0.37	0.36	{0.32 0.40}	0.28
	0.13	0.13	0.09	0.09	0.08	0.08	0.04	0.03
	0.79	0.80	0.81	0.83	0.84	0.85	0.86	0.84
	0.07	0.07	0.09	0.08	0.08	0.06	0.10	0.13
−3.0[e]	6.3	12.7	3.8	4.3	6.1	−1.8	6.0	6.1
0.8[e]	6.2	12.8	7.0	−5.5	7.3	7.2	11.0	−11.7
		1.21[f]	1.36	1.17	1.15	1.20	1.07	
		0.95[f]	1.00	0.98	0.94	0.92	0.95	

TABLE A.1 (*concluded*)

Line No.	Variables	1908–27	1928–30
	PHASE	III–IV	IV
1.2.6	Other		
1.2.6.1	Exports less imports (mill. 1960 U.S. $)	11.2	7.6
1.2.6.2	QR index		
1.2.6.3	Export capacity to import (1965=1.00)		1.03
1.2.6.4	Net foreign reserves held by banking system (mill. U.S. $)		
1.2.6.5	Foreign debt at yr. end/exports for yr.	0.87	1.23
1.2.6.6	Taxes: related to foreign trade/total	0.83	0.63
1.2.6.7	Imports/GDP	0.52	0.38
1.2.6.8	Exports/GDP	0.58[h]	0.44
1.2.6.9	Import taxes/import value	0.13	0.25
2.	Cyclical variables		
2.1	Rate of change of GDP deflator (%)	4.1	−3.0
2.2	Capacity utilization for GDP	0.93	0.91
2.3	Unemployment rate in Santiago in June		
3.	Resource allocation		
3.1	Composition of GDP		
3.1.1	Production sectors		
3.1.1.1	Agriculture	0.21	0.17
3.1.1.2	Mining	0.10	0.10
3.1.1.3	Industry	0.13	0.11
3.1.2	Final demand		
3.1.2.1	Private consumption		
3.1.2.2	Invest. in structures and equip.		
3.1.2.3	Govt. current expend.	0.05	0.11
3.2	Agriculture deflator/GDP deflator	1.07	1.03
3.3.	Role of govt.		
3.3.1	Savings: govt./total		
3.3.2	Invest.: govt./total		
3.3.3	Govt. deficit/GDP		
3.3.4	Taxes/GNP		
4.	Income distribution		
4.1	Aver. wage/consumption deflator (1965=1.00)		
4.2	Wage share of GDP		
5.	Rates of real growth		
5.1	GDP per capita	1.5	−0.9
5.2	Industrial GDP	2.2	−3.8
5.3	Agriculture GDP	2.6	2.2
5.4	Invest. in structures and equip.		
5.5	Marginal gross capital-output ratio		

1931–39	1940–46	1947–51	1952–55	1956–58	1959–61	1962–64	1965–70	1971
I–II	II	II	II	III	IV	II	III	II
7.8	−0.1	0.1	3.2	−9.7	1.2	9.1	19.6	−110.9
	0.94	0.95	0.98	0.96	0.92	0.96	0.95[g]	
0.48	0.47	0.48	0.62	0.65	0.71	0.85	1.23[b]	
	7.0	89.1	79.1	29.9	−60.0	−246.	−17.0[g]	
				1.20	1.31	2.52	2.41	2.51
	0.37	0.35	0.29	0.21	0.21	0.21	0.18	
0.14	0.09	0.09	0.09	0.10	0.12	0.12	0.13	0.14
0.17	0.19	0.15	0.12	0.11	0.12	0.13	0.12[g]	0.12
	0.22	0.24	0.22	0.17	0.20	0.21	0.17[g]	0.26
8.5	15.1	20.8	47.8	37.6	19.3	35.4	31.7	20.0
0.81	0.93	0.90	0.91	0.90	0.92	0.96	0.95	1.00
					0.072[i]	0.053	0.062	0.052
0.20	0.15	0.14	0.12	0.13	0.13	0.11	0.10	0.10
0.09	0.10	0.08	0.06	0.04	0.07	0.07	0.06	0.06
0.14	0.18	0.21	0.22	0.21	0.19	0.19	0.19	0.20
	0.77	0.79	0.79	0.80	0.80	0.77	0.76	0.78
	0.08	0.10	0.10	0.10	0.11	0.13	0.11	0.11
0.08	0.08	0.09	0.10	0.10	0.10	0.10	0.10	0.10
0.92	0.98	1.01	1.14	0.99	0.94	0.92	1.06	
	0.30	0.22	0.13	0.18	0.28	0.24	0.44	
	0.44	0.45	0.56	0.48	0.38	0.35	0.45	
	0.01	−0.00	0.02	0.02	0.04	0.04	0.02	0.10
	0.14	0.15	0.16	0.18	0.21	0.20	0.24	
	0.57	0.67	0.74	0.77	0.78	0.92	1.12	
	0.58	0.64	0.63	0.63	0.60	0.64	0.67	
−1.1[e]	2.2	1.2	0.9	1.4	1.2	1.6	2.5	6.0
2.6[e]	7.5	6.3	6.8	−1.4	2.8	4.9	5.1	12.1
1.5[e]	1.2	0.9	1.7	10.7	−2.9	0.7	2.9	5.8
	7.0	3.8	4.6	2.7	15.1	2.6	4.0	−7.7
	2.7	3.3	3.1	2.8	3.1	3.4	2.4	

Notes to Table A.1

NOTE: The underlying data for virtually all the series listed are from the national accounts of Banco Central [1956b–73b], CORFO, and ODEPLAN, and unpublished data from these three institutions. For 1940–71, exact sources, procedures used to make data from various sources comparable, and evaluation of the data for all series, except as indicated below in the notes for individual variables, are given in Behrman [1974:Chap. 3]. Data before 1940, except as noted below, are based on estimates from Ballesteros and Davis [1963] linked by 1940 values. For the earlier period, it was assumed that the GDP deflator was perfectly correlated with the wholesale price index and that government consumption was perfectly correlated with government product.

1.1 The national accounts exchange rate, which enters into the calculation of series 1.1.1 to 1.1.4, is a weighted average of the various legal nominal exchange rates in effect in each period; it is used by CORFO and ODEPLAN in the preparation of the national accounts.

1.1.1 Indicates the cost of foreign exchange (exclusive of tariffs, related charges, and import premiums) in constant-value escudos. The base date of January 27, 1959, was chosen because Instituto de Economía [1963:203] and Leftwich [1966:407] suggest that, given the trade regime then in effect, this rate was very close to equilibrium.

1.1.2 Number of current dollars required to purchase one escudo or 1,000 pesos (the unit used before 1960), adjusted to 1960 dollars by use of the GNP deflator for the United States (Council of Economic Advisers [1972]). This variable provides a measure of the decline in real terms in the foreign exchange value of the Chilean currency over time. Ratios in 1960 dollars for 1908–60 are from Hurtado [1966:Table 14]. Current dollars, 1960–69, from Ffrench-Davis [1971:286]; 1970–71, unpublished data of the Central Bank.

1.1.3 The numerator is the legal free-market NER, if a legal free-market existed. Otherwise (in most cases), the black-market rate is used. The ratio is an indicator of the dispersion among exchange rates resulting from exchange policy. Since it is a measure of currency demand in illegal markets, it also measures the restrictiveness of exchange control in official markets.

1.1.4 Effective exchange rates are discussed more fully in section 5.1. The ratios reflect the relative favoritism granted under the foreign trade regime to consumption and investment imports.

1.1.5.2 The numerator (1925=100) is that part of the unit value of copper exports by large-scale mining enterprises which is returned to Chile in the form of factor payments, intermediate input purchases in the domestic market, taxes, and related payments. From the point of view of the owners of large-scale mining operations, the exchange rates for these return flows are often unfavorable. See Reynolds [1965:381].

1.1.4.1 and **1.1.4.2** U.S. deflator is from Council of Economic Advisers [1972].

1.1.5.1 Before 1940, from Mamalakis [1971b:527, 661].

1.1.6 Average premium on competitive and noncompetitive imports. For each of these categories of imports the rate equals [(1.0 + implicit tariff rate)/EER] − 1.0 or [(domestic price/c.i.f. price)/EER] − 1.0. The ITRs for 1961 are from Table 5.3; the EERs, from Table A.7; description of the ITRs is given in Appendix B; the source of the ratios of price indices is given in Table A.8. In effect, the rate indicates the extent to which the ratio of domestic to foreign prices for imports exceeds the effective exchange rate. Premiums may be received by importers because of the existence of effective quantitative restrictions. However, several qualifications concerning this interpretation are warranted. (i) Disequilibriums between domestic and foreign prices due to adjustment lags may result in a positive or a negative premium. Given the Chilean history of inflation (series 2.1), such disequilibriums may be of considerable importance. (ii) Water in the tariffs implies a negative premium. (iii) Even if the premium arises purely from effective quantitative restrictions, the government (not only private importers) may be the recipient of part of the premium through government imports.

1.1.7 See Table A.8 and text discussion accompanying the table.

1.2.1 and **1.2.2** In each pair of braced figures for 1965–70, upper figure is for 1965–66 and is comparable with figures for earlier years. Lower figure is for 1967–70 and is comparable only with figure for 1971.

1.2.4.1 and **1.2.4.2** Before 1940, from *Anuarios Comercio Exterior,* as given by Hurtado [1966:Table 10].

1.2.5.1 and **1.2.5.2** From IMF and IBRD [1953–72]. These comparisons are measures of the order of magnitude of evasions of the Chilean foreign trade regime by illegal transactions, under the assumption that all transactions are recorded by the trading partner. If there were no unrecorded transactions in the Chilean trade statistics, a discrepancy of about 10 per cent would be expected due to the difference between the f.o.b. value of exports and the c.i.f. value of imports. For a full discussion of the merits and the shortcomings of this procedure, see Bhagwati [1969]. Chile's eight major trading partners accounted for 76 per cent of imports and 85 per cent of exports in 1948–70. The average percentage share of the eight countries in total Chilean trade in this period was as follows: United States, 41.4; Federal Republic of Germany, 9.5; United Kingdom, 9.5; Argentina, 7.0; Netherlands, 4.2; Japan, 3.1; Italy, 3.1; and France, 3.1.

1.2.6.1 Data before 1940 are from *Anuarios Comercio Exterior,* as given by Hurtado [1966:Table 10]; deflator is from Council of Economic Advisers [1972]. For recent years, this series is not always identical to that implied by the probably more reliable estimates in Table 8.1.

1.2.6.2 For 1952–69, estimate by Ffrench-Davis [1971:302] based on a careful examination of Central Bank documents. For earlier years, I extended the series on the basis of an estimated relation between the Ffrench-Davis series and series 1.1.7; the correlation coefficient between the two is 0.70, which is significant at the 1 per cent level for 18 observations. In the words of Ffrench-Davis, the index is intended to summarize the effects of "prohibitions, quotas, administrative delays, prohibitive tariffs, and import deposits."

1.2.6.3 Value of exports divided by the unit value of imports.

1.2.6.4 Data for 1940–46, 1947–51, and 1952–69 are apparently not comparable.

1.2.6.5 Based partly on Humud [1969:100, 225–228, 241–242]. Public debt only before 1930; public debt plus government-guaranteed private debt after 1930.

1.2.6.6 Based partly on Humud [1969:100, 225–228, 241–242]. Numerator includes import taxes, export taxes, implicit taxes on local cost of production for large-scale mining, and direct taxes on large-scale mining. Denominator includes all taxes (including taxes of the social security system).

1.2.6.7 and **1.2.6.8** Before 1940, from *Anuarios Comercio Exterior,* as given by Hurtado [1966:Table 10].

1.2.6.9 Before 1940, from Humud [1969:100, 238].

2.2 Capacity is defined by the trend-through-the-peaks method; the series is, therefore, a measure of actual production at a particular time compared to the secular trend in production. This method tends to overstate capacity utilization near the end points since the presence of peaks before or after the sample period may change the trend line, but it does provide a useful and definable measure of short-run fluctuations relative to historically feasible levels of capacity. For discussion of the advantages and limitations of the method, see Behrman [1973b].

3.2 Before 1940, based in part on data from the National Statistical Service as given by Mamalakis [1965:131].

3.3.2 Numerator includes government direct investment and government-financed investment.

4.1 Secular trend is used, rather than actual employment data, which is unavailable for the country as a whole for any extended period of time. As a result, the wage level is understated when unemployment is high relative to when unemployment is low. When unemployment is high the number employed is below the secular trend. Since the actual wage bill is divided by the trend rather than the actual number employed to get the average wage, the wage is understated.

4.2 Includes self-employed individuals.

5.5 Defined not in growth terms but as the ratio of gross value of investment in structures and equipment during a phase or subphase to the change in real gross domestic product in the same period.

a. For 1915–27.

b. For 1965–66.

c. For 1925–27.

d. For 1946 only.

e. This rate is an overstatement of the growth which would have had to occur for it to move from the value for the last year of the previous period to the last year of this period at a constant rate because of the initial decline and subsequent increase in the underlying variable.

f. For 1948–51.

g. For 1965–69.

h. Excluding 1917, 1918, and 1920.

i. For 1960–61 only.

TABLE A.2

Exponential Growth Rates and Phase-Coincident Deviations from Growth for Real Values of Exports, Imports, Gross Domestic Product, and Capacity, 1940–65

Dependent Variable: Log of Real Value of	Coeff. of Time	Adjustment to Growth Rate 1940–55	1956–58	1959–61	1962–64	1956, 1959, 1965	Constant	$\bar{R}^2$ *SE*	*DW* ρ
PHASE		II	III	IV	II				
Exports	0.015	−0.024	−0.017				7.45	.74	2.2
	(5.5)	(4.8)	(3.8)				(216.3)	[.09]	[0.12]
Agriculture	−0.018				0.014		5.18	.40	1.8
	(1.7)				(2.0)		(37.3)	[.16]	[0.31]
Mining	0.018	−0.023	−0.016				7.09	.73	2.5
	(3.2)	(2.7)	(3.0)				(75.8)	[.10]	
Large-scale mining	0.001	−0.022	−0.015				7.13	.31	2.8
	(0.2)	(2.2)	(2.3)				(64.4)	[.12]	
Industry	0.019					0.023	4.53	.20	1.6
	(1.2)					(1.6)	(23.5)	[.34]	
Services	0.112				−0.011	−0.022	3.82	.89	2.2
	(5.7)				(1.9)	(4.6)	(13.2)	[.12]	[0.71]
Imports	0.064	−0.023	−0.017	−0.006	−0.010	−0.013	6.73	.97	1.6
	(11.6)	(3.6)	(3.1)	(1.1)	(1.8)	(3.1)	(277.2)	[.07]	
Consumer goods									
Staples	0.045	−0.017					5.18	.75	1.9
	(4.3)	(1.1)					(38.0)	[.20]	[0.46]

(*continued*)

TABLE A-2 (*concluded*)

Dependent Variable: Log of Real Value of	Coeff. of Time	Adjustment to Growth Rate 1940–55	1956–58	1959–61	1962–64	1956, 1959, 1965	Con-stant	$\bar{R}^2$ *SE*	*DW* ρ
PHASE		II	III	IV	II				
Imports (*contd.*)									
Durables	0.040	−0.025	−0.019				4.13	.54	1.6
	(5.3)	(1.8)	(1.5)				(45.0)	[.26]	
Secondary	0.058						3.15	.75	1.7
	(4.3)						(19.0)	[.24]	[0.50]
Capital goods									
Machinery and equipment	0.088					−0.006	4.49	.94	1.8
	(10.3)					(1.1)	(44.7)	[.15]	[0.49]
Transportation-related	0.140		0.020		−0.028	−0.036	3.31	.85	1.7
	(9.4)		(1.1)		(1.8)	(2.2)	(27.1)	[.37]	
Intermediate goods	0.015	−0.024	−0.017				7.44	.74	2.24
	(5.5)	(4.8)	(3.8)				(216.3)	[.09]	[0.12]
Services	0.092		−0.013	0.011		−0.012	4.01	.85	2.0
	(9.2)		(1.2)	(1.2)		(1.4)	(33.5)	[.21]	
Gross domestic product	0.038		−0.002	−0.002			9.13	.99	2.3
	(49.1)		(1.3)	(1.8)			(1,129.)	.03	

Agriculture	0.020		0.007	0.006			7.22	.88	2.1
	(10.3)		(2.14)	(2.2)			(367.)	[.06]	
Mining	0.018	−0.024	−0.039				6.78	.77	2.0
	(4.8)	(3.4)	(6.3)				(140.)	[.11]	[0.17]
Construction	0.064	−0.014					5.18	.95	2.0
	(16.5)	(2.1)					(105.)	[.10]	[0.25]
Industry	0.038	0.012		−0.004			7.49	.96	1.6
	(18.0)	(3.2)		(1.6)			(291.)	[.06]	[0.21]
Services	0.038		−0.004				8.08	.95	1.9
	(21.3)		(1.4)				(406.)	[.06]	
Government	0.051	0.014			−0.006		6.45	.93	2.0
	(16.0)	(2.7)			(1.5)		(189.)	[.10]	
Consumption									
Private	0.040				−0.002	−0.003	8.87	.99	1.7
	(46.2)				(2.5)	(3.1)	(1,182.)	[.02]	
Government	0.047						6.67	.97	1.8
	(28.2)						(353.)	[.06]	
Investment (noninventory)	0.060					−0.007	6.66	.94	1.7
	(11.3)					(2.0)	(107.)	[.10]	[0.45]
Government direct and financial	0.051	0.019		−0.011			5.86	.64	1.8
	(6.4)	(1.3)		(1.0)			(63.4)	[.27]	
Capacity of gross domestic product	0.032			−0.001			9.30	[.998]	1.2
	(7.8)			(1.0)			(101.)	[.01]	[0.93]

Notes to Table A.2

NOTE: Two hypotheses are tested in each case: (i) that phase-coincident deviations in the growth rate occurred for the 1940–55 or the 1962–64 Phase II periods, the 1956–58 Phase III years, or the 1959–61 Phase IV liberalization; and (ii) that deviations in the growth rate occurred in the first year of each of the three liberalization attempts (i.e., 1956, 1959, and 1965).

The sample period is not extended further because consistent data are lacking before 1940 and after 1965. (The components of exports and imports are consistent only for 1947–65.) As of this writing (1971), two sets of Chilean national accounts are available: CORFO accounts for 1940–65 and ODEPLAN accounts for 1960–71. The CORFO accounts, which are used here, are preferred because they contain a substantially larger number of observations. For comparisons between them see Behrman [1974:Chap. 3].

The regressions were carried out by the method of ordinary least squares. For each regression, the dependent variable is the logarithm of the real value of the variable, and the independent variables include a constant, a time trend, multiplicative dummy variables multiplied by the time trend (with nonzero values for the years indicated in the column heads), and a first-order autocorrelation coefficient (ρ), in brackets, estimated by the Cochrane-Orcutt procedure in cases in which the hypothesis of correlation is not rejected by the Durbin-Watson statistic (*DW*). The figures in parentheses are the absolute values of the t statistics. For a two-tailed test with 20 degrees of freedom (approximately the number in each regression), a t statistic of 0.7 is significantly nonzero at the 50 per cent level; a t value of 1.3 is significantly nonzero at the 5 per cent level; and a value of 2.8 is significantly nonzero at the 1 per cent level. The coefficient of any dummy variable for which the absolute value of the t statistic is less than 1.0 is restricted a priori to zero. $\bar{R}^2$ is the corrected coefficient of determination, and *SE* is the standard error of estimate.

TABLE A.3

Implicit Tariff Rates (ITR) and Effective Protection Rates (EPR) for 92 Products, 1967

(per cent)

Sector[a] and Product	ITR	EPR
1. Agriculture, fishing, forestry		
Sunflower seed	−26	−39
Potatoes	−17	−21
Pork meat	0	−18
Rape	−5	−13
Rice	−9	−13
Wheat	−3	−11
Cattle meat	4	4
Corn	16	13
Chicken meat	50	39
9. Food products		
Packing and preserving of fruits and vegetables:		
Canned fruits and vegetables	22	33
Canned peaches	27	81
Packing and preserving of fish products:		
Sardines in oil	28	20
Tuna in oil	28	38
Natural salmon	28	47
Mill products		
Flour	0	0
Rice	50	524
Sugar refinery		
Sugar	100	1,078
Other products		
Spaghetti	0	−5
Oil	41	1,830
10. Beverages		
Wine industry		
Wine (bottling)	14	−21
Beer industry		
Beer	0	−25
11. Tobacco		
Cigarettes	0	−13
12. Textiles		
Fabrication of yarn and fabrics		
Combed wool fabrics	80	63
Carded wool fabrics	80	83
Polyester yarn	92	140
Combed wool yarn	90	152
Dyed linen	130	547
Carded wool yarn	90	821
Cotton thread for retail sale	130	1,641
13. Footwear and clothing		
Shoe manufacture		
Ladies shoes	20	26
Children's shoes	20	32
Sewed men's shoes	20	33
Glued men's shoes	20	46
Clothing manufacture		
Men's shirts	0	−35
Jacket	23	−5
Suit	30	1
Pants	52	33
14. Wood and cork		
Sawmills		
Sawed lumber	0	−4
15. Furniture		
Ordinary wooden furniture	0	−5
16. Paper and paper products		
Papers, cardboard, and cellulose	44	95
17. Printing and publishing		
Books, reprints, 20,000 vols.	0	−24
Books, reprints, 3,000 vols.	0	−20
Books, 1st ed., 20,000 vols.	0	−10
Books, 2nd ed., 3,000 vols.	0	−6
18. Leather and leather products		
Tanyard and finishing shops		
Leather box calf	25	18

TABLE A.3 (*continued*)

Sector[a] and Product	ITR	EPR
19. Rubber products		
Tires	125	304
20. Chemical products		
Fabrication of paints, varnishes, and lacquer		
Anticorrosive paint	54	85
Oil paint	54	103
Enamel paint	54	102
Latex paint	54	113
Toilette articles		
Toothpaste	0	−62
Cosmetics and perfumes	65	42
21. Petroleum and coal products		
Petroleum refineries:		
Petroleum refining	50	900
Derivatives of coal:		
Carbide	60	1,380
22. Nonmetallic mineral products		
Fabrication of glass and glass products		
Plane, cathedral, and mosaic	170	3,500
Fabrication of cement and porcelain		
Sanitaries	0	−6
Table service	25	18
Glazed tile	60	46
Electric isolators	50	56
Fabrication of cement and lime		
Cement and lime	27	29
Cement products for construction		
Rippled sheets	0	−46
Cellulose rippled sheets	0	−25
Plane sheets	0	−17
T-5 pressure pipes	10	−17
Cellulose plane sheets	0	−15
T-4 pressure pipes	10	−14
Pipes without pressure	10	−6
Moldings	20	12
23. Basic metals		
Basic industries of steel and iron		
Cast iron melted for making steel	20	35
Flat steel bars	30	34
24. Metal products		
Metal packing		
15-kg. liquid gas cylinder	61	61
Tools		
90-l. handcart	0	−38
Other metal products		
Bolts and nuts	16	9
12-1. "Califont" (water heater)	73	80
4-plate stove	88	117
"Infrano" stove	244	320
25. Nonelect. machinery		
Metalworking machinery		
20-ton eccentric press	43	58
Winch (1.5 mm. × 180 mm.)	50	69
Drill (column up to 20 mm., 8 speeds)	75	102
26. Elect. machinery		
Elect. industrial machinery and apparatus		
Elect. engine, 5 HP, 1.500 RPM	162	701
Elect. engine, 2 HP, 1.500 RPM	162	780
Equip. for radio and television		
23" TV set	125	113
Radio	345	607
Record player	340	1,400
Elect. equip. and manufacture		

TABLE A.3 (*concluded*)

Sector[a] and Product	ITR	EPR	Sector[a] and Product	ITR	EPR
Household food mixer	94	116	Fabrication of bicycles and other motorless vehicles		
Refrig., 9 cu. ft.	98	121	Bicycles	300	555
Vacuum cleaner	85	132			
Refrig., 7.5 cu. ft.	136	194			
Refrig., 6 cu. ft.	130	190			
Washing machine	105	580			
27. Transportation equipment			Mean	54	217
Naval constructions			Standard deviation	71	512
370-ton barge	0	−14	Range	371	3,562

SOURCE: Estimates by de la Cuadra as presented in de Castro and de la Cuadra [1971:38–46]. For details concerning the calculation of these rates, see the discussion of ITR1 and EPR3 in Appendix B.

a. The sectoral numbers are those of ODEPLAN and, hence, of Jeanneret [1971].

TABLE A.4

Correlation Coefficients Among Alternative Sets of Estimates of Implicit Tariff Rates (ITRs), Effective Protection Rates (EPRs), and Domestic Resource Costs (DRCs), 1961, 1967, and 1968

		Implicit Tariff Rates			Effective Protection Rates				Domestic Resource Costs	
		1961 (1)	1967 (2)	1968[a] (3)	1961 (1)	1961 (2)	1967 (3)	1968[a] (4)	1961 (1)	1968[a] (2)
ITRs										
1961	(1)	1.00		0.60		0.77			0.71	
1967	(2)		1.00				0.50			
1968[a]	(3)	0.60		1.00				0.78		
EPRs										
1961	(1)				1.00	0.43				
1961	(2)	0.77			0.43	1.00		−0.56	0.79	
1967	(3)		0.50				1.00			
1968[a]	(4)			0.78		−0.56		1.00	−0.51	
DRCs										
1961	(1)	0.71				0.79		−0.51	1.00	
1968[a]	(2)									1.00

Source: Table 5.3 contains the underlying data. In the calculation of each correlation coefficient, the maximum number of sectors possible is included after all the blanks in Table 5.3 have been excluded. This table includes only correlation coefficients significantly nonzero at the 5 per cent level. Of course the matrix of correlation coefficients is symmetric but both halves are included to make the table easier to read.

a. For exports only.

TABLE A.5

Correlation Coefficients[a] Between Implicit Tariff Rates, Effective Protection Rates, and Domestic Resource Costs and Selected Sectoral Economic Variables, 1961, 1967, and 1968

Sectoral Characteristics	Implicit Tariff Rates (ITR)			Effective Protection Rates (EPR)				Domestic Resource Costs (DRC)	
	1961 (1)	1967 (2)	1968[b] (3)	1961 (1)	1961 (2)	1967 (3)	1968[b] (4)	1961 (1)	1968[b] (2)
1957 manufacturing census									
Plant/total capital						−.61			
Average wage					−.48				.62
Capital/value added									−.69
Capital per worker						.61			.92
1957 industrial concentration									
Labor force		.56							
Fixed capital									.55
1961/1953 product					−.42				
1961 average tariff rate on intermed. inputs				.72	.58		−.68	.46	
1962/1957									
Gross product									−.88
Gross value added									−.80
1962 input-output table									
Exports/domestic production	−.51		−.79				−.52		
Imports/domestic production		.49							

(*continued*)

TABLE A.5 (*concluded*)

Sectoral Characteristics	Implicit Tariff Rates (ITR) 1961 (1)	1967 (2)	1968[b] (3)	Effective Protection Rates (EPR) 1961 (1)	1961 (2)	1967 (3)	1968[b] (4)	Domestic Resource Costs (DRC) 1961 (1)	1968[b] (2)
1962 input-output table (*contd.*)									
Domestic production ratios									.57
Intermediate/total									−.54
Private consumption/total			.62						
Investment/total	.56								
Government/total			.70				.54		
Import ratios									
Private consumption/total	.56		.54						
Investment/total		.49							
Components of gross value added/ domestic production									
Imported inputs		.62	−.50			.43			
Salaries	−.46		−.78						
Wages	−.44		−.65						

Employers' social security taxes	−.49		−.75				
Total labor payments	−.49		−.75				
Other factor payments		.44					
Indirect taxes and subsidies			.71				
Depreciation	−.45		−.54				
Gross value added			−.72	−.55			
1967 manufacturing census							
Labor payments/domestic production							−.64
Imported inputs/domestic production		.46				.49	
Value added/domestic production				−.43			−.53
Average wage					−.43		.66
Capital per worker							.74
1967 intermediate inputs/gross product						.51	
1967 manufacturing census/1957 manufacturing census							
Average labor price		.59					
Value added/capital							.81
Value added/gross product				.48			
Labor payments/gross product	.42					.43	−.72
Capacity in horsepower		.56					
Plant			−.54				
Electrical energy consumed			−.55				
Value added		.58					
Plant/total capital						.82	

Notes to Table A.5

a. The column headings refer to those of Table 5.3. The sectoral economic variables are from the following sources: 1957 manufacturing census data from DEC [1960a:42–43, 70–71, 95–96, 106–107, 131–132] and Instituto de Economía [1963:100, 103–104], 1957 industrial concentration data from Lagos [1966:80, 96, 97, 170], 1961/1953 production from data in Instituto de Economía [1963:90], 1961 average tariff rate on intermediate imported inputs from unpublished data calculated by Jeanneret and presented in Bacha and Taylor [1973], related data of 1962 input-output table from ODEPLAN [1970], 1967 manufacturing census data from INE [1970:19–80], and 1967 data calculated by de la Cuadra and presented in de Castro and de la Cuadra [1971:38–44]. All correlation coefficients which are significantly nonzero at least at the 5 per cent level are included. Sectoral characteristics for which correlation coefficients were calculated but which were in no case significantly correlated with the variables indicated in the column headings include value added per unit of capital and the ratio of capital to gross value of output for 1957; firm size, firm size plus degree of concentration, and concentration by gross value of output for 1957; the change in concentration of the labor force between 1937 and 1957; the ratio of investment goods of domestic origin to domestic production and the ratios of intermediate goods of foreign origin and of government-consumed goods of foreign origin to imports from the 1962 input-output table; the ratios of the capital stock, of the horsepower capacity, of plant, and of electric energy consumed to gross product, the average tariff rate on intermediate inputs, and the ratio of value added to capital for 1967; capital per worker and the ratio of intermediate imports to gross product for 1967 relative to 1957; and the 1967-to-1962 ratios of gross product and of gross value added.

b. For exports only.

TABLE A.6

Correlations Between Selected Sectoral Economic Variables and 1967-to-1961 Ratios for Implicit Tariff Rates (ITRs) and Effective Protection Rates (EPRs)[a]

Sectoral Characteristics	Ratio of ITR2 to ITR1	Ratio of EPR3 to EPR2
1957 manufacturing census		
Plant/total capital		−.64
Value added/capital		−.49
Capital per worker		.69
1957 industrial concentration: labor force		
1961/1953 product	.49	
1962 input-output table	.44	
Import ratios		
Private consumption	.49	−.46
Government	.55	
Components of gross value added/domestic production: imported inputs	.53	
1967 manufacturing census: value added/domestic production		−.47
1967 manufacturing census/1957 manufacturing census		
Average labor price	.62	.43
Value added/gross product		−.46
Labor payments/gross product		.47
Capacity in horsepower	.47	
Value added	.55	
Plant/total capital		.82

SOURCE: See Tables 5.3 and A.5.

a. Only coefficients that are significantly nonzero at the 5 per cent level are shown. ITR2 and EPR3 are for 1967; ITR1 and EPR2 are for 1961. However, it is assumed in these comparisons that there are no empirically significant definitional differences between ITR1 and ITR2 and between EPR2 and EPR3. See Appendix B for definitions and for a discussion of the importance of the differences in definition.

TABLE A.7

Chilean Average Annual Nominal and Effective Exchange Rates, 1931–72

(escudos per U.S. dollar)

	Nominal Exchange					
Phase and Year	Official (special after 1942) (1)	Export Draft (2)	Gold (3)	Wine (4)	Free Funds (parity after Dec. 1946)[a] (5)	Black or Free Market[b] (6)
I–II						
1931	.00826					0.014[e]
1932	.01405	.03338				0.025[e]
1933	.01334	.03318				0.034[e]
1934	.00964	.02507				0.025
1935	.01933	.02426				0.025
1936	.01938	.02605	.035[e]			0.028
1937	.01937	.02558	.034[e]		.028	0.026
1938	.01937	.02495	.034[e]		.028	0.027
1939	.01937	.02498			.031	0.032
1940	.01937	.02498			.031	0.033
1941	.01937	.02490			.031	0.032
1942	.01937	.02500			.031	0.032
1943	.01937	.02500			.031	0.032
1944	.01937	.02500			.031	0.032
1945	.01937	.02500			.031	0.032
1946	.01937	.02500			.031	0.034
1947	.01937	.02500			.031	0.047
1948	.01937	.02500			.031	0.061
1949	.01937	.02500	.1236		.031	0.075
1950	.01937		.1367		.031	0.092
1951	.01937		.1345	.110	.031	0.090
1952	.01937		.1647	.133	.031	0.122
1953	.01937		.1896	.170	.05175	0.188
1954	.01937			.245	.110	0.335
1955	.01937			.350	.110	0.565
III						
1956	.01937				.110	0.526
1957					.110	0.800
1958					.110	1.100

Rates (NER)							
Bank Market		Special Commer-cial	Pro-visional	Central Bank	Brokers'	National Accounts[c]	Import EER[d]
Spot (7)	Future (8)	(9)	(10)	(11)	(12)	(13)	(14)
						0.0083	
						0.014	
						0.032	
						0.032	
						0.024	
						0.024	
						0.025	
						0.025	
						0.025	
						0.025	0.033
						0.030	0.038
						0.030	0.036
						0.030	0.035
						0.030	0.035
						0.030	0.036
						0.030	0.037
						0.032	0.039
0.0430						0.036	0.044
0.0430						0.038	0.049
0.0430		.050	.060		0.090	0.051	0.063
0.0900[e]		.050	.060		0.085	0.057	0.071
0.1132		.050	.060		0.124	0.066	0.082
0.1102		.050	.060		0.174	0.076	0.094
0.1228					0.290	0.104	0.123
0.205					0.540	0.181	0.219
0.453				0.499	0.534	0.351	0.432
0.621				0.620	0.694	0.624	0.749
0.793				0.788	1.000	0.715	0.846

TABLE A.7 (*concluded*)

Phase and Year	Nominal Exchange: Official (special after 1942) (1)	Export Draft (2)	Gold (3)	Wine (4)	Free Funds (parity after Dec. 1946)[a] (5)	Black or Free Market[b] (6)
IV						
1959					.110	1.059
1960						1.057
1961						1.059
II						
1962						1.750
1963						3.060
1964						4.750
III						
1965						5.35
1966						5.95
1967						6.50
1968						9.50
1969						14.25
1970						22.60
II						
1971						54.70
1972						219.6

Rates (NER)

Bank Market		Special Commercial	Provisional	Central Bank	Brokers'	National Accounts[c]	Import EER[d]
Spot (7)	Future (8)	(9)	(10)	(11)	(12)	(13)	(14)
1.047				1.045	1.055	1.049	1.254
1.051				1.049	1.051	1.049	1.269
1.051				1.049	1.051	1.049	1.292
1.142				1.142	1.751	1.153	1.455
1.875	2.452			1.874	3.011	1.871	2.293
2.372	2.741			2.373	3.204	2.418	2.850
3.128	3.310			3.131	3.739	3.237	3.847
3.955	4.000			3.955	4.649	4.000	4.711
5.031	5.031			5.031	5.697	5.080	5.991
6.787	6.787			6.787	7.818	6.860	8.031
8.974	8.974			8.974	10.145	9.040	10.436
11.552	11.552			11.552	13.503	11.83	13.899
12.36[f]	12.36			12.36	20.285[g]	13.47	
19.67[f]					35.4[g]	21.87	

Notes to Table A.7

SOURCE: The black-market rates for 1931–71 are from Baerresen [1969:17] and Pick's [1948–71]; for 1972, from verbal reports. The national accounts rate is from CORFO and ODEPLAN sources as presented in Mamalakis [1971b:527] for 1931–39 and in Behrman [1974] for 1940–71. The gold and wine rates are from Ellsworth [1945: 56–57] and Baerresen [1969:12]. All other data are from Central Bank sources and are largely presented in Jul [1969:149–150] and in Líbano [1970:730]. Before 1960 the Chilean currency was the peso, which equaled 0.001 escudos.

a. After June 1959, calculations of the IMF for Chilean reserves and balance of payments have been based on the bank rate.

b. End of June for 1948–72. The black-market NER is the EER for nonbulk marginal goods, services, and capital transactions. The black-market rate approximates the EER and not the NER for such transactions because tariffs, taxes, and other charges generally are avoided in those cases in which the black market is the source of foreign exchange. There may be a cost due to risk, however, because of the illegality of dealing in this market.

The black-market rate must be interpreted with care because this market is somewhat narrow (although information about it seems to be widespread in the commercial centers of Santiago and Valparaiso), and may be affected by risk aversion because of its illegality. Risk aversion would shift both the demand and the supply curves downward. The direction of the effect on the price of foreign exchange would be uncertain. One might hypothesize that the supply curve would shift less than the demand curve, since suppliers in this market are largely foreigners for whom the penalties arising from convictions for operating in this market have been less than for nationals. On the other hand, the probability of arrest for black-market operations may be higher for the more visible foreigners than for nationals, which would have a countervailing effect. In any case, attempts to suppress the black market in any manner (except for lessening the degree of overvaluation in the legal market) have been very infrequent—especially before the Allende government. The black-market PLD-NER—or the discrepancy between it and the comparable legal rate—is one useful index of the extent to which demands for foreign exchange are not being satisfied in the legal market(s) because quantitative restrictions are being used to ration the available foreign exchange at the existing overvalued legal rate(s).

The following regression provides some support for this interpretation (t ratios are shown in parentheses; elasticities at sample means, in brackets):

$$
\begin{array}{l}
PLD\text{-}NER^{BM} = \underset{\substack{(3.8)\\[5.2]}}{29.7QRFD} + \underset{\substack{(4.2)\\[0.1]}}{0.113} \sum_{i=0}^{L} (PLD\text{-}NER^{BM} - PLD\text{-}NER^{NA}) - \underset{(3.2)}{23.5} \\
\bar{R}^2 = 0.84,\ SE = 0.532,\ DW = 1.3;\ \text{years covered, 1950–65}
\end{array}
$$

where

BM = black market;
NA = national accounts;
$QRFD$ = Ffrench-Davis quantitative restrictions index (line 1.2.6.2 in Table A.1);
L = first year of start of last stabilization plus liberalization attempt (1956, 1959, 1965).

Variations in $QRFD$ alone are consistent with 65 per cent of the variance in the $PLD\text{-}NER^{BM}$. The second term on the right is the sum of the difference between the PLD-NERs for the black market and for the legal market(s) since the initiation of the last attempt at stabilization with liberalization. It represents the cumulative pressures for another liberalization attempt due to the disequilibrium system and, thus, motivation for speculative capital flight. (A somewhat different interpretation of the regression is possible. The second term may represent a distributed lag of the quantitative restrictions index. In such a case the entire right-hand side is a distributed lag of this index, which may represent expectations concerning future quantitative restrictions.) Together the two right-hand variables are consistent with 84 per cent of the variance in the $PLD\text{-}NER^{BM}$. (Prima facie, the elasticities may be misleading indicators of the relative contribution of the two right-hand variables because the coefficient of variation is much larger for the second than for the first of the two.) The inclusion of additional variables does not significantly increase the correlation.

c. Weighted average of legal exchange rates. For 1971, it is a weighted average of the bank market and brokers' market rates described in notes f and g.

d. The EER for imports is the national accounts exchange rate adjusted to include the average import tax rate (line 1.2.6.9 in Table A.1) and the import prior-deposit-cost rate calculated from prior-deposit cost estimates made by Ffrench-Davis [1971:269].

e. End of year. EER for imports is the average number of escudos paid for a one-dollar international transaction, including all charges for tariffs and other taxes and the interest costs of prior deposits. The figures shown are in each case the higher (by 0.0005) of two rates for gold.

f. As of December 13, 1971, the bank market rate was subdivided into four rates: A at 12.21 escudos per dollar, B at 15.80, C at 19.00, and D at 25.00. As of August 7, 1972, the escudo under these rates was devalued and three new lists were added so that the structure became the following: A or E at 20.00 escudos per dollar, B or F at 25.00, G at 30.00, C at 40.00, D at 80.00, and higher rates for nontraditional exports deemed desirable. The rate in the table is the weighted average of the two basic B rates.

g. The rate of 28.00 escudos per dollar, which was established in July 1971, was replaced by three rates as of August 2, 1972: Area I, 36.00; Area II, 46.00; and Area III, 85.00. The rate indicated in the table is the weighted average of the 28.00-escudo rate and the basic 46.00-escudo rate.

TABLE A.8

Price-Level-Deflated Effective Exchange Rates, Premiums Included, for Major Production Sectors and Subsectors and Demand Components, 1946–70

(1965 escudos per dollar)

Phase and Year	1. Agric. and Forestry (1)	2. Fishing (2)	3. Coal Mining (3)	6. Nitrate Mining (4)	9. Food Prod. (5)	10. Beverages (6)	12. Textiles (7)	13. Footwear (8)	14. Wood and Cork (9)	16. Paper Prod. (10)	18. Leather Prod. (11)
II											
1946	5.872		14.974	3.831	6.257				5.881		
1947	4.864		11.140	2.964	9.877	8.782	8.436		3.623	6.474	
1948	4.359		9.818	3.061	7.796	6.939	6.400		3.498	6.394	
1949	4.946	1.973	9.936	3.337	8.135	8.578	6.908	14.513	4.302	6.052	
1950	5.174	1.959	9.798	3.208	7.789	7.805	7.339	14.147	3.639	6.086	
1951	4.731	2.393	9.788	3.000	7.082	7.488	6.530	12.622	3.530	5.959	
1952	4.817	2.386	10.639	3.024	7.958	8.406	7.623	12.078	3.710	5.967	
1953	5.323	2.023	11.847	3.156	7.483	8.297	9.439	11.769	3.584	5.114	
1954	5.488	2.484	11.605	3.545	7.462	7.498	11.022	12.062	4.181	4.369	
1955	5.940	2.507	31.150	5.852	8.881	7.136	16.942	18.836	6.476	6.814	12.961
III											
1956	5.460	3.628	29.237	3.675	7.969	6.957	17.704	17.171	5.467	6.492	12.417
1957	5.238	3.464	30.078	2.654	7.440	8.220	16.192	14.486	5.160	6.221	10.804
1958	4.557	3.357	4.078	4.711	6.691	9.108	11.633	13.333	4.356	6.924	9.415
IV											
1959	4.501	3.321	5.199	4.241	6.440	7.798	10.566	13.496	3.978	6.219	9.704
1960	4.717	3.583	4.596	3.910	6.254	7.454	9.903	12.571	4.496	5.609	9.827
1961	4.668	3.950	4.472	3.264	5.942	7.247	9.206	11.590	4.407	5.060	8.521

II											
1962	4.725	3.764	4.432		5.915	6.690	9.075	11.449	4.422	4.638	8.713
1963	4.668	3.105	4.679		5.939	6.692	9.956	11.403	5.173	4.809	10.003
1964	4.593	2.800	4.873		5.896	6.869	9.821	11.245	4.959	5.099	10.951
III											
1965	4.120	3.113	5.254		5.969	6.746	9.585	10.938	4.876	5.832	10.457
1966	4.035	3.836	5.924		5.680	5.703	8.611	9.975	4.317	5.268	8.629
1967	4.137	2.780	5.405		5.318	5.238	7.905	8.942	4.166	4.746	8.109
1968	3.867	2.702	3.743		5.202	5.324	7.107	8.205	4.953	4.280	6.939
1969	4.045	2.161	3.687		4.803	5.116	6.922	7.524	4.693	4.028	5.890
1970	3.769	1.640	3.211		4.572	4.515	8.491	8.590	5.995		6.044
Mean	4.745	2.860	9.983	3.590	6.750	7.109	9.722	12.134	4.554	5.585	9.336
Stand. dev.	0.589	0.691	8.271	0.803	1.307	1.227	3.136	2.734	0.814	0.848	2.016
Ratio: stand. dev. to mean	0.124	0.241	0.828	0.223	0.193	0.172	0.322	0.225	0.178	0.151	0.215

(*continued*)

TABLE A.8 (*continued*)

Phase and Year	19. Rubber Prod. (12)	20. Chemical Prod. (13)	21. Petroleum and Coal Prod. (14)	22. Nonmet. Mineral Prod. (15)	23. Basic Metals (16)	24. Metal Prod. (17)	26. Elect. Mach. (18)	28. Other Mfg. (19)	1–28. All Sectors (20)	3–8. Mining[a] (21)	9–28. Mfg. (22)
II											
1946				15.394	12.129				8.982	5.327	11.331
1947		6.426	6.692	12.464	10.049				7.734	4.930	9.504
1948		7.055	5.798	12.035	9.746				6.800	4.506	8.212
1949		8.602	6.744	10.610	9.769				7.519	4.254	8.876
1950		7.634	6.720	10.055	7.833				7.144	4.470	8.242
1951		6.736	6.128	10.099	6.142				6.450	4.079	7.499
1952		7.577	6.230	11.150	7.253				7.029	4.170	8.246
1953		8.912	5.609	11.255	6.514				7.111	4.345	7.985
1954		8.021	4.863	8.297	6.211				6.948	3.792	7.610
1955		7.654	4.378	8.228	5.644	7.210			8.216	3.390	8.805
III											
1956		8.037	4.981	8.778	5.590	6.946			7.824	4.040	8.585
1957		6.702	5.268	9.236	5.546	6.678			7.470	4.123	8.248
1958	6.259	6.364	5.711	9.152	6.008	5.580	8.705	8.491	6.765	4.435	7.797
IV											
1959	6.523	6.716	5.451	8.873	5.890	6.053	7.381	8.334	6.598	3.953	7.531
1960	6.842	6.770	5.236	8.354	5.784	5.676	7.159	7.657	6.505	3.860	7.302
1961	6.595	6.333	4.897	7.803	5.419	5.191	6.692	7.345	6.170	3.526	6.888

II											
1962	6.068	6.095	4.519	7.376	4.888	5.103	6.264	7.631	5.996	3.288	6.686
1963	6.903	5.552	4.166	6.646	4.307	4.902	6.274	7.480	5.977	3.398	6.597
1964	6.751	4.570	4.084	6.760	3.765	4.139	5.924	7.296	5.823	3.134	6.365
III											
1965	5.938	4.541	3.810	7.247	4.772	4.160	6.267	7.152	5.681	3.515	6.373
1966	5.560	4.477	3.536	7.143	5.905	4.013	6.182	7.033	5.353	3.297	5.956
1967	5.060	4.579	3.390	6.402	6.284	4.065	6.204	6.634	5.142	2.913	5.626
1968	4.763	4.752	3.604	6.235	6.919	4.214	6.120	6.126	5.043	2.642	5.514
1969	4.385	4.165	3.947	6.025	6.570	4.153	5.495	5.872	4.884	2.355	5.182
1970	3.669	3.570	3.764	5.899		3.785	5.142	8.880	4.752	2.044	5.103
Mean	5.793	6.327	4.980	8.886	6.622	5.117	6.447	7.379	6.557	3.751	7.443
Stand. dev.	1.036	1.504	1.071	2.341	1.988	1.135	0.901	0.872	1.088	0.778	1.462
Ratio: stand. dev. to mean	0.178	0.237	0.215	0.263	0.300	0.221	0.139	0.118	0.165	0.207	0.196

(*continued*)

TABLE A.8 (*concluded*)

Phase and Year	Construc. Mat. (23)	Intermed. Prod. (24)	Consumer Goods[a] (25)	Invest. Goods[a] (26)	Imports[a] (27)	Competitive Imports[b] (28)	Non-competitive Imports[c] (29)	Raw Material Imports[d] (30)	Exports[a] (31)
II									
1946	9.301	9.087	15.447	12.922	9.948	7.263	12.580		5.385
1947	7.172	7.289	13.979	9.363	8.432	6.158	10.629	10.054	4.906
1948	6.943	7.062	13.081	8.739	7.374	5.626	8.836	8.010	4.253
1949	7.080	7.426	13.244	8.402	7.024	6.382	9.501	7.725	3.926
1950	5.959	6.744	12.948	8.117	7.012	6.343	9.046	7.635	4.178
1951	5.236	5.957	12.108	7.371	6.656	5.708	8.413	7.417	4.328
1952	5.898	6.422	11.900	7.158	6.828	5.948	9.302	6.997	4.757
1953	5.563	6.504	11.714	7.289	5.859	6.376	9.005	6.038	4.284
1954	5.366	6.316	11.846	6.636	4.756	6.311	8.864	5.597	3.123
1955	6.080	7.539	11.719	5.819	4.560	6.555	11.044	5.447	3.380
III									
1956	6.002	7.499	11.167	5.830	5.498	6.353	10.476	6.950	4.104
1957	5.813	7.152	10.647	6.766	7.559	6.038	10.133	8.854	4.338
1958	5.908	7.262	10.346	6.734	6.679	5.604	8.741	8.848	3.521
IV									
1959	5.857	7.002	10.033	7.073	6.861	5.625	8.265	7.458	4.002
1960	5.911	6.972	10.068	6.266	6.065	5.721	7.931	6.913	3.773
1961	5.419	6.497	9.925	6.268	5.517	5.517	7.509	6.497	3.297

II									
1962	5.158	6.202	9.874	5.962	5.174	5.446	7.336	5.893	3.289
1963	5.024	6.235	9.655	6.268	5.229	5.241	7.433	7.169	3.528
1964	4.653	6.107	9.424	6.528	5.462	4.927	7.426	6.823	3.309
III									
1965	4.834	5.976	9.296	6.158	5.489	4.614	7.457	5.318	3.739
1966	4.757	5.666	8.760	6.236	4.793	4.507	6.922	4.632	4.046
1967	4.587	5.650	8.586	5.737	4.734	4.578	6.356	4.438	3.650
1968	4.818	5.583	8.240	5.555	4.564	4.447	6.100		3.640
1969	4.742	5.529	7.779	5.132	4.122	4.450	5.710		3.772
1970	4.365	5.155				4.189	5.684		
Mean	5.698	6.593	10.908	7.014	6.091	5.597	8.428	6.891	3.939
Stand. dev.	1.073	0.861	1.936	1.635	1.392	0.807	1.723	1.416	0.557
Ratio: stand. dev. to mean	0.188	0.130	0.177	0.233	0.228	0.144	0.204	0.205	0.141

Notes to Table A.8

NOTE: To calculate EERs on a disaggregated level for Chile is very difficult. In attempts by the government to pursue stabilization and distribution goals in an environment with very high inflation rates (cf. line 2.1 in Table A.1), foreign-sector policies have been changed with great frequency—and often with great specificity (see Part II, above). To trace the changes in the implicit legal charges related to international transactions on a detailed level, therefore, is an enormous task.

Even if one had adequately chronicled such legal changes, however, a person would not really have EERs because of the large number of exemptions. Many of these exemptions are very difficult to detect, as the following anecdote illustrates: An apparently innocuous three-day suspension of the duties on sugar resulted in a considerable premium to the importer because a shipfull of sugar was waiting for the suspension in the Valparaiso harbor. During those three days, the cargo was unloaded and passed through customs. A quantity of sugar equal to a considerable portion of Chilean annual consumption entered the country duty-free. (In an interview on May 17, 1972, Ana Maria Jul related this and other similar events she had uncovered in Central Bank interviews as part of her research on Chilean international economic policies.)

For 1962, more specific evidence of the importance of such exemptions is available. For that year, I compared the tariff-equivalent rates implied by the legal rates plus prior-deposit costs for 58 categories of goods (Beca, Galvez, and Imperatore [1969:125–126]) with the tariff-equivalent rates actually paid on the same items. The unweighted mean of the actual rates equaled 55 per cent of the mean of the legal rates; the entire difference can be accounted for by the exemptions. The dispersion of the actual rates, as measured by the standard deviation or by the ratio of the standard deviation to the mean, is much smaller than for the legal rates. A regression of the actual rates on the legal rates follows:

$$\text{Actual rates} = \underset{(6.5)}{0.245}\ \text{legal rates} + \underset{(5.2)}{0.348}$$
$$\bar{R}^2 = 0.44,\ SE = 0.37$$

Note that the dispersion of the actual rates is much smaller than that of the legal rates. Exemptions apparently substantially reduce the distortions implied by the legal rate structure. Therefore, the legal rates are quite misleading.

Because of the problems just described, time series for premium-inclusive EERs [EER(PI)s] rather than disaggregated EERs are presented in this study. The former are defined to be the ratio of domestic prices (net of normal distribution costs) to c.i.f. prices. EER(PI)s are equal to EERs if the premium rate is zero (see Table A.1, note for line 1.1.6).

The PLD-EER(PI)s in this table are based on the following procedure:

i. For a number of aggregate domestic price indices and for the 220 most important products underlying the Chilean consumer and wholesale price indices, comparable international price indices were located and examined critically. The most comparable components of the U.S. wholesale price index, consumer price index, and GDP deflator were chosen because all other alternatives were incomplete or unstable. In any case, in 1950–68, the United States provided 440 per cent of the value of Chilean imports from the second-largest supplier country.

ii. Ratios of domestic to international prices were calculated for each of the Chilean price indices for 1946–70.

iii. The time series were normalized to be consistent with the 1961 ratios of domestic to c.i.f. price estimates of Jeanneret [1971]. For this base year, near the end of the most liberal post-World War II phase, the import premium rate was relatively low.

iv. The disaggregated series were averaged with equal weights to obtain the subsectoral estimates and other aggregates.

v. All series were divided by the Chilean GDP deflator, with 1965 equal to 1.00.

The resulting series primarily reflect the combined patterns of PLD-EERs and import premiums for production subsectors and various demand aggregates plus such factors as changes in domestic distribution margins in percentage terms, in those cases in which the consumer price index is used; changes in international shipping costs in percentage terms; changes in the relative quality of Chilean versus U.S. products; changes in the degree of domestic market power; changes in product composition; and time lags in adjustment between foreign and domestic prices. The variances in these additional factors appear to be dwarfed, however, by the variances in the PLD-EERs and the import premiums.

Source: All series are based on aggregations of 220 underlying disaggregated series, unless otherwise noted. Data sources include the Council of Economic Advisers [1972] for the U.S. price indices and deflators; Jeanneret [1971] for the 1961 domestic-to-c.i.f. price ratios; Behrman [1974] for the Chilean GDP deflator; and Banco Central [1945–73b], Behrman [1974], and DEC [1957–70b] for the Chilean price indices and deflators. The means and standard deviations are for all nonzero observations.

a. Numerator based on Chilean GDP deflator.

b. Includes industries identified in columns 1, 12–14, and 16–19 (subsectors 1, 19–21, 23, 24, 26, and 28 in the classification by ODEPLAN [1970] and Jeanneret [1971: 159]).

c. Includes industries identified in columns 2, 3, 5–11, and 15 (subsectors 2, 3, 9, 10, 12–14, 16, 18, and 22 in the classification used by ODEPLAN [1970] and Jeanneret [1971:159]).

d. Based on imported raw materials component of Chilean wholesale price index.

TABLE A.9

Correlation Coefficients[a] Among Price-Level-Deflated Effective Exchange Rates, Premiums Included, for Major Production Sectors and Subsectors and Demand Components, 1946–70

	(1)	(2)	(3)	(4)	(5)	(6)	(7)	(8)	(9)	(10)	(11)	(12)	(13)
1. Agriculture & forestry (1)	1.00												
2. Fishing (2)		1.00											
3. Coal mining (3)	.74		1.00										
4. Nitrate mining (6)				1.00									
5. Food products (9)	.66		.62		1.00								
6. Beverages (10)	.63				.75	1.00							
7. Textiles (12)	.62		.80	.49			1.00						
8. Footwear (13)	.85		.78	.58	.88	.65	.72	1.00					
9. Wood & cork (14)			.38	.61		−.43	.62		1.00				
10. Paper & paper products (16)	.40		.51		.70	.66	.40	.82		1.00			
11. Leather & leather products (18)	.85		.70		.90	.64	.83	.89		.78	1.00		
12. Rubber products (19)	.90	.75			.89	.81	.74	.85		.54	.89	1.00	
13. Chemical products (20)	.83		.53		.78	.76		.74		.46	.73	.76	1.00
14. Petroleum & coal products (21)	.48			−.53	.75	.84		.54	−.59	.60		.60	.75
15. Nonmetallic mineral products (22)	.60				.65	.79		.57		.62	.66	.67	.76
16. Basic metals (23)		−.59			.40		−.42				−.51	−.71	
17. Metallic products (24)	.91		.80		.92	.69	.89	.93		.76	.74	.68	.96
18. Electric machinery (26)	.55	.58		.92	.86	.90	.76	.80	−.60	.87		.59	.80
19. Other manufacturing (28)				.95			.73	.62		.84			
20. All sectors (1–28)	.90		.70		.79	.81	.52	.94		.74	.87	.87	.87
21. Mining (3–8)	.63				.71	.90		.66		.74	.70	.82	.76
22. Manufacturing (9–28)	.82		.58		.76	.85		.90		.78	.86	.84	.86
23. Construction materials	.62				.55	.74		.78		.71	.66	.65	.73
24. Intermediate products	.76		.55		.59	.78	.53	.91		.81	.80	.80	.75
25. Consumer goods	.69	−.44	.40		.74	.73		.70		.60	.87	.89	.79
26. Investment goods	.44	−.42				.67				.52		.80	.49
27. Imports					.45	.77		.43		.68		.72	.43
28. Competitive	.93		.62		.75	.81	.41	.84		.56	.80	.83	.95
29. Noncompetitive	.87		.73		.78	.78	.55	.94		.78	.89	.86	.81
30. Raw materials					.54	.75				.59		.73	
31. Exports										.46			

a. Includes all correlation coefficients among the series in Table A.8 that are significantly nonzero at the 5 per cent level. The results indicate the consistency of the impact across subsectors and demand categories of changes in the foreign-sector regime.

(14)	(15)	(16)	(17)	(18)	(19)	(20)	(21)	(22)	(23)	(24)	(25)	(26)	(27)	(28)	(29)	(30)
1.00																
.90	1.00															
.64	.81	1.00														
.74	.85		1.00													
.83	.92		.80	1.00												
.57	.52				1.00											
.72	.82	.53	.97	.86		1.00										
.87	.92	.65	.70	.91		.84	1.00									
.83	.91	.67	.96	.89	.51	.98	.90	1.00								
.82	.90	.85	.94	.88		.85	.83	.92	1.00							
.66	.77	.59	.95	.91		.92	.81	.93	.92	1.00						
.87	.93	.76	.91	.74	.95	.87	.89	.93	.87	.77	1.00					
.84	.91	.85		.69	.91	.67	.83	.81	.90	.72	.86	1.00				
.85	.88	.72	.49	.86	.93	.69	.90	.81	.85	.75	.80	.90	1.00			
.77	.80	.51	.97	.77		.97	.83	.94	.80	.86	.87	.64	.63	1.00		
.68	.82	.54	.94	.87		.99	.84	.97	.84	.91	.86	.69	.71	.93	1.00	
.75	.63	.47		.76	.89	.52	.79	.66	.69	.62	.58	.69	.89	.43	.53	1.00
.60	.80	.72				.53	.70	.65	.69	.50	.65	.76	.80	.46	.59	.50

The industry numbers in the column headings are identified in the stub. The figures in parentheses are the sector numbers used by ODEPLAN [1972] and Jeanneret [1971].

TABLE A.10

Percentage Changes in Ratios of Effective Exchange Rates, Premiums Included, to National Accounts Nominal Exchange Rate for Major Production Sectors and Subsectors and Demand Components,[a] 1947–70

Phase and Year	1. Agric. and Forestry (1)	2. Fishing (2)	3. Coal Mining (3)	6. Nitrate Mining (4)	9. Food Prod. (5)	10. Beverages (6)	12. Textiles (7)	13. Footwear (8)	14. Wood and Cork (9)	16. Paper Prod. (10)	18. Leather Prod. (11)
II											
1947	−0.8		−10.9	−7.3	88.9				−26.2		
1948	−4.9		−6.5	9.5	−16.3	−16.2	−19.5		2.3	4.7	
1949	28.1		14.2	23.0	17.8	39.5	21.8		38.8	6.8	
1950	−8.8	−13.4	−14.0	−16.2	−16.5	−20.7	−7.4	−15.0	−26.2	−12.3	
1951	−0.9	32.2	8.1	1.2	−1.5	3.8	−3.6	−3.3	5.0	6.0	
1952	7.9	5.6	15.2	6.8	19.1	19.0	23.7	1.4	11.4	6.1	
1953	20.7	−7.3	21.6	14.0	2.7	7.8	35.3	6.5	5.5	−6.3	
1954	25.5	49.5	19.3	36.7	21.4	10.0	42.2	24.8	42.0	4.0	
1955	9.1	1.8	170.7	66.5	20.0	−3.9	55.0	57.5	56.2	57.3	
III											
1956	−24.9	18.1	−23.3	−48.7	−26.7	−20.4	−14.7	−25.5	−31.0	−22.2	−21.8
1957	−30.7	−31.1	−25.7	−47.8	−32.6	−14.7	−34.0	−39.1	−31.8	−30.8	−37.2
1958	−4.1	6.7	−85.0	95.4	−0.9	22.0	−20.8	1.3	−7.0	22.6	−3.9

IV											
1959	−5.3	−5.1	22.1	−13.7	−7.7	−17.9	−12.9	−2.9	−12.4	−13.9	−1.2
1960	14.7	18.1	−3.2	0.9	6.3	4.6	2.6	1.9	23.7	−1.2	10.8
1961	6.7	18.9	4.9	−9.9	2.4	4.8	0.2	−0.5	5.7	−2.6	−6.4
II											
1962	4.2	−1.8	2.0		2.4	−4.9	1.4	1.7	3.3	−5.6	5.2
1963	−11.3	−25.9	−5.2		−9.8	−10.1	−1.5	−10.5	5.0	−6.9	3.0
1964	12.0	2.7	18.6		13.0	16.9	12.3	12.3	9.2	20.7	24.7
III											
1965	−14.0	6.5	3.2		−3.0	−5.9	−6.5	−6.8	−5.8	9.5	−8.5
1966	1.8	28.1	17.3		−1.0	−12.0	−6.5	−5.1	−7.8	−6.0	−14.1
1967	4.7	−25.9	−6.7		−4.3	−6.1	−6.2	−8.4	−1.3	−7.9	−3.9
1968	−9.8	−6.2	−33.2		−5.7	−2.0	−13.3	−11.5	14.6	−13.0	−17.5
1969	9.6	−16.1	3.3		−3.1	0.7	2.1	−3.8	−0.6	−1.3	−10.9
1970	−1.5	−19.8	−8.0		0.5	−6.7	29.5	20.5	34.8		8.3

(continued)

TABLE A.10 (*continued*)

Phase and Year	19. Rubber Prod. (12)	20. Chemical Prod. (13)	21. Petroleum and Coal Prod. (14)	22. Nonmet. Mineral Prod. (15)	23. Basic Metals (16)	24. Metal Prod. (17)	26. Elect. Mach. (18)	28. Other Mfg. (19)	1–28. All Sectors (20)	3–8. Mining (21)	9–28. Mfg. (22)
II											
1947				−3.0	−0.8				3.0	10.7	0.4
1948		16.3	−8.1	−2.3	2.8				−6.7	−3.0	−8.3
1949		37.6	31.3	−0.4	13.1				24.8	6.6	22.0
1950		−22.6	−13.1	−17.4	−30.1				−17.2	−8.4	−19.0
1951		−4.4	−1.2	8.7	−15.0				−2.2	−1.1	−1.4
1952		19.2	7.7	17.0	25.1				15.5	8.3	16.5
1953		28.5	−1.5	10.3	−1.8				10.5	13.8	5.8
1954		9.6	5.5	−3.3	16.1				19.0	6.3	16.0
1955		−3.7	−9.1	−7.0	−8.3				19.2	−9.8	16.7
III											
1956		−14.3	−7.1	−12.9	−19.1	−21.3			−22.2	−2.7	−20.4
1957		−39.8	−23.6	−24.0	−28.4	−30.6			−31.0	−26.3	−30.6
1958		4.6	19.4	9.1	19.3	−7.9			−0.2	18.4	4.1

IV											
1959	−0.1	1.1	−8.5	−7.0	−6.0	3.9	−18.7	−5.9	−6.5	−14.5	−7.4
1960	14.8	10.3	5.1	3.0	7.5	2.6	6.1	0.5	7.9	6.8	6.1
1961	3.9	0.8	0.8	0.7	1.0	−1.3	0.8	3.4	2.2	−1.4	1.7
II											
1962	−5.2	−0.9	−4.9	−2.6	−7.1	1.2	−3.6	6.9	0.0	−3.9	0.0
1963	2.1	−18.2	−17.2	−19.1	−20.8	−13.7	−10.0	−11.9	−10.5	−7.2	−11.4
1964	11.4	−6.2	11.6	15.8	−0.4	−3.8	7.5	11.1	10.9	5.0	9.9
III											
1965	−15.7	−4.8	−10.6	2.6	21.4	−3.7	1.3	−6.1	−6.5	7.4	−4.0
1966	−2.5	2.5	−3.4	2.5	28.7	0.3	2.6	2.3	−1.9	−2.4	−2.7
1967	−7.0	4.5	−2.0	−8.4	8.7	3.5	2.5	−3.6	−1.8	−9.7	−3.4
1968	−9.2	0.0	2.4	−6.1	6.1	−0.0	−4.8	−10.9	−5.4	−12.5	−5.5
1969	−3.4	−8.0	14.8	1.3	−0.4	3.3	−5.8	0.5	1.5	−6.5	−1.4
1970	−11.6	−9.4	0.7	3.3		−3.7	−1.1	59.6	2.7	−8.3	3.9

(continued)

TABLE A.10 (*concluded*)

Phase and Year	Construc. Mat. (23)	Intermed. Prod. (24)	Consumer Goods (25)	Invest. Goods (26)	Imports (27)	Competitive Imports (28)	Non-competitive Imports (29)	Raw Material Imports (30)	Exports (31)
II									
1947	−7.6	−3.9	8.3	−13.2	1.4	1.5	1.1		9.0
1948	2.6	2.7	−0.7	−1.0	−7.2	−3.1	−11.8	−15.5	−8.0
1949	15.1	18.7	14.3	8.5	7.5	28.0	21.4	8.9	4.2
1950	−26.6	−20.8	−14.8	−15.8	−13.0	−13.3	−17.0	−13.8	−7.2
1951	−4.8	−4.3	1.2	−1.6	2.7	−2.5	0.6	5.1	12.1
1952	19.4	14.3	4.1	2.9	8.7	10.4	17.2	0.0	16.5
1953	3.0	10.6	7.5	11.2	−6.2	17.1	5.8	−5.6	−1.5
1954	17.4	18.2	23.1	10.8	−1.1	20.5	19.8	12.8	−11.2
1955	14.3	20.4	−0.1	−11.5	−3.2	4.7	25.7	−1.8	9.2
III									
1956	−19.4	−18.8	−22.2	−18.2	−1.5	−20.8	−22.5	4.1	−0.9
1957	−30.1	−31.1	−31.1	−16.2	−0.7	−31.4	−30.2	−8.0	−23.7
1958	11.9	11.8	7.0	9.6	−2.6	2.2	−4.9	10.0	−10.6

IV									
1959	−4.9	−7.5	−7.0	0.6	−1.5	−3.7	−9.3	−19.2	8.9
1960	10.4	9.0	9.8	−3.0	−3.2	11.3	5.0	1.4	3.2
1961	−1.1	0.4	6.3	7.8	−1.8	4.0	2.1	1.3	−5.7
II									
1962	−2.0	−1.7	2.4	−2.0	−3.4	1.6	0.5	−6.6	2.7
1963	−12.5	−9.7	−12.2	−5.6	−9.2	−13.6	−9.0	9.2	−3.7
1964	5.5	11.5	11.1	18.6	18.9	7.0	13.8	8.4	6.8
III									
1965	−0.4	−6.2	−5.5	−9.6	−3.7	−10.2	−3.8	−25.3	8.2
1966	2.3	−1.3	−1.9	5.3	−9.1	1.6	−3.4	−9.3	12.5
1967	−1.4	1.9	0.1	−5.9	0.9	3.7	−6.1	−2.1	−7.8
1968	1.2	−4.7	−7.4	−6.6	−7.0	−6.3	−7.4		−3.8
1969	3.2	3.8	−0.9	−3.0	−5.2	4.9	−1.8		8.7
1970	−2.7	−1.5				−0.5	5.1		

a. The EER(PI)s are from Table A.8. The national accounts NER is a weighted average of all the legal NERs and is calculated by the national accounts offices of CORFO and ODEPLAN. The data in this table give the variation in the effect of the regime beyond that incorporated in the average NER. Figures preceding sectoral and subsectoral names in columns are those used by ODEPLAN [1970] and Jeanneret [1971].

TABLE A.11

Ex Post General-Equilibrium Elasticities of Important Economic Variables in Chile with Respect to Changes in Foreign-Sector Factors

(1 in a column heading designates the first year of the simulation; 4, the third year)

				1. Changes in Prices and	
		Base Simulation[a]		1.1 All Exports	
Line No.	Variables	1	3	1	3
1.	Balance of payments				
1.1	Exports	−.03	−.01	.1	.2
1.1.1	Agricultural	−.08	−.19	.5	.4
1.1.2	Mineral				
1.1.2.1	Large-scale	−.03	−.01	.2	.2
1.1.2.2	Other	−.05	−.01	.0	−.1
1.1.3	Industrial	.12	.15	−.2	.5
1.1.4	Services	−.03	−.03	.0	−.0
1.2	Imports	.03	−.02	.2	.1
1.2.1	Consumption				
1.2.1.1	Staple	−.05	−.01	−.1	−.1
1.2.1.2	Durable	−.09	−.20	−.1	−.0
1.2.1.3	Secondary	.12	.31	−.4	−.7
1.2.2	Investment				
1.2.2.1	Machinery and equip.	−.00	−.05	.0	.4
1.2.2.2	Transport. related	.06	−.04	.1	−.1
1.2.3	Intermediate	.12	−.00	.7	.2
1.2.4	Services	.06	.03	.4	.2
1.3	Other				
1.3.1	Surplus on current acct.[b]	−.31	.02	−1.1	.4
1.3.2	Net bank intl. reserves[b]	−.23	−.22	.1	.2
1.3.3	Govt. deficit financed abroad[b]	−.95	−.10	−92.2	4.3
1.3.4	Black-market rate	.06	−.02	.3	−.1
2.	Cyclical fluctuations				
2.1	Real capacity utilization	−.01	−.00	.0	.1
2.2	Price stability				
2.2.1	GDP deflator	−.01	.02	.3	−.1
2.2.2	Money supply	−.07	−.01	.2	−.0
2.2.3	Monetary base	−.12	−.07	.1	.2
2.2.4	Govt. deficit	−.09	−.01	−.4	.3
2.2.5	Net central bank foreign reserves[b]	−.35	−.32	.1	.3
3.	Resource allocation				
3.1	Product/intermediate input price				
3.1.1	Agriculture	.08	−.03	.1	.2
3.1.2	Mining	.02	−.03	.6	.1
3.1.3	Industry	−.01	−.03	−.1	.1

Foreign Conditions				2. Changes in Chilean Intl. Economic Policy					
Unit Values				2.1 Exchange Rates					
1.2 All Imports		1.3 U.S. Indus. Prod. Index		2.1.1 All Legal Exch. Rates		2.1.2 Brokers Market Rate		2.1.3 Bacha & Taylor Equilibrium Rates	
1	3	1	3	1	3	1	3	1	3
−.4	−.2	.2	.0	.2	.0	.0	.1	.04	.06
−.2	.1	.1	−.1	.3	.4	.0	.2	.10	.19
−.4	−.4	−.1	.2	.2	.0	−.0	.1	.04	.03
.0	.2	1.5	−.0	.0	−.0	.0	.0	.00	.04
−2.4	−.5	−.1	−.7	.9	−.2	−.1	.3	.43	.29
−.2	−.2	.0	.1	.1	−.1	.2	.2	.04	.01
−.2	−.3	.1	.0	−.1	−.1	.0	.0	−.03	−.05
.1	−.2	−.1	−.1	−.1	−.3	−.0	−.0	−.03	−.21
−.2	−.1	−.1	−.2	.1	−.2	−.0	−.0	.05	−.07
−.4	−1.1	−.2	.3	−.6	−1.2	−.1	−.2	−.18	−.54
.1	−.4	.0	.2	−.0	.0	.0	−.0	.01	.03
.4	.0	.1	.2	−.1	.3	.0	−.1	−.05	−.00
−1.0	−.2	.1	−.1	.0	.0	.0	.1	−.01	.03
−.1	−.3	.3	.0	−.1	.1	.0	.1	−.07	−.03
−1.9	−.0	.6	.1	.9	.2	−.1	.7	.23	.46
−1.0	−.8	.1	.6	.1	.5	−.1	.3	.03	.21
102.2	8.7	−1.3	−6.7	−19.1	2.3	6.6	.9	−.79	−1.66
.7	.3	.2	.0	.6	.2	.1	−.1	.20	.39
−.2	.0	.0	−.0	−.0	.1	.0	.1	−.01	.04
.6	.2	.2	−.0	.6	.3	.1	−.1	.22	.45
−.1	−.1	.2	.0	.2	.3	.1	−.0	.05	.35
−.7	−.3	.1	.4	−.1	.1	−.1	.3	−.05	.17
.5	.6	.0	−.6	−.1	.2	.0	.0	.04	.03
−1.4	−1.0	.2	.9	.2	.6	−.1	.4	.04	.28
.1	.1	.0	−.2	−.1	.1	.0	.1	−.03	−.02
−.7	−.2	−.1	−.0	.1	−.1	−.0	.0	.07	.01
−.1	−.1	−.0	.1	−.1	−.1	−.0	−.1	−.02	−.00

TABLE A.11 (*continued*)

				1. Changes in Prices and	
		Base Simulation[a]		1.1 All Exports	
Line No.	Variables	1	3	1	3
3.2	Labor force (secular movements)				
3.2.1	Agriculture	−.00	−.02	−.0	−.0
3.2.2	Mining	−.00	−.01	−.0	.0
3.2.3	Industry	.05	.10	−.0	−.0
3.3	Capital stock				
3.3.1	Agriculture	.02	.00	−.0	.1
3.3.2	Mining	.04	.03	.0	−.0
3.3.3	Industry	.02	.05	−.0	−.0
3.4	Production capacity				
3.4.1	Agriculture	−.08	−.08	−.0	−.0
3.4.2	Mining	−.07	−.06	.0	.0
3.4.3	Industry	.10	.11	−.0	−.0
3.5	GDP				
3.5.1	Agriculture	−.07	−.12	.1	.2
3.5.2	Mining	−.07	−.10	.5	.1
3.5.3	Industry	.05	.03	.1	.3
3.5.4	Goods/services	−.01	−.03	.2	.2
4.	Distribution of income and resources				
4.1	Factoral				
4.1.1	Real wage	.02	.05	−.1	−.3
4.1.1.1	Agriculture	.04	.03	−.1	−.4
4.1.1.2	Mining	−.02	−.06	−.2	−.2
4.1.1.3	Industry	−.08	−.07	−.2	−.4
4.1.1.4	Government	.04	−.07	−.2	−.2
4.1.2	Wage share in income	.04	.11	−.2	−.4
4.2	International				
4.2.1	Net factor income from abroad[b]	.07	−.19	−1.0	.0
4.3	Intertemporal				
4.3.1	Consumption/product	−.00	−.03	.0	.0
4.4	Public vs. private				
4.4.1	Taxes/deflator	−.03	−.00	.1	.1
4.4.1.1	Import	−.08	.03	−.1	.1
4.4.1.2	Large-scale mining	.01	−.22	1.5	.3
4.4.2	Govt. consumption/product	−.05	.03	.1	−.0
5.	Economic growth-related variables				
5.1	GDP	−.00	−.01	.0	.1
5.2	Gross national savings[b]	−.08	.01	.1	.2
5.2.1	Personal[a]	−.46	1.06	−1.9	−95.3
5.2.2	Business[a]	−.42	−.90	3.8	56.6
5.2.3	Government[b]	.32	−.03	.7	−.3
5.3	Capacity	−.01	.01	.0	.0
5.3.1	Investment	.04	.01	.0	.1
5.3.2	Capital stock	.00	.01	.0	−.0

Foreign Conditions				2. Changes in Chilean Intl. Economic Policy					
Unit Values				2.1 Exchange Rates					
1.2 All Imports		1.3 U.S. Indus. Prod. Index		2.1.1 All Legal Exch. Rates		2.1.2 Brokers Market Rate		2.1.3 Bacha & Taylor Equilibrium Rates	
1	3	1	3	1	3	1	3	1	3
−.0	−.0	−.0	−.0	−.0	−.0	−.0	.0	−.00	−.02
−.0	.0	−.0	.0	−.0	.0	−.0	.0	−.00	.01
−.0	−.1	−.0	−.1	−.0	−.1	−.0	.0	−.00	−.06
−.1	−.0	−.0	−.0	−.0	.1	−.0	.0	−.01	−.01
−.0	.3	.0	−.0	.0	−.0	.0	.1	.01	.12
.1	−.0	−.0	−.1	−.0	−.1	−.0	.0	−.01	−.05
−.0	−.0	−.0	−.0	−.0	−.0	−.0	.0	−.00	−.02
.0	−.0	.0	.0	.0	.0	.0	.0	.00	.00
−.0	−.1	−.0	−.1	−.0	−.1	−.0	.0	−.00	−.06
−.2	−.0	.1	−.0	.0	.2	.0	.1	.00	.09
−.5	−.1	.0	−.0	.1	−.0	−.0	.1	.05	.14
−.2	−.1	.1	−.1	−.0	.2	.0	.1	−.02	.05
−.2	−.2	.1	−.1	.1	.0	.0	.1	.02	.06
−.4	−.4	−.1	.1	−.4	−.5	−.0	−.1	−.10	−.23
−.3	−.5	−.1	.2	−.4	−.5	−.0	−.1	−.13	−.19
−.5	−.5	−.2	.0	−.3	−.6	−.1	−.0	−.08	−.26
−.3	−.4	−.1	.2	−.4	−.5	−.1	−.1	−.09	−.22
−.5	−.4	−.2	.1	−.4	−.5	−.1	−.0	−.09	−.20
−.2	−.5	−.1	.1	−.3	−.7	−.1	−.1	−.10	−.17
−1.4	−.6	−.6	−.1	−1.8	−.8	−.2	.1	−.61	−.79
.1	−.0	−.0	.0	.0	−.0	−.0	−.0	.00	−.02
−.4	−.2	−.0	.0	−.1	−.1	−.0	.1	−.03	−.06
.0	−.7	−.1	.4	−.5	−.4	−.1	.0	−.19	−.39
−1.3	−.6	−.1	.1	.2	−.4	−.1	.1	.16	.19
.1	.1	−.0	.0	.0	−.2	−.0	.0	.02	−.03
−.2	.0	.0	−.0	−.0	.1	.0	.1	−.01	.04
−1.4	.4	.3	−.1	.2	.4	.0	.3	.05	.26
5.3	−122.8	−.7	25.4	−2.9	−151.8	−.4	−13.4	−.81	−51.63
7.8	80.4	3.2	−20.3	8.2	91.7	1.2	17.0	2.28	36.92
−1.7	−1.0	−.2	.7	−.5	−.4	−.2	.0	−.17	−.28
.0	.0	−.0	−.0	.0	.0	.0	.0	.00	−.00
−.0	.2	.0	−.2	.0	.0	.0	.0	.00	−.01
−.0	.0	.0	−.0	.0	−.0	.0	.0	.00	−.01

(*continued*)

TABLE A.11 (*continued*)

		2. Changes in Chilean			
				2.3 Quantitative	
		2.2.1 Import Tax Function × 0.9		2.3.1 All QR Indices	
Line No.	Variables	1	3	1	3
1.	Balance of payments				
1.1	Exports	.01	.02	−.7	.2
1.1.1	Agricultural	.01	.01	2.5	1.3
1.1.2	Mineral				
1.1.2.1	Large-scale	.01	.02	−.7	−.3
1.1.2.2	Other	.00	.00	.0	−.7
1.1.3	Industrial	.11	.06	−8.9	4.0
1.1.4	Services	.01	.01	−.9	−.3
1.2	Imports	.00	.01	−2.4	−.1
1.2.1	Consumption				
1.2.1.1	Staple	−.01	.01	−3.2	.2
1.2.1.2	Durable	.01	.01	−2.2	−1.8
1.2.1.3	Secondary	.02	.02	−3.5	−5.2
1.2.2	Investment				
1.2.2.1	Machinery and equip.	−.00	.00	−1.4	−.9
1.2.2.2	Transport. related	−.00	−.01	−4.2	1.8
1.2.3	Intermediate	.01	.01	−.4	.3
1.2.4	Services	−.00	.02	−4.6	.7
1.3	Other				
1.3.1	Surplus on current acct.[b]	.14	.06	10.6	.6
1.3.2	Net bank intl. reserves[b]	.01	.04	.7	1.4
1.3.3	Govt. deficit financed abroad[b]	4.18	−.16	101.4	−6.2
1.3.4	Black-market rate	−.03	−.01	8.0	2.6
2.	Cyclical fluctuations				
2.1	Real capacity utilization	.01	.00	.1	.2
2.2	Price stability				
2.2.1	GDP deflator	−.03	−.01	1.6	1.5
2.2.2	Money supply	.00	.01	1.0	1.5
2.2.3	Monetary base	.01	.03	.5	.6
2.2.4	Govt. deficit	.02	−.01	.4	−.4
2.2.5	Net central bank foreign reserves[b]	.02	.05	1.0	1.9
3.	Resource allocation				
3.1	Product/intermediate input price				
3.1.1	Agriculture	.00	.01	.4	.7
3.1.2	Mining	.02	.01	−.8	−1.0
3.1.3	Industry	−.00	−.00	−.6	−.9

International Economic Policy (continued)					
Restrictions					
2.3.2 Allocation of Imported Capital		2.4.1 2 × Cost Rate for Import Prior Deposits		2.5.1 Export Subsidies: 10% for Agric. and Indus. Exports	
1	3	1	3	1	3
.03	.04	.02	.10	.01	.00
−.02	.01	.03	.02	.04	.01
.02	.03	.02	.13	−.00	.00
.00	.01	.00	.01	.00	−.00
.26	.20	.20	.23	.18	.01
.02	.02	.01	.05	.00	−.00
.04	.05	.00	.02	.00	.00
.16	.12	−.00	.03	−.00	−.00
.01	.03	.01	.04	−.00	−.00
.04	.29	.02	.23	−.01	−.01
−.00	.01	−.00	−.01	.00	.00
−.00	−.02	−.02	−.07	.00	.00
.01	.03	.02	.04	.01	.00
.03	.05	−.00	.02	.01	.00
−.06	−.01	.20	.54	.04	.01
.04	.02	.11	.56	.01	.01
−46.72	−1.89	−14.09	−2.25	6.92	−.02
−.04	−.05	−.05	−.19	.01	.00
.03	.06	.02	.00	.00	.00
−.04	−.04	−.03	−.17	.01	.00
.01	−.02	.09	−.09	.01	.00
.03	.01	.08	.41	.01	.01
−.08	−.26	−.07	−.18	.03	−.00
.05	.03	.15	.75	.01	.01
.17	.39	−.01	−.04	.00	.00
.05	.06	.02	.09	−.00	−.00
−.06	−.16	.01	.01	−.00	−.00

TABLE A.11 (*continued*)

		2. Changes in Chilean			
				2.3 Quantitative	
		2.2.1 Import Tax Function × 0.9		2.3.1 All QR Indices	
Line No.	Variables	1	3	1	3
3.2	Labor force (secular movements)				
3.2.1	Agriculture	.00	.00	−.0	.4
3.2.2	Mining	−.00	.00	−.0	.0
3.2.3	Industry	.00	.01	−.0	1.0
3.3	Capital stock				
3.3.1	Agriculture	.00	.00	−.1	.1
3.3.2	Mining	−.00	−.01	.0	.8
3.3.3	Industry	.00	.00	−.0	.2
3.4	Production capacity				
3.4.1	Agriculture	.00	.00	−.0	.4
3.4.2	Mining	.00	−.00	.0	−.0
3.4.3	Industry	.00	.01	−.0	.9
3.5	GDP				
3.5.1	Agriculture	.01	.01	1.0	.7
3.5.2	Mining	.01	.01	−.5	.6
3.5.3	Industry	.01	.01	.8	1.5
3.5.4	Goods/services	.00	.01	.8	1.4
4.	Distribution of income and resources				
4.1	Factoral				
4.1.1	Real wage	.02	.01	−1.1	−2.7
4.1.1.1	Agriculture	.01	.00	−.9	−1.9
4.1.1.2	Mining	.02	.01	−1.6	−4.4
4.1.1.3	Industry	.02	.00	−1.4	−3.4
4.1.1.4	Government	.02	.01	−1.5	−3.0
4.1.2	Wage share in income	.01	.01	−1.2	−3.1
4.2	International				
4.2.1	Net factor income from abroad[b]	.06	.02	−4.0	−5.8
4.3	Intertemporal				
4.3.1	Consumption/product	−.01	−.00	−.1	.2
4.4	Public vs. private				
4.4.1	Taxes/deflator	.01	.01	−.9	−.7
4.4.1.1	Import	−.09	.01	−4.1	−1.9
4.4.1.2	Large-scale mining	.04	.02	−2.3	−1.2
4.4.2	Govt. consumption/product	−.01	−.00	−.5	−1.0
5.	Economic growth-related variables				
5.1	GDP	.01	.00	.1	.2
5.2	Gross national savings[b]	.07	−.00	−1.0	−1.6
5.2.1	Personal[a]	.25	2.22	−15.6	−1030.5
5.2.2	Business[a]	−.21	−1.44	34.4	414.2
5.2.3	Government[b]	−.02	.03	−2.7	−1.0
5.3	Capacity	.00	.00	.0	.0
5.3.1	Investment	−.00	.01	−1.3	1.5
5.3.2	Capital stock	−.00	.00	−.1	−.1

International Economic Policy (continued)

Restrictions

2.3.2 Allocation of Imported Capital		2.4.1 2 × Cost Rate for Import Prior Deposits		2.5.1 Export Subsidies: 10% for Agric. and Indus. Exports	
1	3	1	3	1	3
−.00	−.01	.00	.01	−.00	−.00
−.00	.00	−.00	.00	−.00	.00
−.01	−.04	.00	.02	−.00	−.00
1.48	3.60	.00	−.01	−.00	.00
.05	.16	.00	−.02	.00	.00
−.04	−.09	.00	.01	−.00	−.00
−.00	−.01	.00	.01	−.00	−.00
.00	.00	.00	.00	.00	.00
−.01	−.04	.00	−.02	−.00	−.00
−.01	−.01	.02	.01	.00	.00
−.00	−.01	.00	.06	.00	.00
.05	.03	.04	.02	.00	.00
−.01	−.05	.00	.03	.00	.00
.02	.15	.02	.12	−.00	−.01
.01	−.03	.01	.10	−.00	−.01
.01	.02	.03	.16	−.01	−.01
−.01	−.02	.02	.11	−.00	−.01
.01	.01	.03	.16	−.00	−.00
.02	.14	.01	.12	−.00	−.01
.05	.08	.09	.40	−.01	−.01
−.02	−.04	−.01	−.01	−.00	−.00
.05	.07	.03	.09	−.00	.00
.08	.06	.04	.25	−.00	.00
.05	.04	.04	.26	−.00	−.00
−.01	.01	−.01	.01	−.00	−.00
.03	.05	.02	.01	.00	.00
.08	.29	.18	.09	.01	.00
.19	73.39	.55	40.30	−.01	−1.83
−.52	−12.85	−.62	−18.53	.10	1.02
.24	.23	.18	.40	−.01	.00
.00	−.01	.00	.00	.00	−.00
.53	.60	−.02	−.04	.00	.00
.05	.13	−.00	−.00	.00	−.00

(*continued*)

TABLE A.11 (*continued*)

		2. Changes in Chilean			
		2.6 Policy Toward			
		2.6.1 Exch. Rate for Large-Scale Mining		2.6.2 Aver. Direct Tax Function × 0.9	
Line No.	Variables	1	3	1	3
1.	Balance of payments				
1.1	Exports	.2	.2	.01	.01
1.1.1	Agricultural	.1	.3	.00	.01
1.1.2	Mineral				
1.1.2.1	Large-scale	.3	.2	.01	.01
1.1.2.2	Other	.0	.0	.00	−.00
1.1.3	Industrial	−.1	.4	.02	.02
1.1.4	Services	.0	−.1	.00	−.00
1.2	Imports	.1	.0	.00	.00
1.2.1	Consumption				
1.2.1.1	Staple	−.1	−.1	−.00	.00
1.2.1.2	Durable	−.1	−.0	.00	.00
1.2.1.3	Secondary	−.2	−.6	−.00	−.01
1.2.2	Investment				
1.2.2.1	Machinery and equip.	.0	.0	−.00	.00
1.2.2.2	Transport. related	.0	−.1	−.00	−.00
1.2.3	Intermediate	.1	.2	.01	.00
1.2.4	Services	.2	.1	.01	.00
1.3	Other				
1.3.1	Surplus on current acct.[b]	.6	.8	.06	.02
1.3.2	Net bank intl. reserves[b]	.1	.3	−.00	.01
1.3.3	Govt. deficit financed abroad[b]	170.2	2.6	2.99	.01
1.3.4	Black-market rate	.2	−.0	−.00	−.00
2.	Cyclical fluctuations				
2.1	Real capacity utilization	.0	.1	.00	.00
2.2	Price stability				
2.2.1	GDP deflator	.2	−.0	−.00	−.00
2.2.2	Money supply	.2	.0	.00	.00
2.2.3	Monetary base	.1	.3	−.00	.01
2.2.4	Govt. deficit	.8	.2	.01	−.00
2.2.5	Net central bank foreign reserves[b]	.1	.5	−.00	.01
3.	Resource allocation				
3.1	Product/intermediate input price				
3.1.1	Agriculture	.0	.2	−.00	.00
3.1.2	Mining	−.1	.0	−.00	.00
3.1.3	Industry	−.0	−.2	−.00	−.00

International Economic Policy (continued)

Large-Scale Mining

2.6.3 Investment × 1.1		2.6.4 Mining Exports		2.7.1 Foreign Debt Shift Toward Internal Financing of Govt. Deficit	
1	3	1	3	1	3
−.00	.01	.7	−.0	.00	−.03
−.00	.01	.1	.6	.00	−.08
−.00	.01	1.0	.0	.00	.00
.00	.00	1.0	.0	.00	−.02
.00	.02	−.7	−.2	−.00	−.26
−.00	.00	.1	−.2	.00	−.01
.00	−.00	.2	−.0	.00	−.01
.01	−.01	−.1	−.4	−.00	−.00
−.00	−.01	−.2	−.1	−.00	.02
−.01	.00	−.6	−1.0	−.00	.21
.00	−.00	.1	.2	.00	−.01
.00	−.01	.2	.1	.00	−.02
.00	.01	.5	.1	.00	−.02
.00	.00	.9	−.0	.00	−.02
−.03	.07	2.6	.1	−.01	−.17
−.01	.04	.5	.1	.00	−.23
−.13	−.07	50.4	.9	−.84	3.17
.00	−.01	.6	.1	.00	.02
.00	.00	.0	.2	.00	−.02
.01	−.01	.5	.0	.00	.01
.01	−.01	.5	.1	.00	.03
−.01	.03	.4	−.1	.00	.05
−.00	.00	.2	.1	.00	−.08
−.02	.05	.7	.1	.00	−.30
.01	.01	.1	.2	.00	−.08
−.00	.01	−.3	−.2	.01	−.02
−.00	−.01	−.1	−.2	−.00	.07

TABLE A.11 (*concluded*)

Line No.	Variables	2. Changes in Chilean — 2.6 Policy Toward — 2.6.1 Exch. Rate for Large-Scale Mining: 1	3	2.6.2 Aver. Direct Tax Function × 0.9: 1	3
3.2	Labor force (secular movements)				
3.2.1	Agriculture	−.0	−.0	.00	.00
3.2.2	Mining	−.0	.0	−.00	.00
3.2.3	Industry	−.0	−.0	.00	.00
3.3	Capital stock				
3.3.1	Agriculture	−.0	.1	.00	.00
3.3.2	Mining	.0	.1	.00	.00
3.3.3	Industry	−.0	.0	−.00	.00
3.4	Production capacity				
3.4.1	Agriculture	−.0	−.0	.00	.00
3.4.2	Mining	.0	.0	.00	.00
3.4.3	Industry	−.0	−.0	.00	.00
3.5	GDP				
3.5.1	Agriculture	.1	.2	.00	.00
3.5.2	Mining	.0	.1	.02	.00
3.5.3	Industry	.1	.3	.00	.01
3.5.4	Goods/services	.1	.2	.01	.00
4.	Distribution of income and resources				
4.1	Factoral				
4.1.1	Real wage	−.1	−.2	.00	−.00
4.1.1.1	Agriculture	−.1	−.3	.00	−.00
4.1.1.2	Mining	−.2	−.2	.00	−.00
4.1.1.3	Industry	−.1	−.3	.00	−.00
4.1.1.4	Government	−.2	−.1	.00	−.00
4.1.2	Wage share in income	−.1	−.4	−.00	−.00
4.2	International				
4.2.1	Net factor income from abroad[b]	−.9	−.0	−.01	.00
4.3	Intertemporal				
4.3.1	Consumption/product	−.0	−.0	−.00	−.00
4.4	Public vs. private				
4.4.1	Taxes/deflator	−.0	.0	−.00	.00
4.4.1.1	Import	−.1	−.1	.00	−.00
4.4.1.2	Large-scale mining	−.1	.2	−.08	.01
4.4.2	Govt. consumption/product	−.0	−.0	−.00	−.00
5.	Economic growth-related variables				
5.1	GDP	.0	.1	.00	.00
5.2	Gross national savings[b]	.3	.3	.03	.00
5.2.1	Personal[a]	−.8	−72.2	.05	−1.00
5.2.2	Business[a]	3.2	48.4	.05	.59
5.2.3	Government[b]	−.2	−.1	−.03	.00
5.3	Capacity	.0	.0	.00	.00
5.3.1	Investment	.0	.1	.00	.00
5.3.2	Capital stock	.0	.0	.00	.00

International Economic Policy (concluded)					
Large-Scale Mining					
2.6.3 Investment × 1.1		2.6.4 Mining Exports		2.7.1 Foreign Debt Shift Toward Internal Financing of Govt. Deficit	
1	3	1	3	1	3
−.00	−.00	−.0	−.1	−.00	−.01
−.00	.00	−.0	.0	−.00	.00
−.00	−.00	−.0	−.1	−.00	−.02
−.00	−.00	−.0	.1	−.00	−.02
.06	.05	.1	.2	.00	−.01
−.00	−.00	−.0	−.1	−.00	−.01
−.00	−.00	−.0	−.1	−.00	−.01
.00	.00	.0	.0	.00	.00
−.00	−.00	−.0	−.1	−.00	−.01
.00	.01	.1	.3	.00	−.04
−.00	.01	.1	−.0	.00	−.01
.00	.01	.2	.4	.00	−.07
−.00	.00	.2	.2	.00	−.04
−.00	.00	−.3	−.5	−.00	.07
−.00	−.01	−.2	−.4	−.00	.13
−.01	.00	−.5	−.5	−.00	.04
−.01	−.00	−.4	−.5	−.00	.10
−.01	−.00	−.4	−.3	−.00	.05
−.00	−.00	−.3	−.3	−.00	.11
−.01	.02	−1.7	−.2	−.01	.04
−.00	−.00	−.1	−.0	.00	.01
−.00	.01	−.2	.0	.00	.00
−.00	.01	−.4	.0	−.00	.09
−.01	.02	−.4	−.3	.01	−.02
−.00	−.00	−.1	−.1	.00	.04
.00	.00	.0	.2	.00	−.03
.01	.02	.6	.4	.00	−.13
−.02	.97	−2.2	−223.4	−.02	20.00
.07	.25	8.4	81.1	.04	−15.16
−.00	.02	−.8	−.1	.00	.08
.00	.00	.0	−.0	−.00	−.00
.03	−.00	.1	−.0	.00	−.07
.00	.00	.0	−.0	.00	−.00

Notes to Table A.11

NOTE: The simulation period is 1962–64. All underlying data are in constant escudo or index terms, except lines 1.3.2 and 2.2.5, which are in dollars; line 1.3.3, which is in escudos per dollar; and lines 2.2.2–2.2.4, which are in escudos.

All simulations are dynamic in that lagged simulated values of endogenous variables are used whenever it is possible to do so. Elasticities are defined as the ratio of the percentage deviation from the base simulation values for the series listed on the left to the percentage deviation from the base simulation values for the variables identified in the column headings. Instead of elasticities, proportional deviations from the base simulation (or, in the case of the base simulation itself, from the actual data) are given for those simulations for which elasticities are not easy to define; those cases are identified in the notes following.

For either elasticities or proportional deviations, those variables defined as differences between two flows (lines 1.3.1–1.3.3, 2.2.4, 2.2.5, 4.2.1, and 5.2.1–5.2.3) have relatively large deviations from the base simulation value. In all simulations except for columns 2.1.3, 2.2.1, 2.6.3, and 2.7.1, changes indicated in the column heading occurred only for the first year of the simulation, and in all subsequent years, the variable assumed the base simulation values.

Col. **2.1.3** Bacha and Taylor [1973] estimate that the equilibrium rates for the first three years of the simulation period equal the actual national accounts rate multiplied by 1.45, 1.35, and 1.61. The figures shown are the proportional deviations resulting from use of these adjusted rates. The Bacha-Taylor derivation is based upon a Robinson-Metzler–type model in which fiscal and monetary policies are not included explicitly (other than foreign trade taxes), imports and exports depend only on their own prices, an attempt is made to abstract from short-run cyclical effects, and the equilibrium exchange rate is defined to be "that which prevails in a floating foreign exchange market where all import restrictions and export subsidies are removed." The underlying price elasticities utilized for these estimates are −2.0 for import demand, 3.0 for export supply, ∞ for import supply, and −9.0 for export demand. (The absolute values of these import demand and export supply elasticities seem surprisingly large in light of the estimates presented above in Chapters 6 and 7. Bacha and Taylor claim that estimates of elasticities based on historical data are biased downward because of the effects of quantitative restrictions and uncertainty. However, attempts were made to include these effects in the estimation of the functions presented in Tables 6.3 and 7.2.) The Bacha and Taylor partial-equilibrium model clearly differs from the macroeconometric general-equilibrium model utilized in this study in a number of important respects. Nevertheless, the consequences of utilizing their equilibrium exchange rates within the present general-equilibrium model are of considerable interest because of the consensus of a large group of economists that the Chilean escudo was overvalued by the order of magnitude of the Bacha and Taylor estimates in the 1960s: Jeanneret [1971:165] estimates the ratio of the equilibrium to the actual rate to have been 1.68 for 1961; Hachette [1966:50] estimates 1.45 for 1961 and 1.63 for 1962; Selowsky [1970:41] gives 1.35 for the late 1960s; and Bacha and Taylor give 1.50, 1.40, 1.30, and 1.24 for 1965–68 and 1.25 for April 1969.

Col. **2.2.1** The figures shown are proportional deviations from base simulations resulting from multiplication of the tax function by 0.9 in the first year of the simulation. To obtain elasticities with respect to the level of real import taxes, these proportional deviations must be divided by −0.9.

Col. **2.3.1** Each index is changed by the same deviation of 1 percent from the base value, although for some of the indices (in particular, for the widely used Ffrench-Davis index) such a change is relatively large in comparison to historical variations in the index. Other variables in the model, e.g., the black-market exchange rate or the export capacity to import, or various dummy variables, which also represent the effects of quantitative restrictions are not changed exogenously, but some of these variables do change endogenously and substantially (see lines 1.3.2, 1.3.4, and 2.2.4).

Col. **2.3.2** The proportional sectoral distribution of investment-goods imports is assumed to deviate from that which actually prevailed on average from 1962 through 1966 toward an alternative which favors agriculture and mining at the expense of industry.

For all years of this simulation, the sectoral allocation of imported capital in proportional terms is changed from 0.03 to 0.15 for agriculture, from 0.18 to 0.25 for mining, from 0.37 to 0.18 for industry, from 0.16 to 0.17 for the rest of the industries combined, except transportation (unchanged at 0.19) and utilities (unchanged at 0.06). Such imports of capital goods are assumed to enter the sectoral investment functions with fixed coefficients; i.e., the deviation from actual average investment imports allocated to a specific sector, multiplied by a coefficient representing the average ratio of total to imported investment in the sector in 1962–66, is assumed to affect investment in that sector directly by an additive term (the data used for calculating the sectoral ratios and the average sectoral distribution of investment imports are from Meza [1967]). In interpreting the results presented here, it should be kept in mind that the model is specified so that an increment in capital stock during year t results in an increment in capacity only in the year $t + 1$. Therefore, the first-year impacts do not include a shift in the distribution of capacities across sectors even though a shift in the distribution of investment does occur. Note also that the figures shown are proportional deviations from the base simulation, not elasticities.

Col. **2.3.1** For this simulation, investment in large-scale mining was made exogenous and held at the base value except for a 10 percent increase in the first year. Because of the very low level of investment in large-scale mining in the first year, due to growing dissatisfaction of Chile with the *Nuevo Trato* and of the foreign-owned mining companies with the failure of the Chilean government to provide long-term tax and exchange rate guarantees and guarantees against expropriation (see subsection 4.2.1, above), a 10 per cent increase is not particularly large in absolute terms nor is the impact of this increment particularly large.

Col. **2.4.1** The actual import prior-deposit cost rate was very low in 1962, and the rate was therefore doubled in this simulation, from 0.0097 to 0.0194; the proportional deviations shown are for this doubled rate.

Col. **2.5.1** The subsidy is at a rate equal to a 10 per cent increase in world prices for these exports for the first year of the simulation. Since the change amounts to an infinite increase in these subsidies relative to the zero base, elasticities cannot be defined. The figures shown are proportional deviations from the base simulation.

Col. **2.6.2** Function for average direct taxes from large-scale mining multiplied by 0.9. The figures shown are proportional deviations.

Col. **2.6.3** Investment in large-scale mining is made exogenous at the base simulation level except that the first-year value is multiplied by 1.10. The figures shown are proportional deviations.

Col. **2.6.4** Exports from mining are made exogenous at the base simulation level except for a first-year change which is assumed directly to affect mining inventory levels. Assumed changes in mining exports are based on an estimate of −4.0 for the price elasticity of demand for Chilean copper. The figure of −4.0 is based on Chile's share of sales in the world market and estimates of price elasticities in the world market for total world demand and for supply from other countries. For example, see Bacha and Taylor [1973] or de Castro and de la Cuadra [1971:17].

Col. **2.7.1** In each year, half of the government deficit beyond that financed by the banking system is assumed to be financed abroad. For all the other simulations, all the changes in the government deficit from the base level are assumed to be financed externally by a shift in the composition of capital movements between private and public flows, reflecting the great dependence of Chile on foreign sources for such financing in recent phases. Because the government deficit financed abroad in the first year of the base simulation is so small, the change in method is applied in all three years of the simulation. Since this change does not permit a meaningful interpretation of elasticity, proportional deviations are shown.

a. Proportional deviations from actual values.

b. The very large values for this variable in some cases reflect the fact that the actual value and, also, the base simulation value are very close to zero. Therefore, the sign of the elasticity or of the deviation is more pertinent than the magnitude.

Appendix B

Definition of Measures of Protection and Costs Used in Table 5.3

In this appendix, definitions and sources for the ITRs, EPRs, and DRCs included in Table 5.3 are given, and then the empirical importance of some definitional distinctions is explored.

B.1 DEFINITIONS AND SOURCES

ITR1. Jeanneret [1971:153–159] estimated these 1961 rates by the following steps. First, she classified the approximately 5,000 import items for July–September 1961 in conformity with SITC categories and with the 1962 Chilean input-output table. She then determined the tariff equivalent of various protective policies (including special regimes and prohibitive policies) on each item and aggregated the individual-item tariff equivalents to the four-digit SITC level by using domestic import weights. Finally, she further aggregated the four-digit SITC level averages to the subsectoral level of the 1962 input-output table by using world trade weights in order to lessen downward biases due to import responses to the tariff structure.

Although problems exist in the underlying calculations because of a certain degree of arbitrariness in making various sets of data compatible and in averaging and because of price differences that are due to quality differences, this set of estimates is the most thorough and the best available for Chile.

ITR2. These estimates are unweighted arithmetic averages of the 92-item estimates of de la Cuadra [1971] for 1967 (see Table A.3), who used the 1967 manufacturing census, customs data, and direct interviews with producers.[1]

The 92 items include the most important products in each use category and at least one representative item for each two-digit SITC industrial division. The aggregation procedure introduces a bias of unknown direction.

ITR3. Bacha and Taylor [1973] averaged the tax rebate or drawback rates for individual products in order to obtain ITRs for sectoral exports for 1968. The resulting estimates probably overstate average sectoral subsidies because in many sectors very few products received drawbacks.[2] Nevertheless, they are the best available indicators of incentives for sectoral exports in the late 1960s.

EPR1. Jeanneret [1971:159] calculated these estimates for 1961 from ITR1 and from data in the ODEPLAN [1970] input-output table for 1962. She calculated domestic net value added from the input-output data by subtracting depreciation and indirect taxes minus subsidies from gross value added; subtracting trade and transportation costs from both the output and input sides in order to shift from user to producer prices; and adding the value added in the production of nontraded inputs to the value added in the processing industry in question, following the Cordon [1966] procedure.

If, in fact, substantial substitution among intermediate inputs is possible, the use of an input-output table based on 1962 data may lead to an understatement of the use of imported inputs because of the foreign-exchange crisis of that year (see section 1.4). Unfortunately, no other Chilean input-output study is yet available; so all the alternatives based on Chilean input-output coefficients suffer from this same deficiency.

EPR2. Bacha and Taylor [1973] also started from the ITR1 for 1961 and the input-output data for 1962. They corrected for specific differences between world and domestic prices of intermediate-goods imports by utilizing unpublished ODEPLAN data such as that in Table B.1 under the assumption that no arbitrage occurred.[3] They based their estimates on the Hufbauer [1968] formula, with gross value added supplemented by the value added of inputs of nontradable goods as in the Cordon procedure.[4]

EPR3. These estimates are unweighted arithmetic averages of the 92-item estimates of de la Cuadra [1971] for 1967 (Table A.3). The data sources are the same as for ITR2. These rates are focused on gross value added. Nontraded goods are assumed to be supplied at constant costs (or, equivalently, the EPR on home goods is zero), as Balassa [1971:17–18, 321–325] has recommended.[5] The direction of bias due to the aggregation procedure is unknown.[6]

EPR4. Bacha and Taylor [1973] calculated these estimates in the same way as EPR2, except that the 1968 export-oriented ITR3s were used for the final-product prices. Therefore, ITRs for inputs are assumed to be identical to those in ITR1 for 1961, and the intermediate-input coefficients are assumed to be the same as those in 1962. Since the size of sectoral subsidies is probably

TABLE B.1
Ratios of Domestic Prices to c.i.f. Prices by Sectoral Destination and End Use, 1962

Sector[a] of Destination		Use		
		Investment	Intermediate	Consumption
1	Agriculture, fishing, and forestry	1.20	1.31 1.56	1.76
4	Iron mining		2.54 2.32 1.25	
9–13,	Food, beverages, tobacco, textiles, footwear, clothing, and leather	1.40	2.04 1.75	3.31 2.12 4.65 1.80
14–17	Wood, furniture, paper, printing, and publishing	1.51	1.32 2.10 1.20 1.63	2.05 1.79 1.77 4.63
19–21	Rubber, chemical, petroleum, and coal products		1.75 1.58 1.60	2.23 2.28
22	Nonmetallic minerals		2.30	2.87
23	Basic metals	1.55	1.67	
24	Metallic products	1.50 1.40 1.45 1.48	2.12 2.11 2.38 2.54	3.00 4.62 4.11
	Total	1.44	1.69	2.71

SOURCE: Department of Social Accounts in ODEPLAN as presented in Jul [1969: 152].

a. The sectoral numbers are those of ODEPLAN; see Table A.3, above.

overstated in the ITR estimates (see below), effective protection for exports is probably overestimated in EPR4.

DRC1. Bacha and Taylor [1973] constructed these 1961 estimates from ITR1, the 1962 input-output table, and average sectoral capital-output ratios for 1962–1967; they assumed a shadow rate of return of 20 per cent on capital.[7]

DRC2. Bacha and Taylor [1973] calculated these estimates in the same manner as those for DRC1 except that the 1968 export-oriented ITR3s were used for the final-product prices. They assumed that the ITRs and intermediate-input coefficients have been stable since the early 1960s, as they did for EPR4.

B.2 EMPIRICAL IMPORTANCE OF SOME DEFINITIONAL DISTINCTIONS

B.2.1 Aggregation Factors.

i. Guisinger and Schydlowsky [1971:279] conclude that the consistency between ITRs and EPRs increases as aggregation increases.[8] In the limit, of course, they must be correct in that the ITR is identical to the EPR at the one-sector level of aggregation. A comparison of the correlation between ITR2 and EPR3 with the correlation between the ITRs and EPRs in Table A.3 provides a test of their claim because the former pair is only an aggregated version of the latter. For the 28-sector aggregation the correlation coefficient is 0.50. For the 92-product aggregation, the correlation coefficient is 0.52. Thus, this example does not support the Guisinger and Schydlowsky conclusion.

ii. The Jeanneret estimates permit the exploration of the impact of weighted versus unweighted averaging. In addition to the 28-sector estimates in ITR1 and EPR1, Jeanneret presents 57-sector estimates in Balassa [1971: 66–67]. Unweighted averaging of the 57-sector estimates provides alternative ITRs and EPRs at the 28-sector level that are identical to ITR1 and EPR1 except for the weights in the averaging. The more these alternative estimates are correlated with ITR1 and EPR1, respectively, the less important is the choice of the averaging procedure. In fact, this example suggests that the choice of weights is quite important. For the ITRs, the correlation coefficient is 0.67, which is significantly nonzero at the 5 per cent level, but which implies a substantially different cross-sectoral pattern. For the EPRs, the correlation coefficient is not significantly nonzero at the 5 per cent level.

iii. Extreme values on a more disaggregate level may substantially affect the cross-sectoral pattern on a more aggregate level. To investigate this possibility, an alternative set of EPRs was constructed from Table A.3 by excluding the highest and lowest product estimates within each sector that had three or more products. For the sectors so chosen, the correlation between this alternative set of EPRs and EPR3 is 0.99. Thus, the estimated sectoral averages are about the same whether or not the underlying extreme individual product rates are included.

B.2.2 Variations in EPR Definitions.

i. Balassa and Cordon have emphasized the importance of alternative treatments of nontraded inputs (see EPR1 and EPR3 in section B.1). Jeanneret [1971:159] presents alternative EPR estimates which are identical to EPR1 except that the Balassa procedure is followed. The range and the standard deviations are somewhat smaller for the estimates based on the Cordon formula. The correlation coefficient between the two sets of estimates, however, is 1.00. In respect to the cross-sectoral pattern, therefore, the distinction in the treatment of nontradable goods does not seem to be important.

ii. Lewis and Guisinger [1968] criticize EPR definitions in which the difference between domestic and international value added is compared to international value added because such definitions (under the assumption that international value added is positive) give an EPR which is bounded by −1.0 as domestic value added approaches zero. For small values of domestic value added relative to international value added, in other words, quite large proportional differences in domestic value added imply very little change in the EPR. Therefore, Lewis and Guisinger propose that the difference between domestic and international value added be compared to domestic value added, not to international value added.[9] Bacha and Taylor [1973] present a set of EPR estimates which is identical to EPR2 except for this change. De la Cuadra [1971] likewise presents an alternative set of EPR estimates which is identical to EPR3 except for this change. In both cases the correlation coefficient between the estimates in Table 5.3 and the alternatives with domestic value added in the denominator is 0.81.[10] The implications of such an alternative for cross-sectoral patterns in these two cases, therefore, do seem to be significant, but not overwhelmingly so.

iii. The distinctions between EPR1 and EPR2 are primarily two. First, EPR1 is based on net value added, while EPR2 is constructed from gross value added because the depreciation estimates are questionable. Second, EPR2 incorporates information about varying ITRs for different end uses (i.e., lower rates for intermediate inputs), but EPR1 does not. The impact of these two differences is quite substantial. Apparently because of the use of the more gross measure, the EPR2 estimates vary much less across sectors than do the EPR1 estimates. For EPR2, the range and standard deviation are 4.88 and 1.17. For EPR1, the corresponding figures are 28.98 and 5.52. Moreover, the correlation coefficient between the two sets of estimates, while significantly nonzero at the 5 per cent level, is relatively low—0.43 (Table A.4).

B.2.3 Variations in DRC Definitions.

Bacha and Taylor [1973] present alternative sets of DRC estimates which are identical to DRC1 and DRC2, respectively, except that the sectoral returns on capital implied by the input-output data are utilized instead of a 20 per cent shadow rate. The effects of this alternative treatment of the returns on capital are quite substantial. The alternative DRC estimates vary much less across sectors. For the alternative to DRC1, the range and standard deviation across sectors are 3.15 and 0.74 compared to 21.09 and 5.98 for DRC1 itself. For the alternative to DRC2, the range and standard deviation across sectors are 0.30 and 0.10 compared to 3.39 and 0.86 for DRC2. Moreover, the patterns across sectors are substantially different. The correlation coefficient between DRC1 and its alternative is 0.73, and that between DRC2 and its alternative is 0.53. The use of the proper definition of the return on capital, therefore, is of substantial empirical importance.

B.2.4 Consistency Among the Alternative Measures.

i. Cohen [1971:139] concludes that "one learns a lot—but not everything" about the EPR structure by looking at the ITR structure. He finds that in 15 of the 26 cases that he examined the ITR structure could predict more than half of the variance in the EPRs and that 23 of the 26 relevant correlation coefficients were significantly nonzero at the 1 per cent level. The implication of the estimates in tables 5.3 and A.4 is that in the Chilean case less is learned about the EPR structure from the ITRs than Cohen found on the average in his 26 cases. Two of the four correlation coefficients are significantly nonzero at the 1 per cent level, and in only two of the four cases could the ITR structure predict more than half of the variance in the EPRs.[11] For Chile, therefore, the returns to the additional work involved in calculating EPRs are higher than Cohen claims is the case generally.

ii. Under strong assumptions, ITRs, EPRs, and DRCs imply the same shadow price of foreign exchange.[12] Not surprisingly, those special conditions did not exist in Chile in the 1960s. Despite their absence, the extent to which the alternative measures are consistent in their variations across sectors is an interesting question. The off-diagonal blocks of correlation coefficients in Table A.4 provide an answer. If one includes all elements in these blocks, the answer is, "Not very consistent." Of the 26 relevant correlation coefficients, only 5 are positive and significantly nonzero at the 5 per cent level and for only 3 pairs would one set of estimates predict as much as half of the variance in the other. This conclusion, however, reflects more the changes in the regime over time that are discussed in Part II than intermeasure differences.[13] Among the 9 coefficients for which both sets in the pair refer to the same year, in fact, considerably greater consistency is found. Five of these coefficients are positive and significantly nonzero at the 5 per cent level. In their case, estimates for one variable in each pair correlated would predict at least half of the variance in the other.

NOTES

1. De la Cuadra is not clear about the dates of the interviews but the timing of his writing is consistent with interviews as late as 1970, when the international economic regime was more liberal than in 1967.

2. On the basis of Jul's [1969] study, moreover, there is doubt that drawbacks equaled the difference between domestic and f.o.b. prices as generally as Bacha and Taylor claim. The existence of some effective quotas (especially for agricultural goods), for example, implies that the drawback rates overstated incentives to export.

3. The assumption of no arbitrage among end uses may not be as strong as it seems on the face of it because in many sectors the goods for intermediate use are quite distinct from those for consumption or investment use.

4. However, they made no attempt to distinguish between tradable and nontradable inputs used in earlier stages for the production of nontradable goods.

5. The Balassa treatment of nontradable goods tends to overstate the cost of such goods at world prices, and to underestimate value added in world prices and to overestimate effective protection of domestic value added. However, the results in section B.2 below indicate that the choice between the Cordon and the Balassa treatments of nontradable goods makes little empirical difference.

6. Basevi [1971] and Tumlir and Till [1971] discuss some of the relevant considerations for such aggregation. The discussion below, in section B.2, suggests that the exclusion of extreme values before aggregating does not significantly affect the cross-sectional pattern.

7. The studies by Bitar and Trivelli [1971] and Taylor [1973a], however, suggest that the shadow rate of return on capital in Chile may have been somewhat lower than 20 per cent in the 1960s.

8. Guisinger and Schydlowsky find a consistent pattern without exceptions for eight countries, including Chile. For Chile, on a 10-sector level of aggregation, they report a coefficient of determination (corrected for degrees of freedom?) of 0.81. For 56 sectors, they report a coefficient of determination of 0.56. This comparison is based on partially unpublished estimates by Jeanneret.

9. If E_1 is the EPR with domestic value added in the denominator and E_2 is the EPR with international value added in the denominator, then the relationship between E_1 and E_2 is $E_2 = E_1/(1 + E_1)$. If E_1 is zero, E_2 also is zero. If E_1 is not zero but is greater than -1.0, E_2 is less than E_1, but has the same sign. As E_1 approaches -1.0 from above (i.e., domestic value added approaches zero), E_2 approaches positive infinity. If E_1 is less than -1.0 (i.e., if either domestic or international value added is negative, but not both), E_2 is positive.

10. On the 92-product level of Table A.4, however, the correlation coefficient is somewhat lower—0.59.

11. Table A.4 contains correlation coefficients for 28 sectors. The correlation coefficient is 0.52 for the 92-product aggregation. The square of the correlation coefficient indicates the extent which one set of estimates is consistent with the variance in another.

12. Krueger [1972a:54] demonstrates that DRCs and EPRs are identical if "(1) all goods are traded (or tradable); (2) there are no transportation costs; (3) factors of production are perfectly mobile within the domestic economy but perfectly immobile internationally; and (4) all domestic markets are perfectly competitive." However, as Balassa and Schydlowsky [1972:67] note, the first assumption is redundant given the second assumption. The purpose of the fourth assumption presumably is to eliminate any discrepancies between market and shadow prices, but would seem to require the explicit assumption of no externalities in addition to that of perfect competition. In any case, there is no reason why in principle shadow prices could not be used instead of market prices for EPR calculations as well as for DRCs if that would better serve the purpose of the estimation.

ITRs and EPRs, of course, become identical if there are no intermediate inputs or if the nominal protection on the intermediate inputs is identical to that on the final product.

13. The lack of significant coefficients among elements in the on-diagonal blocks (which refer to intrameasured differences primarily because of the different timing of the estimates) also suggest this qualification. Among the 10 relevant correlation coefficients, only 2 are positive and significantly nonzero at the 5 per cent level, and in no case would one set of estimates predict as much as half of the variance in the other set in the pair.

Appendix C

Impact of Devaluation in a Simple Keynesian Model

C.1 A SIMPLE KEYNESIAN MODEL

Consider the following simple Keynesian model: [1]

$$Y = Y(L, K); Y_K > 0, Y_L > 0, Y_{KK} < 0, Y_{LL} < 0, \quad Y_{LK} = Y_{KL} > 0 \tag{C.1}$$

$$\frac{w}{p} = Y_L \tag{C.2}$$

$$C = C(Y - T - \delta K - \frac{M^* + B}{p} \pi, i - \pi); 1 > C_1 > 0, C_2 < 0 \tag{C.3}$$

$$I = I(Y_K - (i + \delta - \pi)); I' > 0 \tag{C.4}$$

$$M = M(Y, p, x, p^M, q); M_Y > 0, M_p > 0, M_x < 0, M_{p^M} < 0, M_q < 0 \tag{C.5}$$

$$X = X(p^X, x, w); X_{p^x} > 0, X_x > 0, X_w < 0 \tag{C.6}$$

$$Y = C + I + G + X - M + \delta K \tag{C.7}$$

$$\frac{M^*}{p} = m(i, Y); m_i < 0, m_Y > 0 \tag{C.8}$$

$$T = T(Y, M, X, \pi); T_Y > 0, T_M > 0, T_X > 0, T_\pi < 0 \tag{C.9}$$

$$S = p^X X - p^M M + F(i, q); F_i > 0, F_q \gtreqless 0 \tag{C.10}$$

C.1 is an instantaneous production function for the output of a single good (Y). The inputs are services from labor (L) and the stock of capital (K). The production function is assumed to be characterized by positive but diminishing marginal products and a positive dependence of the marginal product of capital on employment. As is characteristic of all "Keynesian" analysis, the equilibrium of the economy is considered for a period of time so short that the growth of capital is ignored.

C.2 is the demand for labor under the assumption that firms are perfectly competitive in the labor market. Therefore, they hire labor until its marginal product (Y_L) equals the real wage (w/p), where $w =$ nominal wage and $p =$ domestic price level; w is assumed to be given at a point in time because there are strong unions in part of the modern sector; because a condition similar in its effect to an "unlimited supply of labor" prevails in the traditional sector; and because of government wage policies.

C.3 states that consumption (C) depends on perceived disposable income and the real rate of interest ($i - \pi$), where $i =$ nominal interest rate and π = expected rate of inflation. Perceived disposable income is equal to the real value of wage payments (Lw/p) plus dividend payments, under the assumption that there are no retained earnings ($Y - Lw/p - \delta K$), minus taxes net of government transfers (T) minus the perceived rate of capital loss on the real value of the public's net claims on the government due to expected inflation [$(M^* + B)\pi/p$]. These net claims consist of the nominal money supply (M^*) and the nominal value of variable-coupon government bonds (B). This disposable income concept measures the amount of income that the public expects it could consume and still leave the real value of the sum of its paper and physical assets intact.

C.4 describes the aggregate net investment behavior of firms given that there is no market for existing stocks of capital. The assumed behavior is a neoclassical response to the difference between the marginal product of capital (Y_K) and the cost of capital.[2] The cost of capital depends on the rate of interest on bonds (i), the rate of physical depreciation of capital (δ), and the anticipated rate of increase of prices of newly produced capital goods (π).

C.5 is an import function. Imports (M) are assumed to be positively related to income (Y) and the domestic price level (p) and negatively related to the exchange rate in terms of escudos per dollar (x), the c.i.f. price of imports (p^M), and quantitative restrictions (q).

C.6 is the export function. Exports (X) are assumed to be positively related to the f.o.b. price (p^X) and the exchange rate (x), but negatively related to the wage rate (w).

C.7 is the equilibrium condition for aggregate demand and aggregate supply, where G is government expenditures in real terms.

C.8 is the demand for real monetary balances (M^*/p) as a function of the nominal interest rate (i) and real output(Y). Initially, it is assumed that the central bank exogenously controls the stock of money.[3] In addition to money, another asset is composed of variable-coupon nominal bonds issued by the government (B). Households are assumed to regard bonds as a perfect substitute for equities issued by firms to finance investments. When household portfolios are in equilibrium with respect to the real balance of money, given the household balance sheet, they also are in equilibrium with respect to bonds or equities, or both. Therefore, separate relationships are not required for these alternative assets.

C.9 determines total real taxes (T) as a direct function of total income (Y), imports (M), and exports (X) and as an inverse function of the expected rate of inflation (π). The foreign trade variables are included because of the very important role they have had in Chilean government revenues. Inflationary anticipations have an inverse effect because the legal penalties for delayed payment of nominal taxes often have been outweighed by the reduction in the real value of late payments due to inflation. Given exogenous real government expenditures, the tax function determines the size of the government deficit. C.11 gives the government flow budget constraint at any point of time (where dot accents above variables denote derivatives with respect to time):

$$G = T + \frac{\dot{B}}{p} + \frac{\dot{M}^*}{p} \tag{C.11}$$

C.10 is the surplus on the balance of payments in dollars (S). It equals the dollar value of exports ($p^X X$) minus the dollar value of imports ($p^M M$) plus net capital inflows (F). The last are assumed to respond positively to internal interest rates (i). They also depend on quantitative restrictions (q), but the sign of this dependence is unclear because there are effects in opposite directions. If quantitative restrictions are increased, net capital inflows may rise because outflows are limited by the restrictions. On the other hand, capital flight may occur and potential inflows may be frightened off by the increased restrictions.

C.2 SOLUTION OF THE MODEL

Equations C.1–C.10 are ten relations in ten endogenous variables: Y, L, p, i, C, I, M, X, T, and S. The exogenous variables are w, M^*, G, π, δ, K, x, p^x, and p^M. Under the assumptions that $dk = d\delta = dp^M = dp^X = 0$, the total differentials of the ten equations in the model are the following:

$$dY = Y_L dL \tag{C.1'}$$

$$\frac{dw}{w} - \frac{dp}{p} = \frac{Y_{LL}}{Y_L} dL \tag{C.2'}$$

$$dC = C^1 \left[dY - dT - \frac{M^* + B}{p} d\pi + \pi \frac{dp(M^* + B)}{p^2} \right] + C_2(di - d\pi) \tag{C.3'}$$

$$dI = I'Y_{KL}dL - I'di + I'd\pi \tag{C.4'}$$

$$dM = M_Y dY + M_p dp + M_x dx + M_q dq \tag{C.5'}$$

$$dX = X_x dx + X_w dw \tag{C.6'}$$

$$dY = dC + dI + dG + dX - dM \tag{C.7'}$$

$$\frac{dM^*}{p} - \frac{dp}{p}\frac{M^*}{p} = m_i di + m_Y dY \tag{C.8'}$$

$$dT = T_y DY + T_M dM + T_X dX + T\pi d\pi \tag{C.9'}$$

$$dS = p^X dX - p^M dM + F_i di + F_q dq \tag{C.10'}$$

C.12′ gives the differential of the aggregate supply schedule as derived from C.1′ and C.2′. The slope in the *Y-P* plane is positive (Figure C.1).

$$dY = \frac{Y^2{}_L}{Y_{LL}} \left(\frac{dw}{w} - \frac{dp}{p} \right) \tag{C.12'}$$

An increase in *w* will shift this supply schedule downward.

C.13′ is the total differential of the aggregate demand schedule as derived from C.1′ and C.3′ through C.9′. C.13″ is the same expression except that the coefficients of the differential are replaced by *a*s (where the *a*s are positive or probably positive in value:

$$\left[1 - C_1(1 - T_Y - T_M M_Y) + \left(\frac{C_2 - I'}{m_i} \right) M_Y - I' \frac{Y_{KL}}{Y_L} + M_Y \right] dY \tag{C.13'}$$
$$= \left\{ -C_1 \left[M_p T_M + \frac{\pi}{p^2}(M^* + B) \right] - \frac{C_2 - I'}{m_i} \frac{M^*}{p^2} - M_p \right\} dp$$
$$+ \left[-C_1(T_M M_x + T_X X_x) + X_x - M_x \right] dx + (-C_1 T_M M_q - M_q) dq$$
$$+ (-C_1 X_w T_X + X_w) dw + \left[-C_1 \left(T^\pi + \frac{M^* + B}{p} \right) + I' - C_2 \right] d\pi$$
$$+ dG + \frac{C_2 - I'}{m_i} \frac{dM^*}{p}$$

$$a_y dY = -a_p dp + a_x dx + a_q dq - a_w dw + a_\pi d\pi + dG + a_{M^*} dM^* \tag{C.13''}$$

FIGURE C.1

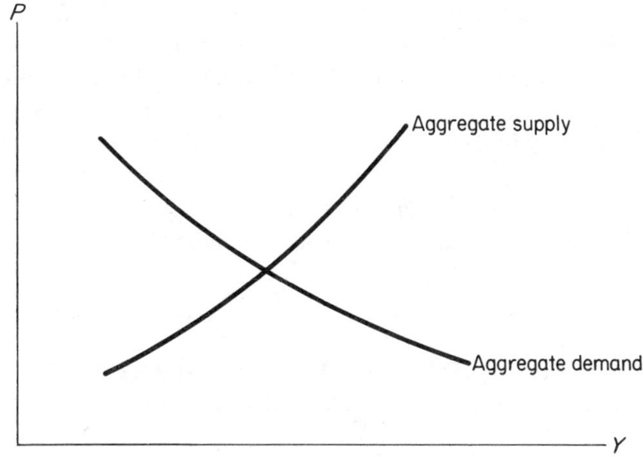

The slope in the P-Y plane is positive. This aggregate demand curve shifts upward with decreases in wages and with increases in the exchange rate,[4] quantitative restrictions, price expectations, government expenditures, and the money supply.

In equilibrium aggregate demand must equal aggregate supply. C.12′ and C.13′, therefore, can be solved to find the impact of any exogenous change on real income and on the domestic price level. C.14′ and C.15′ give these results. Within the model,

$$dY = \frac{1}{a_Y - a_p \dfrac{Y_{LL}p}{Y^2_L}} \left[a_x dx + a_q dq - \left(a_w + \frac{pa_p}{w} \right) dw + a_\pi \, d\pi + dG + a_{M^*} \, dM^* \right] \qquad \text{(C.14′)}$$

$$dp = \frac{-p \dfrac{Y_{LL}}{Y^2_L}}{a_Y - a_p \dfrac{Y_{LL}p}{Y^2_L}} (a_x dx + a_q dq + a_\pi d\pi + dG + a_{M^*} \, dM^*) + \left[\frac{p \dfrac{Y_{LL}}{Y^2_L}(a_w + pa_p)}{a_Y - a_p \dfrac{Y_{LL}}{Y^2_L} p} + \frac{p}{w} \right] dw \qquad \text{(C.15′)}$$

Thus, the comparative static impact of devaluation or of increasing quantitative restrictions is to increase both real product and the price level.

The consequences of a devaluation for the surplus on the balance of payments is ambiguous. C.10′ indicates that this surplus tends to increase because exports rise, capital inflows rise because of the higher domestic interest rate, and imports decline because of the direct exchange-rate response. On the other hand, imports tend to increase because of the higher income and higher domestic prices. If these last two responses are sufficiently strong, they can outweigh the others, causing the surplus to decline. The empirical estimates in Behrman [1974], however, suggest that such an outcome is not probable in the Chilean case.

C.3 ENDOGENIZATION OF WAGES, MONEY SUPPLY, AND PRICE EXPECTATIONS

Three of the variables considered exogenous up to this point in this appendix may well respond to devaluation in the Chilean case. The model in Chapter 2 and in Behrman [1974] provides empirical support for such responses. In this section the simple Keynesian model of sections C.1 and C.2 is not formally expanded to endogenize these variables, but the probable impact of such extentions is discussed.

The exchange rate at times has served as a source of price expectations which have affected wages. C.14 suggests that the increase in real income in response to devaluation is less if wages respond in that way to the exchange rate level than if they do not.[5] The last term in C.15′ implies that the further impact on prices is ambiguous, depending upon which of the two components dominates.

The money supply may respond to devaluations either because the magnitude of the internal financing of the government deficit changes or because foreign reserves change. For a given amount of real government expenditure, C.9′ suggests that the real value of the deficit falls with devaluation unless import taxes are sufficiently responsive and the change in imports is sufficiently strong to cause a decline in tax revenue from imports large enough to offset gains from other sources. Even if the deficit in real terms declines, however, the deficit in nominal terms may increase.

As is suggested in the last paragraph of the previous section, in the Chilean case foreign reserves probably rise in response to devaluation. The impact on the money supply, moreover, apparently is quite substantial and more than offsets any dampening due to a possible reduction in the government deficit. Under such conditions the endogenization of the money supply reinforces the consequences of devaluation on real income and on the price level that are described above in regard to C.14′ and C.15′.

At times in Chile price expectations have been very responsive to exchange-rate policy—in part because some governments have used it as an explicit symbol of stability. C.14′ and C.15′ indicate that if inflationary expectations increase because of devaluation, both real income and the price level rise more than otherwise.

NOTES

1. This model is adopted from the work of Sargent [1972]. Empirical support for the signs of most of the derivatives can be found in Behrman [1974].
2. Empirical estimates of variants of neoclassical investment functions for Chile are in Behrman [1972b].
3. Open-market operations imply $dM^* + dB = 0$, a constraint that is used for relation C.3′.
4. If $a_y > 0$ and $|C_1T_XX_x| < X_x - M_x - C_1T_MMp_x$, then $a_x > 0$, as seems likely.
5. If this response is sufficiently large, real income might decrease.

Appendix D

Definition of Concepts and Delineation of Phases

DEFINITION OF CONCEPTS USED IN THE PROJECT

Exchange Rates.[1]

1. *Nominal exchange rate (NER):* The official parity for a transaction. For countries maintaining a single exchange rate registered with the International Monetary Fund, the nominal exchange rate is the registered rate.

2. *Effective exchange rate (EER):* The number of units of local currency actually paid or received for a one-dollar international transaction. Surcharges, tariffs, the implicit interest foregone on guarantee deposits, and any other charges against purchases of goods and services abroad are included, as are rebates, the value of import replenishment rights, and other incentives to earn foreign exchange for sales of goods and services abroad.

3. *Price-level deflated (PLD) nominal exchange rates:* The nominal exchange rate deflated in relation to some base period by the price level index of the country.

4. *Price-level-deflated EER (PLD-EER):* The EER deflated by the price level index of the country.

5. *Purchasing-power-parity adjusted exchange rates:* The relevant (nominal or effective) exchange rate multiplied by the ratio of the foreign price level to the domestic price level.

Devaluation.

1. *Gross devaluation:* The change in the parity registered with the IMF (or, synonymously in most cases, de jure devaluation).

2. *Net devaluation:* The weighted average of changes in EERs by classes of transactions (or, synonymously in most cases, de facto devaluation).

3. *Real gross devalution:* The gross devaluation adjusted for the increase in the domestic price level over the relevant period.

4. *Real net devaluation:* The net devaluation similarly adjusted.

Protection Concepts.

1. *Explicit tariff:* The amount of tariff charged against the import of a good as a percentage of the import price (in local currency at the nominal exchange rate) of the good.

2. *Implicit tariff* (or, synonymously, tariff equivalent): The ratio of the domestic price (net of normal distribution costs) minus the c.i.f. import price to the c.i.f import price in local currency.

3. *Premium:* The windfall profit accruing to the recipient of an import license per dollar of imports. It is the difference between the domestic selling price (net of normal distribution costs) and the landed cost of the item (including tariffs and other charges). The premium is thus the difference between the implicit and the explicit tariff (including other charges) multiplied by the nominal exchange rate.

4. *Nominal tariff:* The tariff—either explicit or implicit as specified—on a commodity.

5. *Effective tariff:* The explicit or implicit tariff on value added as distinct from the nominal tariff on a commodity. This concept is also expressed as the effective rate of protection (ERP) or as the effective protective rate (EPR).

6. *Domestic resources costs (DRC):* The value of domestic resources (evaluated at "shadow" or opportunity cost prices) employed in earning or saving a dollar of foreign exchange (in the value-added sense) when producing domestic goods.

DELINEATION OF PHASES USED IN TRACING THE EVOLUTION OF EXCHANGE CONTROL REGIMES

To achieve comparability of analysis among different countries, each author of a country study was asked to identify the chronological development of his country's payments regime through the following phases. There was no presumption that a country would necessarily pass through all the phases in chronological sequence.

Phase I: During this period, quantitative restrictions on international transactions are imposed and then intensified. They generally are initiated in response to an unsustainable payments deficit and then, for a period, are intensified. During the period when reliance upon quantitative restrictions as a means of controlling the balance of payments is increasing, the country is said to be in Phase I.

Phase II: During this phase, quantitative restrictions are still intense, but various price measures are taken to offset some of the undesired results of the system. Heightened tariffs, surcharges on imports, rebates for exports, special tourist exchange rates, and other price interventions are used in this phase. However, primary reliance continues to be placed on quantitative restrictions.

Phase III: This phase is characterized by an attempt to systematize the changes which take place during Phase II. It generally starts with a formal exchange-rate change and may be accompanied by removal of some of the surcharges, etc., imposed during Phase II and by reduced reliance upon quantitative restrictions. Phase III may be little more than a tidying-up operation (in which case the likelihood is that the country will re-enter Phase II), or it may signal the beginning of withdrawal from reliance upon quantitative restrictions.

Phase IV: If the changes in Phase III result in adjustments within the country, so that liberalization can continue, the country is said to enter Phase IV. The necessary adjustments generally include increased foreign-exchange earnings and gradual relaxation of quantitative restrictions. The latter relaxation may take the form of changes in the nature of quantitative restrictions or of increased foreign-exchange allocations, and thus reduced premiums under the same administration system.

Phase V: This is a period during which an exchange regime is fully liberalized. There is full convertibility on current account, and quantitative restrictions are not employed as a means of regulating the ex ante balance of payments.

NOTE

1. The present study also includes the concept of the *premium-inclusive price-level-deflated effective exchange rate* [*PLD-EER*(*PI*)], i.e., the PLD-EER adjusted for the premium received by importers.

Appendix E

List of Abbreviations Used in the Study

AID Agency for International Development of the United States Department of State

ALALC Asociación Latinoamericana de Libre Comercio (*see* LAFTA)

CAP Compañía Acero de Pacífico (Pacific Steel Company)

CIAP Comité Interamericano de Alianza para el Progreso (Inter-American Committee of the Alliance for Progress)

COCAIN Comisión de Cambios Internacionales (International Exchange Commission)

CODELCO Corporación del Cobre (Copper Corporation)

CONDECOR Consejo Nacional de Comercio Exterior (National Council of Foreign Commerce)

CONVENSA Corporación de Venta de Salitre y Yodo (Nitrate and Iodine Marketing Corporation)

COPEC Compañía de Petróleo de Chile (Petroleum Company of Chile)

CORFO Corporación del Fomento (Development Corporation)

DEC Dirección de Estadística y Censos (Statistics and Census Department)

ECLA Economic Commission for Latin America

ENAP Empresa Nacional de Petróleo (National Petroleum Enterprise)

ENDESA Empresa Nacional de Electricidad, S.A. (National Electrical Enterprise)

GDP Gross domestic product

GNP Gross national product

IBRD International Bank for Reconstruction and Development

IMF International Monetary Fund

INE Instituto Nacional de Estadísticas (National Statistical Institute)

LAFTA Latin American Free Trade Area (*see* ALALC)

LME London Metal Exchange

NA National accounts (used in reference to national accounts exchange rate)

SOQUIM Sociedad Química y Minera de Chile, S.A. (Chemical and Mining Company of Chile)

UNCTAD United Nations Commission for Trade and Development

Bibliography

Ahumada, Jorge. *En Vez de la Misería.* Santiago: Editorial de Pacífico, 1956.

Allende, G. Salvatore. *La Vía Chilena, el Primer Mensaje del Presidente Allende al Congreso Pleno, 21 de Mayo 1971.* Santiago, 1971.

Anderson, Jack. "ITT Linked to Anti-Allende Plot." Philadelphia *Evening Bulletin* (March 21, 1972a): 60.

———. "Chile Plot: ITT Cash Offer Noted." Philadelphia *Evening Bulletin* (March 22, 1972b): 88.

Assael, Hector, et al. "La Política de Establización: prioridad y oportunidad." *Panorama Económico* (March 1971).

Astorquiza de la Maza, Jorge. *Control de Cambios Internacionales en Chile.* Antofagasta: McFarland, 1942.

Bacha, Edmar. "Una Aproximación a los Tipos de Cambio de Equilíbrio para Comparaciones de Precios en el Area Andina." Santiago: ODEPLAN-MIT, 1969a. Mimeo.

———. "Foreign Exchange Shadow Prices in Chile: Conflicting Theories and Comparative Evaluations." Santiago: ODEPLAN, 1969b. Mimeo.

Bacha, Edmar, and Lance Taylor. "Foreign Exchange Shadow Prices: A Critical Review of Current Theories." *Quarterly Journal of Economics* 85:2 (May 1971): 197–222.

———. "Growth and Trade Distortions in Chile and Their Implications in Calculating the Shadow Price of Foreign Exchange." In Eckaus and Rosenstein-Rodan, eds. [1973].

Baer, W. "The Inflation Controversy in Latin America: A Survey." *Latin American Research Review* (Winter 1967).

Baerresen, Donald W. *The Multiple Exchange Rate System of Chile: 1931–1955.* Latin American Essay Series, No. 2. Milwaukee: University of Wisconsin, 1966.

Baklanoff, Eric N. "Model for Economic Stagnation: the Chilean Experience with Multiple Exchange Rates." *Inter-American Economic Affairs* 13 (Summer 1959): 58–82.

———. "Taxation of United States-owned Copper Companies in Chile: Economic Myopia vs. Long-run Self-Interest." *National Tax Journal* 13 (December 1960): 341–349.

Balassa, Bela. "Tariff Protection in Industrial Countries: An Evaluation." *Journal of Political Economy* 73:6 (December 1965): 573–594.

Balassa, Bela, and associates. *The Structure of Protection in Developing Countries.* Baltimore: Johns Hopkins Press for the International Bank for Reconstruction and Development and the Inter-American Development Bank, 1971.

Balassa, Bela, S. E. Guisinger, and D. M. Schydlowsky. "The Effective Rate of Protection and the Question of Labor Protection in the United States: A Comment." *Journal of Political Economy* 78:5 (September-October 1970): 1150–1162.

Balassa, Bela, and Daniel M. Schydlowsky. "Domestic Resource Costs and Effective Protection Once Again." *Journal of Political Economy* 80:1 (January-February 1972): 63–69.

Ballesteros, Martin A., and Tom G. Davis. "The Growth of Output and Employment in Basic Sectors of the Chilean Economy, 1908–1957." *Economic Development and Cultural Change* 11:2 (January 1963): 152–176.

Banco Central. *Balanza de Pagos.* Santiago, 1966a–1969a.

———. *Boletín Mensual.* Santiago, 1953b–1973b.

———. *Directorio de Exportadores de Chile.* Santiago, 1967c.

———. "Ley de Estímulos a las Exportaciones No. 16. 528 y su Reglamento." Santiago: Gerencia de Fomento de Exportaciones, 1967d. Mimeo.

———. *Manual de Exportaciones.* Santiago, 1968c.

———. *Estudios Monetarios.* Santiago, 1968d.

———. "Bases Juridicas y Administrativos de las Restricciones a las Importaciones de Chile." *Boletín Mensual* 42 (September 1969c).

———. "Indicadores de las Exportaciones Chilenas, 1964–1968." Santiago: Gerencia de Fomento de Exportaciones, 1969d. Mimeo.

———. "Fomento de Exportaciones." Santiago, 1970c. Mimeo.

———. "Régimen de Importación." Santiago, 1970d. Mimeo.

———. "Financiamiento de Exportaciones." (Santiago, n.d.(c). Mimeo.

———. "Ley de Estimulos a las Exportaciones No. 16538 y su Reglamento." Santiago, n.d.(d). Mimeo.

Basevi, Giorgio. "Aggregation Problems in the Measurement of Effective Protection." In Grubel and Johnson, eds. [1971].

Beca I., Raimundo, Thelma Galvez P., and Esteban Imperatore P. "Análisis Cuantitativo de los Impuestos a las Compraventas y a las Importaciones." *Análisis Serie B7* (1969).

Behrman, Jere R. "Forecasting Properties and Prototype Simulations of a Model of the Copper Market." Philadelphia: Report to General Services Administration, 1970. Mimeo.

———. "The Determinants of the Annual Rates of Change of Sectoral Money Wages in a Developing Economy." *International Economic Review* 12:3 (October 1971a): 431–447. Spanish translation in *Cuadernos de Economía* 9:26 (April 1972): 70–88.

———. "Review Article: Trade Prospects and Capital Needs of Developing Countries." *International Economic Review* 12:3 (October 1971b): 519–525.

———. "Sectoral Elasticities of Substitution between Capital and Labor in a Developing Economy: Time Series Analysis in the Case of Postwar Chile." *Econometrica* 40:2 (March 1972): 311–327. Spanish translation in *Cuadernos de Economía* 9:26 (April 1972a): 70–88.

———. "Sectoral Investment Determination in a Developing Economy." *American Economic Review* 62:5 (December 1972b): 825–841.

———. "Short Run Flexibility in a Developing Economy: The Postwar Chilean Experience." *Journal of Political Economy* 80:2 (March-April 1972c): 292–313.
———. "Aggregative Market Response in Developing Agriculture: The Postwar Chilean Experience." In Eckaus and Rosenstein-Rodan, eds. [1973], 1973a.
———. "Cyclical Sectoral Capacity Utilization in a Developing Economy." In Eckaus and Rosenstein-Rodan, eds. [1973], 1973b.
———. "Price Determination in an Inflationary Economy: The Dynamics of Chilean Inflation Revisited." In Eckaus and Rosenstein-Rodan, eds. [1973], 1973c.
———. "Macroeconomic Policy in a Developing Country: An Econometric Investigation of the Postwar Chilean Experience." 1974. Publication due in 1977.
Behrman, Jere R., and Jorge García M. "A Study of Quarterly Nominal Wage Change Determinants in an Inflationary Developing Economy." In Eckaus and Rosenstein-Rodan, eds. [1973].
Bernstein, E. M., Jorge del Canto, Julio G. del Solar, and Henry Murphy. "A Report of the Process of Inflation in Chile Together With Recommendations." IMF report, 1950. Mimeo.
Bhagwati, Jagdish N. *Trade, Tariffs, and Growth*. Cambridge M.I.T. Press, 1970.
———. *Foreign Trade Regimes and Economic Development,* XI, *The Anatomy and Consequences of Exchange Control Regimes*. New York: NBER, 1977.
Bhagwati, Jagdish N., and T. N. Srinivasan. "The Theory of Effective Protection and Resource Allocation." Massachusetts Institute of Technology, 1971. Mimeo.
———. *Foreign Trade Regimes and Economic Development,* VI, *India*. New York: NBER, 1975.
Bitar, S., and H. Trivelli. "The Cost of Capital in Chile." Harvard University, 1971. Mimeo.
Black, Stephen Lounsbury. "A Multi-Sectoral Study of Comparative Advantage in the Chilean Economy." B.A. thesis, Department of Economics, Harvard College, April 1971.
Blitz, Rudolph C. "Some Observations Concerning the Chilean Educational System and Its Relation to Economic Growth." In C. Arnold Anderson and Mary Jean Bowman, eds. *Education and Economic Development*. Chicago: Aldine, 1965.
Bradford, Colin I., Jr. "Economic Planning and Structural Change in Chile." Washington, D.C.: Overseas Development Council, 1970. Mimeo.
Bruno, M. *Interdependence, Resource Use, and Structural Change in Israel*. Jerusalem: Bank of Israel, 1963. Hebrew version, 1962.
———. "The Optimal Selection of Export-promoting and Import-substituting Projects. In *Planning the External Sector: Techniques, Problems, and Policies*. New York: United Nations, 1965.
———. "Domestic Resource Costs and Effective Protection: Clarification and Synthesis." *Journal of Political Economy* 80:1 (January-February 1972): 16–33.
Bruton, Henry. "Productivity Growth in Latin America." *American Economic Review* 57:5 (December 1967): 1099–1116.
Cabezón, Pedro. "An Evaluation of Commercial Policy in the Chilean Economy." Ph.D. diss., University of Wisconsin, 1969.
Cademartori, José. *La Economía Chilena*. Santiago: Editorial Universitaria, 1968.
Campos de Oliveira, Roberto. "Economic Development and Inflation with Special Reference to Latin America." In OECD. *Development Plans and Programmes*. Paris: OECD Development Center, 1964.
Cauas, Jorge. "Stabilization Policy—The Chilean Case." *Journal of Political Economy* 78:4-II (July-August 1970): 815–825.

———. "Short Term Economic Theory and Policy: The Chilean Case, 1964–1972." Harvard University, 1972. Mimeo.

Cauas, Jorge, and Vittorio Corbo. "La Economía Chilena en 1971 y Perspectivas para 1972." Informes de Coyuntura No. 1. Santiago: Instituto de Economía, Universidad Católica de Chile, 1972.

Chenery, Hollis. "Patterns of Industrial Growth." *American Economic Review* 50 (September 1960): 624–654.

"Chile with Allende." *Economist* (March 11, 1972): 25–34.

Clark, Peter Bentley. "An Efficiency Test for Export Subsidies and Tariff Protection." Paper presented at session on Trade and Development of Econometric Society. Detroit, December 28, 1970. Mimeo.

Clark, Peter Bentley, and Alejandro Foxley R. "Sub-Optimal Growth: The Social Cost of Make-Work Employment Policies." Paper presented at session on Numerical Models of Development Planning of Second World Congress of Econometric Society. Cambridge, England, September 8–14, 1970. Mimeo.

Cohen, Alvin. *Economic Change in Chile, 1929–59*. Gainesville: University of Florida Press, 1960.

Cohen, Benjamin I. "The Use of Effective Tariffs." *Journal of Political Economy* 79:1 (January-February 1971): 128–141.

Committee of Nine, Ad Hoc Committee, Alliance for Progress. *Evaluation of the National Economic and Social Development Program of Chile*. Washington, D.C.: U.S. Government Printing Office, 1962.

Corbo Lioi, Vittorio. "An Econometric Study of Chilean Inflation." Ph.D. diss., MIT, 1971.

Corden, W. M. "The Structure of a Tariff System and the Effective Protective Rate." *Journal of Political Economy* 74 (June 1966): 221–237.

———. *The Theory of Protection*. Oxford: Clarendon Press, 1971.

CORFO. *El Programa Nacionál de Desarrollo Económico 1961–1970, Breve Descripción sobre su Contenido, Experiencias sobre su Aplicación y Cumplimiento de las Metas*. Santiago, 1963.

———. "Chile Economic Notes." *New York Weekly*. 1970–73.

———. *Financiamiento Externo*. Santiago, 1968b.

Council of Economic Advisers. *Annual Report*. Washington, D.C.: U.S. Government Printing Office, 1972.

Crosson, Pierre R. *Agricultural Development and Productivity: Lessons from the Chilean Experience*. Baltimore: Johns Hopkins Press for Resources for the Future, 1970.

Davis, Tom. "Eight Decades of Inflation in Chile, 1879–1959: A Political Interpretation." *Journal of Political Economy* 71 (August 1963): 389–397.

———. "Changing Conceptions of the Development Problem: the Chilean Example." *Economic Development and Cultural Change* 14 (October 1965): 21–32.

DEC. *Comercio Interior y Comunicaciones*. Santiago: 1957b–1969b; 1970b in draft form.

———. *III Censo Nacional de Manufacturas*. Santiago, 1960a.

de Castro, Sergio, ed. "Análisis de la Economía Chilena: 1971–1972." Informes de Coyuntura No. 2. Santiago: Instituto de Economía, Universidad Católica de Chile, 1972.

de Castro, Sergio, and Sergio de la Cuadra. "Towards a New Trade Policy for Chile." Santiago: AID, 1971. Mimeo.

de la Cruz, Sergio. "Actualización del Texto Oficial Elaborado en 1965 por el Ministerio de Relaciones Exteriores Relativo a los Bases Juridicos y Administrativos de los

Restricciones a las Importaciones de Chile." *Boletín Mensual del Banco Central* (September 1967).
de la Cuadra, Sergio. "Towards a New Trade Policy for Chile." Santiago: AID, 1971. Mimeo.
de Onis, Juan. "Allende Returns to Rising Tension." New York *Times* (September 5, 1971a): 4.
———. "Chile Devalues Escudo About 30%." New York *Times* (December 11, 1971b): 9.
———. "Economic Crisis in Chile Eroding Allende Support." New York *Times* (October 29, 1971c): 6.
———. "I.T.T. Bank Funds Blocked by Chile." New York *Times* (September 3, 1971d): 3.
———. "US-Chilean Relations Running Into Serious Snags." New York *Times* (June 23, 1971e): 4.
———. "Copper Concerns Appeal in Chile." New York *Times* (October 10, 1971f): 8.
———. "Chile $3 Billion in Debt, Asks Creditors to Accept a Moratorium on Payments." New York *Times* (January 20, 1972a): 4.
———. "Chile Copper Hit by an Output Lag." New York *Times* (January 6, 1972b): 53 and 63.
———. "Chile Takes Fight with I.T.T. to U.N. Unit." New York *Times* (April 14, 1972c): 6.
Díaz-Alejandro, Carlos F. *Exchange-Rate Devaluation in a Semi-Industrialized Country: the Experience of Argentina, 1955–61.* Cambridge: M.I.T. Press, 1965.
———. *Foreign Trade Regimes and Economic Development,* IX, *Colombia.* New York: NBER, forthcoming.
Eckaus, R. S. "Notes on Some Features of the Chilean National Income Accounts." Santiago: ODEPLAN, 1967a. Mimeo.
———. "Questions Concerning the Chilean National Income Accounts." Santiago: ODEPLAN, 1967b. Mimeo.
Eckaus, R. S., and P. N. Rosenstein-Rodan, eds. *Analysis of Development Problems: Studies of the Chilean Economy.* Amsterdam: North-Holland, 1973.
ECLA. *Economic Survey of Latin America.* New York: United Nations, 1970.
Edel, Matthew. *Food Supply and Inflation in Latin America.* New York: Praeger, 1969.
E.I.U. [*Economists'* Intelligence Unit]. *Quarterly Economic Review of Chile* (1960–1972).
Ellsworth, Paul Theodore. *Chile: An Economy in Transition.* New York: Macmillan, 1945.
Ethier, Wilfred. "Input Substitutions and the Concept of the Effective Rate of Protection." *Journal of Political Economy* 80:1 (January-February 1972): 34–47.
Felix, David. "Structural Imbalances, Social Conflict, and Inflation: An Appraisal of Chile's Recent Anti-Inflationary Effort." *Economic Development and Cultural Change* 8 (January 1960): 113–147.
Fetter, Frank W. *Monetary Inflation in Chile.* Princeton, N.J.: Princeton University Press, 1931.
Ffrench-Davis M., Ricardo. "Dependencia, Subdesarrollo y Política Cambiaria." *Trimestre Económico* 37 (April–June 1970).
———. "Economic Policies and Stabilization Programs: Chile, 1952–1969." Ph.D. diss. University of Chicago, 1971.
Ffrench-Davis M., Ricardo, and Samuel Arancibia. "Notas Sobre el Capital Extranjero y America Latina." Santiago: Centro de Estudios de Planificación Nacional, Universidad Católica de Chile, 1970. Mimeo.

Ffrench-Davis M., Ricardo, and Camilo Carrasco. "Chile: Cuatro Años de Experiencia con una Nueva Política de Tipo de Cambio." *Boletín Mensual del Banco Central* 498 (August 1969).

Findlay, Ronald. "Comparative Advantage, Effective Protection, and the Domestic Resource Cost of Foreign Exchange." *Journal of International Economics* 1:2 (May 1971): 189–204.

Fisher, Franklin M., Paul H. Cootner, and Martin N. Baily. "An Econometric Model of the World Copper Industry." *Bell Journal of Economics and Management Science* 3:2 (Autumn 1972): 568–611.

Fishlow, Albert. "Foreign Trade Regimes and Economic Development, X, Brazil." New York: NBER, 1975. Mimeo.

Fontaine, Ernesto. "The Sugar-Beet Industry in Chile: A Cost Benefit Analysis." Ph.D. diss., University of Chicago, 1964.

Foxley R., Alejandro. "Alternativos de Descentralización en el Proceso de Transformación de la Economía Nacional." Santiago: Centro de Estudios de Planificación Nacional, Universidad Católica de Chile, 1971. Mimeo.

García, Eduardo. "Inflation in Chile: A Quantitative Analysis." Ph.D. diss., MIT, 1964.

Griffin, Keith. *Underdevelopment in Spanish America: An Interpretation.* Cambridge: M.I.T. Press, 1969.

Griffin, Keith, and J. L. Enos. "Foreign Assistance: Objectives and Conseqeunces." *Economic Development and Cultural Change* 18:3 (April 1970): 313–327.

Griliches, Z., and V. Ringstad. *Economies of Scale and the Form of the Production Function: An Econometric Study of Norwegian Manufacturing Establishment Data.* Amsterdam: North-Holland, 1971.

Grubel, Herbert G., and Harry G. Johnson, eds. *Effective Tariff Protection.* Geneva: GATT, 1971.

Guisinger, Stephen, and Daniel M. Schydlowsky. "The Empirical Relationship between Nominal and Effective Rates of Protection." In Grubel and Johnson, eds. [1971].

Gunder Frank, Andre. *Capitalism and Underdevelopment in Latin America: Studies of Chile and Brazil.* New York: Monthly Review Press, Modern Reader Paperback Edition, 1969.

———. "La Política Económica en Chile—Del Frente Popular a la Unidad Popular." *Punto Final* (March 14, 1972).

Guzman, Dante L. "Disposiciones Generales, Especialmente Tributaria, Sobre la Importación de Automóviles en Chile." *Boletín Mensual del Banco Central* 514 (December 1970): 1493–1498.

Hachette, Dominique. "Effects de la Sobrevaluación del Escudo en la Distribución del Ingreso en Chile." *Cuadernos de Economía* 3:10 (December 1966).

Hall, Robert E., and Richard C. Sutch. "A Flexible Infinite Distributed Lag." Berkeley: University of California, 1969. Mimeo.

Hammer, Alexander R. "Chile Seeks to Purchase All of I.T.T.'s Subsidiary." New York *Times* (June 11, 1971): 1.

Hansen, Bent. "The Notion of Effective Rate of Protection." Berkeley: Working Paper 34, Department of Economics, University of California, 1973. Mimeo.

Harberger, Arnold C. "The Dynamics of Inflation in Chile." In Carl Christ, ed. *Measurement in Economics.* Stanford: Stanford University Press, 1963.

———. "Some Notes on Inflation." In Werner Baer and Isaac Kerstenetzky, eds. *Inflation and Growth.* New Haven: Yale University Press, 1964.

———. "Economic Policy Problems in Latin America: A Review." *Journal of Political Economy* 78 (July–August 1970).

Harberger, Arnold C., and Marcelo Selowsky. "Key Factors in the Economic Growth of Chile: An Analysis of the Sources of Past Growth and of Prospects for 1965–70." Paper presented at conference on The Next Decade of Latin American Economic Development. Cornell University, April 20–22, 1966. Mimeo.

Hirschman, Albert O. *Journeys Toward Progress: Studies of Economic Policy-Making in Latin America*. New York: Columbia University Press, 1963.

Hobsbaum, E. J. "A Special Supplement: Chile: Year One." *New York Review of Books* (September 1971): 23–32.

Houthakker, H. S., and Lester D. Taylor. *Consumer Demand in the United States: Analysis and Projections*. 2nd ed. Cambridge: Harvard University Press, 1970.

Huddle, Donald L. "Disequilibrium Foreign Exchange Systems and the Generation of Industrialization and Inflation in Brazil." *Economía Internazionale* 25:3 (August 1972a): 1–27.

———. "International Monetary Rules and External Disequilibrium in Developing Countries." *Weltwirtschaftliches Archiv* 108:1 (1972b).

Hufbauer, G. C. "West Pakistan Exports: Effective Taxation, Policy Promotion, and Sectoral Discrimination." Economic Development Report 118. Cambridge: Harvard University Press, 1968.

Humud Tleel, Carlos. "El Sector Público Chileno Entre 1830–1930." Memoria. Facultad de Ciencias Económicas, Universidad de Chile, 1969.

Hurtado Ruiz-Tagle, Carlos. "Population Concentration and Economic Development: the Chilean Case." Ph.D. diss., Harvard University, 1966.

Illanes, Benitez Fernando. *La Economía Chilena y el Comercio Exterior*. Santiago: Imprenta Chile, 1944.

IMF. *Balance of Payments Yearbook*. Washington, D.C., 1969a.

———. *Exchange Restrictions Report*. Washington, D.C., 1950b–1972b.

IMF and IBRD. *Direction of Trade*. Washington, D.C., 1953–72. Before 1957, UN, IMF, and IBRD, *Direction of International Trade*.

INE [Instituto Nacional de Estadísticas]. *IV Censo Nacional de Manufacturas*. 2 vols. Santiago, 1970.

Instituto de Economía. *Desarrollo Económico de Chile, 1940–1956*. Santiago: Universidad de Chile, 1956.

———. *La Economía de Chile en el Periodo 1950–1963*. Santiago: Universidad de Chile, 1963.

———. *Encuesta Trimestral de Cesantía*. Santiago: Universidad de Chile, 1958–1971.

Irigoyen Gonzales, Carlos, and Clemente Torres Toro. "Catalogo de las Estadísticas Aduanderas de Comercio Exterior de Chile." *Análisis Serie B*, No. 1 (1967).

Jeanneret, Teresa. "The Structure of Protection in Chile." In Bela Balassa and associates. *The Structure of Protection in Developing Countries*. Baltimore: Johns Hopkins Press, 1971.

Jensen, Michael C. "Chile Tells I.T.T. Its Unit Will Be Nationalized." New York *Times* (September 16, 1971): 13.

Jobet-Burquez, Julio César. *Ensayo critico del desarrollo económico-social de Chile*. Santiago: Editorial Universitaria, 1955.

Johnson, Harry G. *Trade and Development*. Geneva: Librairie Droz, 1965.

———. "The Monetary Approach to Balance of Payments Theory." Chicago: Department of Economics, University of Chicago, 1971. Mimeo.

Johnson, Leland J. "Problems of Import Substitution: The Chilean Automobile Industry." *Economic Development and Cultural Change* 15:2 (January 1967): 202–216.

Joó Arredondo, Sergio. "Depósitos para Importación." Santiago: Banco Central, 1969. Mimeo.

———. "Distribución Sectorial del Crédito en Moneda Corriente y Extranjera." Santiago: Banco Central, 1970. Mimeo.

Jul L., Ana María. "Diversificación de Exportaciones: el Caso Chileno." Universidad de Chile, 1969.

Kaldor, Nicholas. "Problemas Económicas de Chile." *El Trimestre Económica* 26:2 (April-June 1959): 170–221.

Klein and Saks Misión. *El Programa de Estabilización de la Economía Chilena y Trabajo de la Misión Klein and Saks.* Santiago: Editorial Universitaria, 1958.

Krueger, A. O. "Some Economic Costs of Exchange Control: The Turkish Case." *Journal of Political Economy* 74 (October 1966): 466–480.

———. "Evaluating Restrictionist Trade Regimes: Theory and Measurement." *Journal of Political Economy* 80:1 (January-February 1972a): 48–62.

———. "The Political Economy of the Rent-Seeking Society." *American Economic Review* 64:3 (June 1974): 291–303.

———. *Foreign Trade Regimes and Economic Development,* XII, *Liberalization Attempts and Consequences.* New York: NBER, 1975.

Lagos, Ricardo. *La Concentración del Poder Económico, Su Teoría, Su Realidad Chilena.* Santagio: Editorial del Pacífica, 1962.

———. "La Industria en Chile: Antecedentes Estructurales." Santiago: Instituto de Economía, Universidad de Chile, 1966.

Leftwich, Richard H. "Exchange Rate Policies, Balance of Payments, and Trade Restricttions in Chile. *Economic Development and Cultural Change* 14 (February 1966): 400–413.

Levinson, Jerome, and Juan de Onis. *The Alliance That Lost Its Way: A Critical Report on the Alliance for Progress.* Chicago: Quadrangle-20th Century Fund, 1970.

Lewis Jr., Steven R., and Stephen E. Guisinger. "Measuring Protection in a Developing Country: The Case of Pakistan." *Journal of Political Economy* 76:6 (November-December 1968): 1170–1198.

Lewis, W. Arthur. "Economic Development with Unlimited Supplies of Labor." *Manchester School* 22 (May 1954): 139–191.

Líbano, Doloros. "El Tipo de Cambio en Chile desde 1948." *Boletín Mensual del Banco Central* (1970): 722–734.

Luders, Rolf. "Historia Monetaria de Chile, 1925–1958." *Cuadernos* 20 (April 1970).

———. "A Monetary History of Chile, 1925–1958." Ph.D. diss., University of Chicago, 1968.

McKinnon, Ronald J. "Monetary Theory and Controlled Flexibility in the Foreign Exchanges." *Princeton Essays in International Finance,* no. 84 (April 1971).

———. "The Monetary Approach to Exchange Rate Policy in Less Developed Countries." In H.C. Grubel, and Theodore Morgan, eds. *Exchange Rate Policy in Southeast Asia.* Lexington, Mass.: Lexington Books, 1972.

McNicol, David. "The Two Price Systems in the Copper Industry." Ph.D. diss., MIT, 1973.

Mamalakis, Markos. "Public Policy and Sectoral Development: A Case Study of Chile, 1940–1958." In Markos Mamalakis and Clark Wintor Reynolds. *Essays on the Chilean Economy.* Homewood, Ill.: Irwin, 1965.

———. "Historical Statistics of Chile." 4 vols. Economic Growth Center, Yale University, 1967a. Mimeo.

———. "Negative Personal Saving in the Chilean National Accounts: An Artifact or

Reality?" Discussion Paper No. 36. Economic Growth Center, Yale University, 1967b. Mimeo.

———. "An Analysis of the Financial and Investment Activities of the Chilean Development Corporation: 1939–1964." *Journal of Development Studies* 5:2 (January 1969): 118–137.

———. "Contribution of Copper to Chilean Economic Development, 1920–67: Profile of a Foreign-Owned Export Sector." In Mikesell, ed. [1971], 1971a.

———. "The Growth and Structure of the Chilean Economy." Economic Growth Center, Yale University, 1971b. Mimeo.

Marshall Silva, Jorge. "Inflation and Economic Development; A Case Study: The Chilean Experience 1937–1950." Ph.D. diss., Harvard University, 1957.

Meza, W. "La Inversión Geografica Bruta en Capital Fijo por Sectores de Destino, Periodo 1962–1966." Santiago: ODEPLAN, 1967. Mimeo.

Mikesell, Raymond F. "Conflict and Accomodation in Chilean Copper." In Mikesell, ed. [1971].

Mikesell, Raymond F., ed. *Foreign Investment in the Petroleum and Mineral Industries: Case Studies of Investor-Host Country Relations*. Baltimore: Johns Hopkins Press for Resources for the Future, 1971.

Ministerio de Relaciones Exteriors. *Acuerdo de Integración Subregional, Antecedentes Texto Documentacion*. Publication 18. Santiago: Secretaria Ejecutiva ALALC-Chile, 1970.

Mira, Benjamin. *Las Tendencias y la Política Monetaria en Chile en el Periodo 1950–60*. Santiago: Universidad de Chile, 1963.

Moran, Theodore H. "The Multinational Corporation and the Politics of Development: The Case of Copper in Chile, 1945–1970." Ph.D. diss., Harvard University, 1970.

Morley, Samuel A., and Gordon W. Smith. "On the Measurement of Import Substitutes." *American Economic Review* 60:4 (September 1970): 728–735.

Mundell, Robert. *Monetary Theory*. Pacific Palisades, Calif. Goodyear, 1971.

Muñoz G., Oscar. *Crecimiento Industrial de Chile 1914–1965*. Santiago: Instituto de Economía y Planificación, Universidad de Chile, 1968.

New York *Times*. "Chile Threatens to Seize I.T.T. Unit." (March 30, 1972a): 8.

———. "Columnist Offers More Material Said to Link I.T.T. to Move Against Allende." (March 23, 1972b): 16.

Novitski, Joseph. "Andean Nations Increasing Their Trade." New York *Times* (August 26, 1972): 31.

Nugent, Jeffry B. "Demonstration of the Proposition That the Welfare Cost of any Level of Tariff Increases with the Degree of Dispersion of Tariffs Among Communities." In "Empirical Investigations in Economic Integration: The Central American Case." Los Angeles: University of Southern California, 1971. Mimeo.

ODEPLAN. *Cuadro de Transacciones Intersectoriales Para la Economía Chilena, 1962*. Santiago, 1970.

———. *Cuentas Nacionales de Chile, 1960–1969*. Santiago, 1970a.

———. *La Planificación Bajo el Gobierno Popular*. Santiago, 1971a.

———. *Resumen del Plan Anual 1971*. Santiago, 1971b.

———. "La Economía Chilena en 1971." In *Plan Actual 1972*. Reprinted in *Boletín Mensual del Banco Central* (1972): 305–318.

Papanek, G. F. "The Effect of Aid and other Resource Transfers on Savings and Growth in Less Developed Countries." *Economic Journal* 327 (September 1972).

———. "Aid, Foreign Private Investment, Savings and Growth in Less Developed Countries." *Journal of Political Economy* 81:1 (January-February 1973): 120–131.

Pazos, Felipe. *Chronic Inflation in Latin America.* Translated by Ernesto Cuesta. New York: Praeger, 1972.

Petras, James. *Politics and Social Forces in Chilean Development.* Berkeley: University of California Press, 1970.

Philadelphia *Evening Bulletin.* "I.T.T. Denies Anderson's Chile Story." (March 22, 1972): 88.

Picks' Currency Yearbook. New York, 1960–72.

Pinto, Anibal. *Chile: una Economía Defícil.* México: Fondo de Cultura Económica, 1964.

———. *Ni Estabilidad ni Desarrollo: La Política del Fundo Monetaria.* Santiago: Editorial del Pacifico, 1960.

———. *Chile, un Caso de Desarrollo Frustrado.* 2nd ed. Santiago: Editorial Universitaria, 1962.

Pisciotta, John Lee. "Development Policy, Inflation and Politics in Chile, 1938–1958: An Essay in Political Economy." Ph.D. diss., University of Texas, 1971.

Prebisch, Raul. "Economic Development or Monetary Stability: The False Dilemma." *Economic Bulletin for Latin America* IV:I (March 1961).

Rahman, Md. A. "The Welfare Economics of Foreign Aid." *Pakistan Development Review* 7:2 (Summer 1967): 141–159.

Reynolds, Clark Wintor. "Development Problems of an Export Economy: The Case of Chile and Copper." In Markos Mamalakis and Clark Wintor Reynolds. *Essays on the Chilean Economy.* Homewood, Ill.: Irwin, 1965.

Rufatt, Oscar. "Some Considerations on the Development of Capitalism in Chile in the Second Half of the XIXth Century." Philadelphia: University of Pennsylvania, 1972. Mimeo.

Sargent, Thomas J. "Notes on the Classical Model" and "Notes on the Keynesian Model." Minneapolis: University of Minnesota, 1972. Mimeo.

Schott, Francis H. "Inflation and Stabilization Efforts in Chile, 1953–58." *Inter-American Economic Affairs* 13 (Winter 1959): 3–20.

Schultz, Theodore W. *Economic Growth and Agriculture,* pp. 184–191. New York: McGraw-Hill, 1968.

Seers, Dudley. "A Theory of Inflation and Growth in Under-developed Countries Based on the Experience of Latin America." *Oxford Economic Papers* (June 1963): 192–195 .

Selowsky, Marcelo. "Cost of Price Stabilization Policies in a Strongly Inflationary Economy." Cambridge: Center for International Affairs, Harvard University, 1971. Mimeo.

———. "Política Cambiaria y Asignación de Recursos." Santiago: Centro de Investigaciones Económicas, Universidad Católica de Chile, 1970. Mimeo.

Selowsky, Marcelo, and Lance Taylor. "The Economics of Malnourished Children: An Example of Disinvestment in Human Capital." *Economic Development and Cultural Change* 22:1 (October 1973): 17–30.

Senado, Oficina de Informaciones. *Cobre: Antecedentes Económicos y Estadisticas Relacionades con la Gran Minería del Cobre.* Santiago, 1971.

Sepúlveda, Sergio. *El Trigo Chileno en el Mercado Mundial.* Santiago: Editorial Universitaria. 1959.

Sierra, Enrique. *Tres Ensayos de Estabilización en Chile: Las Políticas Aplicadas en el Decenio 1956–66.* Santiago: Editorial Universitaria, 1969.

Sohmen, Egon. "The Effect of Revaluation on the Price Level." *Quarterly Journal of Economics* 72 (May 1958): 273–283.

Sturc, Ernest. "Stabilization Policies: Experience of Some European Countries in the 1950's." *IMF Staff Papers* (July 1968): 197–217.

Sunkel, Osvaldo. "La Inflación Chilena: Un Enfoque Heterodoxo." *Trimestre Económico* 25 (October-December 1958).

———. "El Fracaso de las Políticas de Estabilizacion en el Contexto Latino Americano." *Trimestre Económico* 30 (October-December 1963).

Sutulov, Alexander. "World Copper Industry: A Time for Change." *Intermet Bulletin* 2:1 (July 1972): 19–22.

Szulc, Tad. "U.S. Government and Business Resigned to a Marxist Chile." New York *Times* (September 21, 1970): 2.

———. "State Department Denies Any Move to Block Allende." New York *Times* (March 24, 1972): 1 and 7.

Taylor, Lance. "Investment Project Analysis in Terms of a Model of Optimal Growth: The Case of Chile." In Eckaus and Rosenstein-Rodan, eds. [1973], 1973a.

———. "Short-Term Policy in Open Developing Economies: The Narrow Limits of the Possible." Economic Development Report 228. Cambridge: Harvard University, 1973b. Mimeo.

Taylor, Lance, and Stephen L. Black. "Practical General Equilibrium Estimation of Resource Pulls Under Trade Liberalization." *Journal of International Economics* 3 (1973).

Theil, H., and C. B. Tilanos. "The Demand for Production Factors and the Price Sensitivity of Input-Output Coefficients." *International Economic Review* 7:3 (September 1966): 258–273.

Torres T., Clemente. "Análisis Evaluativo de los Indices de Comercio Exterior Calculados en Chile." *Análisis Serie* B (1969).

Tumlir, Jan, and Ladislav Till. "Tariff Averaging in International Comparisons." In Grubel and Johnson, eds. [1971].

United States. *Statistical Abstracts*. Washington, D.C.: U.S. Government Printing Office, 1960–1970.

Vúskovic, Pedro. "La Presencia de Chile en el CIAP." *Boletín Mensual del Banco Central* (1971): 385–399.

———. "Exposición del Ministro de Economía ante el Subcomite del CIAP sobre Chile." *Boletín Mensual del Banco Central* (1972): 533–552.

Wachter, Susan M. "Latin American Structuralist and Monetarist Inflation Theories: An Application to Chile." Ph.D. diss., Boston College, 1974.

Weisskopf, Thomas E. "An Econometric Test of Alternative Constraints in the Growth of Underdeveloped Countries." *Review of Economics and Statistics* 54:1 (February 1972): 67–78.

Welles, Benjamin. "Chile Assailed by Rogers for Compensation Stand." New York *Times* (October 14, 1971): 1, 15.

———. "Chile Accuses Washington." New York *Times* (April 15, 1972a): 4.

———. "U.S. Insuring Agency May Face Claim of $216 Million in Chile." New York *Times* (March 6, 1972b): 5.

Wilcke, Gerd. "Kennecott Calls on Chile to Honor Missed Payment." New York *Times* (January 4, 1972): 45, 49.

Wilson, Evan M. "Chile's Economic Position." *Commercial Pan America* 62 (July 1937).

Young, Richard M. "Macro-Decision Making Under Uncertainty: Some Theoretical and Simulation Results." Ph.D. diss., University of Pennsylvania, 1972.

Yver, Raul E. "Dinámica del Ajuste de la Tasa de Inflación: El Caso Chileno." Santiago: Centro de Investigaciones Económicas, Universidad Católica de Chile, 1970. Mimeo.

Zanartu, Mario, and John J. Kennedy, eds. *The Overall Development of Chile.* Notre Dame: University of Notre Dame Press, 1969.

Zorrilla, Américo. "Exposición Sobre la Política Económica del Goberno y del Estado de la Hacienda Pública." *Boletín Mensual del Banco Central* (1970): 1477–1492.

Index